Peaceful Persuasion

SUNY series in Communication Studies
Dudley D. Cahn, editor

Peaceful Persuasion

The Geopolitics of Nonviolent Rhetoric

Ellen W. Gorsevski

State University of New York Press

Published by
State University of New York Press, Albany

© 2004 State University of New York

For information, address State University of New York Press,
90 State Street, Suite 700, Albany, NY 12207

Production by Judith Block
Marketing by Michael Campochiaro

Library of Congress Cataloging-in-Publication Data

Gorsevski, Ellen W.
    Peaceful persuasion : the geopolitics of nonviolent rhetoric / Ellen W. Gorsevski.
      p. cm. — (SUNY series in communication studies)
    Includes bibliographical references and index.
    ISBN 0-7914-6027-4 (alk. paper)
      1. Nonviolence.   2. Rhetoric—Political aspects.   I. Title.   II. Series.

    HM1281.G67 2004
    303.6'1—dc21

                                        2003052614

10 9 8 7 6 5 4 3 2 1

To peacemakers everywhere

Contents

Tables and Figures

Acknowledgments

The myth of the lone scholar, laboring away by herself can certainly be exploded in my case. So many people have helped me along the way I cannot possibly mention them all. Here, for the sake of brevity, I will note only the persons most visibly influential in enabling me to bring this daunting project to fruition. To the rest of you I say, from the bottom of my heart, thank you!

Many thanks go to the following Pennsylvania State University professors for their time and invaluable suggestions for research and revisions along the way. I am grateful to Richard B. Gregg, Tom Benson, Dennis Gouran, Nancy Love, Stephen Browne, and Deborah Atwater.

Earlier versions of some portions of this book have been published previously. For the recommendations for revisions and research, I have many people to thank. For general theorizing of nonviolent rhetoric, thanks go to the editors of *Peace and Change*. For supporting my work on Kiro Gligorov, I thank Dr. Dona Kolar-Panov of St. Cyril and Methodius University as well as Ljubica Arsovska, Editor of *Macedonian Review*, Skopje, Macedonia. I would also like to thank Derek Sweetman of the *Online Journal of Peace and Conflict Resolution* for recognizing the significance of the "Spitfire Grill" research. Thanks go to Edward Lamoureux for encouraging expanded theoretical work on the "rhetorical climate" in *The Journal of Communication and Religion*. For research on Aung San Suu Kyi, thanks go to Gary J. Boelhower and Deborah D. Buffton of the *Journal for the Study of Peace and Conflict*. I also appreciate Rosemary Yokoi for supporting my book review work in *International Journal on World Peace*. Thanks also go to anonymous reviewers of these journals and at the State University of New York Press and its editors.

I'd like to thank Tammie Schnitzer and the Latah County Human Rights Association, for letting me pick her up from the Spokane airport to interview her on the way to her speaking engagement at Moscow, Idaho's 1999 Martin Luther King Day breakfast.

Also, to Tom H. Hastings, I am honored to have had the Foreword of this book written by you, who embody lifelong nonviolent activism, teaching, and scholarship.

At Washington State University, thanks go to the following: To the staff at the Interlibrary Loan Office for tracking down many long distance books and articles; to the College of Education, which underwrote my course, "Peace Rhetoric: Nonviolence in Literature and Media." Thanks also go to Dean Barbara Couture of the College of Liberal Arts and to Victor Villanueva of the English Department for spurring me to understand the political economy of academia and to think creatively about nonviolent responses to exploitation in labor.

Finally, this book is evidence of the love and support from family and friends. Above all, Peter gave me everything I needed to make my dream of this book come true, and for that, I will be forever grateful.

For the strengths of this book, I am indebted for everyone's thoughtful input. Any shortcomings of this book, however, are solely my responsibility.

Nonviolence is not just for an elite few, it is for everyone. It is a way of life based on respect for each human person, and for the environment. It is also a means of bringing about social and political change. . . . It is a whole new way of thinking.

—*Mairead Maguire*

Let us be clear regarding the language we use and the thoughts we nurture. For what is language but the expression of thought? Let your thought be accurate and truthful, and you will hasten the advent of *swaraj* even if the whole world is against you.

—*Mohandas Gandhi*

The conviction that racism is not inevitable rests on an appreciation of the transcendent qualities of human nature and the power of those qualities in the world. . . . human beings do not have to be limited by the tendencies to injustice and prejudice which they inherit from the past. They can choose to think and act differently. There is no limit to the progress people can make when they choose to confront racism in their own lives, because nothing can impede the determination of people to change themselves.

—*Holly Hanson*

The most potent weapon of the oppressor is the mind of the oppressed.

—*Steven Biko*

We can put *more* pressure on the antagonist for whom we show human concern. It is precisely solicitude for his [sic] person *in combination with* a stubborn interference with his [sic] actions that can give us a very special degree of control.

—*Barbara Deming*

If you want to go out and change the world, you should be prepared to be hated for it.

—*Stanton Glantz*

The world is revealed only to an open-minded person.

—*Henry Johnstone*

Foreword

Moments ago, the television cameras left my Portland State University office, where reporters came to ask about the rowdy elements of the antiwar movement here in the Rose City. I told them that our goal was to change public policy through nonviolent action and education. They said, "Well, what about the ones who pull masks over their faces, run into the streets during our peace demonstrations and break things and fight with police?" I said, "They are not operating within our consensed [sic] guidelines in our peace caucus here in Portland and they are thus not a part of our movement, but that if any police arrest any of our nonviolent actionists we will support those people." They said, "What about you being affiliated with these vandals when they come to your demonstrations?" I said, "Well, that's partially up to you, so please don't report their activities as a part of ours."

Our actions are all about ideas, words, rhetoric, in the end. We hear constantly that actions speak louder than words and that those who just talk are doing nothing, but then we learn from Ellen Gorsevski that in fact language matters. Perception is reality. Movement-building is more important than placating everyone. We do not need a diversity of tactics as much as we crucially need a diversity of *people* and those people hear codes in every one of our actions and they see it in every expression on each of our faces. This calls for rhetoric that goes well beyond the forensic or evidence-building, fixed-pie language of the trial attorney or the politician. We need to learn to "beat" our opponents not down and not up but together, on the same problem, in a rhythm that is a celebration of peace, not another war drum. We need to learn the language of power *with*, not power *over*, as psychologist Joanna Macy described it. There is nothing wrong with using nonviolence in a coercive fashion—as it was when Gandhi referred to *satyagraha* as "truthforce," but it is much more effective, we learn, to use our suasive abilities than our subtle or overt *ad hominem* attack linguistic tools. Or, as Martin Luther King, Jr., and others have said, the best way to eliminate enemies is to make them into friends. That is what Ellen Gorsevski illuminates in this timely and much-needed study. Years ago, as I finished my M.A. in mass communications with my thesis focusing on nonviolence, I was told that I needed to do Ph.D. work to bring nonviolence into rhetorical theory. I looked into it and was too daunted at the prospect. With blessed purpose, Dr. Gorsevski has done it.

More nuanced than the examination of written and spoken rhetoric is another of her objectives, which is to reveal when *action* itself becomes language; when the deed speaks for itself, what does it say and how? From Aung San Suu Kyi's synergy of charismatic speech from the pagoda (or from house arrest with her stalwart actions under credible death threat over a long period of time) to King's bold statements from the pulpit or the prison, Gorsevski shows that actions and poses, affect and semiotics all bend and morph messages and send them onto new trajectories. Reading King is interesting; hearing and seeing him was and is inspirational. We can have effective communications by the written or spoken or graphic-image iconic word, but the sum of those is greater than their parts and Gorsevski helps disentangle this welter and thus offers the academy and activist community alike a new platform from which to view and from which to radiate our next message.

Follow Gorsevski through her exegesis of cinema, gender messages, and the propaganda parsing we so vitally need and you will discover that analysis of media messages is much more hopeful than a mere academic problem statement. Nonviolence offers actual solutions, or at least a line of sight toward a better management of conflict. When film shows nonviolent transformation in its true light, it is every bit as moving as the depiction of sweet revenge; once filmmakers internalize this they will expand the genre toward a new era of nonviolent transformative stories, films that will mirror and mold a much better world.

Intercultural communication is well understood and commonly offered to those who work for transnational corporations; this book helps us lift those competencies into the arena of global justice, a key step for those struggling to translate their struggles into language acceptable to the international community. If a Palestinian cannot convince an average American of the justice of his or her cause, will it succeed when the average American is paying for the weaponry that makes injustice possible in that beleaguered region? What can the rhetorician offer to that Palestinian activist?

Ellen Gorsevski has written an important and utterly refreshing book for anyone interested in promoting a new method of conflict management, social change, social preservation and community-building. She has also tossed down the gauntlet to those who wish to offer comment on the theories of rhetoric vis-à-vis nonviolence—and would probably ask that we strike such phrases from our rhetorical toolkit as "tossed down the gauntlet," or, for that matter, "strike." Dr.

Gorsevski is interested in healing; she comes at nonviolence from Dr. King's per-spective of tension-reduction-by-exposure. "We merely bring it out in the open where it can be seen and dealt with. . . . injustice must . . . be exposed, with all of the tension its exposing creates, to the light of human conscience and the air of national opinion before it can be cured" (*Letter from Birmingham City Jail*).

Nonviolence is the language of the heart and the gut; Gorsevski has helped make it available to the head. This is how true creativity is called out and creativ-ity is what we need to have if we seek nonviolent power. Indeed, it is essentially *all* we have when we meet overwhelming arms and propaganda. We had better learn the lessons offered herein and contribute our own in our own time. The lan-guage of nonviolence is the tongue given to invitation and that is the tone Ellen Gorsevski models for us in this critical look at the last best hope for humanity: nonviolence.

Tom H. Hastings
December 2, 2002

Introduction

I had originally approached my research into nonviolent rhetoric with a very different goal in mind. Initially, I thought I would simply highlight for my rather obscure field—rhetorical theory, public address, and criticism—how exciting the rhetoric of peacemakers is. My vision was to simply take what other scholars of peace and nonviolent rhetoric had said, and do something simple, such as cataloging that body of knowledge. But to my surprise and utter amazement, at that time there was next to nothing for me to catalog! Aside from the work of Rod Troester and a handful of others, this lack of information and dearth of serious attention to the rhetorics (that is, persuasive discourse and communication) of peacemakers and nonviolent orators and activists was made even more perplexing and ironic by the following fact: many, if not most, basic courses in rhetoric and public address feature as one of, if not *the* capstone achievement, of 20th-century rhetoric Dr. Martin Luther King, Jr.'s, "I Have a Dream" speech. Indeed, King's photograph at his historic speech at the Mall in Washington, D.C., has often graced the covers of public speaking textbooks or video speech anthologies.

So why was commentary on nonviolence missing from the rhetorical canon? Why did so many analyses of King's rhetoric only discuss his eminent "style" and use of "tropes" or biblical allusions, but ignore the *obvious*: the nonviolent stance and radical *content* of his epic messages? The lack of content analysis of nonviolent rhetoric is also compounded by the American- and Euro-centric nature of the rhetorics of peacemakers. Even when I found studies of peace rhetorics, with the exception of Mohandas K. Gandhi, they tended to focus on domestic or Western orators, activists, or leaders. Even in Gandhi's case, his British barrister training and impeccable English renders him somewhat of a "stand-in Euro" in terms of requisite eloquence for rhetorical studies. Given the relative lack of study on peace rhetoric, especially its American tradition, how could anyone possibly come to understand the peace rhetorics of people who spoke other languages, who lived in anonymity in developing nations?

In the absence of understanding clearly how nonviolent rhetorics work, how could I proceed to spend my career studying the rhetorics of Nobel Peace Prize–winners and other important nonviolent leaders? How can one grasp the equally valuable communicative practices of anonymous nonviolent activists—those whose names never appear in headlines? I had to begin *somewhere*. So this volume represents a start from scratch in trying to figure out what nonviolent rhetoric is. In this book, I begin to divine how nonviolent communicative practices work.

This is an unapologetically interdisciplinary work. As such, it may seem lopsided in some respects. For rhetorical scholars, on the one hand, it may not seem to grapple in sufficient detail with the rhetorical tradition or current studies in rhetoric. For scholars of peace and conflict studies, on the other hand, much of the arcane references to scholars or debates in rhetorical theory or criticism might seem like detours from examining nonviolence in action. The lay reader might view this volume as overly theoretical. However, this collection of essays is designed to point one possible way, and invite others, both in my nano-discipline and in other fields, to do that which, inexplicably, simply has not yet been done. In short, this work pointedly and virtually exclusively discusses and defines nonviolence as a unique persuasive form of communication. It is my hope that this work encourages others to share in my interest in nonviolent rhetoric. I also hope these essays prompt others to join me in puzzling through, and, eventually, articulating a complete theory of nonviolent rhetoric, that is, *peaceful persuasion*.

Vast analyses and knowledge exist concerning hate rhetoric and war rhetoric, but there are comparatively few studies of nonviolent rhetoric and rhetorics of peacemakers. The purpose of this book is to enable interested lay readers, plus students and scholars in disciplines ranging from rhetorical criticism and cultural studies to the social and political sciences to widen their horizons by encouraging the use of theories from peace and conflict studies in general, and nonviolent theory in particular. Through the following different case studies that examine diverse facets of nonviolent rhetoric on the contemporary scene of society, culture, and global politics, this book lays the first blocks of a conceptual and philosophical foundation for developing a theory of nonviolent rhetoric.

Here is a quick sketch of what this book contains. Chapter 1 and Appendix 1 offer background, rationale, and perspective. Chapter 2 encourages nonviolent activists and students of peace studies to better understand rhetoric. Chapter 3 provides the impetus for encouraging the inclusion of nonviolence in the speech communication curriculum.

The first case study (in chapter 4) examines how the popular media uses rhetoric to belittle nonviolent themes. The reviews of a film, *The Spitfire Grill*, are subjected to critique and analysis, with surprising results. What we find is the film is criticized according to the critics' own perspectives on the viability of nonviolence as a means to managing conflict. Popular culture is revealed to be swayed by misconceptions of many reviewers, while, at the same time, other readers seem to have a natural understanding of and predilection for nonviolence in popular films.

The next study (of chapter 5) takes a traditional, public address approach to rhetorical criticism in light of a theory of nonviolence. In it, I discuss the pragmatic nonviolent approach to rhetoric and public address taken by the recent President of Macedonia, Kiro Gligorov, in the face of Macedonia's new nationhood in 1993, as well as the Kosovo crisis of 1999. The hypothesis here is that pragmatic nonviolent rhetoric can be effective in the short term as far as audience receptivity is concerned, but it also can be limited by cross-cultural blockages and tends to take a longer-term approach to attain rhetorical success.

The third case study (in chapter 6) takes a visual approach to the rhetorical criticism of nonviolent communication. In it, I examine the visual rhetoric of Aung San Suu Kyi, Nobel Peace Prize–winner and democratic opposition party leader in Myanmar (Burma). Her oratorical skills are impressive, and she has a prodigious public speaking career by any standard of success in public address. However, I contend that it is her essentialized persona that is most interesting. Her nonviolent uses of her physical body, combined with her striking beauty and photogenic qualities, much valued in this electronic age, create unique rhetorical success, as well as risks, for her nonviolent campaign to press for democracy and to end the military dictatorship in her country.

The fourth and final case study (in chapter 7) diverges most from the conventional approach to rhetorical criticism. Rather than analyzing the oratory of a lone rhetor, as I do in Gligorov's case, or taking a cognitive and cultural studies approach to examining visual rhetoric, as I do in Suu Kyi's case, this final study examines the diffuse rhetoric of a nonviolent social movement. Using extant scholarship from organizational communication theory, I devise and provide ample evidence for the concept of a *rhetorical climate*. I maintain that climates of feeling and experience can be as persuasive, if not more so, than written texts and other forms of symbolic rhetoric. This case shows one way how the nonviolent rhetoric of anonymous people can be studied. In this case, I examine the rhetoric surrounding the nonviolent and collective social movement in Billings, Montana, in 1993, when the entire town rose to the occasion and fought back against neonazi hate crimes and terrorism.

The first chapters and Appendix 1 simply provide an introduction to concepts and theoretical assumptions. The final chapter summarizes preliminary conclusions and offers suggested directions for future research. In short, this book surveys how nonviolent theory supports the notion that humans can argue fairly and arrive at mutual understanding through a risky process of tolerance and self-conversion. Nonviolent theory shows that rhetoric returns in some sense to the classical, Isocratean ideal of *paideia*: nonviolent rhetoric can be an educational tool to achieve

Gandhi's ideal of *swaraj*, the uplifting of all human beings. Nonviolent activists' unique choices and creativity in persuading shows the rhetorical power of using *satyagraha* (soul-force, truth-force) to create a healthy environment in which to make possible social change and equality. Nonviolent theory shows rhetoricians that language and culture, in a sense our way of creating and perpetuating our reality, can be devoid of, or impose minimal, aggression.

I hope this tome directs more attention to the wonderful possibilities, as well as deep responsibilities, of each of us in our respective paths here on earth. There is truly transformative potential in each of us when we recognize the social, cultural, and political value of nonviolence, especially in its form as peaceful persuasion. Peaceful persuasion can foster justice in our hearts, homes, towns, cities, nations, and in countries where democracy is either just beginning or is still a dream.

CHAPTER 1

Everyday Peacemaking: Nonviolent Communication and Rhetoric

INTRODUCTION

In the horrific wake of the terrorist attacks of September 11, 2001, on the thousands of defenseless people inside the World Trade Towers, the Pentagon, and the airplane that went down in Pennsylvania, the overriding story that the media has repeatedly told, in myriad permutations, has been one of retribution, revenge, and war, be it in Afghanistan or in Iraq. It is easy to be led down this seductive trail of pessimism and violence in the name of "justice." It is easy to forget that the overwhelming, pre-media-induced response was *not* a preconditioned violent response: it was of spontaneous prayer and candlelight vigils; it was of reconnection with family members and friends to reaffirm our love for one another.

Somehow, this overwhelming love and need for connection and understanding has become hidden under the military and media drive to act and report on the less universal need for, but seemingly symbolic incidents of, hatred, reprisal, and violence. The incredible, untold story of American and international nonviolence and peace activism is amazing when it is placed in the context of a remarkable and increasingly ubiquitous global phenomenon. In New York City, in protest of police brutality and racist violations of civil and human rights, Oscar-winning actor Susan Sarandon joins other famous and anonymous people in civil disobedience and protests. They and hundreds of other people nonviolently march and submit to arrest without contest.[1] Out West in Billings, Montana, up to 10,000 pictures of menorahs appeared in the windows of homes, churches, businesses, and schools to protest neonazi hatred and intimidation of Jews, African Americans, and Native Americans there. The well-organized protests in Seattle, Washington, and in Washington, D.C., against human rights and environmental impacts of the World Trade Organization's (WTO's) global

1

trade actions have also made headlines for the vast majority of the protestors' respectful use of nonviolent civil disobedience. The *New York Times* gets chastised for underreporting the thousands upon thousands of peaceful people who come to Washington, D.C., to quietly, respectfully disagree with the Bush administration's alleged need to go to war with Iraq in 2002–03.

The peaceful protest phenomenon is occurring overseas as well. In Ireland, the dismantling of Irish Republican Army weapons units is being discussed, if cantankerously. In Myanmar (Burma), a woman leader of a suppressed democratic political party stubbornly sits in her car day after day, refusing to cooperate with soldiers who threaten to shoot her. Years earlier in her fight, she had fasted to the point of starvation and potential blindness while trying to press for getting fellow democratic workers who were political prisoners out of a ghastly prison. Meanwhile, in Israel and Palestine, the Peace Process creaks along, albeit sputtering at times to a full stop, as new crises arise. In South Africa, the publication of findings of Archbishop Desmond Tutu's Truth and Reconciliation Commission has brought bittersweet relief. Internationally, hundreds of countries (except the U.S.) sign a ban on the use of land mines. There is a common denominator in all of these peace-oriented developments on the forefront of international politics. There are tough negotiations, extended inquiries, complex, multiparty agreements, media pronouncements, and often, the plain, stubborn refusal of one person, here and there, to participate with injustice.

It is easiest to think about these events in terms of average people, the Erin Brockovitches among us, performing extraordinary feats of persistence, willpower, and fearlessness in the face of injustice and even mortal danger. What drives human beings to spontaneously behave in selfless, courageous ways? How are we to explain the fearlessness of the firemen running to the top floors of the burning World Trade Towers, with their main concern not being their own lives, but rather the lives of thousands of people they ushered down to safety before the towers fell? As a scholar of communication and the ways that human beings persuade one another, I believe that in all of these events and stories of human drama we find nonviolent communication patterns and rhetoric. In just plain English, it is *peaceful persuasion* that is changing the world.

Nonviolence and rhetoric—as concepts and theories of human existence and communication—are not often discussed together. Rather, these concepts and theories are understood in terms of people. In the early 20th century, it was Gandhi who exemplified nonviolence by using rhetoric, that is, exquisite powers of persuasive communication and civil-disobedient direct action, to achieve a peaceful goal. By midcentury, it was Dr. Martin Luther King, Jr., who led America's civil rights movement and, years later, we see he led all of America in many ways, toward a more peaceful future. As we enter the first years of the new millennium, America's pop culture has embraced Tibet's exiled Dalai Lama, a Nobel Peace Prize–winner. The Dalai Lama's books often grace the *New York Times* bestseller list. His nonviolent campaign to end the terrible human rights abuses in Chinese-controlled Tibet finds him in high-profile places. We see him on the pages of newspapers and magazines, hanging out with U.S. presidents and movie stars such as his friend, actor Richard Gere. Clearly, peaceful persuasion is popular and holds immense global appeal. My question is, What makes it so? How do people peacefully persuade? What makes their speeches, their books, their actions, so compelling?

THE PURPOSE OF THIS BOOK

The purpose of this work, then, is to begin to tip the scales of scholarship, which have weighed so heavily on violence, back in the direction of peace and nonviolence. Through these case studies, I define what nonviolent rhetoric is and identify its key characteristics. My identification is by no means exhaustive, but it is a start. This list includes the rhetorical use of themes and orientations toward community, collectivity, mutual responsibility, and a pointed use of cooperation or noncooperation.

In *The Rhetoric of Reason*, James Crosswhite observes that there are two "forms" of rhetoric, which he calls a "primary" and a "secondary rhetoric" (277–78). The primary rhetoric deals with "civic, public purposes as well as more individual and personal ones" and requires a robust "public sphere, some domain of argumentative discourse within which people can take action in language, resolve disputes, further common projects." In the absence of such a public sphere, "Secondary rhetoric is focused . . . [less] on accomplishing social and civic purposes by way of reasoning and speech as on the forms and techniques of writing." In short, whereas primary rhetoric is "pragmatic and purposeful," secondary rhetoric is "literary and aesthetic" (277–78). The concern of this book, then, is in this form of "primary" rhetoric. While I do analyze and at times appreciate literary and aesthetic qualities in the chapters that follow, I am more concerned here with what effects these unique case studies in the rhetoric of peace and nonviolence have in the public sphere, in the real world.

This book offers no claims to furthering theory expansively; the contribution, rather, is more incremental and introductory.[2] Nor is nonviolence proffered as a panacea to the world's woes. My overarching aim is simply to open a fruitful discussion that may eventually lead to theoretical advances. In turn, such theoretical progress might yield positive political implications. As background, a part of each case study is a brief survey of the literature, which examines what key theorists of nonviolence and scholars of rhetorical theory have to say about rhetoric as (1) a form of communication and (2) evidence of the great potential in humanity for nonviolently managing conflict.

THE PROBLEM DEFINED

One basic problem this book is designed to remedy is that nonviolence, as a theoretical paradigm, is often conspicuously absent from the array of tools of inquiry and theory-building in the field of speech communication (among many other disciplines), especially in terms of *rhetorical theory* and *criticism of rhetoric*. To clarify and qualify the point this chapter makes that rhetorical theorists have not sufficiently examined nonviolence as a major rhetorical form, first let us look at the field of communication writ large, and how conflicts are examined. If we can realistically look at speech communication as a field of study and research, we can observe what tends to be studied in its various branches. The very imperfect and rough dividing line in the field, for the purpose of this discussion, may be thought of as falling between communication theory on one side, and rhetorical theory and cultural studies on the other. Clearly, there is much overlap, but in terms of the ways that attention to nonviolence gets short shrift, some important distinctions may be considered. For example, communication theory entails, for the most part, the study of interpersonal communication, organizational communication, medical field communication, and the like. Scholars on the communication theory side tend to utilize *quantitative* methods (i.e., surveys and empirical forms of study). Statistical analyses abound in communication theory and the journals in which communication theorists publish.[3] Scholars in communication theory are well versed with concepts and studies of violence and nonviolence in contexts ranging from interpersonal relationships to communicative exchanges in international conflicts.

What this book, however, directly speaks to falls on the other side of the theoretical divide in speech communication as a field. The method of study of cultural studies and rhetorical theory tends, by and large, to be *qualitative*; scholars who use qualitative methodologies tend to publish in separate kinds of journals than our colleagues in communication theory.[4] Thus it is those who conduct research in rhetorical theory and cultural studies that I am referring to when I argue that scholars of rhetoric need to be more well versed with nonviolence, and in particular, the rhetoric of advocates of peace and nonviolence. For instance, Kevin DeLuca's book, *Image Politics* (1999), uses both rhetorical theory and cultural studies theories to consider the nonviolent rhetoric of peace activists and social movements ranging from Greenpeace and Earth First! to smaller, local organizations such as Allegany County Nonviolent Action Group

(ACNag). However, the book often becomes cramped in its attempt to explain their peace-minded and nonviolent rhetoric. *Image Politics* labors to examine the nonviolent rhetorics through neo-Marxist methodologies that cultural studies scholars, such as Laclau and Mouffe, who DeLuca cites often, use. For instance, DeLuca uses Laclau and Mouffe's neo-Marxist framework to argue that "new social movements need to disavow an essentialist identity politics that balkanizes and instead link the different antagonisms that give rise to environmental struggles, workers' struggles, feminist struggles, and anti-racist struggles so as to make possible the disarticulation of the hegemonic discourse that constructs these various groups in relations of oppression" (82). However, as I show in Chapter 6 of this book, the nonviolent rhetoric of Aung San Suu Kyi derives its force and power through its marked use of essentializing her feminine persona. Indeed, in early December 2002, under the fomenting of another war in Iraq by the second Bush administration, the *Washington Post* reported that various groups, all relying on their essentialized identities, such as that of mothers, African Americans, Latino/a Americans, veterans, church members, union members, and so on, have organized effectively as identity groups to protest war in Iraq (Nieves A1). The problem with relying on Laclau and Mouffe or other forms of Marxist theory, is that at its core, Marxism often relies on violence to make revolutionary change. How can one be effective in understanding and explicating peace-minded or nonviolent rhetorics and actions when one is using foundationally violent theories? Moreover, while the term *nonviolent* appears occasionally in DeLuca's discussion of visual and protest rhetoric, nowhere is there to be found a clear definition of nonviolent rhetoric. How can nonviolent rhetoric be explained when it is not even transparently defined?

Another recent example of the lack of attention to what "peace rhetoric" means occurs in Francis Beer's *Meanings of War and Peace* (2001), a volume in the Presidential Rhetoric Series. Although the word *peace* figures prominently in the book's title, the entire book only mentions peace a few fleeting times, at none of which is peace, or peace rhetoric, defined or explained. The book focuses heavily on debates about the merits of going to war. Too little emphasis is placed on comparable rhetorical analyses of the merits of "going to peace," that is, keeping the peace when war might have been an option, or the rhetoric of supporting peace and justice in times of relative peace. For example, Beer devotes all of Part I to examining just three rhetorical words: "war, reason, and validity." But where is "peace"? It is conspicuously absent from the analysis. In this way, Peace Studies and even the term *peace* itself is elided as a word, subject, and field of research worthy of serious study and contemplation by political scientists and rhetorical scholars alike—those who Beer draws on for his analysis and who he says are among the intended audience of the book.

It is also problematic that Beer repeatedly uses the simplistic "peace/war" dualism, which, in his context of analyzing pre- or midwar debates, conflates the two terms and essentially nullifies any careful conceptualization or engagement with peace as a valid concept in and of itself. Beer writes, "The meaning of war and peace involves many elements. One of the most important is dying" (117) and "[t]alking about dying is an important dimension of the meaning of war and peace" (138). Certainly dying relates to the meaning of war. However, what most people, texts, or dictionaries say about the meaning of peace usually has something to do with tranquillity and calmness in life; it is absurd to offhandedly equate peace with dying (with the possible exception of someone "resting in peace," by which time the dying has already been done). Elsewhere Beer mentions peace in the context of "an Orwellian twilight zone where peace was war and war was peace" (161). He also notes other forms of "peace," by which he really means "war," such as "hot peace," "guerrilla peace" . . . "'half peace' . . . . [in] which smaller creatures may still fight and the elephants . . . trample the ants" (170). Yet these alleged "peace" terms are ones that have been coopted by war-makers and are hardly encouraging or accurate forms of true peace, nor do they approximate peace with justice, or what Johan Galtung calls "positive peace." Nowhere in the book does Beer even offer a single definition of peace. In short, the book exclusively covers discursive exchanges about war, yet its title, by default, and the content of the book, by omission, allows peace to be wrongly conflated with war. (For the full book review, see *International Journal on World Peace*, June 2002.) These are the kinds of research problems that can be overcome through a careful plotting out of both theories and definitions that more fully and fairly explain what peace is, what nonviolence is, what these rhetorics entail, and which theories might more aptly be used to understand the unique process of persuasion that occurs when peace-minded rhetorical means are used.

So while scholars in interpersonal or organizational communication might study violent or nonviolent conflict-reduction techniques, scholars of rhetoric or cultural studies, in my view, are often somewhat less well versed with definitions of peace and the rhetorical strategies of conflict reduction, as well as foundational concepts of nonviolence in theory and practice. Therefore, this book offers, in part, both a rationale for and a call to study (on the part of students, scholars, and practitioners) more, and well, the nonviolent rhetoric of peace, justice, and nonviolent activism.

Nonviolent rhetoric is important because it is a major feature of geopolitical changes in the 20th century, as well as of changes now unfolding. Political theorists such as Paul G. Lauren and nonviolence theorists like Johan Galtung posit that nonviolence will be of even greater import in the 21st century. In the July 1999 issue of *Spectra* [the official newsletter of the National Communication Association

(NCA)], NCA President Orlando Taylor lists the following as among the "top ten communication events of the 20th century":

- Suffragettes' Protests for Voting Rights
- Mahatma Gandhi's Rhetoric of Nonviolence
- The Martin Luther King, Jr.'s "I Have a Dream" Speech (2)
- Nelson Mandela's Inaugural Address (7)

These communication events feature nonviolent rhetoric; each event features themes of valuing human and civil rights for all people, and noncooperation with systems of institutional and structural violence or oppression. Another defining feature common to, but by no means the sole domain of nonviolent rhetoric, is that each of these communication events comes from women and people of color.

Why Do We Need to Understand Nonviolence?

First, there is a need to study nonviolent rhetoric and rhetorics that encourage nonviolent approaches to handling conflicts. We need to look at the way some traditional characteristics of rhetorical approaches lead to violent or oppositional outlooks. *The significance of developing a critical awareness of nonviolent rhetoric is that its major characteristics often differ from those of conventional rhetoric.* More important, the unique traits of nonviolent rhetoric call for attention to the study of, theory of, and critique of past rhetorics in light of these differences.

Human beings worldwide are beset with problems of overpopulation, gross economic disparity, decreasing resources of viable land, water, air, and energy, as well as various forms of structural violence. Meanwhile, politically based animosities with historic racial, ethnic, and religious overtones are now proliferating with the help of international economic and military systems that operate through ideology. Ironically, this situation runs to the brink of nuclear warfare in Gandhi's own India. So while nonviolence is not a cure-all, it does offer hope and one possible way to address our current conundrums.

Another purpose of this book is to show how nonviolent approaches to rhetoric can differ from existing approaches. The academic and political world too often labors under the *realpolitik* assumption that violence is the only, most powerful, or simply most expedient means to prevailing in hot or cold conflicts around the world. The NATO bombings of Serbia in 1999, Afghanistan in 2001, and the continuous, bombing war against Iraq throughout the 1990s and culminating in 2003 reveal the flaws of the assumption that violence brings or forces a quick "solution" to conflicts. An alternative form of political power can be found in nonviolence in theory and practice.

A subaim of this project is simply to reveal the compelling force and reason of nonviolent civil action. Particularly through rhetoric, nonviolent civil action has been shown by historical precedent to be at least as effective in managing conflicts, if not more so, than using violent tactics. This project is useful because it provides strong indications that human beings can broach conflict in ways that can often exclude guns and violence, whereas more traditional theoretical perspectives (military strategies or Marxist theory, for instance) actually *call for* their use. Each chapter that follows helps to contribute to knowledge in a valuable way by uncovering and drawing out how some of the basic appeals of peace-minded persuasion operate and by identifying and demystifying hidden elements. I explore and explain basic modes of nonviolent rhetoric in different cultural milieus so that nonviolent communication can be widely understood and appreciated.

Once better understood, nonviolent rhetoric can be theorized, so that principles can be applied to assessing future conflict situations. This book is part of an exciting and growing trend in scholarship and social movement activism that (1) aims to prevent or greatly reduce the potential for destroying life on earth, while also (2) vitally enhancing the potential for improved human coexistence, and (3) fostering greater respect for both human and ecological diversity on earth. For a preliminary definition, let us consider that *peace rhetoric* and *nonviolent rhetoric* are comprised of these three facets of research and activism.

Nonviolence Is a Powerful, Global Phenomenon

Violence surrounds us on a daily basis. There is the *interpersonal* violence of school shootings, including, increasingly, ones at college campuses. I shudder to think that on my way to class one morning at Penn State University in 1996, I unwittingly walked right by the site of a shooting shortly *before* it occurred. One young student that day was killed; others were injured. There is also the *structural* violence of corporate-caused environmental pollution, which is exemplified in the nonfiction book, *A Civil Action*. Today more than ever, peace and nonviolence represent both a desire and a potential balm for people living in stressful and unjust conditions. The focus of the case studies in this book is geopolitical rhetoric that broaches conflict *without* the use—or threat of use—of violence and weapons. By better understanding the inner workings of nonviolent communication practices, we can open the door to the exciting opportunity for theorizing how social and political power can exist and be amassed entirely apart from military and other forms of disciplinary power.

Nonviolence is taking hold in the collective psyche of contemporary society: more schools are starting programs to train nonviolent conflict mediators among children; a few progressive corporations support nonviolent working environments by offering flexible work schedules and more egalitarian stockholding plans; even the military has begun to investigate less violent means of crowd control for humanitarian or peacekeeping missions. Three U.S. presidents have, despite serious objections from China, met with the XIVth Dalai Lama of Tibet, a Nobel Peace Prize–winner and world-renowned harbinger of nonviolent rhetoric. So too has the U.S. Congress as a body (via initiatives that have condemned human rights abuses) supported many nonviolent political figures. President Clinton's parting attempt at including the U.S. as part of a United Nations' world-crimes tribunal, which would subject U.S. military personnel to scrutiny over human rights abuses, shows that even the United States cannot escape the world's concern about the excesses of those who wage war.

Learning about and understanding nonviolence is both the interest of citizens and government leaders; it is the world's mandate for a new era. Each of the case studies that follow sheds light on urgent current issues and events. For each case, and although each is very different in terms of geographic, political, and cultural factors, the leitmotif remains nonviolent rhetoric as a means to peacefully broach and manage (if not completely resolve) conflict. There is a degree of cross-cultural and international applicability in this work. I hypothesize that each case is generalizable, in important respects, to other regions and cases around the world.

So, Why Is Nonviolence Ignored in Rhetorical Theory?

The term *passive resistance* has often been misconstrued by rhetorical critics and others to mean a repugnant, cowering weakness. David Cochran, former director of the peace-studies program at the University of Missouri, writes, "The American tradition of nonviolence has been consistently ridiculed and marginalized by those with a vested interest in the status quo. Even the nonviolent activists who make it into the official canon do so in a distorted way."[5] Some people misconstrue nonviolence as pure passivity. For them, it translates into recommending women to passively submit to rape or domestic violence; an accurate understanding of nonviolence, however, would recommend the opposite.

Nonviolence "is seen as cowardly expedience" and "masochism."[6] Nonviolence is considered the tactic of choice among wimps while violence is taken to be, without question, "the strongest and most effective means available to resist injustice, destroy an oppressive system, or counteract a violent attack."[7] Such attitudes stem from status quo representations of nonviolence that do not accurately depict it as a theory or practice.

In the study of public address and rhetoric, when nonviolence is actually included in analyses, it has historically been presented in a distorted manner. For
example, in 1963, speech communication scholar Harry Bowen posed the question, "Do non-violent techniques really change the beliefs and actions of dedicated enemies?"[8] In observing the nonviolent protests of the civil rights
activists, Bowen answers his question in an utterly equivocal manner, saying,
"Against such white people non-violence has had no noticeable persuasive effect,
although the *results of non-violence have compelled some change in the segregationists' behavior*" so that "[African Americans] can sit and eat where they please in
some restaurants and transportation terminals" (emphasis added).[9] If such civil
rights gains were *not* the result of nonviolent action, then what were they? More
frustrating still is the fact that as distorted as it might be, Bowen's article is a
rare one in the range of rhetorical theory because it is one of the few that actually addresses nonviolence outright. Although there is the occasional release of
a book in rhetorical theory that focuses on nonviolent and peace rhetoric, such
as *Women Who Speak for Peace* (2002), it remains a marginalized area of research,
tending to represent the rhetorics of specific interest groups such as women or
minorities, rather than cases of rhetoric of general interest to a wider array of
students and scholars. If not ignored or omitted altogether, nonviolence is simply attenuated; it is only implicitly invoked by the theorist or critic, such as was
shown in the case of *Image Politics*.

When nonviolence is implicitly invoked, nonviolence is distorted because
both its viability and significance are downplayed. It is also distorted because no
clear understanding of nonviolence is first established. Due to the many negative
connotations the term *nonviolence* carries, among other terms pejoratively
deemed "peacenik," clear definitions are crucial to understanding its impact. Yet
nonviolence is left unexplained. For instance, in Richard Fulkerson's essay, "The
Public Letter as a Rhetorical Form: Structure, Logic, and Style in King's 'Letter
from Birmingham Jail,'" Fulkerson finds it important enough to note in the second paragraph of the essay the fact that King's "Letter" was printed ("50,000
copies") and distributed by the American Friends Service Committee; yet there
is *no mention* that the group was a nonviolent organization that supported King's
nonviolent mission.[10] Fulkerson's only other allusions to nonviolence in the *entire* essay occur (1) as a citation of one of his sources, a book title, buried deep in
a footnote, and (2), in the unsubstantiated claim (in the second-to-last paragraph)
that King wrote the letter to a "traditional audience who would generally oppose
civil disobedience."[11] The simple and well-known fact is that King was modeling
his nonviolent approaches to civil disobedience after his own father's and grandfather's nonviolent theological philosophy, and in part after Gandhi's success in
India; Gandhi's forays into nonviolence were in part a result of Thoreau's ideas

successfully taking root in the United States.[12] Such a fact renders the lack of commentary a distortion in that it totally minimizes nonviolence as a significant theoretical and persuasive force in King's letter.

Similarly, in Donald Smith's essay, "Martin Luther King, Jr.: In the Beginning at Montgomery," Smith offers only three remarks about nonviolence in the *entire* essay, all of which are vague and presume an understanding of nonviolence: (1) "Love, not violence, must be the means for redress of their grievances. With these words, the speaker [King] reflected the love ethic of Jesus Christ and *its active application by Gandhi* and thus began to establish the philosophical basis of the movement"; (2) "that this would be a Christian movement, one *without violence*"; and (3) "[King's] talks were directed to four purposes . . . [including] *keeping the nonviolent tone and philosophy* of the movement ever before the boycotters" (emphasis added).[13] Despite the fact that nonviolence is noted by Smith to be *integral* to King's movement, Smith does not include nonviolence as being integral to the effectiveness of King's rhetoric.

By the same token, Malinda Snow's essay, "Martin Luther King's 'Letter from Birmingham Jail' as Pauline Epistle" also downplays nonviolence as an issue worthy of comment; in the whole essay, the only time nonviolence is mentioned occurs (again, in the second-to-last paragraph) when Snow quotes, *without* commentary, King's *own words* that "nonviolence is vital because it is the only way to reestablish the broken community."[14] These are just a few examples of how nonviolence is belittled: it is presumed to be understood as important to King's rhetoric, yet nonviolence as either a theory or persuasive communication strategy is somehow not deemed worthy of commentary by the critic.

In a rare instance of contrast to these examples of how nonviolence has tended to be elided in discussions of rhetorical theory and criticism, Mark McPhail, in *Zen in the Art of Rhetoric* (1996), does acknowledge that nonviolence is central to King's rhetoric. McPhail writes, "Martin Luther King's use of nonviolence as a form of moral action clearly illustrates a coherent metaphysical and epistemological grounding" (86). Likewise, Dorothy Pennington has argued that, for King, nonviolence was "the ultimate form of persuasion" and that the goal of using nonviolent action was "to persuade" (as quoted in McPhail, 86). McPhail adds that King's use of nonviolent rhetoric was "grounded in traditional rhetorical principles and strategies," yet, because it used democratic principles to "[call] into question the social inequities of American society" it was considered "radical" (86). King's famous speech, "Declaration of Independence from the war in Vietnam," can be seen as the textbook definition of nonviolent rhetoric; McPhail writes that "King's emphasis on the interrelatedness of human existence illustrates his reliance on coherent ontological and epistemological assumptions, assumptions which emphasized similarity over difference as a method for transcending the social and psychological divisions that undermine human unity and cooperation" (87). Thus to formulate how argumentation operates in the nonviolent mode, McPhail offers that it "recognizes that which postmodernism privileges most, difference" (127), while also "[creating] common places" that enable the nonviolent rhetor to establish a setting (i.e., social, physical, or psychological) for argumentation in which the "power of argument will be distributed equally" (128).

Such insights into the mechanics of nonviolent rhetoric, however, are presently little known, referred to, or taught in basic courses on rhetorical theory; they remain consigned to the bin of special interest rhetorics at a historic time when the exigencies of global politics could really use them. Teachers and students of communication and persuasion could benefit from better understanding nonviolent theory and seeing how there is nothing "passive" about resisting oppression without resorting to violence. By no means does nonviolence invoke a sense of passivity, or mere waiting. Rather, nonviolent activity is aimed at orienting collective energies in the present into specific, concrete actions. Nonviolent rhetoric is designed to facilitate in one's adversary an acknowledgment of the validity of one's views. Such work is done so that the opponent will want to enter into the hypothetical role of the ideal and humane arguer (Johnstone).

TOOLS FOR ANALYZING NONVIOLENCE

The qualitative methodology employed in this book follows the instructive call of Kenneth Burke to "use all there is to use." Case studies are given of rhetorical-critical analyses of nonviolent rhetoric in action. I contextually situate (1) the growth of nonviolent theory and rhetoric in different cultural milieu and (2) in terms of the place of nonviolent theory in the unfolding events of recent history. This approach stems from Michel Foucault's useful method of the "genealogy," which "entertains the claims to attention of local, discontinuous," and often overlooked sources of data (Foucault, "Two Lectures" 83–84).

It is important to note, as Sara Ruddick has, that while "abstraction is central" to all thinking, it is particularly so for "militarist thinking" (as qtd. in Carroll and Zerilli 68). Therefore, in conceiving of characteristics of nonviolent rhetoric, it is crucial to retain a graspable, tangible element—real-world origins and applications—to the theoretical foundations constructed here. In this way, the theorizing contained in this book attempts as much as possible to work in the nonviolent mode, that is, against the grain of the "abstract" and "militarist" mind-set. On the whole, I employ an interdisciplinary approach to explore the interstices of rhetoric and nonviolence as they play out in global political conflicts. This book demonstrates the ways that nonviolent theory can complement rhetorical theory, expanding it to serve as a mode of political interaction and intervention. Ideally, this book will help to spur a rethinking of existing models of rhetoric and the role of nonviolent rhetoric in both established and budding democratic societies in the world.

Rather than conceptualizing nonviolence through pure abstraction, the design of this project is to examine case studies of socio- and geopolitical conflicts to show how nonviolence works through human symbolic interactions. Accordingly, the focus of each chapter is on (1) why we need to study nonviolence and the nonviolent, political rhetoric of (2) activists as they are (mis)reported in the media; (3) education in Speech Communication as a field; (4) an independent film, *The Spitfire Grill*, (5) Kiro Gligorov, former president of Macedonia, (6) Aung San Suu Kyi, democratic leader of opposition party in Myanmar (Burma), and (7) townspeople of the spontaneous nonviolent social movement in Billings, Montana, who prevailed over neonazi terrorism. Each case study reveals the flaws, shortcomings, paradoxes, and problems with nonviolence in practice, but each also extols the successes and advantages of using nonviolent approaches to conflict management. Each chapter helps pull nonviolence down from the impossible pedestal of saintly perfection, or "principled nonviolence," that many critics use to argue that nonviolence is impractical for the ordinary person, group, or nation (Burgess and Burgess 14–15).

SUMMARY

This first chapter has introduced the reasons why nonviolence deserves more attention from scholars and students of rhetorical theory and criticism, among other fields. (For pivotal terms and assumptions of this treatise as a whole, refer to Appendix 1.) Chapter 1 has introduced the research problems and theoretical context while sketching the potential of rhetorical theory to be expanded in peace-oriented and nonviolent directions. Through examples of a few of the pitfalls of analyzing contemporary political rhetoric and nonviolent civil action, this chapter posits that rhetorical theory can be enriched by the inclusion of nonviolent perspectives.

The remainder of the book unfolds as essays that can be read alone, or in any order. Chapter 2 covers what, in terms of enhanced media and public relations, the peace movement and nonviolent activists stand to gain from better understanding and applying rhetorical theory to their work. Chapter 3 discusses the problem of the inferiority complex that nonviolence has in education in general, in the field of communication, and in rhetorical theory in particular. In chapter 3 I suggest ways for educators to surmount this problem. Chapter 4 examines an independent film that featured nonviolence, and shows how the mainstream press panned it, largely due to the Western cultural orientation of valuing violence and devaluing nonviolence as a means to manage conflict.

Chapter 5 reveals the specifically nonviolent modes of discourse and persuasion that distinguish nonviolent rhetoric from peace rhetoric in general. The focus is on pragmatic nonviolence as a practical mode of communication and conflict engagement, prevention, and management. Chapter 5 takes a traditional, oratorical approach to rhetoric in examining the practical nonviolent rhetoric of a leader in the international political realm. I discuss the nonviolent rhetoric of a leader of a small, beleaguered nation called Macedonia that is struggling to foster democracy in a region at war. Specifically, this chapter provides the rhetorical analysis of the first public address of Kiro Gligorov of Macedonia, when the new nation was finally admitted as a member of the United Nations in 1993. Most speeches delivered in this forum are written off as simply "peace rhetoric." Yet scholars like Michael Prosser, in *Sow the Wind*, are increasingly finding that conflict mediated in this and other international political arenas provides real and tangible results that foster conflict prevention, resolution, and peacemaking processes. Gligorov's speech, analyzed and explained, is a clear exemplar of rhetoric in the pragmatic, not saintly, nonviolent mode. I also relate his rhetoric to a more nuanced understanding of the events of the war in Kosovo in 1999. Gligorov uses nonviolent rhetoric that alternately supports and challenges the notion of a cohesive, mutually responsible, international body politic.

Chapter 6 examines the visual rhetoric of a nonviolent activist—Aung San Suu Kyi of Myanmar (Burma)—and her use of a special rhetoric of the body to further her political drive to create a democratic society out of the totalitarian regime in her country in Southeast Asia. The case analyzed ponders the visual rhetoric of the nonviolent, gendered body of Aung San Suu Kyi, Nobel Peace Prize–winner, and its relationship to the international body politic. This chapter examines the unique role of the textually mediated body—physical, spiritual, and political—in fostering nonviolent persuasion. Questions concerning how nonviolent modes can essentialize or free people from categories are addressed. Culture, gender, territory, and visual/mental maps of displays of nonviolence are shown to pervade individual and political bodies.

Chapter 7 introduces the theoretical concept of a "rhetorical climate." This chapter analyzes a case of how citizens effectively combated violent neonazi anti-Semitism and racism in Billings, Montana in 1993. Although this case could lend itself well to textual analysis in the traditional sense, I provide a different outlook and means for conducting rhetorical criticism. Instead of looking at a single speech or a text or symbol produced by a single leader, I consider the case from a holistic perspective. I examine the rhetoric of collectivity. In rejecting the binary thinking and dichotomies of mind/body and emotion/reason, this chapter explores the important role that new cognitive theories of rhetoric have in enabling us to understand how rhetoric is more than simply a symbolic or linguistic field of study.

Using sociological theory on the influence of the body in persuasion, rhetoric is viewed as a force beyond mere texts and words and the emotions they convey.

The case study in chapter 7 shows how nonviolent rhetoric and social action bolsters democratic community while it values differences among community members in the "asymmetrical" mode of communication. This case study also clarifies and explicates the concept of what a rhetorical climate is and how this concept can contribute to widening rhetorical theory to include nonviolence. Chapter 7, focusing as it does on cognitive aspects of rhetoric and the relationship of rhetoric to the differentiated body, is the culmination of this volume as a whole. This final case points directly to ways that enable us to conceptualize a nonviolent rhetoric. Nonviolent rhetoric focuses specifically on the intersection of nonviolence, rhetoric, and the human body as it reacts to its political and social environment. At the same time, I offer a critique of the problems of privilege and social inequity that nonviolent theories sometimes entail or ignore.

Finally, chapter 8 summarizes and relates the significance of the findings discussed in the preceding chapters. By encapsulating the central concepts explored in each of these case studies, constructs that may be useful in developing a theory of nonviolent rhetoric are advanced. Chapter 8 explores the ramifications and entailments of these constructs, including important areas for future research and scholarly inquiry in fields that include, but are not limited to, rhetorical theory, political theory, history, sociology, women's studies, and peace and conflict studies. The ultimate aim I hope to achieve in chapter 8 is to remind readers that, far from flimsy or utopian, nonviolence in general, and nonviolent rhetoric in particular, is rather sensible and clear-eyed. The implication is that nonviolence, while not always being a perfect or definitive "solution" to social or political conflicts, does provide very real and practical means for engaging in conflicts in a peace-oriented manner; nonviolence can strengthen existing democratic societies and enable budding democracies to take root.[15]

CHAPTER 2

%

Rhetoric, Media, and Public Relations: Evolving Nonviolent Communication with Rhetorical Theory

I f the peace movement is to make progress one of the key problems that its members must surmount is its rhetoric. Rhetoric—that is, persuasive discourse, action, or symbols—is central to successfully getting one's issue reported on, obtaining project funding, being published, getting noticed, or just being taken seriously. Historically, dominant discourses of "violence/war/military = normal" and "nonviolence/peace/peace advocates = abnormal" have been used to marginalize and weaken peace workers such as civil rights activists, environmentalists, or educators (True). Indeed, peace scholars Kai Brand-Jacobsen and Carl Jacobsen write that

> The dream of a world free from the scourge of war is seen by many to be naïve and utopian, if not dangerously unrealistic, against a logic that dictates that violence must be met with violence, and that 'peace' is achievable only through the force of arms. Yet this is a false image. . . . [There is] increasing recognition that humanitarian catastrophes and the structural and cultural violence underlying them are at the core of many of today's wars. . . The need to develop early and effective mechanisms for violence prevention, to identify these patterns and to transform the underlying structures and causes of violence is gaining more and more recognition. (232–33)

The Jacobsens maintain that "peace building or conflict transformation" needs to be more widely accepted by "states, peace researchers and NGO's alike" (233). However, in order to make peace building and conflict transformation possible, there needs to be a stronger campaign to create awareness on the part of the

17

public and the media that informs the public of the real and realistic possibilities and opportunities that peacemakers have to offer. Until the media and the public are better informed, the old images of the out-of-touch, utopian peaceniks will prevail alongside the widely accepted myth that violence works and nonviolence does not work.

This chapter introduces readers, especially those from the field of peace and conflict studies, to concepts from and critical analysis in rhetorical theory to foster awareness of the role of rhetoric in language, symbols, activism, and how they play out in mediated campaigns. There are both empowering and disempowering qualities in peace rhetoric. Some of the rhetorical strategies that peace activists use will be examined for the ways that they can be rhetorically powerful or weak. This chapter also examines rhetorical strategies to more effectively manage the exigencies of the current profit-driven media and of the public relations side of peace activism, revealing ways to reempower peace rhetoric and use it more strategically to challenge dominant discourses. Admittedly, the discussion that follows perhaps poses more questions than it answers. The aim, however, is to simply begin looking at the problem in hopes that other scholars and activists will join in the hunt for more definitive solutions to the quandary posed by the media (mis)representation of peace activism and nonviolent direct action.

Rhetoric is often thought of as empty or hollow discourse (Hauser 2). The term *rhetoric* is frequently negatively associated with propaganda, spin-doctors, and verbal and visual fluff. However, that is just one side of the story. Rhetoric is also a substantive field of study and research, and it has a rich tradition of study and scholarship dating back at least 2,500 years to civilizations of ancient Europe, Asia, and Africa. This body of scholarship and field of rhetorical theory and inquiry is usually understood, studied, and used by the ruling classes and the powerful elites. Rhetoric is studied, for example, by students pursuing law degrees. Rhetoric is also studied by the keepers of culture, such as scholars of Communication and English literature. Rhetoric is also of interest to students of Cultural Studies who analyze how cultural artifacts, norms, and practices persuade people to behave in specific ways. Yet any sustained understanding of rhetorical theory appears to be largely left out of the picture in the field of peace and conflict studies.

A relative lack of understanding of rhetoric as a field of study and practice is becoming a detriment to the peace movement, writ large. If peace scholars, activists, and supporters had a better understanding of the basic underpinnings of rhetorical theory, as well as media strategy and analysis, we might be more agile in our activities, be they fundraising, scholarship, or media management and social movement mobilizing.

RHETORIC IN THE SERVICE OF SOCIAL KNOWLEDGE

So, what does rhetorical theory cover and how can it help those who are working for peace and justice locally, nationally, and internationally? According to Aristotle, rhetoric is the "faculty for observing in any given case all the available means of persuasion." James Herrick writes that rhetoric is concerned with persuasion, that it considers carefully its audience, it "reveals human motives," and that rhetoric is a "response" and that it "invites a response" (8–15). Herrick also summarizes how rhetoric shapes the way political and social events unfold because "rhetoric tests ideas; assists advocacy; distributes power; discovers facts; shapes knowledge; and builds community" (16–23). To expand what rhetoric constitutes further, Sonja Foss, Karen Foss, and Robert Trapp have "defined rhetoric broadly as the uniquely human ability to use symbols to communicate with one another," which includes "any communication medium," be it "the spoken or written word" or "unspoken symbols used by the artist or musician" (11). Barry Brummet updates this expansive definition of rhetoric by conjoining it with critical studies. Brummet maintains that "everyday actions, objects, and experiences" and even "*all* of popular culture works to influence the public" (3). In short, rhetoric is a social, cultural, and political body of knowledge that shapes how people create and perceive reality and how they behave in the world.

According to Gerard Hauser, "the study of rhetoric includes two concerns: the methods followed in constructing intentional discourse [intellectual practice] . . . and the way symbolic performances influence practical choices—a social practice" (12). Because the peace movement is concerned with persuasion, with intentional discourse, and with social practices, it seems only natural and helpful to become more aware of the range of strategic choices that the study of rhetorical theory and media relations would afford the peace scholar and practitioner.

Specifically, there are three ways that a deeper understanding of rhetoric can aid the members of the peace movement. First, understanding rhetoric enhances the ability of the scholar or activist in navigating the oceans of bureaucratic rhetoric that must be traversed in order to obtain funding for scholarship or social movement action. Second, understanding rhetoric can enhance our ability to communicate with disparate audiences to persuade people to support peace, to promote nonviolent resolutions to conflicts, and to better coordinate and amass consensus amongst fellow peace and justice activists. Third, and perhaps most important, a clear understanding of rhetoric can enable scholars and activists to be portrayed more fully and fairly in the mainstream mass media.

This chapter will focus primarily on the role that an enhanced knowledge of rhetoric could play in helping the peace movement get more of a fair shake in the media, especially considering the "distortive tendencies of the press and its proclivity for sensationalism and exaggeration" (Walker 47). For this discussion, I will use Julian Bond's definition of "mainstream news media," by which he includes "national broadcasting networks (NBC, ABC, CBS) and nationally prominent news publications such as *Time, Newsweek* . . . , *Life* . . . and the *New York Times*" (16). Considering global media network expansion, such networks would also include broadcasters such as CNN, and publications that also have international reach, such as the *International Herald Tribune.*

ENGAGING THE MEDIA RHETORICALLY

Members of the peace movement have long been adept at rhetoric, but usually that knowledge comes through a kind of street smarts and experience-based wisdom. This discussion merely submits that that such knowledge can be enhanced and more broadly shared among everyone who works for causes relating to peace and justice. One suggestion here is that if media-savvy rhetorics are used to advantage, peace activists can more fully participate in the current national and international campaign to create a safer, more peaceful nation and world in the post-9/11 era. A benefit of understanding rhetorical theory is that more effective audience analysis yields greater communicative success, which, for the peace movement, could translate into more political and economic opportunities both nationally and internationally for the adoption of nonviolent strategies for conflict resolution and peacemaking.

Rhetoric can inform and enhance our ability to increase the visibility and acceptability of communicative efforts both inside and outside the peace movement. Brian Ward believes that there is a comparative lack of emphasis on the "role of the mass media" in understanding the successes of the early civil rights movement in the United States (2). He emphasizes that music, film, and radio were powerful ways of getting the word out (6–8). Ward reveals that "sympathetic press coverage was vital to the emergence and initial successes of the early southern civil rights campaign" (10). Likewise, Bond maintains that the "wholly white-owned, invariably white-staffed, and largely white-oriented media crucially shaped popular perceptions of the Movement throughout the nation" (16). For contemporary peace activists, the word *white* might now be added to or replaced by terms such as *corporate* or *pro-military.* An important lesson for today's peace scholars and activists can be learned from studying the relationship of the press to the early civil rights activists. Bond says the early movement

> reflected the remarkable skill with which the Montgomery protesters presented themselves to the press, and through the press, to the nation, as models of patriotic virtue and moral respectability. With its church-based

leadership, its much vaunted adherence to nonviolence in the face of enormous white provocation, and its repeated appeals to American constitutional rights and democratic values, the Montgomery Movement had seized the moral high ground from the segregationists. (23)

In an age of visual rhetoric, image rules (DeLuca 4–5). Bond reports that the tidy appearance of the students sitting at lunch counters was contrasted with the slovenly, "ragtail rabble" appearance of the "rowdy white attackers" (30). In the decades since the Vietnam War protests, in which the hippie counterculture dress of "ragtail rabble" became the norm, most nonviolent protesters have been routinely characterized, especially visually, in the press as being slovenly at least and terrorists at worst (DeLuca 88–90). The problematic stereotype of the shaggy, dreamy-eyed, pot-smoking peace activist needs to be taken seriously by the peace movement and actively dispelled because it drastically undermines the *ethos*, or credibility, of the nonviolent messenger. If protesters and activists cannot be seen as credible, then how can the messages they purvey be persuasive to the mainstream public, to voters, and to influential decision makers?

Similarly, the newest stereotype that is an equally challenging obstacle to be overcome by the various peace movement diaspora is that of the spoiled suburban teenager, the proverbial purple-haired punk, dressed all in black clothes, who, out of sheer boredom, takes to the streets to smash things. A friend of mine who attended the "Battle for Seattle" protests in 1999–2000 observed with ironic dismay, for example, when a small band of black-garbed, face-masked protesters, self-proclaimed "anarchists," used crow bars to smash into a Starbucks coffee chain store, then proceeded to help one another to bags of coffee, saying: "Hey! Pass me some of that Mocha Java," or "I'll trade you this Kenya for that Morning blend." Although the majority of the Seattle protesters were nonviolent, it was, sadly, these kinds of symbolic few that the mass media often glommed onto and reported about. After all, these few pests make for exciting reports, and excitement rules in the ratings and profit-driven media. How can nonviolent activists work, both in terms of strategic direct action and rhetorical campaign planning, to separate and distinguish themselves more effectively from these troublemakers?

Likewise, another example of a plain lack of strategic insight on the part of so-called nonviolent protesters appears in the fall, 1996 Patagonia clothing catalog. There is a photo showing a crowd of activists—who, according to the caption underneath the photo, are "Non-violent,"—blocking a road to prevent logging of one old growth forest in the Pacific Northwest. Yet the picket signs that they are holding are stapled to *wooden* posts. Gandhi himself might not approve of this particular protest, for he would not categorize this as true nonviolent action, since the so called "nonviolent" activists are *not* noncooperating with their oppressor. Instead, by buying the wooden posts for their protest signs, they are cooperating with and supporting the very opponent, in this case, the logging and forest products industries, against whom these protesters claim to be protesting. Also, the consumerist context in which the photo is shown is telling. Nonviolent actors need to be more cognizant of the rhetorical implications of their work; a fundamental understanding of rhetoric could enable activists to recognize and prevent such inconsistencies of message. In so doing, the various branches of the peace movement, including the environmental justice movement, could be more persuasive.

The nature of protest itself also needs to be reexamined by scholars of peace and conflict studies as well as by nonviolent activists. Tom Hastings, a veteran teacher and practitioner of nonviolent activism, states:

> In my . . . opinion, the successes of the global justice movement have occurred to the extent they have appealed to the masses who consume mainstream media in whatever country you consider. Thus, I think, Seattle was successful more because tens of thousands of union people were in the street more than a relative handful of window-breaking smash-n-dashers. This is not to take away from their effectiveness when it has occurred, but I would argue that those [so-called anarchist] tactics are effecting a movement diminution, not a movement building. (e-mail)

The problem of maintaining the demeanor of nonviolence in street protests is particularly vexing when the relatively few obstreperous protestors are reported in the mass media as representative of the majority of truly nonviolent protesters. Michael Nagler, founder and chair of the Peace and Conflict Studies Program at University of California, Berkeley, supports the view that "as Gandhi said, 'disobedience must be civil'; that is, polite, not abrasive—obstructive but not *ad hominem.*" But he also cautions, "don't expect the press to treat us well no matter what we do: do the right thing because it's the right thing" (e-mail). To that I would add, however, that if the peace movement does the right thing in a way that's rhetorically appealing, the peace movement might get better press. Using classic rhetorical appeals to virtues such as patriotism constitutes just one lesson of the early civil rights movement that needs to be relearned by current practitioners of nonviolence and civil disobedience.

However, even the successes of the early civil rights movement become diluted in today's media. Ward bemoans the fact that current representation and cultural cooptation of historic peace movement symbols by a sugar-coated, mainstream "master narrative" is routine (9). For example, writes Ward:

> Despite efforts to complicate and deepen this simplistic, static vision of [Dr. Martin Luther] King [as safely frozen in his "Dream"], there is little space in

the public celebrations for the post-Selma King: the democratic socialist who, like many black power radicals to whom he is often favorably contrasted, clearly saw the interconnectedness of racism, militarism, and economic exploitation, and at the time of his death had resolved to fight them all. (9)

Unfortunately, this plays into current media reporting of the anarchist element in nonviolent protests. Jenny Walker says that this "willful media myopia has had a particularly distortive effect on histories of the early southern movement" so that black violence that erupted out of frustrations, even amidst the nonviolent movement, tends not to get much notice. The upshot is that today's activists are unfairly compared to the seemingly more saintly nonviolent protesters of the early civil rights movement, when in fact many of the 1960s nonviolent protests happened despite "black violence—rhetorical and actual—that occurred around the edges, and occasionally in the midst, of the putatively nonviolent movement" (Walker 48). Thus the spurts of violence of the occasional anarchist element that accompany today's largely peaceful protests that involve direct action and civil disobedience are cast as anomalies or proof of the "failure" of nonviolence, when in fact they are side effects to be expected.

At the same time, nonviolent activists would be wise to take a more proactive stance toward anticipating and preventing the rhetorical and actual damage caused by the "smash-n-dash" element. Once the media has labeled the peace movement as "unsuccessful" due to these so-called aberrations of violence in the thick of nonviolence, then the whole peace movement in its current form can be deemed a failure and an aberration by default since it does not uphold the fabled nonviolent perfection of its earlier 1960s incarnation, even if that was to a certain extent a media-generated myth. "If historians do not fully acknowledge the reality of [1960s] black violence," notes Walker, "then they fail to capture what a remarkable achievement any significant display of nonviolent discipline was" (61). This very real and uncomfortable coexistence of nonviolence with violence and its representation in the media needs further attention by both peace activists and scholars of rhetoric and peace studies who examine nonviolent direct action.

Another problem worth studying that Larry Fisk points out is the "fragmentary" and overly contentious nature of the media (170). The media strategy of drastically oversimplifying stories into two sides, says Fisk, feeds the artificially "perceived glamour and excitement of violence" (170). He argues that the most egregious genre to be aware of is TV news because it masquerades as being educational while in fact it is just as fake and ratings bound as any fictional prime time TV shows (171). The harm in TV news, Fisk avers, is that its superficial, soundbite "constraints actually deflect us from long-term reflection and respectfully attending to the violence and pain in human experience" (171). He believes it can even function as a "sophisticated shield from encountering horror," because it serves as a filter and is often just "erudite entertainment" (208). Through peace education and teaching the fundamentals of rhetorical criticism and media analysis, critical thinking skills can be developed. It is also crucial to teach people to actively seek out "[t]he smaller, less conventional media alternatives . . . [to] help us imagine ways around problems and violence" (170). Peace activists need to realize these very real constraints of the news media and work toward developing ways to obtain media coverage that outwits the journalists and outmaneuvers the editorial policies of profit driven media networks. In addition to "[d]emand[ing] professionalism from the media, less violence and elitism and bias; more focus on common people and peace efforts," the peace movement simultaneously needs to think of how to work within and transcend these biases (Galtung 152).

Two recent examples of positive media coverage of peace activism are instructive. With regard to the very persuasive rhetorical appeal of patriotism, National Public Radio's (NPR) Morning Edition reported on a retired couple, Morgan and Marilyn Griffins, who noticed one day all of the political candidate and issue signs stuck in front yards around their suburban Seattle neighborhood. The signs, which appeared during election season, were all done up in patriotic red, white, and blue. Now in their mid-60s, the Griffins had been peace activists in their younger days, but, unaware of the online activism occurring on the Internet, they were looking for a way to get the word out that they were against the idea of renewed war in Iraq. They reasoned, what if we made some antiwar signs like the political campaign ones? So they had some signs made up in patriotic colors with stars that read, "No Iraq War." From Seattle radio KUOW, Kathy DuChamp reported that as of late November of 2002, an estimated 10,000 of these signs appeared around the Seattle area alone, with more being ordered across the nation through the web site, Greenhammer.com. The idea of coopting the patriotism of war hawks clearly worked. "We want to take the flag back," said Marilyn Griffins, "[to show] that it's not a symbol of some kind of right wing, pro-war movement, [and to show] we're all in this together."

Another tactic that has garnered positive media attention came from a group of women of all ages who, using their naked bodies, posed in a field to spell the capital-lettered word "PEACE," to protest the second Bush administration's threats of war in Iraq. The women of West Marin, California, contacted a local portrait photographer, Art Rogers, who shot the image from atop a high ladder, in the style Annie Liebowitz often uses to photograph celebrities. The organizer of the group, calling themselves "Unreasonable Women," was Donna Sheehan (Gale). Sheehan wanted the women to "be heard on a very deep level" (as qtd. in Gale). According to reporter Ivan Gale, "the group first got the idea from a similar protest in Nigeria. . . . [in which] women fighting corporate exploitation stood nude in a vigil that lasted several days outside of Nigeria's parliament." Sheehan said the women "shamed the men and won their cause" (as qtd. in Gale). From a rhetorical perspective, the photograph, rather than just shaming warmongers, works to attract the sensationalized media by using its craving for sex-related stories. The result, however, is much more powerful. The photograph is very artfully done, and at first glance, it looks very antique, almost stylized, like photographs from the 1920s or 1930s, when posing people in the form of letters and words was a popular photographic art form. In short, the image is beautifully constructed, it is at once current and timeless, and, perhaps most important, it exploits the media's need for nudity and sexiness to promote its powerfully embodied message of PEACE. But when can this be considered pure activism and when is it seen as a mere photo opportunity for improved public relations?

PUBLIC RELATIONS AND THE PEACE MOVEMENT

The role of public relations (PR) and propaganda is most often seen as integral to war making. Carl Jacobsen notes, for instance, that the "approach to the [first] Gulf War" was smoothed by an "utterly cynical PR campaign orchestrated by two of Wall Street's leading firms, Ruder Finn and Hill & Knowlton" (8). Perhaps for PR's association to war and gross moneymaking, members of the peace movement tend to shy away from any attempts at creating a slick media image. However, the role of PR and propaganda in promoting peace has always been a strong aspect of peace and justice movements. Gandhi, for instance, ran and wrote for many newspapers to get the word out about the role that nonviolent civil disobedience could play in ejecting the British from India. King's "Letter from Birmingham Jail" was copied and widely distributed by the American Friends Service Committee to ensure his message immediately entered the public's consciousness. King was also noted for being a very dapper dresser—rhetorically speaking, that could not help but enhance his *ethos*. Also, why not do what is taught in PR 101? Work on human relations and rapport-building; send your local journalist a fruit basket.

Another tactic to foster better relations between the peace movement and the mass media bears mentioning. Eminent scholar of peace studies, Johan Galtung, writes that "TRANSCEND," which is a "network of scholars-practitioners" that perform peace activism and education, specifically are involved in "Peace journalism, to contribute to a change in the reporting about conflict from the current focus on violence and war (the 'meta-conflict') to a focus on peaceful conflict transformation" (112). Further, Galtung believes that "[t]hrough training programmes [sic] in peace journalism an increasing number of journalists will understand what this is about and make the media more receptive to news and articles about conflict transformation by peaceful means, empowerment, reconciliation and all the other peace themes" (114). The model of the always necessarily antagonistic relationship between the media and the peace movement simply needs to be rethought in light of the historical record of public relations in nonviolent activism, and considering the work of organizations such as TRANSCEND. In short, why let PR be exclusively the domain of the war makers? In the era of the sound bite and televised reality, why shouldn't peace activists consider more carefully their rhetoric, their dress, how they are perceived and portrayed, even if that means sometimes enlisting the help of those considered to be the friends of the enemy, the PR experts? Especially in this case, why not love the enemy?

INTERNATIONAL MEDIA AND NONVIOLENCE

The relationship of the media to other nonviolent movements on the international scene is also instructive. Looking at the Soviet bloc nations' efforts at nonviolent activism, Lee Smithey and Lester Kurtz write that

> one can hardly overestimate the importance of the media to the success of nonviolent resistance in the Soviet bloc; indeed they constitute a structural element crucial to the success of the insurgencies. An assortment of media sources were used as parallel institutions to disseminate new ideology that contradicted the conventional communist Rhetoric. . . . despite the censorship policies, there were some sources of critical journalism that managed to survive alongside the legal communist ones. (106)

The trick now is to take the lessons learned from stories getting out under the oppressive regimes that used censorship and apply it to the new global media networks that, due to profitability concerns arising from high-level editorial decisions, in a de facto sense constrain or censor stories about peace activism. Smithey and Kurtz observe that "Gorbachev's glasnost policies and modern media technology meant that oppositional material could finally be found not only in underground sources, but through officially sanctioned media outlets" that led to "critical analyses that resonated strongly with [newspapers] readers" (107). Activism already exists that campaigns for global glasnost, such as the media watch group, Fairness and Accuracy In Reporting (FAIR). Peace activists can work in tandem with such organizations to promote more candid reporting of issues relating to social or environmental injustices.

    In another instructive case, Stephen Zunes writes of "the role of the media" in the nonviolent overthrow of Ferdinand Marcos's dictatorial regime in the

Philippines (147). Despite attempts by Marcos both prior and during his over-throw to control the press, his "order was ignored" (147). Further, says Zunes, "[I]t is noteworthy that the few armed encounters between government and rebel forces that occurred during the uprising took place over control of key radio and television stations, underscoring the growing significance of media in modern nonviolent political struggles" (147–48). More interesting still is that even "some of these [armed] confrontations . . . were resolved nonviolently" (148). Even in an age when media is highly vertically controlled and heavily beholden to advertising and ratings (DeLuca 88–93), amazing stories are still amazing stories worthy of reportage. For instance, Zunes and Kurtz highlight the fact that "broadcast . . . tele-vision worldwide lent legitimacy to anti-apartheid forces and undermined the [South African] regime in a way that the armed struggle was unable to do. As nonviolent resistance within the country escalated, momentum grew for external pressure in the form of economic sanctions and other tactics by the international community that raised the costs of maintaining the apatheid system" (312). How can schools of journalism, both at home and abroad, be persuaded that ethics in journalism often means understanding and, under dictatorial circumstances, conducting, civil disobedience?

   Such historic examples of the positive role that the media can play in foster-ing change and an orientation for justice should be considered in the current global context. Freedom from censorship that is imposed by either governments or profiteering exists perhaps most visibly on the Internet. Alternatives to major media or governmental views on the World Wide Web have proven to be difficult to totally squash, even in repressive regimes such as in China or Burma. The lim-itations of the Internet, as always, remain its narrow access by mainly the wealthy and middle classes, however. Yet despite their limits, the Internet and mainstream media still can contribute to nonviolent change. Zunes and Kurtz argue that

> Because of increased global interdependence, the non-local audience for a conflict may be just as important as the immediate community. Just as Gandhi played to British citizens in Manchester and London, organizers of civil rights movements were communicating to the entire nation and espe-cially to the Kennedy administration. Insurgency against the Soviet bloc was disseminated by television broadcasts that spread the news from country to country, legitimating local protests." (312)

More recently, the international protests that popped up from Washington, D.C. to London and other European cities against the WTO, World Bank and Iraq war have echoed this global interdependence. The influence that the mass media ex-erts on leaders and on public opinion, and how these protests are reported needs to be balanced by the peace movement's ability to appeal to, or, if necessary, even woo, journalists.

In conclusion, an understanding of rhetorical theory can help update the strategies of activists in the peace movement so they can make more informed decisions about their media representation. Peace activists can better anticipate and control how nonviolent direct actions are reported on by the media and how mass media audiences receive the nonviolent messages either positively or negatively. Lessons from the past are instructive. "Ultimately," writes Ward, "the generally positive print and electronic news coverage of the early Movement helped to establish its moral authority, recruit activists, and persuade many whites to support black demands for basic civil and voting rights" (10). Current peace scholars and activists need to rethink their strategies for study and activism to regain some of that early good press. In addition to comprehending the foundational principles of rhetorical theory such as audience analysis and what constitutes persuasive appeals, members of the peace movement could benefit equally from undertaking the important study of demographics, media analysis, and public relations. Such enhanced rhetorical message making and improved media outreach could help the peace movement to reposition itself from its current status as an often derided, utopian relic of the 1960s to a reempowered, valued force for democratic change in the millennium ahead.

CHAPTER 3

Peace and Pedagogy:
The Case for Recognizing Nonviolence in the
Speech Communication Curriculum

At commencements, graduates are told to go into the world as peacemakers.
Yet in most schools, peace is so unimportant that no place is found for it in
the curriculum.

—*Colman McCarthy*

I n 1990, Speech Communication scholars Troester and Mester conducted a survey to ascertain "the relationship between speech communication education and peace education at the college level." The survey proved particularly revealing. They concluded that even though "much has been written about teaching peace in some disciplines, very little has been written about teaching peace . . . within a communication curriculum." This blank space in the communication curriculum was especially "noteworthy given that the goals for college level peace education typically mentioned in curriculum guides include communication skills such as exercising influence, practicing decision-making, and resolving conflict."

The goals of this chapter are to (1) define what peace and nonviolence are and how they are integrally related to the speech communication discipline; (2) explore possible reasons for the comparative lack of emphasis on peace and nonviolence in the speech communication curricula; (3) offer a rationale for the value and importance of incorporating peace and nonviolence in speech communication courses; and (4) propose ways that peace and nonviolence can be incorporated into the existing curricula without significantly changing courses that are currently being offered.

DEFINING PEACE AND NONVIOLENCE
AS ASPECTS OF SPEECH COMMUNICATION

Before offering some definitions of peace and nonviolence, what their opposites mean must be established first. The opposite of peace is obviously war. But violence is different. Violence can be physical and tangible harm to others, or it can be *cul-tural* or *structural*, causing more subtle harm to others. Cultural violence is when our social modes of thinking or behaving cause harm to individuals belonging to ostracized groups, such as gays, lesbians, or members of a minority race, such as African Americans. In structural violence, the tangible aspects are only visible in the latent symptoms of its victims. Structural violence, also referred to as institutional or systemic violence, encompasses "material, intellectual, spiritual poverty, or the denial of the opportunity to strive for one's highest achievement . . . [including] the denial of human rights" (Herman 11). It is a "long-lasting punishment" to its victims (Genser 238). Structural violence encompasses interpersonal communication, including "insults, sarcastic remarks, put downs, and other mental/emotional abuses employed" by those in power over those without power (Leyden, 231). Structural violence can be elusive because it is often difficult to prove. An example of the difficulty of proving structural violence would be the high number of formally registered sexual harassment complaints and the comparatively low number of complaints that are proven and settled. How can it be "proven" that a supervisor's or coworker's statement really constituted a *double-entendre*, and a mean-spirited one at that? How can evidence be unearthed to indicate that words are harmful to a person's job performance (as evidence that structural violence was done)? How does an intangible working "climate" constitute an aspect of structural violence (Campbell; Hall)? Scholars in speech communication are on the forefront of studies that delve into these difficult questions (Peterson). One needs look no further than the nearest speech communication or communication theory journal in order to find a plethora of articles devoted to detecting violence in communication, using theories ranging from poststructuralism to rhetorical theory to answer questions like the ones just mentioned. Yet articles on *nonviolence* and peace as areas of research and teaching remain scant. In fact, "[d]espite its widespread diffusion as a conscious movement around the world in recent decades, and its central role in tectonic shifts in geopolitics of the late twentieth century, we still understand little about nonviolence as a technique for social change. 'Nonviolence' is not even a category in the mainstram academic lexicon" (Zunes, Kurtz, Asher xii).

According to Joseph, an anthropologist at the University of California at Davis, teaching peace is a "social responsibility." Joseph avers that "a society that teaches peaceable *methods of communication* is stronger than a society that resorts to brutish means of solving problems (emphasis added; as qtd. in Wright 18). Peace is defined as "the absence of or the ending of military hostilities between contending states or other fighting units. . . . A society at peace will be imperfect and usually will encompass internal conflicts and efforts to improve the society while preserving its meritorious qualities" (Sharp 234). The philosophy of peace, or pacifism, is defined as "the refusal to respond to evil and injustice with force or anger, responding instead with calmness and readiness to suffer" (Herman 6). Where speech communication aids in understanding of the utility of this philosophy is our ability to interpret diverse "cultures and situations" from an interactional perspective (Herman 7), seeing humans as senders and receivers of messages. In strictly speech communication terms, Troester and Mester define "peace communication" as "any exchange of ideas intended to diminish conflict among persons in interpersonal or public relationships" (422).

Nonviolence is referred to as "people power, political defiance, nonviolent action, noncooperation or civil resistance" (Sharp 234). It "isn't just about ending wars," says Colman McCarthy, "It's about creating peace in our own hearts, [which is] often the last place many people ever find it" (6). Theodore Herman defines nonviolence as

> both an attitude and a course of action that seeks to build a community of caring by the reconciliation of adversaries, and/or by active opposition to tyranny and injustice. It also has a positive meaning in working to remove the causes of violent conflict, both human and environmental (3).

One of the points held in common among peace, nonviolence, and speech communication is the concept of empowering citizens through critical thinking so as to reduce or remove the circumstances that enable tyranny and conflict to prevail. As Hart indicates, students are empowered when they "learn to listen critically." Hart adds that it is a "patriotic obligation" for communication educators to enable students to understand and "consume" the forms of persuasion around them so that they will not succumb to tyrannical leaders and misleading messages (111). In an age of antipatriotic terrorists such as Timothy McVeigh, who was an autodidact of antigovernment propaganda, or Islamic *jihad* terrorists, schooled in *madrasas* to hate Jews and Christians, then further steeped in anti-Western propaganda in military training camps, the need for teaching students both at home and abroad how to understand and be critical of persuasion of all kinds becomes all the more urgent. Understanding nonviolence as a tool to resisting violence is an important and sophisticated way that democracy can be promoted and upheld.

Nonviolence as a theory and philosophy of political action uses and relies upon communication. Galtung observes that nonviolence is successful when communication between the oppressor and the oppressed is open and two-way in the form of "speech, writing, or demonstrations" (22). Galtung asserts that "nonviolent action is a communication" in and of itself; nonviolence is also rhetorical in that it uses communication to persuade, to "change the mind, even the heart" of the adversary (23).

Herman delineates seven basic "forms of nonviolence," which are divided between a personal or a group orientation. As shown in Table 3-1 below, each of these forms is already being addressed, though seldom recognized as nonviolence, in the standard speech communication curriculum of many colleges and universities.

The list of examples of courses is by no means exhaustive, but it does provide a clear illustration of the intersection between the study of peace and nonviolence and the study of speech communication. Each of these areas is already included in the standard speech communication curriculum; yet the nonviolent aspects are downplayed so as to enable instructors to maintain the objectivity that is desirable in the social sciences. Social scientific methodology appears to clash with the concepts of peace and nonviolence. Reasons for this clash will be addressed in the next section of this essay.

WHY PEACE AND NONVIOLENCE IS MISSING FROM THE SPEECH COMMUNICATION CURRICULUM

Troester and Mester have highlighted the unfortunate fact that peace and nonviolence are seen as value-laden relics of the 1960s: "There appears to be a perception that teaching peace means indoctrinating students with the personal values of the instructor, a person sometimes perceived as likely to be a throwback to the 'peaceniks' of the sixties" (427). McCarthy, who has taught many college-level courses in peace and nonviolence, asserts that many students are skeptical about nonviolence, thinking of it as "just a philosophy for hugging trees at high tide and full moon" (9). Kounosu dispels the myth that "teaching peace" involves "an authority who acts like a guru writing on the tabula rasa of people in general." Kounosu states that, instead of "teaching peace," it should be considered more as "learning peace," in that "all persons have ideas of peace and how to achieve it" (qtd. in Wright 18).

Another problem that is prevalent in the discipline of speech communication is that the rhetoric surrounding terms peace and nonviolence. "Nonviolence," "alternatives to violence," "peace studies," "conflict/dispute resolution," and "all the other generic names have different meanings to different people" (Leyden 235). For example, "the term 'peacemaking' is often interpreted to mean conflict resolution," which results in faculty considering "peacemaking' to be significantly less important than . . . conflict negotiation skills" (Troester and Mester 427). The distinction is that peacemaking ensures that steps are taken in

TABLE 3-1.
FORMS OF NONVIOLENCE CURRENTLY INCLUDED IN SPEECH COMMUNICATION COURSES

Mass or Group Oriented Communication		Interpersonal Communication	
Type of Nonviolence	Related speech Communication Courses	Type of Nonviolence	Related speech communication courses
Nonviolent struggle and civilian-based defense	• Social movement theory • Communication and responsibility	Personal transformation or psychospiritual change	• Interpersonal oral communication theory • Psychology of speaking and listening • Communication and responsibility • Communication ethics
Conflict resolution	• Communication in conflict resolution and negotiation • Group communication theory • Small group processes in conflict mediation	Pacifism or nonretaliation in kind	• Speech and human behavior • Nonverbal communication • Communication in conflict resolution and negotiation • Cross-cultural communication • Gender roles in communication
Removing the causes of violent conflict	• Studies in public persuasion • Speech criticism • Gender roles in communication • Ethics of rhetoric	Reconciliation with an adversary	• Communication in conflict resolution and negotiation • Cross-cultural communication • Gender roles in communication
Developing a sound relationship with the Earth	• Environmental rhetoric • Rhetoric of the body	Developing a sound relationship with the Earth	• Environmental rhetoric • Organizational communication

Source: Adapted from Herman (1991, p. 5). Sources of course information are Cherkow-Yanoov (1992, p. 286) and the Penn State 1996-98 Graduate Degree Programs Bulletin.

the communication process to prevent conflict from arising or escalating in the first place, whereas conflict negotiation is needed once a communication situation has already deteriorated to a high degree.

Misconceptions about peace and nonviolence abound. The terms *pacifism* and *nonretaliation* are often "seen as cowardly expedience" or even "a clear example of masochism" (Herman 6). Moreover, the history of nonviolent successes is overshadowed by the history of violent "success" stories that feature heroes and a definitive ending (Galtung; Cochran). Nonviolent successes do not lend themselves well to media reporting because they lack individualistic heroes and precise story endings (Galtung). This is at least part of the reason why people do not acknowledge nonviolent theorists and activists as the originators of "many of today's successful . . . [communication tactics and] practices . . . including mediation, arbitration and conciliation" (Genser 240). Media reporting also fosters a "kill the messenger" attitude that makes nonviolent activists out to be the villains, as opposed to the problems that they bring to light through their nonviolent forms of communication (Hubbard).

At the same time, historically, activists who initially were said to have espoused nonviolence often turned to violence in frustration, which resulted in widespread public opinion that *all* nonviolence is just a facade for violence. For example, during the protests in 1999–2000 of the World Trade Organization (WTO) in Seattle, only a tiny fraction of the protesters were violent, yet they were the ones receiving the lion's share of major networks' and newspaper media attention. Still, mere misconceptions about peace and nonviolence are not the only reasons why speech communication curriculum lacks substantial emphasis on these concepts. The idea of grappling with teaching values, which is fundamental to understanding peace and nonviolence, is at times troublesome to speech communication instructors and researchers.

There is apprehension in the social sciences to cover the subjects of peace and nonviolence. In part, this apprehension comes from dealing with morals and values. Troester and Mester note that "values" are sensitive topics for instructors, and that many scholars are anxious about the teaching of values because values, by their very nature, cannot be "uncontested." Nonetheless, they ask: "[A]re we not justified in teaching about peace as we are about truth and honesty?" In the discussion that follows, I answer their question with a resounding, "Yes!" Social scientists are very concerned about, and interested in, issues of values. The emphasis on proper methodology and ethical conduct of research surveys is evidence that values are crucial to the validity of social scientific research and knowledge. At the same time, the emphasis of some values over others is problematic in the social sciences. Kool highlights the fact that

> Whereas studies of violence have ranged from genetic, [to] cultural, to situational effects, and have been pursued through empirical and nonempirical methods over the past several decades, nonviolence did not become a favorite area of study among social scientists . . . [in part this may be due to] a lack of understanding of the concept and a failure to either develop or apply adequate methods. (v)

So the reasons for the absence of research in peace and nonviolence on the part of the social scientific community is not without remedy. If speech communication scholars and others in the social sciences work toward refining and rehabilitating the concepts of peace and nonviolence in terms that are seen as heuristic to the social sciences, then the trepidation or absence of interest could be reversed. Also, offering explicit methods for the pursuit of research into, and instruction of, these subject areas would support this objective. By way of opening up the field to such an effort, the next part of this chapter will provide substantive reasons why peace and nonviolence are valid concepts to include in the speech communication curriculum.

A RATIONALE FOR TEACHING PEACE AND NONVIOLENCE IN THE CLASSROOM

Chetkow-Yanoov maintains that "peace-making knowledge, attitudes, [and] skills . . . should be taught and recycled several times during a person's learning career" (288). Chetkow-Yanoov also declares that learning skills in peace and nonviolence should be part of a total program of education from kindergarten to the university and beyond, including "continuing education for retirees" (288). Likewise, Martha Leyden is convinced that the university curriculum should be imbued with nonviolence:

> The role of the university in the area of alternatives is one of change agent by facilitating the [student's move] . . . toward the use of alternatives to violence skills. [Presently] . . . American society is divided into a number of separate functional sectors: winners and losers, friends and enemies, business and labor, public and personal. The challenge is to move toward a unity rather than to perpetuate continued division. Violence continues to divide. An alternative to violence is essential to the needed transformation toward an *active* nonviolent society. (italics in original) (233)

Accordingly, peace and nonviolence need to be addressed in the speech communication classroom because communication scholars are among the instructors best trained to recognize the negative results of communication that fosters violence. As scholars of communication, we are skilled in understanding how communication can contribute to the prevention, escalation, or reduction of conflict among people on various levels, from the interpersonal to the international. As researchers into the media, speech communication scholars understand the impact that the wide array of communication media, from the Internet and television to Hollywood films, have on society and its norms (Hart; Herman). At the same time, we are also capable of offering insights into the serious entailments that a tacit acceptance of violence has on culture:

> Between 1950 and 1978, the suicide rate among teenagers in the United States rose by more than 170 percent. Some 20,000 murders are committed annually in the United States. Violent sports like football, boxing, and hockey are glorified. . . . The leading cause of injury among American women is being beaten by a man at home.

Observations such as these about violence are often dismissed as just being "human nature." There is a disparity between the understanding of how violence is reproduced, transmitted and reinforced via communication, and how it is accepted. One question that bears asking is this: "If peace is what every government says its seeks, and peace is the yearning of every heart, why aren't we studying it and teaching it in schools?" (McCarthy 6).

Sometimes instructors in the humanities are wary of teaching and researching subjects that are deemed value-laden. Boggs, a professor at Ohio State University, states that teaching peace involves tackling values, and that is part of the educator's role in promoting "civic education." Boggs asserts that "educators can be advocates for greater understanding of any subject, from apartheid to zoning, without taking sides." He also puts concerns about values into perspective, saying, "Civic education is not presenting a point of view or discrediting others, but allowing for learning that permits a search for common ground" (as qtd. in Wright 18). Peace and nonviolence are core concepts to the development of ethical communication. Instructors of public speaking classes normally require, for example, that student speeches should refrain from profanity or breaches of ethics. Instructors also teach that good audience analysis involves avoiding or minimizing hostility between audience and speaker by carefully using words, including using nonsexist and nonbiased language. This is central to ethical communication, and it also supports nonviolent speaking. By choosing language that does not support the structural system of violence against women and other minorities, students participate actively in nonviolence as a verbal and social practice. However, commentary about violence and the role of communication in remediating it nonviolently is not normally included as part of the discussion of ethics in communication.

In addition, as Table 3-2 below indicates, it is clear that the leanings of many speech communication educators favor an approach that incorporates ideas and theories of peace and nonviolence into the communication classroom.

TABLE 3-2.
COMMUNICATION EDUCATORS FAVOR TEACHING PEACE

Survey Question/Statement Posed to Speech Communication Educators	Agree	Disagree	Uncertain
In communication courses we teach, issues of peace are becoming more evident.	21	75	19
Communication educators have an obligation to address issues of peace given the nature of the discipline.	82	21	12
The National Communication Association (NCA; formerly SCA) should become more active in issues related to peace.	70	19	26
With regard to issues of peace, communication educators ought to teach students to be advocates for their ideas.	101	7	7

Source: Adapted from Troester and Mester (1990, p. 423).

It is evident that speech communication educators value peace and nonviolent concepts, and agree with Bogg's contention that it is part of an educator's duty to teach peace through the curricula.

It is also important for us to incorporate nonviolence into the speech communication curriculum because an understanding of nonviolence fosters the nonviolent mission of breaking up the self-perpetuating systems of cultural and structural violence. This nonviolent mission has been part and parcel of the very concept of what constitutes a "liberal education" since the Age of Enlightenment; the very goals of the Enlightenment educational movement were to push back the forces of ignorance and to promote higher ideals, including peace in society. Today, in their use of the theories of deconstruction and poststructuralism, communication scholars have eloquently explicated how these structures of unjust power are reinforced in words, language, and in nonverbal communication. In so doing, these same scholars have been, however unwittingly, performing nonviolent acts. Indeed, as Cochran observes, criticism and theory in communication mesh with nonviolence:

> Teaching the nonviolent tradition allows us to reconstruct . . . social and political contexts . . . It demonstrates that, as the Russian literary critic Mikhail Bakhtin said, "Nothing is absolutely dead; every meaning will have its homecoming festival." American abolitionists like Thoreau and Adin Ballou influenced Gandhi, who then influenced . . . American civil-rights activists like Benjamin Mays, who was [Dr. Martin Luther] King's teacher at Morehouse College. (37)

Theories of communication ranging from feminist theory or gender differences in communication to public speaking to rhetorical criticism all represent the tradition of using knowledge to dispel oppressive social myths and to foster social equality while respecting cocultural diversity (Peterson). It is simply a natural progression for these theories to acknowledge peace and nonviolence as being instrumental to theory and pedagogy. Toward acknowledging peace and nonviolence in the speech communication curriculum, the next part of this discussion will cover simple ways to incorporate these issues productively into coursework and research.

Incorporating Peace and Nonviolence into the Existing Curriculum

Troester and Mester, in recommending to speech communication teachers that peace and nonviolence are areas that need to be addressed in the curriculum, posed the following pragmatic question: "If we are justified in teaching about peace, what approaches might we use?" (428). The humble beginnings of an answer to this question will be now offered. A full answer, of course, requires the participation of students, professors, administrators, and members of the general public who are concerned about education. Here, directions for practical and simple ways that nonviolence and peace might be integrated into the speech communication curriculum will be provided, so that others may take up this question and offer ideas of their own.

McCarthy states that "[c]ourses on nonviolence are easily designed. What isn't easy is shifting people's thinking" (8). He recounts the tale of how it took him seven long years to convince the Board of Education at a Maryland elementary school that a course, "Peace Studies," needed to be taught. In one meeting, he recalls, one board member said, "Look, we don't have a problem with the word 'Studies'—it's that *other* word we find objectionable" (McCarthy "Speech"). The basic subject matter of speech communication already contains the themes of nonviolence; all that instructors need to do is to tap into those themes in order to illuminate and explain how nonviolence works. Accomplishing the "shift in . . . thinking" that must come first can be done by showing that an understanding of human communication and interaction can enhance people's ability to interact more peacefully in conflict situations. Therefore, it would be best to pursue an integrated approach that builds on the existing speech communication curricula, yet amends it in simple ways that open it up to including nonviolence as part of its subject domain. Bowen, who directs a mediation program and who teaches conflict resolution classes, writes:

> Conflict is a normal and essential part of life. The way we deal with differences and conflict, however, often divides us, and inhibits our ability to confront common problems. Complex social issues and increasing global interdependence place new demands on our capacities to work together. When handled constructively, conflict presents opportunities for growth and progress. People of any age can acquire skills and understandings that will help them to deal with conflict in constructive ways. Curriculums are available for learning, modeling, and teaching *nonviolent communication skills such as: how to listen to each other; how to contribute ideas and communicate them clearly*; how to disagree without rejecting; how to label and express feelings—these give everyone insights into their own and others' expectations, misconceptions, fears, differing perspectives, and information, and takes learning to new levels of both comprehension and compassion. (emphasis added; 51)

Certainly, communication skills, including learning how to be an effective listener and communicator, already figure into a curriculum that encourages effective conflict management. All that remains to be done is to recognize these skills for their value not only in enhancing communication skills so as to increase the student's competitive edge in the job market, but also to improve the student's ability to successfully mediate conflicts which are inevitable in life, whether in school, in personal and community relationships, and at work.

Parry affirms how important it is to the success of nonviolence for students to "learn the power of language so they can use it to say how they feel, to protect and defend themselves without being violent" (44). As teachers of communication, we can help show students how language can be used to mediate and reduce conflict in the variety of human communication settings, from the interpersonal to public speaking. Learning to recognize positive (nonviolent, open-minded) and negative (violent, hostile) communication strategies is already part of the speech communication curriculum. Highlighting nonviolent strategies helps enable students to "break the cycle" of "violence as a learned response" (Parry 43).

One approach speech communication instructors can take is that we already teach nonviolence implicitly through in the instruction of these basic skills. All that remains of the instructor is to reveal to the students the positive impact of these skills in that they enable students to reduce and manage conflict in their own lives. In many instances, the students themselves will bring up the subject of nonviolence without even knowing it, as the next section of this chapter will demonstrate.

After a decade teaching at the college level, I have heard my fair share of student speeches and oral presentations. Interestingly, several themes in student presentations have become particularly recurrent. Almost without exception, in each oral presentation round several of my students choose as a speech topic to decry any one of the following kinds of subjects: spousal or partner abuse or violence in the home; environmental abuse; corporate abuse (e.g., Enron's collapse; big tobacco firms); cultural abuse (e.g., in the form of anorexia or bulimia, especially in young women); and racism. With this in mind, it appears that the students themselves are mandating interest in learning about peace and nonviolence by voicing concerns about various forms of personal, cultural, or structural violence. Such topics easily fit into the realm in which education about nonviolence intersects with interpersonal communication, such as the issue of spousal/partner abuse. Likewise, speech topics such as antismoking or anorexia/bulimia fit well into the study of understanding cultural and structural (systemic) violence, for young people are greatly influenced by the media's representations of glamorous, young men and women smoking and being thin.

Accordingly, it seems both logical and feasible to incorporate a unit on understanding nonviolence into one of the oral presentation rounds so that, based on knowledge gained, the students could tailor their speech topics to the general subject of nonviolence. Other student speech topics that recur easily fall into this range, including, but not limited to the following: interracial/interethnic dating; poor treatment of the elderly in nursing homes; some aspect of pollution in the environment; or Sojourner Truth, Ida B. Wells, Martin Luther King, Jr., or other nonviolent activists as model public speakers. The instructor could recommend such nonviolent topics to the students, who are sometimes familiar with the characters already, although they are unfamiliar with any formal theories of nonviolence or conflict management. At the same time, the instructor could explain the significance of the topic and how it relates to issues of human communication and conflict.

In addition to speech topics, speech techniques and strategies for effective delivery can also incorporate tenets of nonviolence. For example, most basic course texts offer the insight that humor is an effective way of getting the audience to relate to the speaker. Humor, as Johan Galtung shows, works well as a nonviolent technique for reducing tensions and improving one's ability for conflict management:

> Humor is another important aspect of verbal communication. . . . Encapsulating our insights in ways that invite smiles, or even laughter, is one way of living with them. . . . Obviously suffering and violence are not joking mat-

ters to be laughed away. Still, whereas the brain may be less readily accessible, the heart can be reached with smiles—including smiles at our ourselves and our own frequent clownish folly. The smile can improve possibilities for dialogue. (qtd. in Gage 39)

Showing how humor can serve to reduce tensions in the context of a speech or in small-group communication provides an opportunity to show that nonviolence, as a theory and communication paradigm, does, in practice, actually work. In short, even if this unit on nonviolence were comprised of no more than one or two lectures and readings, it would be class time that was well spent.

In addition to public speaking courses, learning about nonviolence and peace can also take place in courses ranging from small-group communication and social movement theory to courses in international conflict and mediation. As indicated in Table 3-1 above, many speech communication departments already offer such courses as "conflict management, conflict and negotiation, communication and conflict, intercultural communication, and critical issues" (Troester and Mester 425).

Another area that is central to both speech communication and nonviolence is ethics. Chip Wood notes that "a dominant ethic of care" is a central nonviolent concept that supports the equal treatment of people (7). The vital importance of ethics to all aspects of speech communication, from gathering survey data in an ethical manner, to understanding what does and does not constitute the use of ethical persuasion and rhetoric, also relates to the basic nonviolent concepts of having compassion and respect for others. Forcey states that, "ethically speaking, humanist aspirations for a more peaceful world, in which peace must include an ethic of caring and valuing caring . . . are at the heart of the peace studies endeavor" (11). As ethics and care relates to feminist studies, and to peace studies, it bears notice that they relate to speech communication studies, too, since these "fields rest on a belief in human agency and a confidence that people can change, that individuals can make a difference" (Forcey 9).

Similarly, Early notes how peace studies have contributed to a better understanding of the structural power systems "embedded" in "discourses" (26–27). Since the focus of discourse is central to speech communication, it seems logical that peace studies can contribute a greater awareness of these structural power systems that unfortunately perpetuate societal violence. Early also examines the importance of a "political language," which is a creative, nonviolent construct (25). Discussions of the ethical use of communication and communication research data can be fruitful starting points for students in understanding how violence is embedded in social structures, including academic practices (such as grades), and how the ethical approach to communication research and study supports a nonviolent perspective.

Aspects of speech communication that involve group interaction and study can also pull in key concepts from nonviolence. Wood maintains that "we can learn to structure activities that value cooperation, affiliation, and attachment" and also "de-emphasize competition without eliminating it" (8). Wood believes that a more nurturing strategy for handling education in groups involves listening to, and observing students, promoting interactional ethics, and leaving plenty of room for the students themselves to make choices in their assignments. Kounosu likewise says that "an environment that is open to learning" is one of peace (qtd. in Wright 18). These are all aspects of critical pedagogy that many speech communication instructors are already embracing. Clearly, a better understanding of group dynamics from the pro-social theory of nonviolence could help illuminate the complexity of human communicative interaction. Kohn reiterates the fact that "communication is improved through cooperation," which depends on the key nonviolent aggregates of sensitivity, other-orientation, and trust (150).

At the graduate level of study, the field is wide open for combining the study of speech communication and peace and nonviolence. For example, courses that are available to graduate students include graduate-level courses in conflict management, whether interpersonal, national, or international. Such courses offer concrete, workable, nonviolent methods for conflict remediation and arbitration. Grad students can be invited to learn about the "other history" of humanity that is often overlooked or downplayed in history books, that is, the history of peace, such as the feminist and nonviolent perspective of history offered in books such as *Women Who Speak for Peace* or *Women's Voices* or *The Chalice and the Blade*. In addition, in 2002 at Washington State University, I offered a graduate teaching assistantship in supporting a course I designed and the College of Liberal Arts funded, called "Peace Rhetoric: Nonviolence in Literature and Media." This course taught nonviolence through examining popular American texts, both visual and literary. These are just a few examples of how graduate students in speech communication might become critically engaged in studies and research into the intersection between nonviolence, peace, and communication. Such studies aid in improving our "appreciation of [nonviolent activists]" and their contributions to society (Katz and Kendrick 348). Next, to show how peace and nonviolence fit into the speech communication curriculum, this discussion will now turn to areas of research that unite these subjects.

Areas of Research That Combine Peace, Nonviolence, and Speech Communication

The study of communication and conflict management is a fruitful area for research. Katz and Kendrick, for example, have studied "the dynamics of nonviolent struggle within social movement organizations" (335). There are many areas where peace can factor into research about communication issues. With regard to the study of the communication and action strategies of social movements, Katz and Kendrick conclude that "more attention needs to be given to the development of theory about nonviolent action and movements from the perspectives of . . . participants and from [their] observations . . . as they are engaged in the process of nonviolent conflict" (348). Aside from colleagues in fields such as sociology, political science, or, say, anthropology, who other than communication scholars are better equipped to undertake such studies and to provide the clearest insights as to what is occurring in these social movements? Study of nonviolent social movements is needed because the past few decades have "witnessed a remarkable upsurge in nonviolent . . . [democratic uprisings] against authoritarian regimes. . . . However, there has been little recognition of the significance of the increasing [use] . . . of nonviolent methods in situations where guerrilla warfare was once seen to be the only path to liberation and the extent to which nonviolent struggle has emerged as a central cultural movement throughout the globe" (Zunes et al. xii). The significance and import of this amazing nonviolent global phenomenon runs the risk of being lost on communication scholars in the rush to study rhetorics of "Homeland Defense" and terrorism. While post-9/11 violent rhetorics do merit attention, it is important that they do not deflect all material and intellectual resources away from the equally vital research area of gains made through nonviolent social activism around the globe. Indeed, nonviolence may yet prove to be the most powerful weapon against terrorist violence.

In addition, communication courses and research that focus on gender issues stand to gain from an understanding of nonviolent principles. Forcey regards peace studies as a positive influence on disciplines that are "vulnerable" to slashes in funding; she believes that including peace studies in the curricula strengthens the discipline's viability. Likewise, courses such as cross-cultural communication that include discussions of the ways that language can serve to perpetuate racism and other aspects of ethnocentrism could also feature peace and nonviolence (Will). The "chimera of race" continues to plague America, from campus to inner-city, and Will emphasizes the value that peace studies can have in fostering understanding in order to decrease conflict:

> Although research may help us fathom the causes of such discord and conflict resolution may alleviate it, prevention is best achieved through social policy and education. Scholars in the field of peace and conflict studies should provide leadership in pressing for curricular revisions to address our rampant ignorance about issues of race. (199)

Since speech communication scholars are at the forefront of teaching and research that focus on issues of intra- and intercultural communication (Peterson), including race, there should be a cognizance of the need to include theories about peace and conflict management in the curriculum and research program.

With regard to the nuts and bolts aspects of professional research into nonviolent social movements, Katz and Kendrick offer practical tips for how scholars can best approach and "disseminate" their research "findings" relating to nonviolence. They recommend that the researcher tailor the "design" and the "research results" to a specific "intended audience" (345). They also highlight that "[f]or scholarly research about nonviolent action, the audience may be both academic and non-academic" (345). Further, Katz and Kendrick stress that if the research results are intended to be read by nonviolent activists, that it is best to incorporate those activists into the design process and data-gathering aspects of the research process.

SOME PRELIMINARY CONCLUSIONS

This chapter has defined peace and nonviolence and how they relate to speech communication; dispelled some common misconceptions about peace and nonviolence as concepts; provided reasons why these areas should be stressed in the speech communication curriculum; and offered examples of ways that peace and nonviolence can easily be integrated into existing courses and research. This discussion has, however, only begun to address the major misconceptions that many in the field hold about peace and nonviolence as domains of research and teaching. Continued efforts in this area are necessary for speech communication scholars and instructors to gain a full appreciation for these concepts. Likewise, this discussion has offered simple definitions of peace and nonviolence. (Refer to Appendix 1 for more clarifying information and definitions of how these areas relate to, and strengthen the speech communication discipline, among others.) With regard to incorporating nonviolence and peace studies issues into speech communication, this chapter has provided evidence that courses (or course subunits) in gender and cultural diversity have already rounded out the existing speech communication curriculum in many universities (Peterson). At the same time, however, most programs lack substantial course offerings relating to peace and nonviolence. This lack is ironic considering that most schools' missions usually support training students about the positive impact that respecting cultural diversity can have on their own lives and on society in general.

On a happier note, aside from overcoming simple misunderstandings, there is no reason why knowledge from the studies of peace and nonviolence cannot be seamlessly integrated into the existing curricula. Certainly, the cost of integrating peace and nonviolence into the speech communication curriculum cannot be a prohibitive factor. For example, the Center for Teaching Peace (based in Washington, D.C.) has provided colleges with a complete instruction packet for a college-level course at a cost of about $50 (McCarthy 9).

Incorporating the pedagogical practices, knowledge, and insights gained from peace studies should be thought of as a natural progression of the expansion of speech communication to include insights from women's studies and cross-cultural studies. Mandell, a professor of international affairs at Carleton University, affirms that as university instructors, "we need to train people who can influence politicians to slow down and seek forms of conflict resolution other than force" (qtd. in Wright 18). Mandell cites peace-oriented study areas that speech communication is already advancing in, such as:

> programs for master's level students who will be capable of ethics and social responsibility as active participants in global affairs. The curriculum would include examples of problems and issues beyond our borders. Through simulation exercises, students would learn to empathize with other cultures, learning how . . . [others] view a situation, not ideological absolutes. The curriculum would include peace research on intractable problems, particularly multicultural conflict, so that we are better prepared to deal with future situations. (qtd. in Wright 19)

As the world population increases in tandem with the mobility and cohabitation of people from diverse countries and ethnic and cultural backgrounds, the need for people who possess the ability to communicate well and to mediate conflicts will continue to increase (Chetkow-Yanoov 277). It should be considered the mandate for speech communication educators to do our part to fill this need. Accordingly, Leyden believes that

> Humanity's critical need for nonviolence can be served very well by what already is known. The principles and skills needed have been developed and practiced for centuries at various times and places throughout the world. But, like any good idea or product, it must be made known in order to be implemented. (233)

The speech communication curriculum already offers ideas and skills that promote peace and nonviolence in communication contexts ranging from the interpersonal to the international. By focusing more on the intersection between these areas, speech communication could become more marketable in the university environment, and thus less prone to cutbacks, as it currently is. All that remains is for our discipline to capitalize on what we know. This is difficult but worthwhile work that would benefit the speech communication discipline, its students, and as a result, society as a whole. Coleman McCarthy acknowledges that teaching non-violence and peace is not easy, for it "is an act of faith: the belief that students will dig deep into their reserves of inner courage and love to embrace the highest calling we know, peacemaking" (9).

CHAPTER 4

The Spitfire Grill:
Nonviolence as Social Power

Our non-violence is as yet a mixed affair. It limps. Nevertheless, it is there and it continues to work like a leaven in a silent and invisible way, least understood by most. It is the only way.

—*Mohandas Gandhi[1]*

In *A Certain Tendency of the Hollywood Cinema, 1930 to 1980*, Robert Ray highlights the notion that violence in film is continually reaffirmed "as the only possible solution" to conflict (146). Ray cites the increasing progression of films' depictions of violence in American film history, noting that in later films, "violence . . . far exceeded" what would have transpired in a similar plot in an earlier film (172). Ray attributes to "Right"-wing ideologies the use of 'violence as a solution' to conflicts; Ray shows how "Left" movies such as *Taxi Driver* are "corrections" of this ideological vision (358–59). It is troubling to relegate the issue of violence in film to a notch on an ideological continuum from left to right or even to genre status, such as *film noir*. It is dissatisfying to people who support democratic ideals to view violence in film from a perspective that warps the possibility for social regeneration while it excludes critical perspectives that perceive violence in a nontraditional light.

REDISCOVERING NONVIOLENCE

Films that feature overt violence, such as Westerns, *film noir*, Mafia films, war films, constitute a "genre," as do films that lack so much violence, like romantic comedies. But critics and Hollywood moguls alike seem blinded by what they deem as a gender-oriented subject matter. Movies that feature human interest stories that downplay or omit overt violence are given the pejorative term, "women's movies." But there are plenty of stories that minimize (or even lack) overt depictions of violence that escape this *sobriquet*. Such films feature the ways that ordinary people overcome systematic, totalizing structures of violence by employing

47

creative, nonviolent solutions to the problems in their lives. The "men-viewer"-oriented range of films in this nonviolent category would include films such as *An Everlasting Piece* and *Billy Elliot* on the lighter, more humorous side, and, on the more serious side, *Gandhi* and *Cry Freedom*.[2]

It is significant that the stories in these films feature what seems to be a human desire to handle social conflict—from the large scale to the interpersonal—by reducing the possibility and occurrence of violence to happen. Filmic story lines that feature nonviolence reveal the strategy in the nonviolent method as a type of maximized cost-benefits analysis: How can the protagonist(s) of the plot overcome the problem without, or with minimal, violence or damage to the plot's villains and protagonists alike? Although there are countless films that present this perspective, unfortunately few critics recognize nonviolence as a theory, and as a form of rhetoric, social resistance, and political power.

The same perspective holds in Hollywood. For example, in commenting on his work on the screenplay for Richard Attenborough, John Briley writes that he had initially viewed Gandhi's "non-violent philosophy . . . as benign, but unrealistic"; but over the course of the project, Briley came to see nonviolence as "indeed a tough and formidable political tool, something the world should be more aware of and could benefit from" (Briley 4). Briley's first impressions of nonviolence are common in Hollywood, for he notes that "no studio would finance *Gandhi*. It was shot with private money and only purchased for distribution after it had been finished" (12). Similarly, critically acclaimed, and at least moderately financially successful films with nonviolent themes like *An Everlasting Piece, Endurance, Hoop Dreams*, and *The Spitfire Grill* were independently made and financed, only later to be bought for major Hollywood distribution.

By following the Hollywood distribution lines, as well as traditional and conservative perspectives on film criticism, film critics may be failing to see larger issues at work in the rhetoric of the films. Critics may also be missing why movie viewers pay to see certain films over and over again in video format.[3] It is important to distinguish between these traditional modes of film criticism and a fundamentally nonviolent mode of analysis. The difference is that nonviolence is (as a worldview, philosophy, core motive and means to understanding rhetoric and the world around us) largely what drives the other forms of criticism. These forms of analysis, however, seldom cite nonviolence while they often misunderstand it in theory and in practice.

The result of this misunderstanding is that traditional modes of film criticism tend to overemphasize the *symptoms* of structural violence in their critiques. A focus on symptoms renders the social situation as more rigid than it is. As a consequence of such theoretical rigidity, the problems film critics study are viewed as being more hopeless than they actually might be. While nonviolence is certainly neither a panacea nor a Pollyanna worldview, its characteristic hope for humankind does starkly contrast with existing approaches to the study of film. Traditional theoretical constructs can sometimes lead to an overly narrow way of understanding the rhetorical workings in film. These constructs even support cynicism in popular film reviews as well as in academic criticism. Ray's book, for instance, is immensely wise and helpful, but viewing the use of violence in film from a strictly ideological and historical perspective limits our range of possibilities for understanding its ramifications.

By the same token, the use of Freudian theory leads to contradictory conclusions in feminist film criticism. For example, in Tania Modleski's *The Women Who Knew Too Much*, Modleski brings to light insightful visions of Hitchcock's presentation of women in his films. Unfortunately, the patriarchal theories of Freud that she uses tend to constrain and drown the critical voice at moments when a creative feminist theory might better explain how a given scene unfolds. Likewise, the use of Freudian theory in generic film criticism, such as that found in Stanley Cavell's *Pursuits of Happiness: The Hollywood Comedy of Remarriage*, only perpetuates a constraining worldview of human beings as primarily *aggressive* and *sexual* beings, rather than as primarily, *creative, human* beings. These theoretical constraints simply mirror the general social beliefs and structures that perpetuate the myriad forms of structural violence around us.

It is difficult to theorize human forms of resistance to social and structural violence and persuasion *while* cooperating with, and perpetuating, the very violent structures that exist through the theories we use and validate. Although the identification of social violence using critical frameworks is certainly an important means to understanding social violence and its causes, it seems to me that nonviolence in theory and practice offers the added satisfaction of finding concrete means or paths *out* of our conundrums, beyond simply labeling or categorizing and complaining about them.

Therefore, the film criticism that is presented in this chapter attempts to circumvent, to the greatest degree possible, this sort of theoretical rut. The goal here is to break the repeated cycle of structural violence that is perpetuated through the use of theories that are embedded with the very violence that they claim to expose. Breaking this cycle can enable critics to create just one of many possible new visions for understanding the rhetoric of film. A careful reading of the rhetoric surrounding the film, *The Spitfire Grill*, illustrates that there is much nonviolence at work in this film in particular. It also illustrates how our conventional, theory driven worldviews and culture can taint film criticism, revealing the bias that violence in the world is *the only* reality.

Hollywood has been, and is responding, to a significant block of cinematic viewers who desire to see films that focus on how ordinary people use nonviolent strategies to overcome and transcend obstacles presented by cultural hegemony or by an Orwellian, Kafka-like bureaucracy and social structure that entails a quiet, deadening violence. The wild success of *My Big, Fat, Greek Wedding* in 2002 shows that films taking on and making light of intercultural misunderstanding can be commercial successes. Popular movie themes in such films indicate that filmmakers and moviegoers alike are interested in stories that show how people deal with issues such as the uncertainties of life in corporate and bureaucratic settings, domestic abuse, poverty, social and economic inequalities, cross-cultural miscommunication, and lack of opportunities. People are similarly interested in seeing films that show characters that devise ways of dealing with conflict *other than* through shoot-outs or explosions.

This chapter shows that applying nonviolent theory to film criticism presents a useful new perspective. Nonviolent theory, properly applied and understood, can be a more hopeful and humane way to theorize how human persuasion operates in film. A nonviolent attitude invokes empathy, identification, and the acceptance that human beings can broach conflict in ways that can often exclude guns and violence whereas a more traditional theoretical perspective (Marxism, for instance) might actually call for their use. What Griffin and Foss have identified as an "invitational rhetoric" (2–17) comes closer to what is operating in the myriad films that display nonviolent themes. Invitational rhetoric, while a new twist on rhetoric, actually harkens back to the *paideia* of Isocrates, a vision of community and influence exerted in the public sphere for the good of all. Nonviolent rhetoric operates in this Isocratean tradition.[4]

If we dismiss nonviolence as Briley at first did, as "benign, but unrealistic," we are missing out on a potentially creative, insightful, and heuristic critical tool. By approaching film criticism with a solid understanding of nonviolent theory and practice, we may be able to (1) move beyond the shortcomings of using overly rigid theories and simplistic categorizations of gender, class, and genre in film; (2) observe at the base how oppression operates, and is perpetuated; and, even more important, (3) observe how we can move beyond simply identifying and *bemoaning* categories of oppression (such as misogyny, racism, anti-Semitism, ethnocentrism, homophobia, and so forth) to actually *discovering and appreciating creative means to overcoming* such problems and the conflicts that arise from oppressive, and violent social structures.

The beauty of nonviolence is that its very interdisciplinarity lends itself as a creative and potentially unifying force for critics from many perspectives to find reasons to listen to one another and build on one another's theories. So while a nonviolent worldview embraces an "invitational rhetoric," it likewise accepts Foucault's belief that power is not "exercised in a naked manner" but is instead "operating in much more complex, relationally-situated ways" (Nakayama and Krizek

296). As the following discussion shows, theories of nonviolence better enable us to comprehend the complexity and hidden qualities of social power as it exists in our culture today.

Nonviolent Cooperation

In order to help create a better society through scholarship, we must cooperate. Nonviolence requires cooperation. Its benefits are creative sharing and a kind of rhetorical invention that promotes understanding and insight. As shown by the growing scholarship in the field of conflict and mediation, of which nonviolent theory is part and parcel, we can see that human conflict and its resolution is not necessarily a mysterious process. It can be broken down into steps. Problems can be taken apart in light of theories that provide helpful means to resolving the problems. By the same token, understanding and incorporating nonviolent theory to film criticism can be considered as a meaningful way to solve theoretical problems, and transcend artificial borders of disciplinary theoretical constructs or perspectives. Nonviolence is like a Burkean "unifying perspective," which is not to say that it is not without its paradoxes, inconsistencies, and theoretical self-contradictions, but it does present a helpful way to look at rhetorical texts and it offers a means for critics to draw more openly from various perspectives without appearing to betray one disciplinary paradigm.

A NONVIOLENT READING OF FILM

Instead of calling the *The Spitfire Grill* a "woman's movie," it can be recast as a film that features characters—men and women—who are grappling with issues of structural violence. Nonviolence is used here as a critical tool for understanding, at least in part, why the film was received—positively and negatively—as it was. Following an overview of the critics' reviews, nonviolence and structural violence are defined, and nonviolence is then distinguished from pacifism. Last, this chapter illustrates how nonviolence can be an effective means to overcome the structural violence inherent in many cultures and worldviews.

The primary focus here is not looking at the film from the individualistic perspective, but rather from a nonviolent perspective that is collectivistic, that observes the plausibility of the interplay among the characters and events in the film. By no means is this is an exclusively "nonviolent" film; to label it as such would be misleading. Instead, the film is simply shown to feature many elements that lend themselves to a nonviolent critique, which is the purpose of this essay. In short, instead of performing a close reading of the film as a text itself, this chapter reveals nonviolence via a contextualized and interrelational reading of the critics' interpretations of the film. Nonviolent theory informs this reading of the film and other critics' perceptions of the film. By contextualized, I mean that the film's enthymemes and the contradictory cultural mores displayed in critics' commentaries can be better understood through their sociocultural context. By interrelational, I refer to how and why many reviewers reject the "reality" of the film's nonviolent portrayal of characters as a collective organism; these reviewers prefer to see human beings as discrete, individualized people. In short, theorizing is done here via nonviolence—what Briley concludes is a "tough and formidable political tool, something the world should be more aware of and could benefit from" (4).

THE DIFFERENCE BETWEEN NONVIOLENCE AND PACIFISM

> Who cannot protect [one]self or [one's] nearest and dearest or their honor by non-violently facing death, may and ought to do so by violently dealing with the oppressor. (36)
>
> —Mohandas Gandhi

To avoid the confusion of pacifism with strategic nonviolence, at the outset pacifism needs to be distinguished from nonviolence. Nonviolence is to be distinguished from the general ideology of pacifism because whereas pacifism advocates the rather nebulous goal of peace for society, nonviolence recognizes the situational and contextual requirements and methods for broaching conflict while promoting peace.[5] Robert Holmes writes:

> A commitment to nonviolence will be unqualified if the nonviolentist renounces the use of violence in any circumstances whatsoever; it will be qualified otherwise. The Jains were unqualified nonviolentists. Gandhi, on the other hand, said that although nonviolence is always preferable, if the choice is between cowardice and violence, one might better use violence. Some pacifists likewise have only a qualified commitment to nonviolence; for pacifism, strictly, is the renunciation of (and opposition to) war [specifically], not all violence. Though many pacifists are nonviolentists as well, many are not. And some people subscribe to nonviolence only because they believe it is effective and do not rule out the use of violence in principle. Still others view nonviolence merely as a tactic, to be used in certain specific circumstances and not in others. (2)

Holmes summarizes the distinction between pacifism and nonviolence in noting that a pacifist may not approve of nonviolence, while a nonviolent activist may not be a pacifist. While pacifism relates specifically to a view that denounces *going to war* and *war making*, pacifism may still cooperate with, and exist within, a warring nation. On the other hand, nonviolence takes into account the violence that occurs on various levels from the interpersonal to the international, and proposes specific measures for handling immediate conflict so as to reduce or prevent a greater future conflict.

Nonviolence is equipped to deal with the seemingly invisible, structural, and cultural violence that occurs in the range between the conversation between two people to inequalities in international economics, such as the unwillingness of developed nations to nullify vast debts of developing nations.[6] As Holmes indicates, a pacifist may also espouse nonviolence, but in general, nonviolence does not need to address issues about "war." Instead, nonviolence centers on conflict, and proposes means to avoid or reduce, as much as possible, violence in human conflicts. Also, as Holmes concedes that one finds in Gandhi's theories of nonviolent action, in the absence of all other desirable nonviolent alternatives, the "nonviolentist," as he terms the nonviolent activist, may need to resort to individual acts of violence in order to overcome the all-encompassing violence of the oppressor. Such violence must always be seen as a last resort, and most successful programs of nonviolent direct action do not require the use of violence at all.

In observing how films have represented individual acts of last-resort violence (or qualified nonviolence), two examples are illustrative. In *Miracle on 34th Street*, there is the scene where the usually very compassionate, gentle Kris Kringle (Santa Claus) acts with violence. Kringle, indignant over the company psychologist's cruel mistreatment of one employee (Kringle's friend), takes his cane and raps the uncaring doctor on the head. In *The Sound of Music*, there is the scene in which two nuns from Maria's convent use sabotage to help the Von Trapp family to escape the Nazis and exit the country. The scene shows the nuns holding wiring they have ripped from the engine of the Nazis' car. Thus they have prevented the soldiers from chasing the family.

The fact that these scenes in film work so well, and are understood by the viewer as examples of permissible violence (hence qualified nonviolence), reveal our intuitive understanding and appreciation for nonviolent behavior in everyday life. By the sardonic expressions of mirth and guilt the film viewer observes on the faces of the nuns, we see that what they have done is "wrong" in a technical sense, but in a situational and contextual sense, what the nuns have done is perfectly consistent with their nonviolent mission to support the word of God and His purpose here on earth. By the same token, the usually peace and goodwill bearing Santa Claus becoming uncharacteristically angry is instructive. Out of context, it would be hard to understand why a benevolent mythic figure would use violence, but in the situation, the viewer is invited to observe with satisfaction the unmasking of the inappropriate behavior of the doctor. Kringle is understandably upset at the abuse of people and power manifested through the corporate doctor, who Kringle raps on the head. Kringle's use of violence is qualified because the viewer sees that the doctor is unhurt, aside from his pride. Also, in a later scene, the viewer sees the doctor's abusive use of his position revealed before the courtroom, thus Kringle's act is shown to be consistent with Santa Claus's general mission of bringing joy and happiness to children and adults alike in an increasingly stressful life that is often tinged with structural violence, which the doctor's character symbolizes.

These two scenes illustrate qualified nonviolence. For nonviolence to appear convincing, one does not even need to know what nonviolence is in a pure sense. It is convincing because the viewer is invited to recognize that human beings are to a great extent fundamentally peaceful, amiable, and cooperative creatures, albeit ones that must face conflict. These scenes show characteristically nonviolent people using qualified violence. Thus a film that does contain violence can still be categorized as a generally nonviolent film. By the same token, just because people are polite or appear "nice" to one another, does by no means indicate that a film is nonviolent. Martin Scorsese's *The Age of Innocence*, for example, is full of the beauty and accoutrements of the rich, and the polite pleasantries of people obsessed with etiquette. On a surface level, the film may be seen as lacking violence because there are no beatings, rapes, or gory murders to witness. Yet *The Age of Innocence* reveals perfectly the hidden, structural violence and its devastating effects on the lives of people trapped in a suffocating class system during the Victorian era.[7]

On the opposite end of types of films, nonviolent theory can be usefully applied to the critical analysis of films with largely bloody, violent content. As Neil Postman and others have posited, we may, indeed, be amusing ourselves to death; nonviolent theory offers a means to understanding how and why. While pacifism deals exclusively with opposing war, nonviolence may or may not deal with war. Nonviolence, in dire circumstances, may even be violent. But it is not especially useful to label a film as violent or nonviolent, pacifist or bellicose; to do so is to set up a false dichotomy. Nonviolent theory presumes that violence and conflict are inevitable aspects in human life and society; however, nonviolent theory maintains that this violence is not a human being's sole makeup, but rather the result of artificial social pressures, since humans are deemed fundamentally benign. Moreover, nonviolence asserts that anyone can transcend violence by invoking what is more attuned to what humans are, that is, amiable, cooperative, and intelligent. It can be productive to employ nonviolent theory to film analysis and criticism, just as feminists find it useful to employ feminist theory to film, or as deconstructionists find it useful to use new theories in appraising, analyzing, and understanding the rhetoric at work in film.

CRITICS' REVIEWS

Human dignity is best preserved not by developing the capacity to deal destruction but by refusing to retaliate. If it is possible to train millions in the black art of violence, which is the law of the . . . [irrational], it is more possible to train them in the white art of non-violence, which is the law of regenerate man (65).

—*Mohandas Gandhi*

We all recognize the story line: a mysterious stranger with a dark past but a good heart enters a new town; the narrow-minded townsfolk do not wish to give the good-hearted stranger a fresh chance; and through their own misperceptions and mistaken biases, they drive the stranger out, only to discover their mistake in the end. The critics' reviews of *The Spitfire Grill's* take on this familiar tale generally fall into three groups. First, there are those critics who outright panned the film, citing poor acting and an overly "sentimental" plot. Next, there are the mixed reviews; critics generally liked some aspect of the film, such as the cinematography, but disliked the acting or the theme, which many critics deemed too oriented toward women viewers. Last, there were critics who liked the film, citing solid acting, a refreshingly quirky and quiet filmic look at small-town America. Beyond these three groups, though, the reviewers shared a few opinions on specific aspects of the film or its production.

Shared Themes

Across the board, film critics offered four key observations about the film. One observation common to most reviews, regardless of whether not the critics liked the film, was that the film "was financed by an order of Roman Catholic priests" (Rottenberg 126). The second point that reviewers made much of was that the film contains "themes of redemption and forgiveness" (Rottenberg 126). Third, reviewers remarked that the film's plot centered on "empowering female bonding" (*Sight and Sound* 64). Fourth, reviewers made it clear that this was the director's first foray into major motion picture directing (Klady 65).

According to the film's reviewers, the film's themes center around "human values" (*Sight and Sound* 64). Rita Kempley calls it a film "about the power of goodwill in the face of nasty community gossip" (F1). John Petrakis says that the film "teaches us lessons about life, love and matters of the heart and soul"; further, he says it "reminds us how sacrifice can still play a role in our daily lives and how resurrection is not restricted to the pages of our family Bibles" (D4). Other similar descriptions are that the film is "chock full of spiritual uplift: it features redemption, martyrdom" (Rafferty 93); the film has "small-town values"

(Dauphin 45); "this story . . . conveys any number of messages about the power of forgiveness and the true meaning of resurrection" (Petrakis D4).

The female bonding that critics found central to their interpretation of the film reminded them of "sleeper" films such as *Fried Green Tomatoes* and *Gas, Food, Lodging,* among other "women's flicks" (Klady 65). Travers called the film one of two "movies about women opening . . . in one macho summer" (69). Terry Lawson calls it "the next 'woman's movie' . . . [that] brings together women of variant ages, personalities and backgrounds for the purpose of showing us what they all share" while filling the bill of Hollywood moguls' search for profitable "movies about women relating to other women" (69).

Writing about director Zlotoff's major motion picture debut, one critic said that, on the one hand, he "overstates his intent with long dialogues when simple action would suffice"; yet, on the other hand, "to Zlotoff's credit, he eschews pat, happy endings" (Klady 65). Another critic states that "Zlotoff's feature-film debut" is "noteworthy in its attempt to turn back the clock" (Simon 94). Others felt that the picture ultimately fell short of its aims: "Narratively, this dramatic balancing act requires a far more skilled craftsman [than Zlotoff]" (Klady 65).

Bad Reviews

Having looked at themes common to all of the film's reviews, I now summarize representative remarks from critics' reviews that were specifically disapproving of the film. Critics commonly remarked that the acting in the film was poor. Dauphin writes that the film is a "sappy mess" and that as Percy, Alison Elliott "only has two notes here: dreamy" or hardened (45–50). Rafferty writes that Ellen Burstyn, as Hannah, "struggles with her wretchedly written role" (93). He also contends that the actors' renditions of the Maine accent were unconvincing (Rafferty 93).

Another common criticism is that the theme and the plot of the film are overly sentimental. "We're meant to be awed by the spectacle of all this human potential being realized, but the spiritual landscape of 'The Spitfire Grill' looks phony and remote, like retouched mountains on a picture postcard" (Rafferty, 93). Travers writes that the film "sells human values like a preacher who thinks he can win a soul for every tear he jerks" (69). Dauphin states that Zlotoff "favors the cloying look and feel of a Hallmark Hall of Fame presentation" (50). Bruce Williamson calls the film a "sloshy little drama" that only won the 1996 Sundance Film Festival's audience award because there at the Festival "filmgoers often get swept up in schmaltz"; he adds that the film is rife with "gobs of sentimentality" (28). Kemply complains that the "essay-writing contest" that is so central to the plot "gives rise to a corny, feel-good sequence in which Gilead archetypes (from kids in bike helmets to older folks in porch chairs) cheerfully help Hannah read through the huge pile of raffle application letters" (F1).

Mixed Reviews

The mixed reviews included remarks such as the fact that the film seemed to mean well. Some reviewers liked the plot and not the acting, whereas for other critics the reverse was true. Terrence Rafferty states that the actor Alison Elliott, whom he finds it important to label as "a former model," brings "a lack of technique [that] makes her seem . . . refreshingly natural"; however, Rafferty finds the other aspects of the film "solemnly berserk" (93). Leonard Klady likewise writes, "The emotionally charged material is abetted by a strong cast, but the familiarity of the subject matter limits the picture to niche audiences"; he also says Zlotoff "has devised a complex tale that tends to bog down as he attempts to weave together its many plot strands" (65). Typical of the mixed and negative reviews, Simon notes that "some things are hard to believe" (90). In contrast, the reviewers who were able to suspend their disbelief tended to like the film on all counts.

Positive Reviews

Plenty of reviews were positive. Overall, these critics characterized the film favorably as "a pleasantly picturesque fable" (Rottenberg, 126); "a distinctive and affecting film" (*Sight and Sound*, 64); "a stray, eager-to-please puppy that has wandered into your yard—virtually impossible to kick out" (Simon 95); "always appealing" (Kempley F1); a "good allegory" (Petrakis D4); and "heartwarming" (Williamson 28). The rationales behind the positive reviews centered on the film's solid acting cast and interesting, modern spin on what would otherwise be considered as simply retro, that is, wholesome, "mainstream fare Hollywood made in the 50s" (*Sight and Sound* 64).

The reviewers who liked the film cited solid acting. John Simon avers that the film's plot "hinges on . . . likable performances" of a "good acting company" (95). With Ellen Burstyn as Hannah, the matriarchal figure in the plot, the film's cast of characters was deemed convincing. The performance of Alison Elliot as the protagonist, Percy, was called "mesmerizing" (Rottenberg, 126). As "ex-con Percy," Elliot's performance is "a rare mix of enigma and blue-collar grit, [and] suggests real star potential" (*Sight and Sound* 64). Klady writes that Elliot performs well in "a daunting role layered with natural smarts, youthful energy and painful regret; she weathers the mood shifts with aplomb and grace" (65). Also, Marcia Gay Harden as Shelby was praised as "excellent . . . thanks to Harden's ability to suffer silently, she becomes the moral center of the story"

(Petrakis D4). Similarly, says Lawson, "Watching Harden cast off her [character, Shelby's] cloak of self-contempt is almost worth a repeat visit" in what would be an otherwise "predictable" character slot (G9). Such superb acting and plot turns help make the film refreshing for viewers who are willing to set aside cynicism if only for 117 minutes, and may be one alternative explanation for the film's (1996) Sundance Film Festival Audience Award.

Aside from good acting, critics stated that the major strength of the plot was its real-world origins from three different news items; one about a restaurant being raffled off because the owner could not find a buyer; another about convicts operating a state tourist call-in center; a third about the poor in the rural Eastern states (*Sight and Sound* 64). The *Sight and Sound* reviewer believes that such "'small' details with big implications imbue the film with a low-key ironic awareness that lifts it clear of sentimentality" and, further, that "this is no idealized rural idyll defined by the gaze of privileged city-dwellers" (64). Likewise, Kemply maintains the film's "mystical qualities are wonderfully offset by subtle, restrained humor" (F1).

Perhaps in counterbalance, the plot's realistic overtones are tempered by the visuals, which are painterly in quality. Favorable reviews often cited the "stunning naturalistic camerawork" (*Sight and Sound*, 64). The film was described as featuring "a grey-white winter range of colors for the surroundings and a generally dark, earthy palette inspired by the paintings of Andrew Wyeth" (*Sight and Sound*, 64). Kempley asserts that "There's a warm, almost Capraesque glow" to the film (F1).

So, we see that for some viewers, the film was a "success" in the rhetorical sense, while for others it was a mixed bag, and still others felt it was a "failure" and unbelievable. What can account for such a disparity among viewers? Would it be fair to cite the film's so-called woman centeredness or its niche orientation as the reason for this disparity in the film's reception? I have reason to believe that much more is at work in this film, which leads me to point to an understanding of nonviolence and structural violence as a way to comprehend the film's "believability" factor.

Next, to better understand the film's message, a working definition of structural violence is offered. In addition, nonviolence in "real-life" situations— and thus, in 'reel-life' ones as well—will be shown to be an effective means to surmount structural violence.

STRUCTURAL VIOLENCE

> We have all—rulers and ruled—been living so long in a stifling, unnatural atmosphere that we might well feel in the beginning that we have lost the lungs for breathing the invigorating . . . [air] of freedom (59).
>
> —Mohandas Gandhi

In this section of the essay structural violence will be defined and shown to be integral to the plot of *The Spitfire Grill*. Zlotoff wrote the script from the starting point of three real news stories. Two of the news stories—the one about rural poverty and the one about prison inmates being used as travel agents—are fine instances of *structural violence* at work. Johan Galtung defines violence as "the cause of the difference between the potential and the actual, between what could have been and what is . . . [it] is that which increases the distance between the *potential and the actual*, and that which impedes the decrease of this distance" (9-10). This emphasis on the gap between the "potential and the actual" shows that, as with nonviolence, violence too occurs in the contingent, mobile realm of rhetoric.

Galtung lists many types of violence, ranging from the physical to the psychological. He shows how interpersonal violence is deemed "material" while structural violence is less visible (10-11). Like Pepinsky's understanding of crime, Galtung's research proves that much violence "is structural" that is, it is "built into structures" and thus seems invisible (11). The danger of this invisibility, according to Galtung, is that it then appears "the natural state of affairs," and, even worse, that our "ethical systems . . . will easily fail to capture structural violence in . . . [our safety] nets" so that we focus on overt or personal violence, such as "murder," while "ignorance" may be more socially detrimental (11). Structural violence operates, exists, and is perpetuated in a rhetorical manner:

> It is not strange that attention has been focused more on personal than structural violence. Personal violence shows. The object of personal violence perceives the violence, usually, and may complain—the *object of structural violence may be persuaded not to perceive this at all*. . . . Structural violence is *silent*, it does not show—it is essentially static. . . . Thus a research emphasis on the reduction of personal violence at the expense of a tacit or open neglect of research on structural violence leads . . . to acceptance of [hierarchically based] 'law and order' societies (emphasis added). (12-13)

Galtung explains how structural violence is made to seem a normal part of social order, when in actuality it functions to warp that order and prevent human beings from reaching their highest possible levels of self actualization and social contribution.

Let us turn to specific examples of structural violence. There are the systems of economic maldistribution that engender poverty, like that represented by the character of Percy in the film. There are systems that perpetuate the construction and political use of prisons in the economy, like the tourist office inside the prison of the film's opening scene. Films such as Michael Moore's *The Big One* and *Bowling for Columbine* also clearly reveal systems of structural violence. The *Spitfire*

Grill's prison scenes reveal the tacit cultural acceptance, through structural violence, of things that might otherwise seem off kilter or even bizarre. Thus structural violence is made manifest through the material functions in our social order while it is hidden through rhetorical means.

The structural violence of poverty is hidden by the word poverty itself, which connotes a lack of means. Through a structurally violent lens of discourse, poverty appears to be a kind of weakness that society can attribute to the *person* who experiences it; in the Burkean sense, such terms are deflections of a reality that could be changed but that seems fixed. The structural violence of roles, such as that of housewife as personified by the character of Shelby, exemplify how language and rhetoric is implicated in creating this invisible reality where society quietly sanctions the stunting of a human being's emotional, intellectual, social growth. It is the very stunting with which this film is most concerned, and which is shown to be offset through nonviolence, as I shall show in the following reading of the film.

THE ISSUE OF "BELIEVABILITY" IN
NONVIOLENCE AND VIOLENCE

> Perceptions are perceptions of our body, feelings, mind, nature, and society . . . Perception should be free from emotions and ignorance, free from illusions. . . . Guarding knowledge is not a good way to understand. Understanding means to throw away your knowledge. . . .The technique is to release . . . to transcend (146).
>
> —*Thich Nhat Hanh*

Next, my interpretation of the critics' reviews is given along with an explanation of the pertinent tenets of nonviolence as they relate to a critical rendering of *The Spitfire Grill.* Without waffling, I can say the three camps of critics were right about the film's being good, so-so, and bad. By and large, the critics who found the film annoying did so for two key reasons. First, the film's reviewers dismissed the artistic value of the sentimental as being too "womanly" or feminine. Second, the film was deemed bad in large measure because the reviewers rejected the premise that people can become empowered nonviolently. This is not to say that the film is perfect.[8] But what this analysis reveals is how critics perpetuate twin individualistic, structurally violent world views: first, violence is seen as "natural" in society, and therefore it is acceptable. Second, nonviolent behavior is rejected out of hand as not only unrealistic, but also as unproductive. Further, if these "popular" film critics do it, it must also, at least to some degree, filter into academic treatments of film criticism and theory (and vice versa), which needs to be questioned. Indeed, Roger Courts, Director and CEO of the Sacred Heart League, who helped get the film made, believes that one negative article that he felt was "extremely harmful to the film was one written by Caryn James of the *New York Times* and which ran, at great length, in a Saturday and Sunday edition. It was particularly mean spirited and intimidating (to Castle Rock Pictures, the studio that had just bought the film)" (Courts 2). In the end, Courts is glad that the film did as well as it did nonetheless, because "the total profit from the film was used to build a new 450 student, state of the art school . . . in northern Mississippi. And, not surprisingly, the cafeteria is named 'The Spitfire Grill'" (Courts 1).

If a film has "gobs of sentimentality," as *The Spitfire Grill* was condemned for having, it does not necessarily mean that it is a poorly conceived, filmed, or acted work of art; but such a film is dismissed for snobbish artistic reasons. In *Cinema and Sentiment*, Charles Affron writes that "Art works that create an overtly emotional response in a wide readership are rated inferior to those that engage and inspire the refined critical, intellectual activities of a selective readership" (1). But Affron asserts that an "inferior" rating ignores the fact that such films remain influential "meaning-generating" forms of rhetoric (1). Affron traces the particularly affective form of film from its origins in Renaissance art (especially painting) to later forms in theater and novels, to classic films such as *It's a Wonderful Life, Mr. Smith Goes to Washington, A Place in the Sun, The Merry Widow*, to more contemporary films such as the first and second *Godfather* films. Affron asserts that the epithet of "woman's film" being synonymous with "tearjerker" is actually "ambiguous and inaccurate. It suggests that such a film is only about women or that it appeals only to women. Neither is true" (16). Affron's book illustrates the generic transcendence of the affective in generating meaning in myriad kinds of films and film plots.

With regard to the negative reviewers' claims that *The Spitfire Grill* just had too much going on to be believable, Affron's research points to the effectiveness of exactly this mode of unreasonable reason. "Many sentimental narratives," says Affron, "tend to generate improbabilities in proportion to the strength of the feelings they express" (23). The "emotional engagement" is set in place by the paradox that in these "narratives the very activity of fiction making becomes so expressive that it reflects a measure of incompatibility between feeling and necessity, between emotion and logic" (23). Affron very sensibly reminds critics that while "we may snicker at . . . [the teary scene's] excessive familiarity; we may object to their manipulatory power," nonetheless "the way they are designed to produce almost automatic reactions in viewers . . . we cannot deny that power's existence or afford to overlook its sources in the medium's capacity for infusing us with the anguish of loss and the joy of fulfillment" (34–35). Affron explains how the affective aids in audience identification and bonding, even in spite of what might be considered as unrealistic renderings of individual scenes or plots in their entirety. So there is power of sentiment and feeling in moving audiences (irrespective of gender or plot design).

Second, the most crucial reason that probably contributed in large part to the film's negative reviews was the simple fact that people in contemporary society often dismiss nonviolence as a viable means to dealing with social conflict. Decades ago, Gandhi recognized this mind-set; he wrote that "It is a bad outlook for the world if the spirit of violence takes hold of the mass mind. Ultimately it destroys" us all (30). Today, Jamil Salmi, a professor of educational planning, has documented the phenomenon of how violence "takes hold" and is naturalized in modern democratic societies.

Salmi has determined that the process of naturalizing violence occurs mainly through the institutional presentation of violence in a superficial manner. Through presenting violence out of proportion, through trivializing it, and through excessive individualization, our understanding of violent acts dims (1-9). Salmi writes that our understanding of violence is warped because any sense of interconnectedness is lost in "individual factors" so that "the possibility of a causal link between the violence observed and the surrounding social structure is systematically dismissed" (8). Salmi's research indicates that a nonviolent perspective that values human rights is continually quashed, along with the socially redeeming possibilities it entails.

So, when seen from a skeptical person's point of view, overcoming injustices through teamwork, cooperation, creativity, and sacrifice would indeed appear to be "corny" and "phony." Nonviolence is a perspective that is based on a totally different worldview than that belonging to those of us who espouse the modern, scientific, Darwinian tradition. For our modern, scientific worldview, hate is considered an innate, thus "natural" aggression, and as in Freud, sexuality is posited as the defining motive for human action. To the contrary, a nonviolent worldview is based in the assumption (religious or atheistic) that the most fundamental human tendency is that of love.

In his groundbreaking essay, "The New Litany of 'Innate Depravity,' or Original Sin Revisited," Ashley Montagu takes issue with the notion that humans are fundamentally aggressive beings. Montagu writes that by blaming our human fallibilities on our supposed "natural inheritance" or "innate aggressiveness" we are really just opting for the easy way out, and we are thus "absolved from any responsibilities" for "juvenile delinquency, crime, rape, murder, arson, and war, not to mention every other form of violence" (11-12). Instead of seeing people as self-centered or inherently violent, Montagu, like Kenneth Burke, Alfie Kohn, and others, believes that humans are characterized by "cooperation," and have been, "throughout the five million or so years of [hu]man's evolution . . . or else there would be no human beings today" (17).[9] Moreover, Montagu cites the importance of rhetoric in our socialization to believe that social ills merely 'exist,' through no fault of our own; he maintains that we learn this cynical worldview from sources ranging from Darwin's theories to popular literature (such as Golding's novel *Lord of the Flies*).[10] The issue of human nurture, or its lack caused by contradictory or dysfunctional social norms, is at the heart of *The Spitfire Grill*.

Like Montagu, criminologist Harold Pepinsky supports the notion that violence and crime in society are only viewed from a status quo perspective, which further perpetuates social problems by ignoring their sources. Pepinsky writes that prevailing norms about social justice ignore "the dynamics of a hierarchical social structure that allow[s] some people to gain wealth, power, position, and legitimization by impoverishing and killing others" (4). Our modern worldview, according to Pepinsky, is such that "Violence is instinctively perceived to be a symptom of social illness, of death and decay"(6), whereas his research leads him to conclude that in reality violence is simply the result of the simple fact of "power over others" (8); "domination—power over others—is the fundamental cause of crime and criminality" (9). He writes that "crime is a politically arbitrary subset of violence" (7), which obfuscates power as the base cause for violence. His research indicates that "those who victimize more often and more seriously are those who are less closely supervised, who command greater resources, and who have greater capacity to resist detection and punishment" (8). He concludes that "murder" really occurs in corporate board rooms (14), and even in the "office of the President"[11] (8), and less so on the mean streets, the latter being the scapegoat for the politics of the former. Pepinsky's research takes on new meaning in the wake of the wave of corporate scandals in the era of post-Enron collapses and President Bush's alleged war imbroglios as well as Vice President Cheney's alleged abuses of power when he was at the helm of Halliburton. Pepinsky maintains that the Darwinian, naturalizing perspective about violence further perpetuates the illusion that certain social groups, such as minorities or the poor, are inherently stupid, lazy, violent, and otherwise socially undesirable and problematic. Meanwhile, powerful elites get away with everything.

Hegemonic Positions of the Critics

Because Percy is an ex-con, the issues of "nature" versus "nurture" and of crime and criminality bear on her role in *The Spitfire Grill*. She is a "criminal" just released from prison, so some townspeople regard her with suspicion and mistrust, like the film viewer who sides with the "innate depravity" side of the "nature" versus "nurture" debate, or the viewer who regards her as being from a poor, rural background, imputing to her traits of stupidity, laziness, uselessness, or violence. However, other characters in the film, such as Shelby or Joe, just as the film's reviewers who liked the film, take the nonviolent perspective, that "crime is a disease like any other malady and is a product of the prevalent social system" (Gandhi 49). Thus Percy is given a second chance in life, to redeem herself—not once, but several times in the course of the film.

Perhaps it appears here that I am putting words in the mouths of the reviewers, who may have more serious problems with the film for its ample use of sentimentality. But the recurring commentary among the reviewers that the film's plot was patently unbelievable centers most on the nonviolent acts of the characters in the film. It is not that I wish to disagree with these reviewers, again, in light of their prevailing worldviews, it is important to add that these reviewers are totally "correct" in their assessment of the "unreal" nature, hence "unbelievability" of the film. All I aim to show here is how such distaste for the "unreality" of nonviolence is culturally based, rather than based in particularly insightful readings of the film.

Moreover, in light of the mixed and positive reviews of the film, it appears that some film critics found the plot realistic enough. Thus in bold relief this illustrates how the film critic's "taste" runs deeper than a simple like or dislike. The rhetorical stakes of critical tastes are higher than that. My point is that the negative reviews stem at least in part from the cultural logic that renders nonviolence untenable. Rather than disagreeing with these film critics, we can see they are perfectly correct in their assessments in light of their worldviews. But there is another perspective that is just as valid, and, in a different way, as logical, as theirs. Thus the positive reviews to some degree reflect the viewers' ability to suspend the Darwinian, dog-eat-dog logic. The good reviews also indicate some viewers' tacit understanding of nonviolent human behavior.

From a nonviolent perspective, hatred is believed to be a learned trait, and as such, it may be unlearned or overturned through love; whereas the opposing worldview, which is exemplified, for example, in the theories of Darwin, Marx, or Freud, accepts our "animal" side as superseding our "rational" side. In contrast, nonviolence presupposes that, as Thomas Merton writes, "human society is naturally nonviolent" (44). Of this tendency, Gandhi wrote: "All society is held together by nonviolence . . . as the earth is held in her position by gravitation. . . .What is happening today is disregard of the law of non-violence and enthronement of violence as if it were an eternal law" (44). Thus whereas the modern citizen is trained to see violence as a routine part of everyday life, other traditions enable us to see that we can use compassion and nonviolence to overcome conflict and violence.

To a critic schooled in the logic of violence as "eternal law," the possibility of "kids in bicycle helmets" helping do the raffle-contest reading certainly appears not only unrealistic, but "cloying" like a "Hallmark" production. For when violence rules, society separates into hierarchies which Pepinsky's research, among others, has shown are both undesirable and avoidable. Hierarchies create artificial social boundaries: children are confined to schools; adults to corporations; the elderly to nursing homes; the poor to welfare projects or prisons. Of course, in this kind of hierarchy, it would be more difficult to imagine children, adults, and the elderly joining together in reading raffle letters in a contest organized by an ex-convict.

But in the decidedly affective realm of the idyllic small town, Gilead, where the story takes place, the film creates an atmosphere of possibilities of all sorts, including removing artificially constructed social boundaries and structures. In this sort of nonviolent world, people are accepted as beings in flux, ever in process. These beings are fully in the realm of rhetoric because they are in the realm of the contingent, the probable. The *Sight and Sound* reviewer writes:

> In a lesser film, Percy would go through a hard but finally rewarding struggle to win the townspeople's hearts, but here the process is more complex. Instead, in a town where the postmistress regards any mail arriving from beyond the state borders as a sign of criminal activity, support for the ex-con newcomer is rare and stays that way throughout. (64)

The complexity of the film signals the nonviolent approach to understanding conflict. While conflict is considered an inevitable part of life, the nonviolent orientation opts for creative solutions that transgress artificial borders placed by hierarchies; nonviolence encompasses suffering, forgiveness, sacrifice, and people giving other people the benefit of the doubt. Nonviolence accepts youth and aging as processes that are rhetorical, but not necessarily as limiting. Nonviolence proposes actions for otherwise powerless people, especially women and children. Moreover, in a rural setting where hierarchies may be more malleable, why couldn't an adult entrust a letter to an eight-year-old, or to an eighty-year-old, to ponder the letter's merit?

As film viewers in the modern, scientific perspective, so many of us have been trained to suspend our disbelief at the sight of massive violence in the name of "realism" that illustrates our "innate depravity." Note, for example, the critical acclaim, Oscar buzz, and huge box office returns of *Pulp Fiction* or *Fargo*, and the so-called comedies (in reality, violent farces) *To Die For* and *Get Shorty*. But when nonviolent themes appear in an overtly affective plot, we have been socialized to promptly reject it as impossible, improbable, or "preachy" and "sappy." To be sure, sustaining an illusion matters in film; illusion is needed for a film to appear "realistic." But what makes the over-the-top use of extreme violence or profanity in film seem "real," or "funny," while its lack seems "phony" and "remote"? What is it in the viewer's or film critic's "taste" that causes these rote reactions? Take, for instance, the comments of this reviewer:

Some things here are hard to believe. Why does the supposedly rich quarry remain unexploited? Why would the rest of the country know about the essay contest so much earlier than Gilead? How can a whole town participate in adjudicating it? Why would the hermit in the forest remain unknown to all but Hannah and Percy? (Simon 90).

In view of these comments, it is important to acknowledge the viewer's willingness (or unwillingness) to participate in an illusion—one that is necessary to make the film seem more "real." There are plenty of logical answers to these questions, which the positive reviews indicate that viewers had no problem supplying. The lack of corporate interest in the quarry could be attributed to tax structures or other disincentives to expand the town's rock quarry. Regarding the town being the last to know about the raffle, fewer people in rural small towns subscribe to major city newspapers, which is where Jolene placed the ad for the raffle contest. From a collectivistic orientation, there is no real reason why a whole town could not adjudicate a contest. Many corporations today use collectivistic work teams with greater productivity than individuals had formerly been achieving working on projects alone—Why could not a similar principle work for a raffle contest? In addition, the existence of the hermit exemplifies that homelessness is easily ignored in towns both large and small, where the homeless are often actively ignored, or characterized as lazy or criminal. Films with nonviolent themes such as *The Fisher King* illustrate well how the homeless are often treated. Perspective is central to interpretation.

In another representative negative review, the critic was displeased with the "myriad personal dilemmas" in the plot, including "Percy's dark past, Hannah's grief for . . . [a lost son], and a mysterious, unseen woodsman" (Rafferty 93). Here again, the plot shows the interconnectedness of people who live and work in close proximity. Do we not learn about each other's personal lives when we live and work together? From a disconnected, city-slicker's perspective, perhaps we do not. Rafferty's reading makes sense. But from an interconnected, compassionate view, other readings are not only possible, they are probable. Indeed, the favorable reviews covered the bonds as if they were natural. Kempley writes, "Percy forms a much closer bond with Shelby," and in general, "the movie weaves a pleasing tapestry of fantasy and humor, with strong performances" (F1). The difference between opinions in these readings forms a pattern that appears to make sense in light of differing attitudes toward social power and possibilities.

What I am highlighting here is not that the negative reviewers' found the film distasteful not only for its ample use of emotion, but also that their dislike clusters around the film's obvious portrayal of nonviolent social actions. I am merely pointing out the very clear pattern that many critics' "taste" finds the portrayal of violence in film as "natural," but the portrayal of nonviolent social action is seen as unnatural, or, as one critic put it, "completely contrived" (Lawson G9). The interconnectedness of people that is characteristic of nonviolence is dismissed while violence is viewed as "normal." There are social and cultural reasons why this occurs.

Salmi has documented how "standard analyses of violence are . . . trivialized presentations in that the phenomena studied are seen as mere occasional disturbances" (7). In this way, violence in media is trivialized because "there is hardly any attempt to look for explanations and causes, for links and patterns" and the end result is "trivializing the meaning and impact of the event" (7). Violence in film is thus reported as *trivial* to the film's general import, to the film's rhetoric and aura of realism. Conversely, in a film that is sentimental and features nonviolence, those features are reported as *crucial* to the film's being rated as inferior, unrealistic, and, in short, a bad movie.

This is not to say that nonviolent themes necessarily make a movie a good movie, or that violence makes a bad movie. It should, however, be noted that film criticism is very tightly bound to the customary worldviews of the critic, which can cause the critic to overlook or downplay important elements in the film's composition. Take, for instance, Guthmann's remark that film viewers should never "abandon our suspicion" of films based on "the assumption that humility" is a "purifying quality that ought to be nurtured in this cold, overinformed world" (D3). When the preferred reading of film in general is shown to be open to violent themes and immediately "suspicious" of compassionate or nonviolent ones, the film's reviews (positive, so-so, and negative) make more sense. Salmi's work opens up a space for us to see how academic and popular discussions of film invite "attitudes and statements that are out of phase with the reality of the phenomena observed" (4). Specifically, he has found that reporting in the media is a significant factor in the warping of our worldview to accommodate and perpetuate violations of human rights and the dismissal of nonviolent perspectives (11–13).

Whereas Salmi's work shows that many of us in modern society are frequently biased to accept violence and reject nonviolent or pro–human rights orientations, Affron's research demonstrates that many audiences—regardless of gender—are indeed willing to participate in plots featuring the affective play of possibilities, even in filmic alternatives to violence. Affron shows how viewers actively participate in the "illusion" of emotions of love, in the Platonic sense. There is also the Greek concept of *storge*, which refers to a love that is a caring and enduring bond that does not require sexual activity; Freudian (ultra)sexuality is thus rendered an exaggeration of just one aspect of what it is to be human. Viewers can be drawn into an affective realm in which they confirm their hopes, maybe even beliefs, that nonviolence is a viable way to deal with human conflict.

SOME CONCLUSIONS ABOUT
NONVIOLENCE IN FILM

Non-violence is the greatest and most active force in the world. One cannot be passively non-violent. . . . One person who can express [active non-violence] in life exercises a force superior to all the forces of humanity (44).

—Mohandas Gandhi

This analysis began by showing the predominantly accepting orientation that rhetoric and film critics hold for the idea that human beings are characterized by "innate aggression" and violence. Violence in society, as mirrored by violence in film, is seen as a "realistic" depiction of "criminal" activity, and of a kind of Darwinian natural order. A few nonviolent theories were offered here that tend to debunk, or at least challenge, the idea that humans are characterized solely by aggression or sexuality; or that hatred and violence are our most fundamental, "natural" human tendencies. This discussion has also illustrated how it is likely that the critical reading of the film, disguised in a rhetoric of "taste," can be influenced by the viewer's perspectives and worldview. Supported by Salmi's media research revealing that modern views of reality are warped to privilege violence as "normal," I have drawn a connection between the positive and negative reviews of the film, and their relationships to the worldviews held by the critics producing their respective commentaries. This analysis also showed how nonviolent theory allows us to look at crime from a human rights perspective. From the nonviolent view, crime often arises from inequalities in power, rather than from some "innate depravity" in people who are poor or otherwise disadvantaged. I have inferred that negative readings of the film can be, at least in part, attributed to a rejection of the nonviolent perspective, while positive readings support it.

Contrary to popular misconceptions of a kind of unrealistic, utopian nonviolence; in actual nonviolent theory and practice, the nonviolent theorist or actor does not exclude the reality of violence or conflict, but rather she or he *embraces* dealing with the conflict. The nonviolent goal, however, is to reduce any ultimate violence through the use of creative ideas, disarming surprise, humor, telling of the truth, and, on a more serious end of the scale, through the use of self-sacrifice.[12] Theorists of nonviolent action recognize that there is a proper context for its success, and democracy is both a precondition and an end goal. Yet despite the careful documenting of the many successes of nonviolent action,[13] advocates of the "innate aggression" theories of human behavior ignore or dismiss nonviolent perspectives. Disbelievers of nonviolence are eschewing useful critical tools and a valuable means to understanding rhetoric. Either giving or not lending credence to nonviolence results in the way the texts such as film work to influence how we perceive what is "realistic" or what is, as one film critic put it, "solemnly berserk." The simple reason for this reliance on a worldview that "might makes right" or "might is natural" is that it is easier for a critic to remain within the structurally violent theoretical world in which he or she resides; it is difficult to buck the system. Status quo theories about aggression constitute a kind of self-sustaining microclimate for the critic, one that is difficult to escape because it does superficially appear to nourish the critical mind.

The film *The Spitfire Grill*, in its modest way, shows how people can cooperate to fight both structural violence and personal violence. The film invites the viewer to acknowledge that life entails conflict, struggle, and pain. But the moral of the story is that there is, indeed, "a balm" to heal wounds and create the possibilities for handling and reducing conflict and for improving society. Nonviolence engenders humor and goodwill; it takes the opponent by surprise; it is disarming without the need for using arms. Forgiveness and understanding, and the ultimate act of self-sacrifice if need be, show that nonviolent resistance works to manage conflict, and to bolster democratic society.

CHAPTER 5

The Politics of Nonviolent Pragmatism: Kiro Gligorov at the United Nations

Herodotus called them the "*Makedoni*" (Poulton, *Macedonians* 12). Like the people of most nations in Europe, for Macedonians, it is impossible to talk about the events of today or yesterday without also discussing the events of one hundred or even one thousand years ago.[1] "The Balkan peninsula," Hugh Poulton observes, "with Macedonia at its center, is one of the most ethnically, linguistically and religiously complex areas of the world" (4). Wars and mass migrations of peoples have taken place regularly over the past 2,500 years in the Balkan region.[2]

In 1991, Kiro Gligorov was elected president of the Republic of Macedonia. This was to be a fortuitous event. Today, Macedonia is—however tenuously—the *only* republic of all five former Yugoslav republics not to have become part in the bloody civil war in what was once a unified Yugoslavia. Dubbed "Gligorov the Gritty" (*Economist* 56), the President of Macedonia has been instrumental in keeping the peace in his small country. Warren Zimmermann, American ambassador to Yugoslavia during the first Bush administration, calls Kiro Gligorov "a wise old [politician] . . . Yugoslavia's first economic reformer" (116). Zimmerman avers that Gligorov "came through the Yugoslav crisis with honor" (126) and that Gligorov "tried valiantly to bring the Yugoslav republics back together" (136). Gligorov negotiated the withdrawal of troops of the Yugoslav People's Army by April of 1992; he was persuasive in garnering for Macedonia a place as a member of the United Nations by April of 1993.

In May of 1999, as NATO bombs continued to fall on Macedonia's northern neighbor, Serbia, Gligorov persevered in his struggle to keep his country out of the ever-burgeoning conflict. Gligorov was criticized for "remarks that Kosovar Albanians would be better off in their 'natural homeland' of Albania" (Padilla A22). Both Gligorov and Macedonia's government were condemned, especially in

71

much mainstream American media, for the Macedonians' apparently insensitive treatment of the hundreds of thousands of ethnic Albanians who poured across the northern Macedonian border to escape the bloodshed in Kosovo (Padilla A22).

In *Negotiating across Cultures*, Raymond Cohen writes that Americans are obsessed with fast-track diplomacy and speedy results (28–29). The more collectivistic and slow-paced approach to diplomacy that the Macedonians exhibited in the latest crisis exasperated many Americans. Some, however, in the diplomatic corps, as well as in scholarly circles, were less quick to criticize Gligorov, even in light of his apparently callous recent remarks that ethnic Albanian refugees ought to be taken from Macedonia's refugee camps and sent to Albania. In August of 1998, Gligorov foresaw that events would be likely to unfold as they have (Boudreaux). "In light of our [serious lack of] economic capacities," said Gligorov, "this [influx of ethnic Albanian refugees] would be excruciating for us" (Boudreaux).

Gligorov is, above all, a pragmatic politician. To provide for better understanding of the ongoing crisis in the Balkans and how Macedonia and its former leader have behaved as they have, this chapter discusses an earlier crisis during which Gligorov exhibited tendencies of nonviolent pragmatism. Nonviolent pragmatism entails noncooperation or defiance of political adversaries in order to decry a perceived injustice. This kind of political nonviolence means that the nonviolent practitioner need not subscribe to any personal or moral authority as a Gandhi or a King would, but rather would utilize nonviolent strategies to achieve political objectives. The nonviolent approach is seen as politically expedient, and not necessarily morally superior or pure in any way. In fact, nonviolent pragmatism clearly shows that violence and nonviolence are not opposed as a binary, but rather in a sliding scale of actions and consequences. In pragmatic nonviolence, to a certain extent, a successful approach to crisis management could entail a measure of violence.

Gligorov and his government's rationale for their handling of the refugee crisis can be better understood by looking back at their handling of earlier crises. This chapter examines the crisis of Macedonia's entrée into the United Nations in 1993. Gligorov's background is discussed, and the more distant and recent history of Macedonia is summarized. Finally, in a traditional approach to rhetoric, a textual reading of Gligorov's first speech before the UN is undertaken in light of pragmatic nonviolence.

GLIGOROV THE PEACEMAKER

At 82 years of age, Gligorov stepped down as president. He has a remarkable record as a political mediator and peacemaker. In 1994, the American Bar Association's (ABA) Central and Eastern European Law Initiative (CEELI) "honored

Kiro Gligorov . . . as its first-ever award winner" for his role in "promoting the rule of law, pursuing a market economy, and respecting human rights" in the Republic of Macedonia (Keeva 106). In 1995, Gligorov was also honored with the prestigious Kran Montana Peace Award for Eastern Europe. Gligorov has proven himself to be an ethical and effective statesman. For instance, in July of 1995, Gligorov "acted to curb corruption in order to reposition the [Macedonian] state on the democratic track. He fired fourteen officials, including four deputy ministers" (Perry, *Miracle* 117).

As far as ethnic strife is concerned, Gligorov, while not achieving the integration standards set by some American observers, has nonetheless created a climate of interethnic tolerance that "can be regarded as non-typical of a Balkan country" (Hooper 10A). By 1999, and despite complaints about Macedonians discriminating against the ethnic Albanian minority in Macedonia, "five of 27 seats in Macedonia's democratic parliament [were] occupied by politicians who are ethnic Albanians" (Hooper 10A; Boudreaux). Having miraculously survived a car-bomb attack on his motorcade—in which he nearly lost his life in October of 1995—Gligorov continued to serve as president of Macedonia as vigorously as before. As a result of the November 1999 Presidential elections in Macedonia, which Boris Trajkovski won, Gligorov left office. Gligorov "is credited with guiding Macedonia's peaceful transition to independence" and for "[leaving] this country of 2 million people as . . . an example in its progress toward democracy" (Gall). Of this transition, says Gligorov: "The important thing is that there is no vacuum of power without a president, and that a new president is elected democratically" (as qtd. in Gall). Fostering democracy in the Balkans is a tall order.

For example, alluding to the insurgence of the recent Kosovo Liberation Army (KLA) against Serbian control, Gligorov believes the attempt on his life and nine other bomb attacks on police stations and military barracks in 1998 in Macedonia "have the aim of sending us a message that similar developments in Macedonia as those in Kosovo are possible" (Boudreaux). Still, Gligorov's aim has been to "keep the peace" with both "U.S. aid and close ties with NATO" (Boudreaux).

Gligorov has been a vital, if overlooked, player in keeping Macedonia peaceful and viable while a war has raged on for many years just north of its borders (1991–1995; and through much of 1999). This chapter examines the pragmatic nonviolence exhibited in a speech Kiro Gligorov gave to the United Nations General Assembly on 30 September 1993. The speech was attended to by influential leaders worldwide, especially in Eastern Europe. In the speech, he argues that to achieve a lasting peace, Macedonia must be supported in its efforts to "reject the changing of borders by force, the use of ethnic cleansing and the failure to respect the rights of minorities." Gligorov is particularly concerned with the role of the

Balkans in promoting a regional peace and warns the UN that "to condone the use of force for territorial expansion could increase the potential for permanent inter-ethnic wars."

THEORETICAL SIGNIFICANCE OF NONVIOLENT RHETORIC

Why would a student of rhetoric or peace studies examine the nonviolent and cross-cultural rhetoric of a virtually unknown leader of a diminutive Eastern European nation? There are important reasons. In particular, this chapter focuses on the potential role that Gligorov's nonviolent rhetoric has played in securing Macedonia's peace. Gligorov's rhetoric is noteworthy for his insistence on nonviolent means to handle conflict situations. On a grander scale, considering the continued migrations and intermingling of peoples from all over the world, cross-cultural rhetoric can provide clues to understanding how and why diverse peoples coexist peacefully or violently.

Unveiling the inner workings of communication that fosters harmony among peoples and nations would be useful to present leaders who face rhetorical situations that are rife with ethnic and religious disagreements, border disputes, and historical animosities passed down from generation to generation. In view of racially and ethnically charged events such as the 1993 riots in Los Angeles, the more recent riots in Cincinnati, to the current attacks on immigrant and minority communities in cities from London, Paris, and Bonn to Beijing, nonviolent rhetoric is posited herein as an area of study worthy of better understanding.

Apart from a handful of articles and essays on Dr. Martin Luther King, Jr.'s rhetoric, there are few studies in public address and rhetorical criticism on significant, nonviolent orators and advocates for peace. Aristotle's mandate for an ethical rhetoric entails expanding criticism and the history of public address to include and appreciate the works of *nonviolent* orators—those women and men who use persuasion for the betterment of society and of all human beings. In short, more investigation into how the nonviolent rhetoric of diversity operates in language and society is long overdue.

Nonviolent perspectives include valuing the uniqueness of ethnic, religious, racial, and cultural groups and actively opposing ethnic cleansing. At the same time, many critics of nonviolence believe that everyone who subscribes to nonviolent political and rhetorical strategies needs to be squeaky clean or saintly to attain the martyred stance of a King or Gandhi. This chapter challenges that assumption by taking nonviolence down from its pedestal and revealing its messier, more human side. Pragmatic nonviolence is about achieving political results by using as little violence as possible, without necessarily excluding the occurrence of violence.

Nonviolent perspectives often necessarily entail cross-cultural themes. Critics like Xiaosui Xiao and Mary Garrett have amply shown the value of learning from cross-cultural rhetoric.[3] Yet, in general, critics have not sufficiently invested efforts in comprehending the messages of those who can transform the rhetoric of hatred into a rhetoric that fosters understanding, mutual respect, diversity, and peaceful coexistence. In part, for this reason as well, Kiro Gligorov's rhetoric merits analysis.

The central hypothesis of this chapter is that Gligorov's use of pragmatic nonviolent rhetoric enhances the resonance of his message in the long term. Specifically, I examine how the rhetoric of pragmatism operates in his speech, including how he takes the concept of peacekeeping force and transforms it into a symbol of pragmatic nonviolent action. Throughout, I focus on his use of the themes of "community," mutual responsibility, and the sliding scale of cooperation to noncooperation.

Bowen affirms the significance of investigating nonviolent rhetoric in saying, "Once understood, nonviolent persuasive theory and practice will expand our knowledge of rhetorical forms far beyond the customary, accepted modes used today" (*Realistic* 10). The efficacy of Gligorov's inaugural address before the UN owes much of its success to its having incorporated rhetorical techniques that evince nonviolent pragmatism. Gligorov's rhetoric, like much nonviolent rhetoric, differs from the usual fare for the following reasons:

- it empathizes with, rather than demonizes, the opponent(s);
- it portrays all people as deserving of human rights, equality, and respect;
- it generally eschews metaphors that are violent (and which, therefore, to a certain degree confirm and condone violent behaviors);
- it relies on mutually agreed on feelings, facts, and history;
- it is cross-culturally respectful and aware;
- it relies on a sense of community and mutual responsibility;
- it evinces stubborn noncooperation with actions or systems perceived to be unjust; and
- it displays an *ethos* of being an underdog.

These are the main features that form nonviolent rhetoric in general and that are manifest in Gligorov's speech, in particular. Some of these aspects may be found here and there in various other kinds of rhetoric, but to find *all* of these features at the same time is a strong indicator that a nonviolent perspective is at work.

Development of Nonviolent Rhetoric

Nonviolence is a concept present in political, philosophical, religious, and social systems ranging from Christianity to Judaism to Asiatic Philosophy. In the United States, Henry David Thoreau's ideas concerning nonviolence were largely articulated in terms of civil disobedience. Thoreau's perspective of political and rhetorical action on nonviolence was primarily confined to the action of nonpayment of taxes to protest policies deemed unjust. In 1872, Karl Marx delivered a speech entitled "The Possibility of Non-Violent Revolution," in which he expressed the opinion "that there are countries . . . where the workers can attain their goal by peaceful means" (522). However, even in Marxist and neo-Marxist scholarship, the promise of nonviolent potential for transformative change and promoting justice tends to be ignored.

Mohandas K. Gandhi of India would later expand this idea of transformative nonviolent change, influenced by Henry David Thoreau's conceptions of nonpayment of taxes and Leo Tolstoy's formative understanding of structural violence. Gandhi extrapolated strategically noncooperative action to all forms of political, social, commercial, and spiritual life in a nation. Gandhi's definition of nonviolence encompassed the rhetor's (or social actor's) noncooperation with the oppressor in any way, shape, or form, provided, of course, that the noncooperator's actions did not include violence and anger.

Nonviolence, for Gandhi, entails compassion, humility, and morals; it ranges from boycotts to marches to use of rhetoric, the media, and the legal system. Gandhi called it *satyagraha*, meaning "pure soul-force," winning over (persuading) one's adversary through "this power of love"; it is also "soul-force," "Truth" that is "persistently held on to" and, contrary to popular misconceptions, it is *not* passive; rather, nonviolence requires "intense activity" (Gandhi, *Satyagraha* 52–53). Gandhi's more spiritual form of nonviolence has tended to be the defining one, which opens up nonviolence in theory to much criticism and dismissal of nonviolence as lacking any relevance to political practitioners in current events. This narrow focus on spiritualism has obstructed from view the real and more often used side of nonviolence, which is *pragmatic* nonviolent action.

The crux of pragmatic nonviolence is that people must do the unexpected, they must "resist" against "power," even "war . . . but resist nonviolently" (143). Gene Sharp, scholar of nonviolence theory, writes, "nonviolent action is not passive. It is *not* inaction. It is *action* that is nonviolent" (*Technique* 147). At the same time, nonviolence also features *cooperation*. Nonviolence assumes that cooperation is the mark of civilized society and humans' orientation toward other humans in that context. Therefore, from its essence in cooperation, Sharp divides "nonviolent action" into acts of omission, commission, or a combination of the two

(*Technique* 149). Nonviolent "symbolic action," that is, "*persuasion*," is key to this discussion (149–50).[4] This is also the point where I shall part ways with Sharp's definition of pragmatic nonviolence, for Sharp excludes "simple verbal persuasion and related behavior" (*Technique* 148) from being a constituent part of nonviolent action. I join others who assert that "speeches" *are* a crucial element of nonviolent action (Ackerman and Kruegler 6). This point imbricates rhetoric in a discussion of nonviolent practices.

Harry Bowen offers the following helpful insights toward revealing nonviolence as a theory of action and rhetoric:

> [Nonviolent] Resisters commonly are neither masochists or saints: they may feign humility and may steel themselves to accept enormous amounts of verbal and physical abuse without flinching or resorting to violence. *Non-violent resisters adopt humble statures to create morally superior contrasts between themselves and their opponents.* (emphasis added) (*Realistic* 10)

Bowen notes the tactical and strategic advantage of "adopting humble statures" to engage one's adversaries. The rhetor must express sentiments that paint him or her as the underdog in the scenario. Bowen further declares that although "some theorists are quick to assign sympathy evocation as a prime reason for non-violent [persuasion's] efficacy," he maintains "such a view is narrow," since it does not consider the other persuasive factors involved (*Realistic* 10). Such factors include the likelihood that using "violence against non-violence can tarnish a governmental image or create a lawless appearance within a community," so that the government must accede to the nonviolent resisters' demands and persuasion rather than face consequences of "possible political and economic injury"; this, avers Bowen, is what makes nonviolent rhetoric a "potentially powerful leverage" (*Realistic* 10).[5]

The rhetorical status of the nonviolent advocate is crucial to the efficacy of the message. Bowen explains the relationship between the suasory power of nonviolent rhetoric and its "attached moral aura" (*Realistic* 10). He states that "[b]ecause non-violent protesters frequently are the underdogs within a system, it is tempting to ascribe a rightness to their causes"; Bowen also states that "[this] halo effect is not unknown among other persuasive stratagems" and cites the orator's invocation "of God to substantiate . . . arguments or *ethos*" (*Realistic* 10). Cal Logue and Eugene Miller argue, however, that "status or background characteristics are not a part of *ethos*" (23). Logue and Miller maintain that "the formation of rhetorical status" is based on "the personal qualities of the parties to the communicative interaction—their motivations, aims, beliefs, and habits of character" (27). The rhetorical status of a rhetor is further complicated by consistency and cross-cultural factors. In a nonviolent message, for instance, the personal qualities of the rhetor must be shown through the language choices; that is to say, for example, that a nonviolent rhetor must eschew violent metaphors (such as "kill two birds with one stone").[6] The nonviolent rhetor travels the dual linguistic path of speech and action; each must confirm the other nonviolently. Also, what may appear to be nonviolent, less violent, or innocuous to one culture may be offensive to another.

CROSS-CULTURAL RHETORIC AT THE UNITED NATIONS

One problem associated with cross-cultural rhetoric is that it has often been regarded as falling exclusively in the domain of propaganda and belligerent communication. However, cross-cultural rhetoric is just as often (even perhaps far more often) used to communicate peaceful messages to foster harmony among nations and cultures. One site where cross-cultural rhetoric is invoked for nonviolent and peaceful ends is the United Nations. "The United Nations," says William Starosta, "is a starting point for international communications analysis, since it is a landmark in international organization and because it is a microcosm of a greater world perspective of communicative exchange" (243). The UN presents to an orator the peculiar communication constraints that are presented by international diplomacy, cross-cultural exchange, and the vagaries of translation.

Particularly in times of conflict, global leaders prefer to convene at the UN "face-to-face" in order to "restore communication and allay . . . mutual suspicions" (Prosser *Summitry* 256). The UN is a special place for communication because it "has always paid special homage to visiting heads of state and of government," and, absolutely crucial to Kiro Gligorov's rhetoric, the UN "has provided as one of its fundamental services the legitimizing of states, large and small" (Prosser, *Summitry* 258). Themes of "universal morality, progress in human welfare, and the laying of the foundations for peace and disarmament" have long been staples of communication exchange at the UN (258).[7]

Prosser observes that there is a rhetorical tendency to use "basic elements," while short of producing immediate resolutions, has actually resulted in enabling "leaders . . . to approach each other on a saner and more even basis" (273). Prosser's research also prompts him to state that at the UN member nations' leaders "are attempting to communicate not only to their fellow leaders but often to what they imagine to be the conscience of [hu]mankind" (284).

Starosta calls the UN a "dramatic stage" on which conflicts are acted out (245–46). He underscores the critical importance of examining rhetoric at the UN: "While the view of the United Nations as a symbolic . . . 'playhouse' answers questions relating to the . . . impotence of the Organization, it also obscures a more fundamental distinction, that 'props' for the 'sacred drama' are semantical, and the 'religion' of the United Nations is first *a worship of words*" (emphasis added) (246). Starosta believes that rhetorical attempts at consubstantiation among UN members represent "realistic hope" for a given "disputant" in an international conflict (253).

Now that the theoretical concepts of this chapter have been posited, we must understand the complex history and rhetorical situation that Kiro Gligorov faced in giving his inaugural speech before the UN in September of 1993, as the depths of the Balkan war loomed ahead.

HISTORICAL BACKGROUND

To understand contemporary Macedonia and the extremely difficult situation President Kiro Gligorov has had to surmount in keeping Macedonia out of the Balkan wars, one must first understand the distant past. Poulton writes that "the pre-Ottoman history [of Macedonia] gives ample scope for nationalists of a variety of persuasions to claim rights for their 'nation' by referring their putative ancestors and the relationship which they at times had with Macedonia" (*Macedonians* 24). Currently, *all* of Macedonia's neighbors proffer varying degrees of expansionist pretensions that are historically based.[8] The lure of this land is great, even though the price paid in blood in the past has been far greater. David Fromkin likens Macedonia to a "jewel stolen from an Indian goddess or from a pharaoh's tomb, [which] brought ruin to its possessors" (69).

Geographic Macedonia, to be distinguished from today's Former Yugoslav Republic of Macedonia (FYROM), is the entire Balkan region stretching northwest to northeast from the Sar mountains to the Osogoveska Mountains to the Rila mountains, then over to the eastern Pirin and Rhodope mountains; across to the southwest, geographic Macedonia is cupped by the Pindus mountains; to the south is Mount Olympus, Greece, and the Aegean Sea (Poulton, *Macedonians* xvii). It must be underscored, however, that "virtually no two scholars agree on the precise borders of geographic Macedonia" (Perry, *Miracle* 113).

Macedonian History

In the writings of Herodotus, this geographic area is conceived of as a "Macedonian homeland" (Hammond 120). In "describing the origin of the Temenid dynasty," Herodotus named "the inland Macedonia' . . . (ἐκ δὲ Ἰλλυριῶυ ὑπερβαλόυτες ἐς τὴυ ἄυω Μακεδουίηυ)" (121).[9] Thucydides also "used the term 'Macedonia' in the same geographical sense" (120). Figure 5-1. shows Macedonia's location today in relation to neighboring countries.

Macedonia has long been the crossroads of Eastern Europe. Ancient invaders traversed Asia Minor and Europe, first bringing the Vlachs (descendants of the

FIGURE 5-1.
Macedonia Today in Relation to Neighboring Countries

Romanic Thracians) to mix with the Greeks and smaller indigenous tribes. The Albanians inside Macedonia's western border are thought to be the descendants of the early Illyrians and possibly also the Thracians (Poulton, *Macedonians* 18). In Classical times, Macedonia was permeated by "Greek influences," although total control of Macedonia by Greece was inhibited by the harsh "geographic and climatic differences" between the two regions (12–14). According to Hammond, in the fourth century BCE, while the Greek language was spoken in royal court, rulers "also spoke the language of their people, 'Macedonian'"; moreover, these people "did not consider themselves Greeks, nor were they considered Greeks by their neighbors" (Poulton, *Macedonians* 13).

By the early 20th century, the Ottoman empire ended with the closure of the Balkan Wars of 1912–1913. The Balkan Wars instigated the current land-grabbing and "irrendentist" tendencies of Serbia, Albania, Greece, and Bulgaria, to name a few[10] (Perry, *Miracle* 113–14). At this time, the Treaty of Bucharest was signed, and Macedonia was again placed under Serbian rule. At the end of the second Balkan War, "Bulgaria lost out to a coalition of Romania, Serbia, Montenegro, and Greece. Lower Macedonia . . . became a province of Greece; upper Macedonia was taken by Serbia" (Fromkin 70). Bulgaria was able to secure a part of eastern Macedonia, which is known as Pirin Macedonia (Vesilind 131).

World War I is viewed as "a continuation of the second Balkan war" (Poulton, *Macedonians* 76). Serbia, Greece, and Romania sided with the Allies while Bulgaria stood with the Axis nations (75). After the First World War, the "Macedonian Question" became a focus of the Balkan political scene (80). Macedonia had been divided among Greece, Serbia, and Bulgaria. Rebel Macedonians organized under VMRO and renewed their guerrilla activities, especially in Bulgaria (80-85; 92-93). Meanwhile, Macedonians in what had become Greek territory (Aegean Macedonia) were punished severely for speaking the Slavic language, Macedonian (Poulton, *Macedonians* 89; Vesilind 131).

As World War II unfolded, Yugoslavia was bombed, and the nation disintegrated into civil war. Bulgaria was rewarded for supporting Hitler by regaining portions of "Vardar Macedonia, eastern Aegean Macedonia . . . and a small part of western Aegean Macedonia" (Poulton, *Macedonians* 100-01). Josip Broz Tito was gaining power with his communist Partisans in Yugoslavia; Tito had begun to formulate plans to incorporate Macedonia as a portion of Yugoslavia. Tito fought against the Germans and rose to power after the civil war in Yugoslavia (Zimmermann 6). Tito's break with Stalin in 1948 also enabled him to gain support from the United States, whose foreign policy experts "believed that Yugoslavia could become a model for independence as well as for an Eastern European political system that, though . . . communist, could be more open politically and more decentralized economically than the Soviet satellites" (7).

Thus, by the end of World War II, several separate republics had been incorporated into Yugoslavia; Macedonia was the southernmost of these republics. With its "republican status, Macedonian national consciousness was allowed to develop unimpeded" (Perry, *Miracle* 114). This consciousness was further enhanced by the "reestablishment of an independent Macedonian [Orthodox] church in 1967" which served as both "a religious benchmark . . . [and] an emotional reaffirmation of identity" (Vesilind 127).

Recent History

Macedonia (like the former country of Yugoslavia, of which it was a member republic from World War II to 1991) remained stable until Tito's death in 1980. Afterward, the Yugoslav government became increasingly decentralized, with power "flowing down to the republics, where, in the hands of . . . [each of the Yugoslav republic's] leaders, it could be used to foment nationalism" (Zimmermann 16). Tito had managed to quell ethnic strife among the Bosnians, Albanians, Macedonians, Serbians, Croatians, Turks, Roma, and the other ethnic and cultural groups in Yugoslavia by executing, jailing, expelling, or intimidating those who attempted to surmount the unifying communist authority and imperil the Yugoslav federation of states (Ramet 41).

Without Tito, however, not only did these ethnic groups in Yugoslavia lose the imperative to coexist peaceably, Yugoslavia also lost the status as "pampered child of American and Western diplomacy"—losing advisory know-how as well as financial backing (Zimmermann 7).[11] By 1989, with the end of the Cold War, "Yugoslavia no longer enjoyed its former geopolitical significance as a balance between the North Atlantic Treaty Organization and the Warsaw Pact" (7). With this loss of significance also went a loss of understanding of Yugoslavia's precarious union and its potential to destabilize the whole Balkan region.[12] In this way, centuries-long ethnic animosities, now unchecked in the absence of the Tito regime, grew. Croats were pitted against Serbs, Serbs against Bosnians, Albanians versus Serbs, and so on.

Also, in part as a result of strategically nonpublicized human rights abuses by Serbs against the ethnic Albanians (and vice versa) in Kosovo, the potential for conflict became explosive (7). Serbs resented the presence of the ever-exploding population of ethnic Albanians in Kosovo. Serbs have an ideal of Kosovo as their mythic homeland, which they do not wish to cede to ethnic Albanians. Serbs also resent the fact that the "ethnic Albanians have among the highest birthrates in Eastern Europe, while the Serbs have among the lowest" (Spence). The Serbian republic's leader, Slobodan Milošević, seized advantage over the increased powers of Serbia and advocating Serb nationalism. As fate would have it, the capital of Yugoslavia, Belgrade, and thus the political and military power, was located in Serbia.

The other Yugoslav republic capitals were: Ljubljana in Slovenia; Zagreb in Croatia; Sarajevo in Bosnia-Herzegovina; Titograd (today called Podgorica) in Montenegro; and Skopje in Macedonia (9). In terms of industry and business, Macedonia was the least well developed of all the republics, as Tito's plan had been to develop and promote industry and tourism in the northwest part of Yugoslavia first, and then to move gradually to develop the central and southern republics. By the time Tito died, Slovenia and Croatia were the most developed and prosperous of the republics.

Early in 1991, the "republics conducted a series of summit talks to avert civil war and find a path to interrepublican agreement, but none of these meetings produced any progress" (Ramet 48). The most cohesive plan was developed by Kiro Gligorov and Alija Izetbegović (of Bosnia), but it too was rejected by the combative Franjo Tudjman of Croatia and Serbia's Milošević (Zimmermann 131–37). In "late June, 1991, Yugoslavia was caught between the poles of Serbian and Croatian nationalist extremism" (111). So at that time, as the civil war was breaking out, Slovenia and Croatia were the most developed of the republics, and had amassed most of the financial capital of Yugoslavia, whereas Serbia controlled most of the political power, troops, and weapons of the entire Yugoslav federation.[13] The Yugoslav National Army (JNA) was stationed in every republic, and on announcements of secession by the other republics, the troops "were seen as occupiers" (143).[14]

Acknowledging these realities, Gligorov had to act wisely to keep Macedonia out of the civil war. He "helped win peaceful independence in 1991 by renouncing claims to all property of Yugoslavia's 3rd Army" and negotiated for "its removal from his new nation" (Boudreaux). Before the fighting had even begun, Macedonia's own parliament had held democratic elections and made plans for the inevitable conflict to the north (Perry, *Politics* 33). Over vociferous objections from Greece, in July of 1992 Kiro Gligorov applied for membership to the UN, averring that to admit Macedonia as a UN member nation would be "a very significant step towards the peaceful solution of the crisis in the territory of the former Yugoslavia" (*UN Chronicle* 12). Also in 1992, the UN established a no-flight zone over Bosnia-Herzegovina but a year later, 465 violations of the zone had been recorded (6).

Obviously, Macedonia's proximity to the warring area made it a potential target of armed aviational attack. In April of 1993, Macedonia was admitted to the UN, over strenuous objections from the Greeks, who feared their northernmost province, which is inhabited by a large population of ethnic Macedonians, would wish to secede from Greece and join a "greater Macedonia."

By June of 1993, the UN Protection Force (UNPROFOR) was stationed along Macedonia's borders to "monitor" and "report" activities that could "undermine confidence and stability in Macedonia or threaten its territory" (5–6). Peace talks were stalling in Geneva, since none of the parties could agree on newly drawn territory maps; the so-called ethnic-cleansing (genocide and forced mass exodus migrations of ethnic groups) had taken place at such horrific frequency that territories that had been "cleansed" were claimed by the Bosnian Serbs, who refused to cede them to the Bosnian Croats (7). Even worse, as the peace talks continued, so did "military attacks in eastern Bosnia by Serb paramilitary units" (9). Meanwhile, although Macedonia stayed out of the war, the internal and external threats to Macedonia's stability seemed almost insurmountable.

Coupled with the onerous history of the Balkans, contemporary cultural and ethnic disputes intermingle with territorial disputes. As is common elsewhere in the former Yugoslavia and Balkan region as a whole, Macedonia is rife with interethnic conflicts. Macedonia is comprised of roughly 60% ethnic Macedonians, between 30% and 40% ethnic Albanians (any census taken to date remains disputed by all parties), and the remaining population includes Vlachs, Roma, Turks, Serbs, Bosnians, and other minorities.[15]

GLIGOROV'S RHETORICAL ACE: "THE NIGHTMARE SCENARIO"

It bears repeating here that many historians believe that *both* World Wars I and II began in the Balkans. Frequently referred to as the "nightmare scenario" by scholars, a Balkan war specifically involving Macedonia would be likely to involve *all* of Macedonia's neighbors, and possibly Turkey, too, because of these nations' views on Macedonians as a people (Kaufman 238). "Serbian nationalists view Macedonia as the heartland of 'old' (medieval) Serbia, and Macedonians as a sort of . . . group of Serbs; they would like to reabsorb Macedonia into a new [Serbian] federation" (237). While the Macedonians need to maintain good relations with Serbs for trade, and while the Macedonians tend to empathize with the Serbs in terms of their fears of being overtaken by the ever-expanding population growth of ethnic Albanians, Macedonians retain a strong sense of their distinct national identity and they have no desire to join with the Serbs.

The Greeks believe that "Macedonia [has] had no right to the name 'Macedonia,' which Greeks regard as their exclusive birthright" (Perry, *Miracle* 115). Greeks "insist that the legacy of ancient Macedonia is part of Greek heritage and the Slavic Macedonians have no right to claim either the name or the associated symbols" (Kaufman 236). Symbols in contention have included the original Macedonian flag, the "sixteen-point yellow sun . . . that [Greeks] consider purely Greek because it was found on the grave of Philip II, Alexander [the Great's] father" (Vesilind 132).[16] The Greeks also claim to fear the extreme nationalist Macedonians' proclamations of wishing to join the Macedonian people who reside in northern Greece (Aegean Macedonia).[17] In 1992, the Greeks imposed a crippling trade blockade on Macedonia to retaliate for the republic's refusal to select a national name that excluded the term *Macedonia* (Perry, *Miracle* 115; Kaufman 237). Not surprisingly, too, the Bulgarians "claim that the Macedonians are simply Bulgarians" and, "like the Greeks, do not recognize the existence of a separate Macedonian nationality" (Kaufman 237). Gligorov had to broach these delicate issues of contention carefully, as all of Macedonia's citizens and her neighbors jealously watch economic and diplomatic exchanges.[18]

"Rhetorical Status" and Pragmatic Nonviolence

Despite being a virtually unknown newcomer to international politics at the UN, Gligorov's ability to maneuver successfully in the face of such circumstances is no accident. Duncan Perry has remarked that Gligorov "has managed to give the office [of the Macedonian Presidency] great prestige and place it in the forefront of national decision-making" (*Politics* 31–32).[19] A graduate of the Law Faculty of the University of Belgrade, Gligorov has extensive experience in legal affairs and in politics after spending years as a government bureaucrat and researcher at the Yugoslav capital. Gligorov is also a veteran of World War II, having fought on Tito's side with the Partisans.

After the war, he served in various governmental and related nongovernmental posts, as well as teaching at the University.[20] Gligorov's extensive experience in Belgrade politics proved beneficial to his stature and ability to know exactly how to negotiate with the Serbs for the withdrawal of Yugoslav troops from Macedonia as the civil war to the north worsened. By the time Macedonia achieved independent and internationally recognized status, Gligorov's statesmanship was further put to the test on a global scale. To ensure internal peace and promote economic viability, Gligorov needed to solicit international financial and advisory aid for Macedonia.

In 1993, in the midst of the civil war raging only a few hundred kilometers north of Macedonia's border, Macedonia was in the depths of economic strife due to both the Greek blockade and UN embargo of trading with Serbia, Macedonia's former trading partner. It was then that Kiro Gligorov addressed the United Nations for the first time as the leader of the fully recognized independent nation, the Former Yugoslav Republic of Macedonia (FYROM). An official UN translation of the text of that speech is included in Appendix 2.[21]

ANALYSIS

Cross-cultural complications preclude an exceedingly close textual reading of the speech because the text being analyzed here is an English translation of the original Macedonian language text of the speech. Therefore, the analysis concentrates on the general themes, strategic moves, and images in the speech, rather than, for example, the nuances of rhythm and poetic or linguistic devices such as alliteration, which would largely be obliterated in the process of translation. At the same time, where historical and cultural research yields insights that offer potential reasons why certain themes or key phrases were used, such information is included in the analysis.

The overarching theme of this deliberative speech is to advocate supporting peace through pragmatic nonviolent action on both regional and global levels. The key points that Gligorov makes are: (1) to declare the absolute autonomy of Macedonia; (2) to promote "peace and stability" in the international community at large and in the internal system of the Macedonia as a nation; (3) to emphasize the pressing need to advocate and support "human rights" and "human dignity"; (4) to encourage action toward preventing a "spillover" of the conflict to the north of Macedonia into Macedonia proper; (5) to request financial and advisory aid to promote trade and economic advancement, which goes hand in hand with democracy and social "stability"; (6) to uphold the rule of *legitimate* international law; (7) to condemn "ethnic cleansing" and distrust; and (8) to affirm Macedonia's prodemocratic stance in the "post-cold war" world.

The first rhetorical move that Gligorov makes is to support firmly the nonviolent idea of peace and cooperation among the member nations of the UN. This move is reiterated throughout the speech; Gligorov uses the word "cooperation" 13 times, and various forms of the word *peace* 20 times. Other nonviolent words repeated in the text include: *human rights, human dignity, community,* and *friendship.* Thus, Gligorov emphasizes his nonviolent perspective toward the "Bosnia and Herzegovina" and the general conflict situation to the north into which Macedonia was (and remains) in peril of being drawn into.

Next, Gligorov affirms Macedonia's autonomy in no uncertain terms. Indeed, Macedonia was admitted into the UN under the FYROM label, so that Greece's objections could be at least somewhat allayed. Despite this, and despite the fact that the president of the 48th session introduces Gligorov as "President of the Former Yugoslav Republic of Macedonia," Gligorov proceeds to refer to his nation throughout the speech as simply "The Republic of Macedonia." Fitting the form of UN speaking, Gligorov is formally "legitimizing" Macedonia (Prosser, *Summitry* 258). This sends a strong, clear message to the Greeks that despite their ongoing trade blockade, Macedonia will not bow to political demands to withdraw the Macedonian State name and identity from its historic people. This shows Gligorov's resolve and pragmatic nonviolent resistance in the face of extreme odds.

Indeed, noting the Greek protests and blockade, Gligorov highlights the terrible cost that this tenacious persistence in retaining the Macedonian name for the nation: "[T]his year alone, our gross national product has been cut in half." At the same time, Gligorov shows that his opposition is a nonviolent one: "In the same spirit, our efforts are aimed at establishing good-neighbourly relations with all our neighbours and at resolving all existing problems with our *southern* neighbour" (emphasis added). The "southern neighbor," of course, is the obstreperous Greece. Through this opening depiction of Macedonia as both defiant and independent, while also evincing what Bowen calls a "humble stature" (*Realistic* 10) in that Macedonia is shown to be economically crippled and militarily weak, we see the nonviolent strategy and rhetorical status of Gligorov put into play.

Gligorov's nonviolent commitment to peace is highlighted in his repetition of "human rights," "human dignity," and his avowal that he and the "citizens of the Republic of Macedonia" abhor the "ethnic cleansing" occurring just north of Macedonian borders. Gligorov uses "truth-force" to remind the member states of the UN and the European Community that their floundering and lack of ability to assert strong negotiations and preventive measures in the past was partially responsible for the egregious results, since, in spite of "[n]umerous international conferences and activities . . . undertaken in order to bring about an end to this war" nothing positive has resulted. Quite the contrary: "The most terrible post–cold war drama is unfolding in the heart of Europe: massive killings, massive destruction, over 2 million refugees, insane acts of ethnic cleansing and genocide." In effect, Gligorov states that international efforts were too late to stop the war from worsening; but he alleges there is still time to prevent the war from spreading to Macedonia, which is "situated in the immediate vicinity."

Also in line with nonviolent resistance, Gligorov rejects, through a rhetorical move of noncooperation, the notion that *all* laws should be recognized and are binding. In the theory of nonviolence, laws that are perceived as being unjust must and should be obviated. This is a critical point to note, especially for Gligorov, who holds a law degree and was a professor at the University of Belgrade Law School. For a legally trained person to imply that not all laws are to be observed is quite peculiar, yet this implication is logical in light of nonviolence. Thus, Gligorov recognizes the injustice of the "resolutions" and "negotiations in Vienna" that patently ignored the "rights of ethnic, religious, and linguistic minorities." In fact, testifies Gligorov, "borders cannot be changed by force" even if those changes are sanctioned through "negotiations." He shows his disgust for the idea that the program of "ethnic cleansing" in order to grab land has been sanctioned by de facto laws: "The international community does not recognize or accept 'ethnic cleansing'; and . . . the rights of minorities must be respected."[22] This nonviolent affirmation not only shows Gligorov's ethical stance toward the horrors occurring in the ongoing civil war in the former Yugoslavia, it also serves to assuage the ethnic-Albanian minority's fears and concerns of being marginalized in Macedonia proper.

Through the use of a distanced tone and diminutive connotations by which he paints an image of Macedonia, Gligorov fosters the sense that Macedonia is neither a threat to the Greeks nor to developed nations with interests in the Balkans. Macedonia is depicted as an island of calm and "stability" in a sea of regional and global problems: "The Republic of Macedonia is a country with foreign policies based on the principles of peace, friendship and cooperation," says Gligorov, despite her location "in the crisis-ridden region of the Balkans." It is a vivid oxymoron, for in actuality, Macedonia is an island of *land* in a sea of potentially land-grabbing neighbors, all of whom have literal access to the sea, which is vital to trade. This oxymoron is recurrent, for Macedonia is elsewhere described in the speech as "a landlocked country," "a small country," and simply "my country."

The central metaphor of the speech is of the body. Europe is presented as being a body politic and a body of trading countries, which are interconnected according to "natural . . . principles." Gligorov maintains that Macedonia, by "attaining independence in a peaceful and legitimate manner," has transformed "our historic position from a bone of contention to a factor of peace and stability in the Balkans." Thus, Macedonia as the "bone," possibly even the backbone nation of the Balkans, is crucial to the viability of the peace, the health of the entire European Community. Misha Glenny supports this view in calling Macedonia "the strategic hub of southeastern Europe, the only territory through which it is possible to cross the Balkan Mountains by land from north to south and east to west" (Glenny "Victims").

Gligorov also warns of the dangers to the health of the Macedonian state by broaching the issue of the crippling effect that the trade embargo and Greek blockade have had on Macedonia as part of this greater European body. As a blocked artery stops the life's blood from flowing, "[e]conomic and cultural ties, communications, the free flow of people, goods and ideas have . . . been severed" due to these economic sanctions.

The development of the body metaphor is punctuated by two interesting examples of world peace's becoming possible. Gligorov cites the "extraordinary significance of the historical accord between Israel and the Palestine Liberation Organization for peace in the Middle East." He also says that he is "deeply convinced that . . . we will soon be speaking of South Africa as a region of successful development and human dignity" and that everyone has reason to "hope that the forces of peace in that region will ultimately prevail over the forces of regression and apartheid." These examples function to show that even the most "serious" and "adverse" of conflicts can be resolved. Both the Israeli-Palestinian and the native or tribal South African versus the white Afrikaner ethnic conflicts constitute apt analogies to the Balkan ethnic conflicts. Gligorov's use of these examples supports Rentz's claim that "in international crises, . . . [diplomats find] deductive arguments, based on commonly accepted premises, the most useful tool in creating support for their positions among representatives of divergent nations" (179).

Following this deductive move, Gligorov returns to the imagery of the body to propel his argument. The war in Bosnia and Herzegovina, like European blood of the UNPROFOR troops, may "spill over." It is in "dead earnest" that Gligorov speaks of this conflict. In fact, the "situation . . . is . . . grave" and, like death, it is "tragic and incomprehensible." The war is like a disease "unfolding in the heart of Europe." Like the worst kind of "heart" attack, it is "massive . . . massive." The current, "heated" state of the European body is the "post–cold war" result: it is war renewed, leaving cold dead bodies, the "killings," "destruction," and "2 million refugees"; it is "insane."

To address specifically Greek concerns regarding Macedonia's potential for nationalist expansion into northern Greece (Aegean Macedonia), Gligorov asserts, "We see the interdependence of interests and mutual respect as the future of successful international cooperation." More to the point, Gligorov claims that

Macedonia's "foreign policy is consistent with the *internal* development of the Republic of Macedonia, which is oriented towards a market economy, democracy, a State of law, human rights and harmony in inter-ethnic relations" (emphasis added). Thus, by referring to Macedonia's "foreign" policy in terms of its "internal" state of affairs—a contained, finite imagery—the Greek fears of outward movement and expansionist intentions are addressed and allayed.

Also, the United States and other western European nations' concern for upholding democracy and the capitalist entailments of democracy are supported. For instance, to assuage U.S. and western European fears of Macedonia serving as a transit point for dangerous illicit commodities, such as nuclear fuel and arms, Gligorov avows that his government is committed to "the promotion and development of a policy of good-neighbourly relations" and to "forestalling the proliferation and use of weapons of mass destruction." Macedonia's housing of UNPROFOR, KFOR, and NATO troops to date has borne out this commitment as steady and true.

The dangerous regional position in which Macedonia finds herself is amplified through such phrases as: "a country situated in the immediate vicinity" of the "war in Bosnia and Herzegovina" and as one of the beleaguered "Balkan States." The support that Macedonia needs to avert the "spillover" of war into her borders is likewise underscored: "my country belongs to a group of countries that can survive and develop only in conditions without war." Gligorov alludes to the "nightmare scenario" of which diplomats and scholars alike are well aware, that, without "assistance from the international community," Macedonia will be susceptible to "social tensions, and the probable collapse of the economy" that will turn the tiny country into "a new crisis spot"—one that could very well spark World War III.

The "nightmare scenario" is without doubt one of the strongest elements of persuasion in his enacting the role of underdog and pragmatic nonviolent leader. Whereas the imperiled Poland prior to Nazi takeover, and the weak, timid Tibet (circa 1949) were easily ignored by the international community in their pleas for protection and support, Macedonia, because of the frightening "nightmare scenario," must be heeded. Decades ago the UN saw Poland and Tibet, respectively, as expendable, isolated.

In stark contrast, Macedonia's cornerstone geographic location and her role in a long history of Balkan wars and, more recently, World Wars I and II, renders Macedonia vital to maintaining peace. The 19th-century German chancellor Otto von Bismarck said, "Those who control the valley of the River Vardar in Macedonia are the masters of the Balkans" (Glenny, "Victims"). Knowing this, Gligorov's allusions to the "nightmare scenario" serve to bolster his rhetorical status as an underdog, but one that is not expendable; to the contrary, as small as Macedonia is, the international community needs it as much as Macedonia needs the help of the UN.

Gligorov heightens the exigency of the situation by repeatedly emphasizing the crucial need for international support in keeping the peace in Macedonia. The horrific potential for an expanded war serves as both a reminder and an impetus for the international community to act quickly to "prevent" such a global war: "[A]ll the unresolved issues involving ethnic minorities can well lead to future military conflicts," says Gligorov, "particularly in certain regions of the world, thus endangering international peace. . . . [I]t is essential to take immediate preventive measures." Of course, the Balkan region, and Macedonia in particular, is among these "certain regions."

At the same time, Gligorov strategically aligns Macedonia in a futuristic sense to the "stability" of western European nations by calling Macedonia "a European country in transition," "a developing country," and by affirming that, with the appropriate international support and "aid," Macedonia will play a possible role in "a world where everyone will have respect for human dignity." Gligorov reminds the Europeans especially of the fact that they are beholden to Macedonia for holding up its end of the bargain by complying with the UN embargo, the "sanctions imposed on Serbia and Montenegro." A tiny and defenseless country has done its part for the greater good of "international" and "world" "stability"; now, intones Gligorov, it is pay-back time. "It is inconceivable to expect a small country to bear the damage of an international action of this type on its own, without solidarity and timely assistance." Thus, the international community must, in its turn, help Macedonia: "Aid should be provided now as a preventive measure, instead of after the outbreak of those likely social clashes which may grow into new conflicts." Put simply, the choice is theirs: either help Macedonia now in a comparatively minor way, or be forced to stem the tide of a conflict of potentially global magnitude.

Implications of Gligorov's Nonviolent Rhetoric for Future Peace in the Balkans

In the end, Gligorov has been successful in garnering the desired international aid for Macedonia, which he requested in both nonviolent terms and context. Soon after the speech was delivered, extra UNPROFOR troops (almost exclusively American troops) were stationed along Macedonia's borders, despite the fact that "peacekeeping is nowhere described in the U.N. Charter" (Norton and Weiss 9). Also, financial and advisory aid has ever since been likewise supplied to Macedonia by the United States and the UN. In addition, the Greek blockade was finally ended, and now free trade and access to Greek ports for the import and export of Macedonian and international goods is once again enjoyed. In April 1997, the International Monetary Fund (IMF) approved $80 million in aid to Macedonia for a three-year period. Additional, if belated, support has been received in the wake of the NATO bombings and the influx of refugees, both officially (in refugee camps) and unofficially (in villages, cities, and towns) in Macedonia.

In short, Gligorov's use of the rhetoric of pragmatic nonviolence enhances the resonance of his message and that it provides indicators of why he and his government reacted to the 1999 crisis in Kosovo as they did. Gligorov's repugnance of NATO's actions in bombing Serbia (which critics found ill conceived and poorly planned) might seem less baffling to observers if seen in light of his past rhetoric of pragmatic nonviolence. Gligorov's statements that the ethnic Albanian refugees who gushed into Macedonia ought to be absorbed by NATO member countries, as well as "sent to Albania," appeared callous and perhaps downright shocking to American observers. The statements also appeared to fly in the face of what most people perceive as nonviolence, which they view as saintly, purely moral, and spiritual. Yet, Gligorov's rhetoric is one of *pragmatic* nonviolence, which espouses a view of noncooperation with powers and parties that he perceived were threatening to the very existence his tiny, impoverished country.

Gligorov's pragmatic nonviolence can be understood through his past rhetoric, which showed his proclivity toward not cooperating with parties who might be conceived of from the Macedonian perspective as more powerful bullies. Pragmatic nonviolence need not be moral or spiritual, as nonviolence is often portrayed. The 1999 dilemma Serbs imposed on the Macedonians, and NATO's response to Serbian ethnic cleansing, is clear. As Ljubco Georgievski, Macedonia's former prime minister, put it, Macedonians "have been made to choose between the Albanians and the Serbs. It should not be a question for a country that already has a quite complicated political life" (Gall). Macedonians thought keeping the refugees for an extended period of time would signal to the ethnic Albanians that the KLA's violent tactics are a successful means to attain a greater Albania, at the cost of breaking up the fledgling country of Macedonia.[23] So far, that fear has proven true.

Under these difficult circumstances, by positioning himself as a representative of his small, landlocked country, Gligorov played the role of the underdog. At the same time, his defiance of western scapegoating of Macedonia for its apparent ill treatment of refugees from Kosovo shows his *pragmatic* nonviolent stance. As such, Gligorov sends conflicting messages, rhetorically, which have confused and even angered many observers. On the one hand, his stance as underdog heightens the probability for invoking empathy and cooperation among listeners who liken an underdog with a nonthreatening rhetorical status. This stance has resulted in increasing amounts of aid coming into Macedonia recently. On the other hand, his pragmatic nonviolent stance appeared only as callous leadership through his nation's treatment of refugees. In the face of so much human suffering displayed on TV screens worldwide, observers could not fathom Macedonia's defiance of

NATO's macho action. Little did Americans (or others critical of Gligorov's lead-ership) know that Macedonians perceived NATO's attack as occurring from, at best, a lack of planning, or at worst, an excuse for a sideshow to deflect attention from President Clinton's Monica Lewinsky scandal. In any case, NATO's actions left Macedonia—an economically poor, and politically weak new democracy—holding the bag (Gourevitch 21–22; Glenny "Victims").

The tensions in nonviolent rhetoric between pragmatism and the allure of sup-porting an underdog can help or hinder one's stance in the eyes of observers. Many observers are normally inclined to agree with a stronger power, such as NATO. But this is not always the case. In Gligorov's rhetoric in 1993, the undeniable appeal to magnify the rhetorical status of an underdog worked to his advantage. Greece's view was ignored in the UN, and Gligorov achieved the goal of having Macedonia enter the UN as a member nation, while attaining the important symbolic goal of keeping the country's proper name.

The persuasive tactic of underdog *ethos* is common to pragmatic nonviolent rhetoric (Bowen *Realistic* 10). As Logue and Miller state, "[R]hetorical status op-erates in some contexts to empower some while placing others at a disadvantage" (20). In Gligorov's rhetoric in the 1993 speech examined in this chapter, the rhetorical status of Macedonia becomes empowered while the respective statuses of her irredentist neighbors, especially Greece, become disadvantaged.[24]

Gligorov employed the rhetoric of diversity in his 1993 UN speech to prove to both the neighbors and inhabitants of Macedonia that the rights of all "persons be-longing to national or ethnic, religious and linguistic minorities" will be respected. Gligorov framed his cross-cultural audience in the natural metaphor of a body that can flourish in "international cooperation" and "peace." Today, as then, Gligorov renders Macedonia as a tiny, landlocked nation with few financial assets into a nation worthy of being guarded by U.S. troops because Macedonia is the key to regional, and due to the potential of the "nightmare scenario," global peace.

In 1993, Gligorov incorporated the roles of Greece, as Macedonia's "south-ern neighbor," and of Turkey, Macedonia's powerful nearby ally, as well as Mace-donia's other nervous Balkan neighbors, into the rhetorical picture. Gligorov used pragmatic nonviolence by alternatively defying Greece and other nations' ir-rendentist ideals, and by emphasizing "community," the "prevention of conflict" and "cooperation." In 1999, Gligorov deflected international relief agencies' crit-icisms of his country's seemingly bumbling or even malicious (mis)handling of the refugees by reminding them of both Macedonia's underdog ethos and its com-mitment to upholding international agreements.[25]

In disagreeing with both NATO's decision to bomb Serbia and with Serbia's decision to ethnically cleanse Kosovo, Gligorov's rhetoric again emphasizes his pragmatic nonviolent stance:

If you ask me as a human being, from a humane . . . humanitarian point of
view, I cannot justify any kind of bombing. But nonetheless, Kosovo has its
own very long history, [and its recent] history . . . dates back to 1989. We
have a 10-year period in which the present regime of Serbia . . . abolished all
the legal institutions which the Albanians in Kosovo had according to the
constitution of the former Yugoslavia of 1974. (King)

By disagreeing in principle with the tactic of using violence to overcome violence, Gligorov does take a higher moral ground that is characteristic of the
kind of nonviolence with which most people are familiar and feel comfortable.
By disagreeing with Serb practices that flout legal norms and human rights,
Gligorov likewise evinces a rhetoric of nonviolence that is on an elevated moral
plane. However, as political pressures within Macedonia mounted with each
passing day that the country housed thousands of the people who make up the
political minority that Macedonians fear will shear their nation asunder, Gligorov's rhetoric returned to pragmatic nonviolence and its characteristic defiant
noncooperation with greater powers.

PROSPECTS FOR PEACE

Until his last day in office, Gligorov's leadership remained strong. As Macedonians voice concerns over the long-term implications of managing the ever expanding ethnic Albanian minority, including well-founded fears it could throw
their country into civil war, Gligorov's position remained most of all pragmatic.
His rhetoric revealed his stance of noncooperation with NATO member countries' wishes for Macedonia to blithely bend to Western wills without regard to
Macedonia's needs.

As the foregoing analysis illustrates, Gligorov's negotiation and political
skills translated into a skillful, diplomatic oratory that has been targeted toward
a diffuse and often disunited audience of UN members. In the turn of a phrase,
Gligorov either assuages or arouses the disparate fears of the United States and
the international community. His use of the theme of "community" and mutual responsibility, and the deductive manner in which his 1993 speech, as well as later
rhetoric, unfolds, has strengthened his argument for supporting an economically
and democratically strong Macedonia in the crisis ridden, post–cold war era.

The rhetoric of pragmatic nonviolence is evident in Gligorov's reliance on such
tactics as (1) being the "underdog" in terms of a rhetorical status, (2) using "soul-
force" or "truth-force" to open the world's eyes to the "reality" of the ongoing "genocide" that could "spill over" throughout the region, and (3) ironically, supporting
both "cooperation" and "noncooperation," through either *supporting* or *subverting*

the rule of law: the law is to be supported when it constitutes "timely preventive measures in cooperation with the United Nations"; the law is to be subverted when it disenfranchises "the rights of ethnic, religious and linguistic minorities" or when it threatens the very existence of his nation's infant democracy.

Finally, the cross-cultural colorings of Gligorov's rhetoric are evident in his adept and liberal sprinkling of examples of mutual concerns between and among all UN member nations. Gligorov displays an omniscient view of the situation. He deftly moves between the local and the global; the "Balkans" and the "European Community"; between the "developing" and the "developed" nations; between the "international" and the "regional"; between the "we" and the "I." He illustrates his concern for the "world economy" while showing that the economy of his own nation is dependent on both the strength and the largesse of "developed countries." Fitting the UN venue, Gligorov invokes the themes of "disarmament and peace" (Prosser 258). Gligorov invokes the General Agreement on Tariffs and Trade (GATT), peace progress in the Middle East, and the strong potential for peace in South Africa as points of identification and success in the global community.

Throughout his 1993 speech, given in the depths of war, Gligorov presented a fair-minded perspective, one that was thoughtful and distanced, yet intensely firm in guarding the interests of his "small," "landlocked country." This examination of Gligorov's first UN speech reveals a uniquely *nonviolent* perspective on rhetoric, one that illuminates how persuasion works when it is squeezed into the narrow space between bravely broaching conflict so as to prevent its ultimate escalation and flirting with a sense of righteousness that could foment conflict. True to the genre of communicating at the UN, the use of nonviolent rhetoric "is . . . itself a humanizing factor . . . our world leaders produce and receive symbols concerning the messages that are vital to human survival and the preservation of the highest values relating to the improvement of the human condition" (Prosser 284).

Gligorov uses the truth (*satyagraha*), but provides his argument methodically, deductively. There is a surprising absence of emotional appeals; he uses pathos sparingly. Nonetheless, the message, propped as it is by the heightened rhetorical status of a dark horse, can be powerful. It is a message carefully balanced between the possibilities of what the world community can and will do, and what his small country can and must do—or will not do—to stay viable. It is an easily translated, cross-cultural message.

It is pragmatic nonviolence in words, denigrating inaction, promoting, where possible, "preventive" action. While Gligorov deflates the morality that is most often associated with what many people perceive as the Gandhian or

Kingian modes of nonviolence, his rhetoric nonetheless meets the criteria for pragmatic nonviolence. As Carlotta Gall states, Gligorov "avoided bloodshed and kept his fragile state together despite its volatile mix of [ethnic] Slavs and [ethnic] Albanians and its historic frictions with neighbors." In all, his is a rhetoric of both defiance of perceived injustices and of the will to work toward promoting geopolitical peace.

CHAPTER 6

֎

Nonviolence in Pink:
The Visual Rhetoric of Aung San Suu Kyi

> The distinctions between sex (physiological, bodily characteristics), gender identity (the socio-cultural and psychic construction of a 'female' and a 'male' type supposedly corresponding to these differences), and lived sexuality (whether a woman with female physiological characteristics expresses herself sexually as a 'female' in relation to a man, or as a male or female in relation to another woman) is interesting and useful.
>
> —*Seyla Benhabib ("Subjectivity" 115)*

Since 1988, a dramatic struggle in nonviolent resistance has unfolded in Burma (Myanmar). This struggle is emblematic of a globally expanding public sphere. The Nobel Peace Prize award in 1999 to Doctors without Borders (*Médecins Sans Frontiers*) likewise epitomizes that nonviolent intervention in sovereign countries constitutes a proliferating form of rhetoric and action. As a ubiquitous mode of discourse and politics for the new millennium, nonviolent rhetoric bears inquiry. This chapter explores the nonviolent, visual rhetoric of Aung San Suu Kyi, Burma's Nobel Peace Laureate.[1]

Examining the visual rhetoric of the gendered body of a woman leader and its relationship to the international body politic illuminates how rhetoric permeates culture, gender, and territory. Visual rhetoric remaps the geopolitical arena, impacting individual and political bodies. Gender is a "construction of what it means to live in a world that has created [people] . . . not human, but always woman or man" through means including the "conceptual and experiential, individual and systemic, historical . . . contemporary, cross-cultural . . . culture-specific, physical . . . spiritual and political" (Minnich 136). Gender can be a means to perpetuate structural violence (systems of institutionalized oppression) because its constructs enable and hide the "systematic and unreciprocated transfer of powers from women to men" (Young 50). Conversely, gender serves as strategic "meta-concept" and "subject matter" so as to "demystify" human habits and guard against injustices of power distribution (Minnich 136–40).

Essentialism and universalism trouble nonviolent and feminist theories. Indeed, "whether moral and political universalism is philosophically plausible without essentialism or transcendentalism of some sort or another" remains the "more controversial issue" explored (not resolved) here (Benhabib "Subjectivity" 118). Essentialism or universalism yield transformative potentialities as well as pitfalls. Universalism, for instance, can be helpful in fostering justice and fighting oppression since it fosters "reflective solidarity" (Dean 142). On the other hand, universalism is decried as enabling "dominant groups [to] project their own experience as representative of humanity" (Young 59).

Essentialism refers to the notion that specific categories or communities of persons exhibit some inherent, essential or "natural" qualities. For instance, it is an unlikely essentialism that *all* women everywhere share certain, specifically "female" or "feminine" characteristics, such as being "communal (rather than individual), noncompetitive, and nonviolent" (Brummet 127). Also, "essentialism occurs when generalized statements are asserted that make no reference to cross-cultural differences or previous historical variation. This is . . . called universalism."[2] Essentialism can be seen as a move to "suppress the participation of dominated groups" in history (Nicholson 3). Diana Fuss, however, believes

> essentialism is typically defined in opposition to difference. . . . The opposition is . . . helpful . . . it reminds us that a complex system of cultural, social psychical, and historical differences, and not a set of pre-existent human essences, position and constitute the subject. However, the binary articulation of essentialism and difference can also be restrictive, even obfuscating, in that it allows us to ignore or deny the differences within essentialism. (xi–xii)

Thus, my questions are: How does nonviolent rhetoric as visually expressed essentialize women, especially Aung San Suu Kyi? How does this essentializing process affect Suu Kyi's audiences; in what ways might essentializing help or hinder a nonviolent advocate's aims in attaining political goals?

In this chapter, I first discuss the problem of essentializing as it relates to nonviolent theory. Next, I summarize picture theory. Then I explain who Suu Kyi is and how her nonviolent rhetoric and essentialized persona are significant. I conclude by noting some of the democratizing tendencies that nonviolent rhetoric, especially a visually oriented rhetoric like Suu Kyi's, can foster.

ESSENTIALIZING AND NONVIOLENT THEORY

Lisa Adler and L. H. M. Ling argue that "advocates overlook the inherently gendered nature of nonviolence *as both theory and practice*" (emphasis theirs) (2). They characterize nonviolence strictly in conservative, Gandhian or Kingian forms as a straw-person to knock down easily.[3] For them, nonviolence is "individualist and essentialist in nature" as well as "androcentric . . . Western and elitist" (9; 11). Such circumscribed assumptions regarding nonviolence simply do not reflect contemporary theory and practice. Essentialism is presumed detrimental and disempowering rather than amenable to being used in subversive ways that are empowering to women and all oppressed people.

Elizabeth Minnich deconstructs essentialisms. Men and women are depicted, she says, through cultural norms that foster an unjust "dualism" such that "man is what it means to be human; woman is his Other . . . as . . . slave is . . . to master, and the 'primitive' is . . . to 'civilized man'" (54). Minnich maintains that throughout history "differences from men were, for women, encoded as failures, not merely as distinctions" (54). Rhetorically, this operates so as to disadvantage women in terms of being respected and having their message(s) heard (76). The net result of this difficulty in visualizing an empowered Other is that in communication and dialogue people loathe the apparent reversal of values undergirding their entire worldview. Essentializing women, people of color, and others through *dominant discourses* impedes democratizing tendencies of empathy and justice since it reinforces stereotypes and blocks members of dominant groups from visualizing nonviolent change.

Minnich characterizes traditional theory and thinking as steeped in "mortality" rather than "natality" (134).[4] The seemingly innocuous basic syllogism begins: "All men are mortal." Minnich maintains this outlook is pernicious because it causes people to "feel a need to identify with death, and so, too, often, also with killing" (134). The nonviolent alternative, believes Minnich, is to identify with "natality," which "has been treated as Other for mortality, as woman has for man, as peace has for war" (134). In rhetorical terms, *strategic* essentializing, such as characterizing humans not by mortality but rather by natality, can be effective in enabling nonviolent activists to convey messages and achieve political goals through uplifting and transformative persuasion in the public sphere.[5]

PICTURE THEORY AND SPECTACLE

Enter picture theory. Picture theory and seeing democracy as spectacle offers alternative ways of thinking about essentializing and nonviolence in rhetoric. In *Picture Theory*, W. J. T. Mitchell contends a major shift in philosophical thinking—a "pictorial turn"—has long been occurring. In this pictorial turn, words complement, compete with, and lose ground to visual icons . . . pictures . . . images (11–13). "Characterizations of our age" by Guy Debord as one of "spectacle" or Foucault as one of "surveillance" define the pictorial turn (13). Mitchell describes "visuality as a cultural practice of everyday life" the world over in which "the observer/spectator's body [is] marked by gender, class, or ethnicity" (20). Mitchell highlights the "interactions of visual and verbal representation in a variety of media, principally literature and the visual arts" (5). Picture theory fosters understanding of political realities, he says, because of "the commonplace notion that we live in a culture of images, a society of the spectacle, a world of semblances and simulacra" (5). Mitchell emphasizes the "metapicture," meaning "a picture that is about itself" (Reilly 2–3). He also underscores the "image/text" as "a nexus where political, institutional, and social antagonisms play themselves out in . . . representation" (Mitchell 91). The power and widespread use of the internet's visual technology (at least among the affluent), which mixes text and images, is a testament to the continuing pictorial turn.

In *The Politics of Pictures*, John Hartley argues that pictures have become the prime force in today's political domain. He contends that "the creation and politicization of readerships is a key feature of politics in contemporary society, while . . . the public domain as traditionally understood has become increasingly mediated, transformed from a place on the ground into a space . . . [in TV] schedules" (5). For Hartley, the pictorial turn occurs through "two moves . . . the textualization of politics, and the politicization of texts, accomplished within the ambiguous frames of public/private, secret/confessional, talkative pictures" (5). The "*visualization* of the public" means that media enable "direct democracy" to become "representative democracy" because journalists are "creators" of both "popular reality" and "the public itself" (italics his; 5).[6] "Journalism," he finds, "is at the heart of democracy" (220). He avers the popular press is increasingly "a celebration of fecundity" that "feminizes and sexualizes 'our' body politic" (220). Not only have pictures become a prime force in politics, the overwhelming prevalence of particularly femininely gendered pictures emphasize "fecundity."

Pictures and symbols comprise visual rhetoric. Pictures are crucial to nonviolent rhetoric that often must rely on cross-cultural universality to traverse international borders and reach disparate audiences of diverse races, classes, and affiliations. From the *New York Times* to *In Style* magazine to illicit, frayed photocopies passed secretly in the "media underground" in totalitarian states, photographs of nonviolent resistance leaders are rhetorically powerful. The smile of the Dalai Lama, for example, has become as mysteriously pervasive as that of the Cheshire cat.[7] "Smiling," writes Hartley, "has become one of the most important public virtues of our times, a uniform that must be worn on the lips of those whose social function it is to create, sustain, tutor, represent and make images of the public . . . to call it into discursive being" (121–22). To convey political messages effectively, states Hartley, requires "good . . . media" (122). Above all, "Smiling . . . is now the 'dominant ideology' of the 'public domain,' the mouthpiece of the politics of pictures" (122). In film, video, or photographs, the "visualization" of a smiling leader occurs in a media-created public. Aung San Suu Kyi is a fine example of this visualization process.

AUNG SAN SUU KYI

One of only nine women in Nobel history to have received the prestigious Peace Prize, Aung San Suu Kyi (pronounced "Awng-Sahn-Soo-Chee"[8]) has been a paragon of nonviolent political demonstration for over a decade in Burma (Myanmar). "Elegant and well-spoken in both Burmese and English, she often demonstrated her courage, facing down armed soldiers who threatened . . . her rallies."[9] The Nobel Committee cited her "non-violent struggle" and declared its "wishes to honour . . . [her] for . . . unflagging efforts and . . . support . . . the many people throughout the world who are striving to attain democracy, human rights and ethnic conciliation by peaceful means."[10] Suu Kyi holds myriad awards and honorary degrees.[11] She is often compared to "Mahatma Gandhi, Nelson Mandela, and Martin Luther King, Jr."[12] Coincidentally, Suu Kyi worked at the United Nations in New York during the civil rights movement; she recalls, "There was a feeling of tremendous vigor. I had been moved by . . . King's 'I Have a Dream' speech and how he tried to better the lot of . . . black people without fostering . . . hate."[13]

Aung San Suu Kyi is the daughter of the Burman national hero, Aung San, who fought with the Japanese during World War II to rid Burma of the British colonials. He later fought and succeeded in expelling the Japanese from Burma. In 1948, just months before Burma achieved independence, General Aung San was assassinated, becoming Burma's first modern leader and martyr for democratic ideals. His daughter, Aung San Suu Kyi, was then two years old.

Burma's fledgling democracy lasted until 1962, when General Ne Win's forces seized power, instituting totalitarian rule. From then on, several forms of totalitarian, military rule prevailed.[14] Popular unrest boiled over in 1987, when a program of demonitization "wiped out savings without compensation" and the United Nations bequeathed Burma with the dubious title of "Least Developed Country" in the world.[15] After ruling for 25 years, Ne Win abruptly resigned in 1988. People flooded the streets, demanding democracy. Another military regime replaced Ne Win, onomatopoeically named SLORC (State Law and Order Restoration Council). The acronym's unsavory sound in English is perhaps why SLORC was later euphemized as State Peace and Development Council (SPDC). SLORC's vacuum of leadership escalated chaos. From August 8 to 13, 1988, over 3,000 unarmed civilians were killed.[16] Although this has been documented as an incident of ghastly human loss, it received barely any coverage in Western presses, in stark comparison to major coverage of the massacre in China's Tiananmen Square that same year. According to Amnesty International and other human rights organizations, Burma remains one of the world's worst countries in terms of ongoing human rights abuses.

The Crisis

At age 43, as the mother of two young boys, a student writing her dissertation, and wife to a professor at Oxford University, leaving England seemed to her unthinkable. In March of 1988, however, Suu Kyi's mother suffered a stroke. Suu Kyi went to Burma, planning to care for her mother and then return to England. As her mother's condition worsened, Suu Kyi decided to move her from the hospital to their family home in Rangoon (Yangon). Meanwhile, Suu Kyi observed pandemonium unfolding in Burma, sensing great urgency in the moment. "On August 26 she stepped into the open," holding a political rally at the Schweidagon pagoda, which "drew over half a million people."[17] Martial law was instituted to quell further gatherings. Suu Kyi stayed. Until SLORC arrested her a year later, Suu Kyi traveled throughout the countryside of Burma, giving over 1,000 public speeches advocating democracy.

In 1989 she was placed under house arrest and began a hunger strike, refusing to eat until the authorities transferred her so she could join her fellow democratic protesters at the aptly named Insein prison. Finally, in critical condition, she ended her strike, which by then had gained international attention for the political prisoners' plight. In December 1989, she agreed to be a candidate in the state run elections, which SLORC conceded to administer as a concession to widespread popular unrest. In 1990, to the utter surprise of the military junta, Suu Kyi's National League for Democracy (NLD) won 82% of the vote. SLORC immediately annulled the election results, citing alleged irregularities. Suu Kyi remained in house arrest for the next six years.

In 1991 when the announcement was made that Aung San Suu Kyi was the winner of the Nobel Peace Prize, she was still in house arrest, cut off from contact with the outside world, unable to attend the award ceremony in Oslo, Norway.[18] Suu Kyi was released from house arrest in 1995, and renewed her campaign of speeches advocating democracy and nonviolent direct action. She gave daily speeches at the gate of her house, drawing intrepid crowds of people who braved armed soldiers milling nervously about.[19] By autumn 1996, students once again filled the streets, calling for democracy. In early 1997, SLORC again reconfined Suu Kyi to her house for "security reasons."[20] At this writing, she has been compelled to discontinue her speeches; her movements are watched and limited. As recently as "the summer of 1998, she attempted to leave the city to meet with

NLD officials, but military officers stopped her car at the Yangon border; after a standoff lasting several days . . . officials 'escorted' her . . . home."[21] The drama reiterated both Suu Kyi's life threatening commitment to furthering Burma's transition to democracy as well as her ability to garner excellent press coverage through nonviolent resistance and rhetoric.

Performing Nonviolence

Suu Kyi's message flourishes in Western media and in Burma's communications black market. Her text, body, and subject position are purveyed in nonviolent and often visual rhetoric. Judith Butler writes, "[a] performative act . . . brings into being or enacts that which it names, and so marks the constitutive or productive power of discourse" (134). The past decade for Suu Kyi has been a nonstop series of such performative acts. Suu Kyi is radiantly portrayed in the 1996 film "Beyond Rangoon," which secretly circulates "underground" in Burma.[22] Her calls for divestment,[23] while being obviated at present, have made some headway: in 1996 President Clinton signed a U.S. law that specifically invokes Suu Kyi's physical body, even if it flouts her nonviolent principle; the law "prohibits investment in Burma if Suu Kyi is imprisoned or harmed, or if there is a large-scale crackdown on the pro-democracy movement."[24] Conveniently ignoring structural or institutional violence as an ongoing form of "large-scale crackdown," international investors still conduct business with SPDC. The limits of the "productive power" of nonviolent discourse lie in the economic realm. Attention lavished on Suu Kyi's performatively gendered persona averts focus from interrelationships between political and economic interests.

The democratic hopes for Burma seem super concentrated into the person of Suu Kyi. In 1999, as it became clear that her husband, suffering from cancer, would soon die, SPDC representatives offered to release her to travel to visit him in England. However, because Suu Kyi feared she would be prevented from returning, she remained in Burma. Suu Kyi's stoic decision was widely reported in Western media. Michael Aris died in London; a Buddhist ceremony was held at Suu Kyi's home a week later.[25] In this drama, Suu Kyi's dilemma as a nonviolent activist resurfaced. As ostensibly the one embodied, living hope for a democratic future in Burma, Suu Kyi is immobilized and cannot do physical campaigning outside of Burma on behalf of the political prisoners and oppressed inside Burma. Also, violence in Burma is only condemned by the United States in terms of Suu Kyi's *own body* rather than her forced silent, political body. Yet her mediated picture and story creates awareness abroad of abysmal human rights abuses ongoing in Burma. Benhabib maintains that hope is vital to any movement. "Without such a regulative principle of hope, not only morality but also radical transformation is unthinkable"

(Benhabib 30). Suu Kyi clearly believes her presence and rhetoric is advancing toward that end, affirming that "Burma *will* become a democracy."[26]

NONVIOLENT RHETORIC IN VISUAL FORM

Suu Kyi's physical appearance, as the consummately essentialized woman, has been fortuitous for her publicity and cause. Photographs in Western media and in her book, *Freedom from Fear*, showcase herself in the mandalic stages of life: as a smiling baby; as a pretty little girl; as a reserved debutante; as a beautiful bride (Fig. 6-1); as a glowing mother; as an accomplished orator and stateswoman (Figs. 6-2 and 6-3).[27] These pictures, in Mitchell's words, are "metapictures" because they reiterate themselves along with Suu Kyi's nonviolent message.

Supporting photographic documentation, Suu Kyi's physical being (body) has been described variously as "elegant";[28] "petite, feminine";[29] she is "a woman of subtlety."[30] The people of Burma reflect Suu Kyi's persona clearly: many refer to her simply as "The Lady." Fig. 6.1 is a metapicture that emphasizes two of her nonviolent themes: cross-cultural understanding and interethnic tolerance. By marrying across cultures, the audience/spectators are invited to see that both she and her spouse evince cross-cultural sensitivity and interethnic acceptance. According to one scholar, vicious interethnic conflict and animosities in Burma today are among the last great stumbling blocks to starting a democracy there since power hungry politicians often pit one ethnic group against another, which prevents interethnic unity and democratic coalitions from forming (Matthews 7–23). By sharing intimate photographs as "talkative pictures" with her audiences worldwide, Suu Kyi confirms Hartley's hypothesis that contemporary political discourse must easily traverse realms of "public/private" and "secret/confessional" (5).

Figure 6-2 is a metapicture representative of Suu Kyi's photogenic persona; she wears a brightly colored yellow blouse, sophisticatedly subtle yet evident eye makeup, ruby-red lipstick, demure pearl earrings, and white flowers in her hair. Similarly, in her sitting for her photograph, which appeared in two issues of *Vogue* magazine, Suu Kyi emphasizes her femininity by wearing a tight, long, fuchsia-colored sarong and matching blouse of a slightly paler shade of pink. She wears gold earrings and the ruby color on her lips. On her feet, *à la* Jesus, she wears simple flip-flop sandals. In both photographs, her hair seems slightly unkempt, as if she's been hard at work for hours, and (flowers aside), too busy to fix it. In the *Vogue* shot, she has dark circles under her eyes; she wears an expression of determination, only faintly offset by a Mona Lisa–like shadow of a smile. Encapsulated visually as attractive and nonthreatening, each metapicture's residual message is one of practical nonviolence: sensuality and good breeding put in the service of

FIGURE 6-1.
The Newlyweds: Aung San Suu Kyi and Her Husband, Michael Aris

Source: *Freedom From Fear,* © Aung San Suu Kyi, 1991.

FIGURE 6-2.
Aung San Suu Kyi Addresses the Crowd in 1996

Source: Agence France Presse; photographer: Emmanuel Dunand.

public relations that will reach a stubbornly sex starved/saturated media and *Entertainment Tonight*-style audience.

In contrast to her physical, gendered self, her intellectual and spiritual self has been described in eerily disembodied terms: she is "a noble voice for freedom"[31] or the "Burmese whose silenced voice echoes."[32] Suu Kyi embodies the essence of selfless, spiritual (noncorporeal) nonviolence. Of Suu Kyi, her husband once wrote: "In . . . daughter as in . . . father there seems an extraordinary coincidence of legend . . . reality . . . word and deed."[33] Such statements elevate Suu Kyi. In appreciating sympathies after the death of her husband, Suu Kyi's rhetoric reflects a distance from herself: "On behalf of my sons, Alexander and Kim, as well as on my own behalf, I want to thank all those around the world who have supported my husband during his illness and have given me and my family love and sympathy."[34] The phrase, "as well as on my own behalf" is reminiscent of the stylistic choice in the first line of Lincoln's Second Inaugural speech, which "establishes a relentless tone of passivity and self-effacement" (Leff 81). Suu Kyi's distancing of her embodied self from her political persona in her rhetoric is common. The distance subsumes her personality into the collective of her family and supporters, while it confirms her subject position in Burma's culture, in this instance, as that of a dutiful widow. Thus she distances her feminine-gendered self from the political, masculine-gendered self in order for her rhetoric to be acceptable in a culture in which politics has been dominated by men.

Kathleen Jones declares the rhetorical articulation of the sovereign being and body is masculine. For women to even assume the subject position and role of speaker, much less to be powerful, they must assume the role of man. Jones asks critics to examine "marks of authority . . . codes of being in authority" to see which codes help "establish claims to rule" and which ones "mask . . . [feminine] characteristics . . . [thus] colonizing the feminine while displacing women symbolically from the founding moment of public life" (80–81). Suu Kyi's rhetoric is interesting because she relies heavily on the "feminine" to shore up her power through the dominant cultural mores of Burma. Suu Kyi's visual rhetoric contradicts Jones's observation that "in order for women to be recognized as authorities, women rulers must either defeminize themselves, by taking up the masculine position, or they must desexualize themselves, representing themselves as 'exceptional women,' as women who will not be women" (81). Suu Kyi distances herself through written discourse that emphasizes a disembodiment to fulfill the masculine political role requirement. Yet in visual rhetoric she appears to actively pursue being represented visually as feminine, sexy, or motherly.

Her message extrudes from and mediates outwardly via her body and metapictures. For example, here is a typical correspondent's report of her:

FIGURE 6-3.
Aung San Suu Kyi on the Campaign Trail

Source: *Freedom From Fear,* © Aung San Suu Kyi, 1991.

She appeared above the gate, smiling and waving, dressed in a brightly colored *longyi*, or sarong,[35] and wearing three different kinds of flowers in her hair. Later, at her home, she was wearing more fresh flowers. "People give me flowers all the time," she explained, "and I wear as many of them as I can. My mother often quoted a Burmese saying: 'A man without knowledge is like a flower without a scent.' I prefer scented flowers."[36]

Suu Kyi's rhetoric is literally *incorporated*; meanings are derived from culture, displayed bodily, and reflected back into the political realm. With "flowers" and smiles, her message combines both feminine and political bodies. Well-timed proverbs in her rhetoric resonate Burma's rich, ancient culture.[37] Discourse and image unite in a metapictorial jab at her political opposition. Suu Kyi's brightly colored sarongs and customary public appearances with flowers in her hair constitute a *visual rhetoric of culture* and *nonviolence* that contrasts sharply with the drab, military garb, cultural disowning, and violence of her opposition: members of SPDC.

This is Woman, perfectly possessing the gender qualities that dominant norms in Burma's and other cultures the world over, value, encourage and laud in the sex/gender of women. Whether she does it intuitively or purposefully, by coopting the dominant mode of what an idealized, gendered version of what a woman "ought" to be, Suu Kyi uses visual rhetoric to her advantage to get attention needed to further political goals.

Appearance is vital in this televised, "visualized" era. Appearance makes or breaks political careers of highly visible women. All of the *Saturday Night Live* skits and Jay Leno jokes about the "manly" appearance of Janet Reno point to the continuing problem that women as political leaders face in their subject positions as Other to, and therefore deviant from or inferior to, men. Jodi Dean describes the "media massacre" of Lani Guinier, who, marked as Other, became the target of career-crushing savagery in popular presses (152). Dean writes, "institutional histories of racism and sexism functioned to deprive Guinier of her own words" (152). Dean reveals as representative of the media's (mis)characterization of Guinier that "an article on Guinier in *U.S. News and World Report* opened with 'Strange name, strange hair, strange writing—she's history'" (152). Note, too, Guinier's purported *visual* appearance is decried first, before the alleged content of her writing. Often, the best press women in highly visible, especially political offices gets entails her superficial style, not her skills or substance. With "infotainment" and an increasingly visualized public sphere, Hartley thinks "there's no such thing as bad publicity" (21). But this is not the case for women in politics.

In essentializing herself through highly pictorial and visual stories as a beautiful, glamorous, aristocratic lady, it becomes easier for auditors/spectators to reach the other side of Suu Kyi's image and attend to her nonviolent message.[38] In addition to Suu Kyi's well-heeled appearance, she maintains the symbolic trappings of the elite to draw, as bees to honey, media to her story. Symbols of upper-crustiness, the kind that is journalistically irresistible, abound. Suu Kyi is known for her piano playing, a telltale sign of refinement and education. She lives in a large home with a garden in a city and country—and, by media extension of the public sphere, much of the world—where most inhabitants cannot afford such luxuries. With all of the fuss over the charity work of the late Diana Spencer, ex-Princess of Wales, similar rhetorical processes occurred in Diana's audiences as they do for Suu Kyi.[39] Using *bourgeois* ideals of womanliness to further political agendas is not a new idea. The "cult of true womanhood" was actively fostered by 19th-century women orators and activists to heighten their moral standing and render their political messages compelling to conservative audiences of the day.

Pitfalls in Pictorializing Nonviolence

Pictorializing nonviolent acts or ideas in the public sphere means that nonviolence in theory and practice is represented at the whim of media bureaucrats. Summarizing nonviolence as elitist or only effective for upper classes is erroneous considering the media's role in perpetuating elitism by running stories deemed fitting for dominant discourses. Hartley observes that while "open, offensive prejudice is rare . . . racial stereotyping and racism in . . . media is institutional and not individual" since it "results from news values, from editorial policies, and from routines of newsgathering" (210). Thus "news is organized around strategies of inclusion and exclusion from 'our' community" (207). For example, in Australian news media, "[a] story featuring Aboriginals is . . . more likely to be covered . . . [and] to survive subeditorial revision . . . if the story represents Aboriginals as 'they' rather than as 'we,' and makes sense of them as in need of protection, correction or welfare, and not in terms of what they . . . wish to say and do for themselves" (210). For nonviolence to make news, its advocates must market themselves in ways that can be editorially manipulated to sell newspapers, magazines, or to increase TV viewer ratings. For nonviolent proponents to cross over from liberal/radical to accepted/normal, they must present themselves as maintaining traditional trappings (206–07).[40]

Indeed, Johan Galtung affirms that "events will register more easily, the more they are identified with male and non-lower class leaders like . . . Gandhi or . . . King. A major event emanating from black, lower class women . . . would not easily register with persons with the opposite rank. . . . As women are prominent in nonviolence, this factor alone accounts for . . . the invisibility" (26–27). The vagaries of media processes, which Hartley calls "fake journalism," mean that, to the unwitting spectator, nonviolent activism is enacted by or favors elites when this is seldom the case.

"Substantive Unity"

Likewise, the charge of excessive individualism and pernicious essentialism in nonviolent action or rhetoric is not accurate in Suu Kyi's case. For instance, the text of her Nobel Prize acceptance speech embodies Suu Kyi's nonviolent, collectivistic message. The speech was a joint writing effort of her husband and the far removed Suu Kyi; it was a joint presentation effort of her son, who gave the speech, thereby reembodying her voice. In this way, the speech accomplished more than if Suu Kyi had been present to deliver it herself. Mary Rentz labels this rhetorical process "substantive unity" between a rhetor who mediates a message on behalf of another person.[41] Rentz finds "simple, but pervasive, linguistic devices" reveal profound "unity." Referring to others in joint statements, saying, "so-and-so and I believe . . ." or "[s/he] is . . . principled, disciplined . . ." fosters profound discourse "unity."[42] This method of combining speech originator with messenger creates a strategically split or unified front, depending on the interlocutor's goals.[43] A strong unified front of "substantive unity" redoubles the speaker's agency and power, while it reinforces the benefits to people of acting in concert and community.

Suu Kyi's visual and written texts reflect a message of mutual responsibility, nonviolent political action, reverence for family, tradition, religion, and country. It is important to note that "as ideology, rhetoric associated with the traditional family ideal provides an interpretive framework that accommodates a range of meanings" (Collins 62). Suu Kyi's own family, and, as daughter of a national hero, her extended family of Burmese people are foremost in her rhetoric. The family theme is a highly effective rhetorical ploy that "is a common strategy for conservative movements of all types" (Collins 62). Yet Suu Kyi appears to use the theme of family, which is an accepted conservative norm in Burmese culture, to promote democracy, which is suspect there (Matthews 7–23).

Still, her essentialized self as Woman and Other causes rhetorical shortcomings. As Other, she can be perceived by dominant spectators as "deviant" or "deficient." Since much publicity highlights her striking beauty, critics discount her political savvy. A researcher comments, for example,

> The political thought of . . . Suu Kyi is not offered as . . . that of a scholar or reflective thinker at work in the abstract. Rather, it is presented as an example of a special person[44] who, because of her name and family, gained an immediate audience and, by using language and expressing ideas the [Burman] people understood and related to, was pushed into . . . leadership . . . against totalitarian rule.[45]

The discounting of her mental acuity by critics such as this one occurs because she is essentialized as Woman and as Other. Another critical commentary evinces a more patronizing tone:

> Poor, gorgeous . . . Suu Kyi. She spent the entire week in her large white sedan on a tiny wooden bridge, not . . . far from her luxurious bungalow. Unable to see her [NLD] supporters [whom she was en route to visit], there sat her Nobel laureate self, getting weak with hunger, lack of water and stress; the police refused to let her proceed and she refused to return. The adoring western press reported her every move on a daily basis, the coverage always accompanied by a well-framed photograph of a smiling, resplendent oriental woman." (Sardar 24)

The pitfalls of her nonviolent approach and visual rhetoric are evident. Although Suu Kyi remains, and is acknowledged as, a leader to be reckoned with, her essentialized personage sometimes harries her.

On the other hand, if Hartley is correct foretelling pictorialization of democratic politics, Suu Kyi's "smiling, resplendent" image, as "feminized" politics, may prove most powerful. Hartley calls "smiling professions" those "jobs where work, preparation, skill and talent are all necessary but hidden, where performance is measured by consumer satisfaction, where self is dedicated to other, success to service, where knowledge is niceness and education entertainment" (135). Both dedication to other and success defined by selfless service form key underpinnings to nonviolent theory, practice, and rhetoric. Service "professions" have long been "associated with women." Hartley believes these professions enable "you [to] . . . get ahead and achieve public approval on the strength of your smile." Hartley finds "the whole New Age is smiling" (135). Nonviolence today, part and parcel of New Age concepts such as valuing social and ecological diversity and preservation, entails such good public relations skills. Often in pictures we see Suu Kyi at work at meetings with journalists, sometimes she is casually brushing her hair aside and wearing a minimicrophone that clings to her blouse like an orchid to a tree. One cannot help but notice her poise, perfect posture, and the ubiquitous flowers in her hair.

Undoubtedly, Suu Kyi, in "using language and expressing ideas" Burmans "understood and related to," has been a formidable opponent to the military junta. Yet the criticism that she is not "a scholar or reflective thinker," while unfounded,[46] illustrates her persona's limits. Clearly, Suu Kyi was not "pushed into . . . leadership." *Freedom from Fear* recounts intimately, including personal letters, that as a young woman she presaged, as daughter of revered hero Aung San, she might be summoned. Her rising to leadership echoes her subject position as essentialized Woman: reliable, long-suffering, giving, selfless.

Covering Ground

In house arrest, unable to travel or to speak out,[47] she employed mediated communication to continue her campaign for a free democracy in Burma. Suu Ky's rhetorical efforts have required collective effort and risk. Except when she was held *incommunicado*, during most of her years in house arrest, she has communicated with her supporters via "weekly letters, distributed worldwide." In these letters, she has been noted for using "metaphor and allegory to shed light on current events [in Burma] . . . and to attack her political opponents"; indeed, playing on notions of an idealized, traditional Woman, "Suu Kyi . . . [alludes to] ancient ritual to . . . paint a vivid portrait of her troubled country."[48] Through letters citing Buddhist tenets and Burman cultural norms, Suu Kyi's "voice for freedom" resonates.

The same can be said of her rhetoric in public address. In 1993, her husband delivered her address, "Towards a True Refuge," at Oxford University. Also, her opening keynote address in 1995 for the NGO Forum on Women, in Beijing, China, was videotaped and smuggled out of Burma so she could "present" it, televised, at the Forum. The metaphorical cliché, Don't shoot the messenger, reverts to a literal connotation in Suu Kyi's case. While the disembodied Suu Kyi lives on videotape, the messenger smuggling it out of Burma tempts death: He or she becomes Suu Kyi's nonviolent risk taker in the real world. Enacting community, real persons cooperate to bring her message to the outside world. By bringing the message to the outside, they hope to bring change back inside Burma.

Suu Kyi's mediated rhetoric shines in her son's delivery of the Nobel acceptance speech. By reciting his mother's words, Alexander embodies multiple nonviolent quests that become one in the speech. Suu Kyi's own thoughts and discourse are mediated through space and time, reembodied in her son and the audience/spectators. Although essentialized as Woman, as Burma's opposition leader, she is also an honorary "man" who will "realize . . . the quest for democracy" that turns "man" as dualism into "human" as universalism. She has written, her husband selected, and her son spoken words transcending distance; her message traverses cultural, national, ideological borders. As Hartley notes, "boundaries of . . . [one's community] are not coterminous with national boundaries" (207). More than simply advocating collective action and highlighting every individual's role in that action, the poignant collective enactment of her speech indicates she practices what she preaches.

Suu Kyi's transcendent rhetoric abounds in cyberspace, too. Experiencing any of the numerous web sites devoted to her or to a "Free Burma" features listening and watching Suu Kyi's audio- and videotaped speeches. This experience can be cognitively transformative.[49] Leonard Shlain posits that with the ever-increasing rise of pictorialization in today's media driven world, right-brain tendencies toward nonviolence (such as empathy or intuition) are exercised and fostered. This peace-minded brain activity, coupled with spatial discourse, suggests interesting possibilities for nonviolent rhetoric.

Goddess of Democracy

While Suu Kyi's voice and rhetorical prowess resonate, her gendered/sexed body complicates the picture. Suu Kyi's subject position as wife (and now, widow) of a British citizen has been the object of much attempted ridicule by the propagandists of SLORC/SPDC. In one noteworthy instance, authorities "went so far as to put up posters around the country with sexual caricatures of her with her husband."[50] Specifically, the posters were described as "obscene . . . showing her locked in sexual intercourse with an English devil." To their misfortune, instead of discrediting Suu Kyi, the posters only served to "add to her glamour."[51] Suu

Kyi, as essentialized Woman, here turns potentially damaging rhetoric to her advantage. "What makes . . . [Suu Kyi] 'news' is the attraction we have for the 'waiting' . . . woman. Add the extra layer of modernity and we reach Viagric heights" (Sardar 24). As Hartley puts it, "This, then, is the politics of pictures, journalism in a post truth society, where the body politic is naked and smiling. . . . [The public sees] . . . an image of themselves . . . more ancient than Leviathan" (223). The smiling nakedness of the femininely gendered protagonist may represent the type of collectivistic, egalitarian, proto-democracies that are believed to have existed long ago, and which some scholars believe are rising again.[52]

The junta also ignored the fact that myriad Asian and Buddhist deities (commonly worshiped in Burma and throughout Asia) are female. Many of these goddesses derive powers from the mysteries of feminine reproductive powers: here Minnich's sense of the nonviolent power of "natality" is apt.[53] These deities reaffirm that "sexuality allows us to participate in the ultimate act of creation"; such goddesses remind us that in the act of "[making] love we become God-like in our capacity to produce new forms of life. Sexual love . . . allows us to connect with the spirit that unites us all" in the world.[54] Robert Thurman, professor of Indo-Tibetan Studies at Columbia University observes,

> Buddhas possess beauty marks. The bodhisattvas [compassionate deities] are depicted as sexy androgynous beings. I used to look at the women in fashion magazines and think, 'That's Mara [a deity].' . . . Maybe at some level an issue of *Vogue* could introduce an element of respect for female beauty. Fashion can be dharma. The great fashion editors may have been teachers of the dharma without realizing it. (as qtd. in Trachtenberg 115)

Suu Kyi's nonviolent rhetoric encapsulates this visual sense. Her rhetoric thrives on the mass media's endless needs for themes like sex, heroism, beauty, elitism, and drama. While these themes may downplay the tragic, real sacrifices Suu Kyi has made to promote a democratic vision for Burma's future, her nonviolent message has been flamboyant enough to gain token Western sympathy, if not real economic and political support. By reaffirming her interconnection with the 'unifying spirit' in the world, Suu Kyi's subject positions as stateswoman, mother, and sensuous wife (now widow) to an English "devil" have enhanced her aura of having goddesslike powers.

Suu Kyi's detractors downplay her political prowess by focusing on her gender and sexuality. Ziauddin Sardar complains that very capable and effective stateswomen in Asia such as Begum Khaleda Zia and Sheik Hasina Wajed of Bangladesh have been totally overlooked by Western media. He avers it is because they are less photogenic than Suu Kyi (or Pakistan's Benazir Bhutto). Sardar observes, "Because they were not educated at Oxford or its colonial outposts . . . they are just too plain and traditional to be part of anyone's erotic, orientalist imagination" (25). Photogenic stateswomen like Suu Kyi, Bhutto, or Chandrika Bandaranaike Kumaratunga (of Sri Lanka), he says, "represent the culmination of the colonial project of making the world more like the west" (24). These women, he muses, "trigger all the stereotypes . . . [of] oriental sexuality that lie buried deep in western consciousness." Such women "oriental leaders" are palat-able to the west since they are "chic" and "they don't just speak pukka English, they speak our political language, a language of democracy, human rights and modernization" (24). Sardar reduces Suu Kyi to a mere tool of postcolonialism: "Suu Kyi combines within her person . . . two irreconcilable poles—the old allure of oriental woman and the compatibility of a westernized modernizer" (24).

Sardar's analysis on Suu Kyi's subject position in Asian democracy and its complex relationships to postcolonialism is useful. It appears, however, that, in addition to a cynical and suspicious view of the likes of Suu Kyi, he overly es-sentializes (Woman as deviant) and simplifies the notion of colonial influence on Asian women leaders. By proxy, cynical oversimplification of the subject po-sition of these women belittles the real work and intellectual efforts that women like Suu Kyi expend in assuming roles of leadership at all in a part of the world where the life of most women is not easy and the prospect of political power is even more uncertain.[55]

Suu Kyi and other high-profile Asian women have, to varying degrees, both profited from their subject positions and succeeded in assuming roles of leader-ship in their respective countries. That does not, however, mean that those roles are based on willy-nilly adherence to mythic colonial ideals without regard for the best interests of their respective countries and peoples. Last, the appeal of god-dess worship remains strong throughout Asia, and as Thurman notes, a celebrity formula of it exists in Western countries; perhaps such reverence for visually stim-ulating female deities enables womanly gendered rhetoric and figurehead status to be accepted by many audiences/spectators worldwide.

Suu Kyi's critics aside, Bruce Matthews, a scholar of Asian studies, believes that her power is real, based on wide popular support from the Burmese people, though presently the military junta prevents them from voicing that support. Matthews writes that people in Burma are "living in increasingly sullen despair" and resent the junta while "Aung San Suu Kyi has captured the loyalty of the masses" (7; 15). Matthews discloses an economic reason why a democratic revolution has yet to have occurred in Burma: four million people, or "ten percent of the population . . . ma-terially benefit from [SPDC's] regime." In addition, SPDC runs "systems of surveil-lance that are unsurpassed in the scope of their intrusiveness," so that democratic protests and activities are easily, quickly quashed (Ghosh, as qtd. in Matthews, 10).[56]

Such political, economic, and social blockages to democratic free expression make for less flashy news, so the alleged failings of Suu Kyi are easier and simpler for some journalists and audiences to grasp or to use as means to criticize her.

What may prove most irresistible to audiences/spectators is *not* that visual rhetoric of Suu Kyi (or other aesthetic Asian stateswomen) reflects sexuality, but rather it evinces above all "natality." So, despite what anyone says or tries to do—aside from assassinating Suu Kyi, and that threat remains real—she figures prominently in Burma's democratic future (Matthews 16–23). Suu Kyi's rhetoric reveals the strength of the theme of *life* through an emphasis on regenerative willpower: "The quintessential revolution," she has said, "is that of the spirit, born of an intellectual conviction of the need for change in those mental attitudes and values which shape the course of a nation's development."[57] Following the botched devil-goddess cartoon campaign, SLORC lamely "announced that anyone married to a foreigner should be barred from becoming president" of Myanmar.[58] To date, such actions by SPDC have accomplished little in terms of attempting to influence the Burmese people into withdrawing support from Suu Kyi's democratic platform and cause. Moreover, now that Suu Kyi is a widow, SPDC's dictate is obsolete. As Matthews says, "Despite repeated attempts by the military regime to defame and insult her, she retains vast popularity and respect" (16).

ENGENDERING DEMOCRACY

"The idea of freedom in Burma has two sources," writes Josef Silverstein, "one deeply embedded in Burma's religion and culture and the other, ideas and values brought to Burma by the British . . . [T]oday, the idea of freedom in Burma is a mixture of the two traditions."[59] It is ironic that Suu Kyi married a British national, a descendent of the men her father fought arduously to expel from Burma. At the same time, that union endowed her with the essentialized role of wife and mother that is needed for her to conform to the cultural norms of her country and dominant discourses of audiences/spectators abroad as well. As essentialized Woman, Suu Kyi best embodies Burma's tentative political ideal of democracy as conservative and culturally tailored. "She is 'Burma' in every direct and definite way" (Sardar 24).[60] While democracy remains just an idea in Burma, Suu Kyi's subject position as a femininely gendered personage who favors family, is respectable, refined, and a woman of class normalizes and imparts a sense of constancy and reliability to democracy, a culturally suspect concept (Matthews 7–23).

The totalitarian regime isolated Suu Kyi in house arrest to squelch the democratic movement in Burma; her isolation only added to her courageous aura, helping her to win landslide democratic elections and the internationally acclaimed Nobel Peace Prize. Her enforced isolation was designed to crush her spirit through loneliness and total separation from her family; from all reports, it has only appeared to renew her strength and redouble her resolve: after all, in her omnipresent metapictures, she is still smiling. Her appearing to enact the role of Woman so well enhances the receptivity of audiences/spectators to her speech and images.

Rather than individualistic, her message is fully mediated; it is a team effort. For instance, her son, who presented her Nobel speech for her, is the physical, cultural, and ideological embodiment of the Burman political ideal of freedom: Alexander Aris is himself, "a mixture of the two traditions"—Burman and British cultures, societies, political ideas, and people. His body reunites Suu Kyi's voice—her thoughts, language, and body, all distanced in space and time—with her message, and the universal political ideal of democracy and human rights.

The removal of Suu Kyi's physical presence—her body—from her international public address presentations could easily be misconstrued as rhetorically debilitating. Her disembodiment, however, and subsequently required mediation of her metapictured self (with her vying subject positions as statesperson, goddess, mother, or servant) has symbolized and strengthened the impact of her collectivistic, other-oriented messages. Suu Kyi is current, she is cool, she is even hip. For example, on inside flap of the rock band U2's year-2000 album, adjacent to slick, glossy, black-and-white images of the band members (who are among the world's hottest pop music stars), one finds the message: "Remember Aung San Suu Kyi, under virtual house arrest in Burma since 1989," followed by information of web and mailing addresses of The Burma Campaign.

In requiring mediation, her nonviolent rhetoric subsumes her individual self, subject and body, while it assumes the collective. Her nonviolent rhetoric exists as an ongoing performative act, unifying others to and for whom it is directed. Judith Butler believes performative acts inherently efface individual agency, collectivizing it:

> For a performative [act] to work, it must draw upon and recite . . . linguistic conventions which have traditionally worked to bind or engage certain kinds of effects. The force or [effectiveness] . . . of a performative will be derived from its capacity to draw on and reencode the historicity of those conventions in a present act. This power of recitation is not a function of an individual's *intention*, but is an effect of historically sedimented linguistic conventions." (italics hers; 134)

The collective message and "force" of the performative act both amplifies and collectively embodies Suu Kyi's "voice" of compassion and "natality." For example, her interactive web presence enables web surfers worldwide to participate in her message and in campaigning to "free Burma." In this manner of visual, nonviolent rhetoric, the discourse becomes at once universal and transspatial as well as particular, personal, and embodied.

Patricia Hill Collins writes that "peace without justice constitutes an illusion" (8). This idea pervades the nonviolent rhetoric of Suu Kyi and her supporters.[61] When Suu Kyi advocates "freedom from fear" she is urging an end to the junta, whose soldiers and secret police actively foster a climate of debilitating fear. This polite phrase, representative of her as essentialized Woman, is misread by critics as fuzzy, lacking a call to action. Yet nonviolent rhetoric "recites . . . linguistic conventions" understood by the international community and by Burmese people who, nearly a decade ago, elected her to the presidential office to which SPDC has denied her.

Suu Kyi invokes space in her rhetoric; her discourse is mediated across space and time in epistolary, photographic, video, or human form so that the totalitarian-state-imposed debilitating space and distance are gradually transformed into rehabilitating, collective space and optimal rhetorical and aesthetic distance.[62] Suu Kyi's nonviolent rhetoric evokes human sensations regarding distance and space, while attempting to bridge the class gap between rich and poor, envisioning a democracy in which the populace can share in Burma's resources more equitably. Ultimately, for her, space can be conceived as being "equated with a sense of freedom."[63]

Suu Kyi's mediated message surmounts space and time, inspiring "freedom from fear" in a country known as the "prison without walls."[64] The renewed sense of collective agency and empowerment is realized through the growing public sphere, with an awakened sense of responsibility toward others. Asian rhetoric and philosophy embraces "a sense of community" which "may help bring new vigor and life to the 'body' of Western culture."[65] Asian rhetoric and philosophy continue to complement that of the West as part of the rising puissance of the "New Age," one of Hartley's "smiling professions." While some aspects of the New Age have clearly been coopted by advertisers as a marketing ploy, some New Age proponents have been influential in their calls for people to be mindful of human exploitation of the natural environment, its creatures, and one another. Gail Presbey affirms that "political action helps [people to] . . . reveal themselves and thereby discover themselves; it affirms human dignity; it gives people a chance to shape the political world in which they live; it gives people a chance to develop skills of creative imagination, persuasion, and conciliation."[66] Suu Kyi "recites" precisely this discovery to Burmese and audiences/spectators abroad.

CONCLUSION: METAPICTURES IN NONTERRITORIAL DEMOCRACY

The rhetoric of democracy in Burma and other totalitarian states expands the public sphere. Collins writes, "not only have self-contained borders . . . [among

family, neighborhood, nations] . . . collapsed, but time and space . . . have entirely
new meanings within a new global context" (8). Overall, "new time and space relationships require . . . reorganization of [all] boundaries . . . especially nation-
state borders. . . . [F]ree movement of global capital and displaced populations
needs weak nation-states" (9). Burma is precisely such a "weak nation-state." Reportedly, with multinational corporations and ample tourism, SPDC's elite members grow richer, while most Burmans remain impoverished (Matthews 7–23;
Pilger *Land of Fear*).

William Connolly echoes Collins on geopolitical/economic duress:

> . . . . [d]emocratic politics must either extend into global issues or deterio-
> rate into . . . nostalgia for a past when people believed . . . the most funda-
> mental issues of life were resolvable within the confines of the territorial
> state. The contemporary need . . . is to supplement and *challenge structures
> of territorial democracy* with a politics of *nonterritorial democratization of
> global issues.* (emphasis his; 218)

Suu Kyi's rhetoric represents this nonterritorial, democratizing shift, which pro-
pounds two themes. Her political rhetoric inculpates the global community in the
problematic entailments for Burma of sizable foreign investments, such as oil companies overlooking egregious totalitarianism to make money. Also, her nonviolent
rhetoric provides encouragement and a transformative, compassionate ideology to
people worldwide who crave justice and peace. Nonterritorial democratization is
fruitful because it is "creative" and "energizing" to citizens (Connolly 218–19).
Such creative energy symbolizes natality, Minnich's nonviolent concept.

Superspatial thinking and action prompts criticisms of nonviolent rhetoric,
theory, and practice. Nonviolence "exudes an air of unreality. . . . It lacks . . . a stable set of electoral procedures through which accountability could be organized"
(Connolly 219). Suu Kyi's critics focus on such issues, citing the inability of her
rhetorical and political efforts thus far at getting wealthy foreign investors to divest
from and thereby weaken SPDC (Pilger *Land of Fear*). Suu Kyi's critics pooh-pooh
her "gorgeous" and smiling persona as so much hollow, feminine fluff.

However, there is no reason to take a cynical view of Suu Kyi's visible role in
pressing for democracy in Burma. Seyla Benhabib argues that there are "sources
of utopia in humanity" (30). Connolly offers examples:

> [nonviolent organizations] . . . Amnesty International, Greenpeace . . . di-
> vestment movements aimed at global corporations doing business with
> states that trample on human rights . . . movements to assist "boat people,"
> Palestinians, and others . . . outside the protection of territorial states . . .

[N]onstate movements . . . to foster arms reduction between states . . . provide reflection in . . . specific . . . [ways] to proceed. (219)

The nonviolent rhetoric of Suu Kyi, particularly her metapictures, points to the reformative, transformative possibilities of a representative democracy based on natality, not mortality. The "possessive individualism" of "Leviathan," whose name Hobbes used for his idea of a "competitive, private" form of representation "required not . . . participation but representation" (Hartley 123). Suu Kyi's rhetoric and image, in contrast, invite participation, a hallmark of nonviolence in theory and practice. Benhabib believes people can "develop a view of collective identities . . . at once discursively constructed *and* complex, enabling of collective action *and* amenable to mystification, in need of deconstruction and reconstruction" (italics hers; 72). As Diana Fuss says, there are "differences within essentialism." Suu Kyi's metapicture entails collective effort; it represents a cross-cultural, "nonterritorial democratization" that is gradually, if fallibly, evolving.

For Linda Nicholson, nonviolence is "an openness to challenge one's basic organization of the world" (8). As a woman leader in a state and borderless public sphere where simply entering such a contested subject position is politically absurd yet factually real, Suu Kyi's gendered self, mediated in pictorial form, embodies the nonviolent challenge.

Finally, Suu Kyi has another advantage: time. She and her political party, NLD, can potentially wait, like Nelson Mandela did in South Africa, for democracy to emerge. It remains to be seen what will materialize following her house arrest in 2003. Her visual rhetoric has universal appeal in natality. Gordon Lauren, scholar of political science, maintains Suu Kyi's chief message is one of setting universal standards for human rights; she is saying, in effect, "do not be seduced by standards of relativism on human rights and authoritarian regimes."[67] Her rhetoric asks us to understand the world through collective nonviolent action: diverse people cooperating inside one shared nonterritory, our fragile earth.

CHAPTER 7

A Rhetorical Climate:
The Power of Hope in Big Sky Country

> They came after the Jews and I was not a Jew, so I did not protest. They came after the Trade Unionists, and I was not a Trade Unionist, so I did not protest. They came after the Roman Catholics, and I was not a Roman Catholic, so I did not protest. Then they came after *me*, and there was no one left to protest.
>
> —*Pastor Niemoeller, survivor of Nazi concentration camps*

Why is it important to investigate—as rhetorical artifacts—the feelings and emotions of people in a given physical milieu? While feelings and emotions in a particular setting have been valued in rhetorical theory as factors or variables that, for example, influence a speechwriter, or that determine the reception of, say, a speech, there has been less attention on them as the primary font and focus of rhetoric. Nonviolent theory enables critics to shift perspective so that rather than being a peripheral consideration, feelings, emotions, and environmental influences form the basis of an entire rhetorical analysis. This is an important shift toward a more inclusive, nonviolent theory of rhetoric that prizes not only the eloquent and powerful, but also embraces the indistinct mutterings of the inarticulate and dispossessed.

Many years have passed since Lloyd F. Bitzer wrote of the "experience" of a rhetorical situation. Since that time, the trend in rhetorical criticism has evolved to the point at which rhetoric in social movements is often seen as leader centered, rather than as diffuse and decentralized. Arguably, the core of the tradition of rhetorical criticism has been to laud and analyze the work of the lone hero, the text by the single-orator, Cicero's "good man speaking well." This chapter examines the value of renewing our understanding of Bitzer's term, "experience." The question posed here is this: Were critics to extend Bitzer's perspectives in a collectivistic direction, what might that rhetorical theory look like? Investigating the implications of this question first entails discussing key views on Bitzer's "rhetorical situation." The focus then narrows to an explication of one aspect of a rhetorical situation: the term *climate*. Within this definition, the question of whether or not human emotion and feeling can be used as a valid tool in rhetorical analysis will be examined.[1] Finally, a case study of a town's response to neonazi hate rhetoric and terrorism will be offered as an illustration of a rhetorical climate.

THE PROBLEM WITH SITUATION

Bitzer began this conversation with the idea that a situation in which a motivating transaction takes place is often "rhetorical." This situation is "located in reality"; is "objective and publicly observable . . . in the world we experience"; is spurred by an "exigency" that sets in motion "decision and action needed to modify the exigence" (Bitzer "Situation" 11). In part from its unscientific, "intuitive appeal," the rhetorical situation has been questioned (Garret and Xiao 30). Vatz, for instance, believed that rather than an exigency existing *outside* the discourse, an exigency exists *in* the discourse itself, as created by the speaker ("Myth" 159). Vatz's position is characteristic of the single orator paradigm. William Benoit has argued that situation is less important than the rhetor's purpose and agency (354). Again, Benoit harkens to the tradition of the individual rhetor. A newer twist comes from the deconstructionist view, which renders the situation into a socially constructed identity based on Derrida's notion of "*différence*" (Biesecker 1).[2] Here, too, the social construction impinges on the "identity" of a single person.

Although complete consensus about what constitutes a rhetorical situation is lacking, critics such as these seem to focus on the lone rhetor in the situation, rather than on a collective rhetorical experience. Bitzer, however, in revisiting the rhetorical situation, defended his position that situations do exist, apart from the lone individual. For Bitzer, such situations are measurable in some way by astute observers ("Forum: Tompkins" 101; Benoit 2). Bitzer's later focus is on "perception" accuracy or error on the part of the participant(s) in a rhetorical situation ("Forum: Tompkins/Patton" 93; Benoit 3). Overall, Bitzer emphasizes the situation and the experience as a totality; his focus is less on the rhetor and more on situational elements inviting reaction on the part of one or many people.

Situation, Context, or Climate?

While certainly less so than it used to be, there remains a strong focus on the classical ideal of rhetor rather than on situation because so much is known about the rhetor. This "good man speaking well" is familiar terrain. Less is known or understood about the situation (Porrovecchio 58). Parts of the murky territory of situation are still uncharted; there remain sketchy portions on the rhetorical map.

Perhaps for practical reasons, situation is often simply called context. For instance, in his textbook explanation of how one ought to go about doing rhetorical criticism, James Andrews highlights how important it is for a critic to determine the context of a given rhetorical text. Andrews says that context entails the "social and cultural values" of the audience, plus their "*perceptions*" and "*public consciousness*" (emphasis in original) (17-19).[3] On the one hand, context, for Andrews, is simply a rallying influence on the text and speaker. Text and speaker are deemed most relevant to the rhetoric the critic seeks to understand. Context, on the other hand, is merely an expedient to understanding the text better. With a nod to the "scene" in Burke's pentad, Andrews defines context by likening it to a "painted backdrop against which the principal scene is played" (19). Context is comprised of "the swirl of events and perceptions of events." Context determines "what really *is* at issue" and is based on observations of surrounding events (Andrews 19-20). Context is an influence on a text or speaker, but it remains in the background.

Interestingly, in middiscussion of context, Andrews shifts terms. Whereas he defines context at first in scenic terms, he later gives it a more mysterious, intangible connotation. "Of utmost importance to the rhetorical critic is what might be called the ethical *tenor* of the times," says Andrews. He concedes that "determining the ethical *climate* of a period is never easy. Major problems confound any attempts that one might make to discern the ethical *climate*" (emphasis added) (23). Climate, then, is like a rocky, foggy coast, and the critic as explorer here is warned that these are barely navigable waters. Without differentiating the term *context* from *climate*, Andrews adds that "the ethical *climate* that permeates a rhetorical situation will vary from setting to setting" (emphasis added) (25). He explains that it is the critic's duty to try to "understand the prevailing codes" of the audience and speaker that the critic is studying (25). In this subtle shift from the word *context* to the word *climate*, from a visible "backdrop" to a variable, virtually indeterminate, and elusive "climate," something interesting is happening.

It would be instructive to slow down, return to, and deconstruct this shift in terms. What might a critic overlook by conflating the discrete concepts of "situation" or "context," with attitudes that create an "ethical climate"? What is more, "culture" is also tossed in with context. Andrews, like many critics, uses the terms context, culture, and climate interchangeably (or at least culture and climate figure in under the general rubric of context). This is problematic for several reasons.

Interesting problems arise when terms such as context, attitudes, culture, and climate are used synonymously or are presumed to be interchangeable by critics. In his take on the rhetorical situation, Mark Porrovecchio asks, "[H]ow can [Bitzer's] model be refined so as to avoid complications in analyzing situational elements, and (2) how can critics arrive at more concrete determinations of an audience's response to a 'fitting response' by the speaker?" (58). This chapter addresses both these questions and poses new ones that might lead to mapping this unknown terrain, and, thereby, advancing rhetorical theory.

First, consider Bitzer's point that a rhetorical situation can feature manifestations of physical or emotional "reality" that may or may not be perceptible to all parties present in a given situation ("Functional Communication" 24). This contrasts with William Benoit's point that "If the rhetor fails to provide the 'correct,' 'fitting,' or 'proper' response [in a rhetorical situation], it is only through incompetence" (348). Benoit also maintains that the idea of a situation is, in itself, overly constraining to the agency of a rhetor because it then "subordinates the rhetor's purpose and the nature of the rhetor to the situation" (348). Benoit seems to be arguing that all rhetors are created equal in terms of their individual agency. There is, however, at least one category of cases in which agency is greatly circumscribed by situation, and there is much scientific evidence to demonstrate it. That category is hate crimes.[4] In such cases, it is not incompetence, then, on the part of the rhetor or participant(s) to surrender to a situation. It is merely a difference of feelings and perceptions that varies from person to person. In Bitzer's own explanation, he accounted for this variance of experiential capacities and tendencies. Bitzer's rhetorical situation is packed with terms. These terms were later interpreted and used somewhat arbitrarily, while also taking on individualistic shades of meaning as opposed to collectivistic ones.

Particularly where hate rhetoric is concerned, the blend of terms like *context*, *attitudes*, and *climate* becomes a stumbling block to effective rhetorical analysis and critical interpretation. Therefore, let us call rhetorical manifestations that are visible and sensible (and sometimes invisible and imperceptible to some people) a *rhetorical climate*. A rhetorical climate can be analyzed as a "text" in the traditional sense of the term. This concept can help to "open and refine the notion of 'text.'"[5] Scholars in rhetoric often look at written or oratorical texts that have come about as the result of a crisis or turbulent situation, and seek the meaning of the text in coming to terms with the "exigence" out of which it arose (Bitzer, "Situation" 6). It would be equally revealing to observe the situation itself, as "experienced." This is a perspective that mediates the seemingly competing views of Biesecker's deconstruction and Vatz's traditional, orator-centrism, as well as among the conflicting views of Bitzer, Tompkins, and others.

It would be illuminating to observe the "exigence" as it is felt, acted on, and communicated by the people involved as a *multiplicity* (Garret and Xiao 39). Such a view extends beyond Porrovecchio's concept of the "rhetorical field." The rhetorical field does account for "situational complexity," including "multiple audiences and exigences," and it enables critics to take a "more adaptive and focused situational approach" (61). On the other hand, Porrovecchio's rhetorical field remains somewhat stuck in the Platonic view of the predominance of the lone orator over an audience and the assumed divide between them. Porrovechio fears a "skewing of rhetorical practice" in valuing the role of the audience in a rhetorical situation (58). Entrenched in the idea of a rhetorical field are the artificial barriers among rhetor, audience, and exigence. The notion of a rhetorical climate, however, transgresses these barriers and enriches rather than "skews" rhetorical practice by moving beyond the limits of the individualistic paradigm.

Critical conceptualizations of context with their dramaturgical metaphors have been highly heuristic. Therefore, the second point made here is to recommend extending and clarifying existing formulations of context beyond the classic metaphor of a stage set or scene.[6] It would be helpful in the analysis of some situations to focus on the dramatic appeal of *vision, feeling, and bodily sensation.* Critics can expand the dramatistic metaphor, and, thereby, enable it to take on a more pervasive rhetorical meaning.

In other words, critics need not relegate the context of a persuasive speaking or acting event to the role of a mere "backdrop." Instead of viewing context as a static "backdrop," critics can analyze a situation as a text.[7] Robert Branham and W. Barnett Pearce have already shown that "texts and contexts are interactive" (20). Contexts, texts, and actors are likewise interactive. The move is one of a shift in focus, such as shifting a camera's view from a close-up shot to a far distant one. As climate is clarified and distinguished from context, attitudes, and other terms, the critical reliance on the heavily demarcated separation of pentadic terms blurs and recedes. In the familiar Burkean pentad, the experiential aspect of "scene" becomes itself a living, moving, prime "actor" in unfolding events. This acting organism is a rhetorical climate.

Also, climate should be considered as a distinct and separate concept from a rhetorical situation, or context, even though it is certainly related to them. A social participant often creates a text that "functions as a fitting response to its situation" (Bitzer, "Situation" 6). A context is usually thought of as being somewhat static, like a frame for a picture. A context is a perspective and window for viewing the landscape of a text or act. The term itself, con-text, shows that it is a force pushing on or weighing against a specific text or act; it is a superimposed view over a particular audience in a particular place and time.

In contrast, a climate pervades the text(s), participant(s), and context fluidly. Increasingly, critics are becoming interested in situations in which more than one persuasive person, text, or event commingle at the fore, or interpellate.[8] Critics are looking beyond the tradition of focusing on a single, lone speaker or writer and are interested in understanding how collective experience operates rhetorically. By checking the pulse of a group of people, by acknowledging the collective thinking and feeling states of diverse people in a given situation, the critic gains a tool for understanding complex rhetorical events.

Climate as Understood

In the preview for Ang Lee's 1997 film, "The Ice Storm," the voice-over says, "It was 1970, and the climate was changing." In common terms, we understand what it means when someone gives us "the cold shoulder" or an "icy stare." In a guide to corporate annual reports, writers are advised to start early and "try to anticipate the socioeconomic and political climate that will prevail when the report is issued" (Wilcox and Nolte 378). As these examples show, climatic metaphors abound in everyday language. People simply just *understand* what climate means. The problem with this common understanding is that it leads to an assumption that climate is merely metaphorical and, therefore, does not exist in any "real" or "objective" or "factual" sense.

There is a perception that there is no real way to articulate or measure an actual climate. Climate is a problematic term because even though it has been invoked in rhetorical criticism, it is seldom clearly defined. Instead, it is taken for granted as understood. For instance, in "The Classroom Climate for Women," Roberta Hall mentions and describes the "climate" for women, but never actually says what a climate is. Hall presumes from all the descriptions of the problems with which women are confronted in the classroom (such as being ridiculed, denigrated, harassed, excluded, or victimized) that the readers will understand what the climate is, or at least what it is like.

Similarly, in "The Communication Classroom: A Chilly One for Women?" Karlyn Kohrs Campbell laments the lack of a curricular focus on women and minorities, which contributes to what she calls a "chilly climate." The closest Campbell ever comes to defining climate, however, is an oblique allusion to what a climate might include: "The conflict between the role of woman and the role of rhetor persists into the present and perpetuates the problems women confront in speech communication classrooms" (69). Such an allusion is too vague to conceptualize a theoretical construct of a rhetorical climate.

A pamphlet on display at a university campus is called "Classroom Climate: A Chilly One for Women?" Again, in the pamphlet, nowhere is a precise definition of climate to be found.[9] Instead, it only mentions that "three of the elements . . . contributing to a 'chilly classroom climate' are. . . [lack of] faculty representativeness . . . academic curriculum . . . teacher-student interactions . . . [and] women students [being] particularly at risk." Still, these are "elements" that make up a climate for women, but the reader is left to guess (or presumed to already know) what that climate is.[10] Finally, in "Community Service, Religious Commitment, and Campus Climate," Robert Serow titles a major section of his essay "norma-tive climates" but does not define what they are. Serow, like others, assumes that readers *just know* a climate is real, and not metaphorical. Sans definition, Serow writes that these "normative climates" are persuasive and influential in people's lives and decision-making processes (109).

Substantiating Climate as Real

Descriptions of or allusions to a "problem" of "climate" or "elements" in a "cli-mate" cannot serve as sufficient evidence for scholars' arguments because they lack any clear definition of climate.[11] Until the concept of climate itself is explained clearly and fully, it cannot be taken as seriously as it ought to be. An unfortunate consequence of the lack of a clear, specific, and viable definition of climate is that assertions of victimization by minorities, women, and others will remain unsub-stantiated in the eyes of people who are not oppressed by a given climate. For ex-ample, if people who are key decision-makers do not perceive or believe in the existence of a "chilly climate," the problem will receive less attention than it de-serves. Despite its being an urgent problem needing to be remedied, the "exi-gency" would go unnoticed or unaddressed.

Indeed, workplace complaints often hinge on a person, sometimes a member of a minority group, expressing discomfort in a given climate—a climate that may not be bothersome to anyone else. Organizational climates are touted as an impor-tant deciding factor in whether or not a prospective employee should take or remain in a job.[12] At the interview, job seekers are encouraged to take stock of an organi-zation's climate by asking questions such as: "Do the people [who work there] seem happy? . . . Do you feel welcome? Does this seem like a good place to work? Do you feel comfortable with the people, site, facilities?" (Nat'l. Assoc. of Colleges and Em-ployers 69). The descriptions that enable the job seeker to ascertain the workplace climate hinge on such perceptual words as *seem* or *feel*, which are highly subjective.

The validity of climate might be questioned on the purely logical grounds that climate as a concept is too "metaphorical," too "descriptive," or that it might just as readily be replaced with words like "context" or "feeling." Still, climate is "a construct . . . [of] intuitively logical explanatory power—it seems to make sense" (Falcione, Sussman, and Herden 196). Feelings and experience have, in fact, long constituted legally valid bases for argument in courts of law. Feeling- or experi-ence-based pleas such as the "insanity defense" are routine in legal rhetoric. A de-fendant's descriptions that establish her or his state of mind—whether in premeditation of an alleged crime, or in the heat of the moment a weapon was used—comprise a valid data set in a court of law. Legal precedent provides one source of proof that climates do exist in a real and objective sense.

In addition, a well-accepted tool for organizational management relies on the validity of climatic data sets of "Feeling," "Sensing," and "Intuition" (Briggs Myers 4–5). The Myers-Briggs Type Indicator test, or MBTI, is, "after more than 50 years of research and development . . . the most widely used instrument for understanding normal personality differences" (Briggs Myers 1). "The MBTI is used in" government, business, and academic settings worldwide for purposes ranging from "academic counseling" and "organization development" to "management and leadership training" (Briggs Myers 1). The wide acceptance and use of the MBTI shows that feelings, intuitions, and sense perceptions are all valid sources for logical decision-making and theory building.[13] Why, then, cannot descriptions of feeling states or bodily sensations or metaphors that indicate the existence of a climate be likewise applied to rhetorical criticism?

Metaphors and descriptions of feelings and bodily states *are* appropriate sources of data. If experience or feelings are rejected as overly descriptive or seen as lacking scientific merit, the effect is to silence large blocks of people. For many people, feelings and experience are often all that are available to articulate (and in some cases prove) the injustices they suffer are real. There is a danger of writing off the analysis of grass roots rhetoric, including the use of symbols, marches or riots, as illogical, unwarranted, or poorly executed. Critics are discouraged from attempting to discern climates for fear of being "confounded" by "major problems" (Andrews 23) or "skewing rhetorical practice" (Porrovecchio 58).[14] By ignoring feelings, body states, and environmental influences, rhetorical critics potentially close off one avenue of opportunity for revealing injustices. On the other hand, the potential for criticism to serve justice and ethics is reinfused by acknowledging, rather than dismissing, feelings, bodily sensations, and environmental cues, all of which constitute rhetorical climates.

If descriptions of feelings and experiences are viable data in courts of law and in organizational communication research, then their role in constituting climates of rhetorical action may also be reasonably considered as valid. A climate is rhetorical when that climate shapes a certain logic of belief and subsequent action. As Serow states, climates are "normative." A climate is all encompassing; it is persuasive, motivating. A climate only remains silent, invisible, and nonexistent *if* critics ignore descriptions of feelings, intuitions, and experiences. Thus, it may be surprising to see what can be learned from examining, rather than excluding, internal states of mind and physiological (body) states as expressed and conceiving of them as rhetorical.

At present, climate is only a problematic concept because although it remains understood, it is as yet unsubstantiated in the canon of rhetorical theory. As long as rhetorical climates are theoretically unsubstantiated, those who exist comfortably within (or even profit from) structurally or culturally violent social frameworks may elude critical capture. Perhaps since collective nonviolent community action or other forms of resistance to oppression often (1) do not feature a lone orator and (2) stem from rhetorical climates, nonviolent rhetoric tends to be overlooked in rhetorical criticism and theory. It could also be that most approaches to rhetoric assume difference and conflict, and focus on cases that obviously feature both. Rhetorical climates, transitory or imperceptible to some, may rightly appear flimsy or superficial to those who labor to understand rhetoric and influence under present critical frameworks.

The discussion that follows uses the available definitions of climate (mainly from scholars and researchers in organizational communication) as a means for revisiting and revitalizing Bitzer's rhetorical situation. By focusing especially on the term "experience" and by unraveling what is wrapped up in an "exigence," a definition of a *rhetorical climate* is offered so that critics may regain the collectivistic orientation that is ingrained in the essence of Bitzer's theory.

Defining Climate

Climate is a "rich" but complex concept (Falcione, Sussman and Herden 195). It would be hard to review the vast literature on climate in this short space; consequently, this analysis concentrates on the points most salient to understanding climate as a rhetorical phenomenon.[15] Climate theory arises from "symbolic interactionism . . . cognitive social learning and interactional psychology . . . and . . . organizational socialization literature" (Falcione, Sussman, and Herden 203). In general, there are three overarching views of climate: (1) it is "an attribute, or set of attributes, belonging to an organization" or social entity; (2) it is comprised of the perceptual consensus of subgroups; and (3) it is also an "individual's summary perceptions of his or her encounters with an organization" or a particular milieu (Falcione and Kaplan 286–88). Each of these views is grounded in the fact that "climate is a phenomenon that is intersubjective in nature and continuously being structured and restructured by organizational members as they *interact with their environment*" (emphasis in original) (Falcione, Sussman and Herden 203). This interaction of people with context blurs the separations of Bitzer's speaker, exigence, audience, and constraints in the rhetorical situation (Porrovecchio 52).

Climate resides in the interaction with an environment as experienced by a specific group of people as a collective (or by a member of that collective). William Glick avers that "the evolution of climate, the process of . . . sense-making, and the social construction of reality . . . may be viewed from a psychological perspective . . . [and] they also are dynamic social/organizational processes" (603–04). Tagiuri defined climate as "the . . . enduring quality of the total environment that (a) is experienced by the occupants, (b) influences their behavior, and (c) can be described in terms of . . . a set of . . . attributes of the environment" (as qtd. in Poole 80). These environmental "attributes" may be the very elements that Bitzer argued existed objectively and in reality.

Climate abides in the liminal space between the environment and its inter-actor. Rhetorical exchanges feature interactors rather than single speakers. Den-nis Saleebey facilitates the theoretical move from a flat context to a rich and embodied climate in asserting that "[t]o be 'in' a situation requires *sensuous at-tendance* and a *vibrant contextual sense of self,* for the body knows context in a way that the intellect does not" (emphasis added) (114). Winnifred Gallagher also emphasizes that "'set and setting' . . . are crucial . . . to experience" (91). Gallagher maintains that "an individual and [her or] his environment is best un-derstood not as separate entities but as a dynamic feedback system" (103). Bitzer himself has noted that "a fundamental proposition grounded in individual and collective experience [is that]. . . *the environment and persons invite change*" (ital-ics in original) (Bitzer, "Functional Comm." 26). Note Bitzer's emphasis on "col-lective experience." A given physical and emotional environment and the people experiencing it mutually create and amplify suasory influence.[16]

The second component of climate is, to use Bitzer's terms, "mental elements" or "entities" (Bitzer, "Functional Comm." 24; 31). A climate is "perceptual and psychological in nature"; it is also "abstract" and "descriptive" (Al-Shammari 30–32). A climate does "influence [the] . . . motivation and behavior" of people living and working in it (Al-Shammari 30–32). Climate accounts for the fact that "[m]ind, body, and environment continually interact in a variety of changing and complex ways" (Saleebey 113). In short, then, Serow's phrase, "normative cli-mates," is redundant. To be in a rhetorical climate is to be mentally and physically moved and influenced.

The term closest to a rhetorical climate is perhaps a "climate of opinion." Ken-neth Burke identifies "climates" in discussing attitudes that groups of people hold either synchronically or diasynchronically. A "climate of opinion" may be consid-ered as an "orientation," an attitudinal frame of reference that people will accept or reject. It will provide the grounding for judgments and constrain the directions of various attitudes. It will provide direction for terms developed and for proce-dures adopted. It will coach the knowledge of the day. It will mark what is accept-able and what is unacceptable. It will operate, to some extent, on Burke's principles of "piety." In short, a climate of opinion merges with the rhetorical because it is an all-consuming milieu—often steady and unquestioned.[17]

Climate is to be distinguished from culture; climate arises from Bitzer's exi-gence. A climate is time-bound and transitory, whereas a culture is entrenched and is a more long-term phenomenon. Daniel Denison writes that although the two concepts share linking elements, there are clear differences between climate and culture: "Culture refers to the deep structure of organizations, which is rooted in values, beliefs, and assumptions held by . . . members. . . . Climate, in contrast, portrays organizational environments as being rooted in the organization's value system . . . but [exists] as relatively temporary, subject to direct control, and . . . limited to those aspects of the social environment that are consciously perceived by organizational members" (624). Thus, while culture may reside in unconscious thought and behavior that occurs in a given value system of a given societal group, climate resides palpably and very consciously among members of that group. Falcione and Kaplan write that "*culture* may be . . . viewed as the organization's system of values, norms, beliefs, and structures that persist *over time*, while climate is the assessment of these elements *at a given moment*" (emphasis in original) (301). The key difference is that climate exists in its "temporary state" and in the fact of its being "perceived" by people at a specific "moment" in time.

CLIMATE: CONCEPT DEFINITION AND SUPPORTING DATA

A key question now arises: What are the data to be analyzed in assessing a rhetorical climate? Researchers in organizational communication theory maintain that one good data set (but certainly not the only one) is the descriptive statements of people who interact in a given environment. "Questionnaires, interviews, or direct observation" have been some of the tools of choice for determining climates (Poole 105). The data are what social group members describe about their experience of existing in a specific place and time.

Critics can investigate descriptions of internal feeling and sensory states, including very personal ones, such as emotions, sights, sounds, physical contacts, and touches. In short, one effective data source for determining a climate is a sum of the participants' experiences of their overall *interaction* with their environment in a specific time period. Descriptions can be gleaned from participants in contemporary settings by means of interviews and surveys; descriptions can also be culled from historical documents, such as letters, diaries, or newspaper accounts.[18] In the case study that follows, newspaper accounts, verified by interview and documentary evidence, constitute the primary source of descriptive data that enabled me to establish the existence of a rhetorical climate.

Building on social scientific definitions of climate,[19] *a rhetorical climate* is defined as follows: A rhetorical climate (1) is a mobile and time-bound, cognitively structuring, feeling, intuitive, and sensory experience; (2) is an experience individuals perceive and construe individually and collectively; (3) is motivating or persuasive enough to mobilize one or more persons to react to it; and (4) causes those who experience it to act in a unified or characteristic manner on the basis of those feelings and sensations.[20] It is important to underscore the mobility and transitory nature of a rhetorical climate, for that is what can make it singularly powerful. Like the darkening sky in a coming storm or the gentle breeze of a spring day, *feelings* about what is occurring at that moment in time contribute to the intensity of resultant actions on the part of the people who experience those feelings.

Bitzer explains that "situations may be expected to change because of forces and tendencies in the environment" ("Functional Communication" 24). He also underscores the idea that "situations are not fixed or unchanging. Some of their elements . . . are physical objects and events caught up in streams of history" ("Functional" 24). These changing "forces," "objects," and "events," in "situations," I believe, comprise a given rhetorical climate. A rhetorical climate occurs as a social phenomenon that can be explained in terms of the interactions of the members of a social group with their environment. People still remain thinking, feeling, and acting individuals within the environment (Berlin 327). At the same time, however, they are influenced by "a social reality" (331).[21]

It is also important to bear in mind that a rhetorical climate appears silent and may only exist through the chimera of perception and description. Bitzer affirms this in noting that there are motivating aspects in each situation that may or may not be "apprehended." For Bitzer, the objective reality of the environmental influences does exist, "whether or not anyone apprehends or acts to alter them" ("Functional Communication" 24). Someone may tell you he or she feels afraid, and though you may see no reason why, there are valid reasons for taking that fear seriously. Descriptions, metaphors, and articulated feeling states are theoretically sound sources of data. Feelings-based data (e.g., social work guidelines, the MBTI, and emotion based arguments in the legal code) are routinely used to assess scientifically the actions of human beings in specific locales. In organizational communication, these are quantified and used in verifying the objective reality of a given climate.

In rhetorical theory, Philip Wander, for one, has opened a space for the utility of using feeling- and experience-based data. In "The Third Persona: An Ideological Turn in Rhetorical Theory," Wander writes: "There are two kinds of texts, sociopolitical texts and highly *personal* texts focusing on *attitudes, consciousness,* and ideal worlds" (emphasis added) (201). A rhetorical climate arises from these "personal" texts of feelings and mental formations. A rhetorical climate can be accepted as sound theory building when the critic follows a *pattern of descriptions* to their logical ends. Critics can apply the climate concept to a given case by analyzing the *attitudes* and the *descriptions* of shortfalls between the "ideal world" and the "real world" in the eyes of people who inhabit that particular space and place in time.

Because a rhetorical climate is based on feelings that are felt, and often shared, but which are sometimes silent (or not orally specified or overtly articulated), it can alternately exist.[22] An example of this alternate existence would be the "chilly climate" Campbell and Hall believe women experience on college campuses or in the corporate boardroom; for men, the "chilly climate" might exist alternatively; that is, it might exist for the men only in relative obscurity, if at all. Therefore, rhetorical climates can exist in a kind of silent or invisible parallel universe. A rhetorical climate exists truly in the realm of the contingent. Bitzer himself underscored the fact that unstated, unseen "mental states" form the linchpin of "exigences" ("On Tompkins" 90–91). This helps explain how exigences may go unanswered or rhetorical climates may be discounted by some people while they are vouched for by others in the same place and time.

In noting these parameters for a rhetorical climate, the utility of expanding the rhetorical critic's array of analytical criteria becomes evident. Critics can escape the confines of a tangible, written, or reproducible "con-*text*" by embracing as data the expressions of transitory feeling states. Critics can transcend the material "backdrop" by appreciating descriptions of intuitions or sensations that have largely been construed, until now, as too subjective to serve as proper data for analysis. The idea of a rhetorical climate goes beyond "the discourse tradition" as part of the rhetorical situation while it empowers the audience with suasory influences heretofore reserved for rhetor alone (Garret and Xiao 39). A rhetorical climate removes any division between audience and rhetor, making them one.

A rhetorical climate also contradicts Biesecker's assertion that "the rhetorical situation [is not] an event structured . . . by a logic of influence" (126). In fact, experiences constitute the greatest influence on a person's decision-making actions and reactions in diverse environments or situations (Haley 187–88). Rhetorical climates may thus exist beyond words and "articulation"; they are often manifested silently in experience. The task of the critic is to retrieve and elicit the descriptions of experiences in order to determine what the climate is/was and then proceed to "read" these data as a cohesive text.

A transcendence comes from investigating the feeling states of actors in the inner- and outer-worldly social conflict, and from musing over the "ambiance" and the descriptions these actors provide of the given climate (of opinion and of *being*). Critics gain insight into the influences and persuasion taking place in the minds and bodies of the people experiencing a given situation. A rhetorical climate displaces traditional notions of "scene" and "text" or "audience," or the triangulations between and among such elements.[23] In a rhetorical climate, there is no discrete rhetor and audience or singular material text; all are mutually influential to the point of being indistinguishable. Let us now turn to examine more closely this interplay of influence.

"RHETORIC AS A WAY OF BEING": THE EXPERIENCE OF HATE CRIMES

Despite foundational ideals of freedom, United States history is rife with discrimination against certain groups of people or individuals who exhibit defining attributes. Prejudices and hatreds on the basis of religious affiliation, ethnicity, or sexual orientation, to name a few, have a long legacy that continues to haunt Americans today. Hate crimes are on the rise throughout the United States (*ABC News*, "Hate Groups"; Martin 303-04; Cooke 44; *Harvard Law Review* 1314). As with Native Americans, African Americans, Asian Americans, people of color generally, and in the wake of 9/11, Muslim Americans, this alarming situation is also potent for Jewish people, who, since first immigrating in large numbers to the United States during the early 19th century, have been targets of prejudice.[24]

Hate crimes are particularly insidious because they affect the tenor of *interactions* within the communities in which they occur. Hate crimes are a peculiar form of lived rhetoric because "actions" of some people result in a radical change in other people. In short, "the *being* of each is constituted by their interaction" (emphasis in original) (Benson 293-94). What, then, exactly are hate crimes, and how do they operate rhetorically? Michael Lieberman defines them in this way:

> Hate crimes are designed to intimidate the victims and other members of the victim's community in an attempt to leave them feeling isolated, vulnerable, and unprotected by the law. These crimes can have a special *emotional* and *psychological* impact on the victim and [her or] his community; exacerbate racial, religious, or ethnic tensions; and lead to reprisals by others in the community. By making members of minority communities fearful, angry and suspicious of other groups—and the power structure that is supposed to protect them—these incidents can damage the fabric of our society and fracture communities. (emphasis added) (37)

Noting the "power structure" is helpful because it brings up the question of the more subtle form of violence occurring in society: structural violence.[25] Hate crimes are especially effective when perpetrated in social systems that feature institutional or structural violence.[26] On the other hand, passive acceptance of violence is not always prevalent. Lieberman cites an exemplary case in which police leadership and community support turned back the rising fear and destructiveness of a wave of neonazi hate crimes (42). This successful result was accomplished by the active nonviolent stance of community members. This particular case—the focus of this chapter—is interesting because, in being a model for success, it offers hope to other communities that are plagued with hate crimes.[27] This case also aptly illustrates the concept of a rhetorical climate.

Climate as Antidote for Hate Crimes

Hate crimes affect victims both psychologically and physiologically. The balm for the victims of these crimes includes reinstilling in them faith and hope. In other

words, intangible states of mind, attitudes, and feelings (mental/physical) are crucial to offsetting a victim's mental and physical duress that is the result of a hate
crime. Featured in organizational communication researchers' descriptors of climate are nine measures: structure, responsibility, reward, risk, warmth, support,
standards, conflict, and identity (Falcione and Kaplan 295; Poole 87; Denison
623). These descriptive measures of communication climates (as used in organizational communication studies) coincide with law enforcement and victim descriptions of hate crimes. Other descriptors of climate have focused more on the
reactions that the climate itself induces, such as "leadership" or "creativity" (Poole
88). Overall, the majority of climate descriptors are measures of the agency people
perceive they collectively or individually possess in a given place and time.

Warmth, which is the perceived "degree of interpersonal warmth in the organization" or social group, and support, which is the "degree to which members
support each other," are both measures that reveal agency and collective experience (Poole 87). High degrees of warmth and support can foster positive attitudes.
Positive attitudes create the possibility for positive outcomes that foster "creativity" and "leadership." In the case studied here, both creativity and leadership were
evident in transforming the rhetorical climate set in place by neonazi propaganda
and guerrilla and terrorist tactics.

Aside from communication studies, research in modern medicine also validates what members of organized religion have long believed: that positive attitudes foster healing. Medical research, particularly studies in healing and
neurology, indicate that spirituality, faith, and hope can change a person's prognosis for the better.[28] As Lieberman defines them, hate crimes create climates that are
detrimental to people's minds and behaviors. As science and communication theory reveal, so too can *nonviolent* action create countermeasures of "warmth" and
"support" to foster hope and faith, which function to help people to collectively
change their minds and behaviors in healthy and productive ways.

Faith is a key element in rhetoric. "[T]here is always some element of faith involved in one's communication with other people" (Johnstone 241). Faith also
emboldens and enables people to take risks. Risk, according to communication
theorists, is a key determinant in measuring climate (Falcione, Sussman, and Herden 202). On a grander scale, hope combined with faith can transform a small
community, a city, or even a nation.[29] Feelings of hope can be intensified when
hope is fostered by religious organizations, especially since religious activities
feature confirmatory behaviors and patterns of thought that serve to reinforce
sensory and cognitive states.[30]

Attitudes and feeling states of faith and hope, along with the support of social organizations, can influence the way people in a conflict react. Attitudes and
feeling states are persuasive and, therefore, influence the ways social conflicts

escalate or deescalate. Any number of feeling and sensory states contribute to a pervasive rhetorical climate in which people interact. Altruism, faith, and hope are the feeling states that altered the rhetorical climate analyzed in the following case study. The climate change influenced the behavior of most of the inhabitants of a city and, as a result, influenced the outcome of an ongoing conflict.

The feeling of hope changes the climate of a bleak situation. Richard Weaver explains that it is the discourse "about real potentiality or possible actuality" that infuses a situation with hope.[31] In Weaver's example, it is the direct rhetorical action of a single leader that supplies the hope that "transfigures" the scenario. However, just as often, the rhetorical action of a *community of people acting as a unit* is what transfigures situations. Again, the shift is away from the lone rhetor and toward the rhetoric of a given collectivity.

Of course, initial rhetorical acts of one or more persons may take place. These rhetorical acts are what organizational communication scholars refer to as the measurable "outcomes" of climates (Poole 88). Yet incitement from a single, identifiable leader is often *absent* (Mathews 400).[32] Moreover, initial persuasive efforts that incite the activity of the people depend on community based experience. It takes the "will" and cooperation of a group of people for one to realize fully what can "exist by favor of human imagination and effort" (Mathews 400; Weaver 20). At the level of one person, it is the feeling of hope that can help heal a patient (Damasio 120).[33] Weaver's paragon of the lone rhetor is Winston Churchill, who fuels the faith of the people to fight Nazi Germany.[34] Looking beyond individual rhetors, feeling states can be collectively asserted and equally as motivating as the rhetorical act of one person. Therefore, shared feeling states can be conceived of as all encompassing; these states of mind and being are as persuasive as a written or spoken text by a single person. Unified experiential collectives are constitutive of rhetorical climates.

Scholars in rhetorical theory have emphasized the great rhetorical power of cynicism;[35] this case, however, provides a counterpoint by showing the equally powerful sway of goodwill and benevolence. Scholars in communication theory characterize climate not only in terms of perceived levels of warmth and support, but also in terms of "friendliness," "openness of expression," "open-mindedness," and "cooperation" (Falcione, Sussman, and Herden 202). For people interacting in society, Damasio claims there is a "powerful connection" between "social phenomena and biological phenomena," which contribute to a natural orientation toward "altruism" (124).[36] All this, he says, is "something . . . unique to humans: a moral point of view that, on occasion, can transcend the interests of the immediate group and even the species" (126). Here, too, the shift is away from the individual and toward an emphasis on the group as a whole. Damasio stresses that our cognitive make-up contributes to altruistic behaviors (175–76). Similarly,

Alfie Kohn, agreeing with others in the fields of conflict analysis, peace studies, and nonviolent theory, has noted that amiable cooperation should be considered as the defining characteristic of human beings.[37]

Most significant for this discussion, Damasio, among others, offers compelling evidence that human reasoning and behavior are based on *feeling* states. Feeling states arise from sensations, such as sight, touch, smell, and hearing, rather than from what have traditionally been thought of as "objective," "rational," "thinking" or "logical" states of mind (177-79).[38] What this means for the rhetorical critic is that perceptions and feelings of people in a given scenario can provide clues to the rhetorical climate they are experiencing individually and collectively. These clues can help critics understand why people are behaving the ways they are within that climate. Gallagher supports this analytical strategy in remarking that "the senses convey to the brain far more information than we can consciously be aware of; it is the totality of all that undifferentiated input that we perceive in a general way as ambiance. At special places . . . this diffuse essence is somehow stronger and more poignant" (24). The influence that "ambiance" or "essence" has on people, in a given rhetorical climate, is evident in the case study that follows.

This case illustrates how a series of events, including speech and other symbolic acts, but more importantly, *feelings*, comprise a rhetorical climate. With an analysis of the *feeling* and *sensory descriptions* of the participants in that climate (as data), we can understand incipient action. Rather than shying away from the intangible and elusive quality of metaphor and feeling, this case demonstrates that critics have much to gain by embracing descriptive data. Berlin supports this position in stating that researchers interested in social interaction "should . . . invest creative energy in understanding the nature and meaning of incoming environmental cues" (332). This case study examines these cues as rhetoric and analyzes the behaviors that the cues invited while conceiving of them as Bitzer's "fitting response": nonviolent collective action.

The following section examines the experiential measures of a collective effort in a small American city in the West—Billings, Montana. The altruistic effort of townspeople in Billings created a successful reversal of a series of frightening and ominous hate crimes that took place there. The collective altruistic feelings and actions of the townspeople altered the course of history/"herstory" there. In examining this case, both the concept and reality of a rhetorical climate are illustrated.

THE CASE: A CHANGING CLIMATE IN BIG SKY COUNTRY

In Hayden Lake, Idaho, there was a "ten-acre Aryan Nations compound" (Sochocky and Siegner 15), from which its white supremacist leader, Richard Butler, issued an ominous proclamation in 1986 (Rosenblatt 23).[39] The proclamation announced that the "five state area of Washington, Oregon, Idaho, Wyoming, and Montana" was their "white homeland" (Rosenblatt 24). The white supremacists "and growing numbers of kindred skinheads, Klan members" and their followers "have targeted nonwhites, Jews, gays, lesbians for harassment, vandalism, and injury, which in some cases has led to murder" (Hartsig and Wink 54; *Billings Gazette* "Hate Groups Get Aggressive" A7).

In one particularly horrific example of neonazi hatred, "in 1988, in Portland, Oregon, three skinheads . . . surrounded an Ethiopian student named Mulugeta Seraw on a street and beat him to death with a baseball bat" (Rosenblatt 24). In such a place and time, designated as amenable to white men and dangerous to those targeted by white supremacists, the murder of Seraw is more than contextualized (McCracken, "Ex-white Supremacists" A1). Seraw's murder followed a predictable pattern from the motivating forces of the rhetorical climate in which the murder took place.

Rhetorical climates exist throughout history. Waldo Braden explains that Hitler's mythic tales resulted in ultraviolent outcomes in Germany (121). Hitler's strategy echoes in the new myth of the "white homeland," which is fostering similar violence in the Pacific Northwest and throughout America (McCracken, "Windows" A1). It has not gone without notice that, since this "homeland" proclamation took place, "the *climate* for the[se] incidents had . . . been established" (emphasis added) (Rosenblatt 24). Since observant reporters call patterns of events which evoke feeling states "climates," and scholars like Karlyn Kohrs Campbell identify "chilly climates," it stands to reason that rhetorical critics can theorize that the intangible or immaterial is, in fact, material.

Feeling states, like textual material, influence the outcomes of events and the way people run their everyday lives. Events, such as the terrible hate-driven murders of James Byrd (for being African American) in Jasper, Texas, and Matthew Shepard (for being homosexual) in Wyoming, do have a vast effect on the attitudes and behaviors of people in the communities in which those events occur. It is a small theoretical leap to posit that events, descriptions, and the subsequent feelings and attitudes of those living in an affected community, are motivating. Influential, all encompassing, and persuasive, these shared feelings comprise a uniquely rhetorical climate.

Environmental Cues

In May 1992, a prominent resident of Billings, Montana, Tammie Schnitzer, "noticed something on the stop sign" close to the town synagogue; "[s]he got out of her car to take a closer look, and a *shiver shot down her spine*. A sticker showed a swastika over a Star of David and the words 'Want more oil? Nuke Israel' " (emphasis added) (Dobb 96). This was not Schnitzer's first brush with hate. She had earlier discovered that being Jewish in Montana meant enduring threats and fear. In 1989, when she had organized a gathering for Montana's Jewish families, which she had advertised in the local paper, she "received a *chilling* [phone] call. 'Stop or we'll make you stop,'" said the man on the other end of the line, who added, "Die Jew Bitch!" before abruptly hanging up (emphasis added) (Safran 82; Schnitzer "Speech"). For Schnitzer, the climate of hate and fear had begun to take hold of Billings ("Interview").

By October 1992, during presidential campaign visits, "hate literature appeared in Billings" (24). Schnitzer also "saw a flyer that named Brian [her spouse]," as a target, since he had just become president of the Montana Association of Jewish Communities. Schnitzer says of that moment, "*I felt sick. It really hit home*" (emphasis added) (Safran 82). The analysis of this isolated experience, as a text, is broached by asking: Why should her feeling states matter? How does the way *she feels* influence her household, her community? Wander validates this rhetoric of experience by noting that audiences of Heidegger's last lectures in Germany were

> well aware of the awesome disaster . . . [of the First World War]; that this audience had experienced, was experiencing, and knew people who were experiencing . . . the *threat of insanity* brought on by the collapse of what is and the *fragile hope* and *sense of purpose* anchored in existing institutional arrangements . . . this audience would . . . have found the details . . . the sort of common knowledge, the sort of *shared experience* a speaker may call upon to *flesh out* an argument or *breathe life* into a figure of speech. (emphasis added) (208)

In Wander's description of Heidegger's audience, the audience is influenced both by its experiences and by the way Heidegger calls on that experience to "breathe life" into his lecture. The incipient climate of Billings is less evident in the clear-cut fashion of Heidegger as orator and Germans as audience. In a rhetorical climate, there is no distinction among pentadic elements. Instead, the climate moves fluidly, and the persuasive trajectory is multidirectional.

It is an awful irony that Heidegger serves here as an example of how to foment a rhetorical climate since one aim of this discussion is to extol the use of a rhetoric of nonviolence to counter hatred.[40] Heidegger, a Nazi sympathizer, knew people's experiences could be manipulated through rhetorical means.[41] It is horrifying to realize that neonazis today foster hatred and violence by posting Klan leaflets and hate literature or web sites to seduce or intimidate people. Today's neo-nazis create a shared malevolent experience in the deeply connected space between living flesh and virtual reality. However, just because Hitler followers past and present used and continue to exploit rhetorical climate for violent means does not exclude the potential for rhetorical climate to be used by others to resist and oppose intolerance and bigotry. Critics seeking social justice through nonviolent means are beginning to acknowledge there is an equally positive power of shared experience of the rhetorical kind.

A rhetorical climate arises from the lived or vicarious experience communicated by the participant. Ms. Schnitzer described how she felt to her neighbor; that neighbor described it, in turn, to her neighbor's neighbor: it is partially in this way that climate diffuses. The spreading rhetorical climate is ascertained by asking, what did the whole neighborhood, as a collective, feel when they found out? What evidence can the critic provide of people's reactive and felt vicarious experiences? Observing environmental cues (such as the Klan posters) and the descriptions of feelings about experiencing such cues ("I felt sick") or interpersonal actions (such as organizing meetings) enables the critic to start assessing the existence of a rhetorical climate.

Dale Hample's research shows that people are more susceptible to persuasive arguments when they hold little or no opinion on a given issue (158). If experiences, like opinions, are new or barely conceived of, experiences may be said to function like persuasive arguments. In short, a lived or even an imagined experience can be like a persuasive text; an experience (felt or perceived) is motivating.

In response to the harrowing experience of being subjected to the hate-leaflets and stickers she saw posted in town, Schnitzer, who is "a Billings native . . . called Wayne Schile . . . of the Billings *Gazette*, to talk about the problem of hate groups in their community. 'What problem?,'" Schile asked (Dobb 97). Soon after, Schnitzer went to visit Schile with the . . . [leaflet] in hand: "This problem." Reportedly, Schile was "*stunned*" by it (emphasis added) (97). In response, the *Gazette* "ran a front page story" about the problem. This was to be the first of a series of articles that would help to alter the atmosphere of hate and fear looming over the town. The altruistic tone of the newspaper's stories became compelling to the residents of the town (Gantz, Trenholm, and Pittman 730). When the power and influence of the mass media become involved in personal experience, the fact that there is a rhetorical situation at hand is confirmed. The critic's next task is to cull from the rhetorical situation the existence of a rhetorical climate.

Observing the interactions between people within and outside local power structures, such as government, police, or community groups, is one way to understand the experience of a rhetorical climate. When Schnitzer initially pursued other government officials and business leaders about the problem of the hate literature, she recalls that, "They thought the incidents were isolated, and weren't that concerned. But I wanted them to look into [my children's] . . . eyes and see who was being *hurt*" (emphasis added) (Safran 82; Schnitzer, "Speech"). Also during this period, Margaret MacDonald, part-time director of the Montana Association of Churches, was attempting to obtain signatures for a petition that denounced hatred and bigotry (Safran 82; *Not in Our Town*). MacDonald also noted the resistance to recognizing the problem: "There'd been an emphatic hard-line stance in the town, like a brick wall, that the less said about the skinheads and other racists, the better" (Safran 82).

By spring 1993, Schnitzer, MacDonald, and others had formed the Billings Coalition for Human Rights (*Not in Our Town*). Schnitzer wanted to enlist community support for the victims of hate crimes: "This wasn't just a Jewish issue, it was a human rights issue" (Safran 82; Schnitzer "Speech"). A rhetorical climate can entail a range of emotions from hatred to loving kindness. A peace-oriented theory of rhetoric that allows a critic to identify and claim as *real* a rhetorical climate is a theory that presupposes a collectivistic, nonviolent worldview. To deny even the possibility of the existence of a given climate is, by the rhetorical standards of Henry Johnstone, to shut oneself off from true and fair argumentative possibility.

Some members of the local government of Billings, such as those desiring reelection or secure positions in the power structure, had neither the vested interest nor the empathic attitude required to use their power to help turn the climate of hate into one of hope. Others, however, did. The *Billings Gazette* reported, for example, that in early December, 1993, the entire "Billings City Council officially spoke out . . . against local hate-group activity" and that "Mayor Richard Larsen read his entire proclamation denouncing hate groups" that "all nine members at the meeting" signed and ratified ("Hate Groups Denounced" C8). The climate assessment measures of "warmth" and "support" are evident in this action.

MacDonald succeeded in garnering signatures from about 100 organizations and 3,500 people community-wide, but the hate activities did not stop (Safran 82; *Billings Gazette* "Crime Stories" A1). A few months later, after a

> celebration of Martin Luther King, Jr.'s birthday . . . people found Ku Klux Klan fliers on their cars. One showed a drawing of a Klansman on horseback, bearing a blazing cross. Around the drawing were numerous anti-Semitic phrases, like "juden Raus," "Jews Out" and "Go Back to Israel, Jew Scum." And under the drawing: "We are the Klan . . . bringing back the dream." (Rosenblatt 24; *Not in Our Town*)

The fliers had been distributed "during [the] interfaith . . . observance at the First United Methodist Church" (Dobb 97). Without more help and support of local authorities, nonviolent community groups would have a difficult time of prevailing over the hatred of the neonazis who were creating the climate of fear in Billings.

At the same time, an altruistic, collectivistic perspective recognizes that because hate-mongers and "skinheads" are frequently from a low socioeconomic bracket, often unemployed, and undereducated, they, too, can be considered as victims of structural violence in their own right (*Billings Gazette* "Hate Groups" A4).[42] Again, the feelings of hatred that foster a fearful rhetorical climate arise from material conditions that are, in Bitzer's words, "factual" and "observable" out in the real world. In a sense, the "skinheads" and "racists" are just as much victims as the victims of the hate crimes they target. Fortunately for Billings, however, people came forward to help change the tense conflict and recognized the very real problems that needed to be addressed between the beleaguered camps.

Wayne Inman, who was chief of the Billings police department at the time, "knew . . . that a group of angry young men . . . most of them poorly educated and underemployed, were followers of the KKK" (*Not in Our Town*; Dobb 97). Inman "worried" and anticipated how these initial acts of intimidation might grow into something worse (Dobb 97). Inman was particularly sensitive to the growing climate of hatred in Billings because, as fate would have it, "he was a precinct captain in the section of Portland where the killing of Seraw [the Ethiopian college student] took place" (Rosenblatt 26). The brutal killing of Seraw "*shaped* much of [Inman's] *thinking*" (emphasis added) (Rosenblatt 26).[43] Thus, one collectivistic-minded person, whose past experiences "shaped" his attitudes about hate crimes and the social inequalities from which such crimes often arise, was better situated to come to terms with the conflict in Billings. Being empathic, Inman understood both the victims of poverty as well as the victims of hate crimes. Because he was a member of Billings's governmental power structure, he was poised to be an important influence in deescalating the conflict and altering the climate.

Following the Martin Luther King Day incident, Inman called a press conference (Dobb 97). This was now the second time the media reported concern about the incidents in Billings. In his statements to the press, Inman recounted how he had been in Portland when hate "leafleting had escalated to vicious crimes" culminating in the murder of the student (97). Inman went on to say:

> Only then, did the people of Portland acknowledge the problem . . . Silence is acceptance. These people are testing us. And if we do nothing, there's going to be more trouble. Billings should stand up and say, "Harass one of us and you harass us all."

From the local government's side, Inman's press conference was one of the first key moves on the part of authorities that would begin to alter the rhetorical climate in Billings. From the grass roots' side, Schnitzer's initial action in informing the newspaper of the hate leaflets and MacDonald's antibigotry petition were likewise important first steps toward altering attitudes of the people of Billings as individuals and as members of social groups in the community. Also, a local human rights activist, Sarah Anthony, figured heavily in the grassroots initiatives against hate (McCracken "Symbol of Unity" A1; *Not in Our Town*). Schnitzer herself confirms that the events unfolded toward a positive end result because of community leader involvement and the widespread support of nonviolent means to handle the conflict (Schnitzer "Interview"). The motivation to support an informed and empathic solidarity against the hate crimes was more encompassing because it emanated from the grassroots level and moved upward.[44] Characteristic of a rhetorical climate, the persuasion migrated multidirectionally, rather than exclusively top-down, as in the orator/audience paradigm.

Once the influence permeated to responsive leaders in Billings's power structure, they began to seek "creative" solutions to the problem. For instance, Police Chief Inman, "through his vigorous investigation of the crimes and public statements denouncing bigotry and encouraging community support for the victims, *established a high moral tone* and sent the strong message that residents should not remain silent in the face of bigotry" (emphasis added) (Lieberman 42). Where does a "high moral tone" reside? It resides in the attitudes, and sometimes behaviors, of those who hold, or perceive, the "tone." A tone may be invisible, but it is palpably present for those who experience it. In Bitzer's words, "we engage the environment in a rhetoric of adjustment . . . through patterns of response . . . of which we are seldom conscious" ("Functional Communication" 38). Little by little, through moral tone and political action from those in and out of the official power system, the rhetorical climate in Billings was changing.

Still, as Bitzer states, "situational elements" are uneven and unpredictable ("Functional Communication" 24). Following Inman's public stand, the "leafleting increased" (Dobb 97). In addition, on September 11, 1993, it was discovered that "19 headstones" in the Beth Aaron Jewish cemetery had been deliberately knocked down, while gravestones in the bordering Catholic cemetery were left alone (*Billings Gazette* "Crime Stories" A1). Particularly painful for Tammie Schnitzer was the fact that the gravestone of her infant son had been both urinated and defecated on (Schnitzer "Speech"). Making matters worse, Inman was under "pressure" from "town officials not to label the cemetery incident a hate crime" (Rosenblatt 26). This illustrates how structural violence operates. Certain town officials feared political retribution or for their own personal safety. Their passivity—as a specifically motivated inaction—was abetted and rationalized by a climate of fear. By calling them mere "pranks," they downplayed the real nature of the hate crimes. The neonazi actions thus "explained away" had the net effect of influencing the behavior of other town leaders and citizens alike to avoid

addressing the problem. "Even my own police department chose to call it vandalism at first," said Inman. But when the Beth Aaron synagogue received a bomb
threat only a few days later, the police and town leaders began to acknowledge the
earlier incidents as hate crimes (Rosenblatt 26). As Schnitzer puts it, although a
bombing was not carried out, "a bomb did go off that day." It was an emotional
and sensory explosion because she and everyone at the synagogue services that
day had to run the frightening gauntlet of fire trucks, paramedics and police to get
inside; once inside, no one knew what would happen, and everyone was terrified
(Schnitzer "Speech").

The climate of fear further manifested itself on Sunday, September 26, when,
"during the . . . worship service at the African Methodist Episcopal Wayman
Chapel, three white men entered and stood glowering at the [handful of African
Americans who comprised the] congregation" (Rosenblatt 26; Not in Our Town).
The church's minister, pastor Freeman, described the scene this way:

> They'd sit a few minutes, and then they'd get up and stand by the door with
> their arms folded, in a kind of belligerent manner. I think they were trying to
> make us say something to get them started. We ignored them, but a lot of our
> people were *frightened* (emphasis added). (Rosenblatt 26–27; Not in Our Town)

Pastor Freeman's description of the climate of fear is palpable. With only a little
empathy and imagination, a critic can "see" and "feel" the isolation of the two
groups of "victims" in a world of structural violence: the propagandized ruffians,
the "skinheads," on the one side, and the racial minority, the churchgoers, on the
other. At this point, it seemed as if the climate of fear would snuff out any budding
hope that some town leaders and nonviolent activists had created.

Fortunately, however, a climate of hope was beginning to compete with that
of fear and hatred. What happened next was evidence that Chief Inman's press
conference and the activists' door-to-door work had touched the people of
Billings. In small groups, supportive Euro-Americans began to attend the beleaguered church's services; they came and sat in quiet solidarity with the usual
African American congregation. Eventually, the "belligerent" skinheads gave up
on their attempts at intimidation and stopped coming (Not in Our Town).

Still, the mobility and transience of the competing rhetorical climates was evident. Not long after that, the "home of Dawn Fast Horse," a Native American,
and her Euro-American partner, Jason Miller, "was spray-painted with four-letter
epithets, [huge] swastikas, and the words 'Die Indian'" (Rosenblatt 27; Billings
Gazette, "Memories of 1993" F2). The house is located "literally on the other side
of the tracks" in the section of town where many African Americans, Latinos, and
Native Americans of Billings reside. When word of the hateful graffiti got to Bob

Maxwell, who is head of the local Painter's union, he and other local painters
agreed to repaint the house, free of charge (Rosenblatt 27; Not in Our Town). The
graffiti stayed on the house for three days until the painters came (Safran 82).
Here, too, it requires a critic just a little thought to imagine how the neighborhood's residents—children and adults alike—felt passing by that hurtful eyesore
each day.

Finally, while the painters did their work, about 150 women, men, and children in the neighborhood rallied around them and showed their support of the
pro bono community action (Rosenblatt 27; Not in Our Town). Once again, the
soft breeze of altruism and nonviolent action had prevailed over the climate of
hate in the town. A rhetorical climate is suffused with a sense of the potential for
a shared experience and for a probable experience; it is contingent, transitory. A
rhetorical climate has an ephemeral quality and immateriality, which may exist
in a period of time or in the passage of events. Time and events coalesce while
malleably shaping various pockets of attitudes, behaviors, and social influences.
These influences exist through experiences and compete for prevalence in social
interactions and settings.

In this way, critics can acknowledge that experiential recalcitrances are in-
evitable. On November 27, "a beer bottle was thrown through the glass door" of
Uri Barnea, a Jewish immigrant and the director of the Billings Symphony (Mc-
Cracken, "Symbol of Unity" A1; Billings Gazette, "Racicot" B1). Barnea took it as
a logical progression in what he had experienced as a long-term climate of fear.
Barnea commented:

> For nine years, since it was known that I'm a Jew, I had been receiving
> derogatory phone calls, and the trouble stayed at that level. But then . . .
> things suddenly got worse. In January 1993, Ku Klux Klan literature was
> left at my front door, tucked into the folds of the morning paper. So here
> was someone coming up to my house. *I felt violated.* (emphasis added)
> (Rosenblatt 27)

Thus the climate of hate remained recalcitrant in Barnea's personal experience of violation. As experts on hate crimes indicate, this feeling on the part of a
victim of a hate crime leads to a physical and psychological change (Cooke 44).
Hate crimes are indeed influential, in a sense *un*motivating, changing the victim's
attitudes into a mindset of defeat and frequently of passivity. "Barnea mentioned
the K.K.K. note to the police, but said nothing publicly. His *attitude* may have represented that of many in the Jewish community, who *felt* that the less said about
[the matter] . . . the less likely the incidents were to recur" (emphasis added)
(Rosenblatt 27). Bidirectional "confidence and trust" are also climatic measures

(Jones and James as qtd. in Falcione, Sussman, and Herden 202). Here, Barnea exhibited some confidence and trust "up" at the level of the police, but less at the "down" or lateral level of the general public of which he was a part.

Similarly, Tammie Schnitzer, who had become president of Congregation Beth Aaron, noted the decision of the temple officers not to speak out. Schnitzer observed, "They seemed to *feel* that to acknowledge a problem or identify ourselves as being different would make us stand apart" (emphasis added) (Safran 82; Schnitzer "Speech"). This attitude shift from confidence to fear is common among victims of hate crimes. This defeatist attitude, in turn, influences the people who interact with the victim (Lieberman 36); can it not, then, be said to be rhetorical? Bitzer maintains that the diffusion of emotion and feeling throughout a community is transmitted through forms of communication ranging from "poetry, drama, ritual, education, philosophy, religion" ("Functional Communication" 38). This diffusion of messages and the "interaction of . . . [people] and environment" is part of the changing and unpredictable essense of a rhetorical climate (38).

The resistant climate of hate continued, keeping hope in check. On December 2, at about 7 p.m., a trespasser threw a "chunk of cinder block" through the window of Schnitzer's house (Ehli, "Mother Denounces Hate Crime" A1). Most frightening was that it was the window of her young son's bedroom. Fortunately, Isaac, then only five years old, was not in his room. Schnitzer's husband had come home to find the distraught baby-sitter with the boy in the other room. Tammie Schnitzer had been out at a meeting and arrived home to find her husband had thoroughly cleaned up the shards and splinters of glass from the room and stripped the bed. She found her husband sitting in the cold, and now partially emptied room, weeping. "He reacted just like a rape victim," she remarks, in that he wanted to feel as if he had completely cleansed away the violation of the hateful act (Schnitzer, "Speech"). Apparently, the cinder "block left an indentation on the [child's] bed" (Ehli, "Mother Denounces Hate Crime" A1). In fear of greater retribution, he begged her not to call the police, but she called anyway (Schnitzer, "Speech").

When the police officer arrived, he agreed with Ms. Schnitzer that it wasn't "just mischief" (Safran 83). The police officer's advice was to take down the banner on the window that read, "Happy Hanukkah" (Ehli, "Mother Denounces Hate Crime" A1). Schnitzer was concerned by the advice, understanding the safety issue, but at the same time wondering, "How do you explain that to a child?" (Mother Denounces Hate Crime" A1; Rosenblatt 30). She thought about whether or not she should go public with her own very personal story. She decided to go to Schile of the *Billings Gazette* and recommend that the paper run her story. "You're setting yourself up for more trouble," said Schile. "I don't care," Tammie replied. "This is a quality of life issue, not a Jewish issue" (Dobb 98). The paper ran the story (Ehli, "Mother Denounces Hate Crime" A1). The featured quotation on the front page captured the climate of fear: "So at night, as a parent, you lie in bed with your eyes wide open" (Ehli, "Mother Denounces Hate Crime" A1).

The results of the article were heartening. Because "the safety of a child was involved, everyone could identify with the parents. Public outrage was immediate" (Rosenblatt 30). When MacDonald "read Schnitzer's quote in the paper, she tried to imagine telling her daughter . . . that they couldn't have a Christmas tree . . . because it wasn't safe" (Safran 83). In her capacity as director of the Montana Association of Churches, MacDonald knew about nonviolence in history. MacDonald

> remembered the story of King Christina of Denmark. When the Nazis informed him that all Jews would be forced to display the yellow star of David on their coats, the king responded that he would be the first to wear it, and all Danes would follow his lead. The Nazis withdrew their order. Now MacDonald reasoned, *What if, instead of the Jews removing menorahs from their windows, Christians placed menorahs in theirs?* (emphasis in original) (Dobbs 98–99)

She then called her pastor, Keith Torney, with her idea, asking, "What would you think if we had the children draw menorahs in Sunday school? If we . . . [copied] as many pictures of the menorahs as we could [and then] told people to put them up onto their windows?" (Safran 83). Torney agreed and spent that day calling other churches, encouraging them to do the same. By the end of the week, "hundreds of menorahs appeared in the windows of homes in Billings" (Safran 83).

The people who put the paper menorah images on their windows understood the implications. "It wasn't an easy decision, with two young children, I had to think hard about it myself," said MacDonald (Safran 83). Of her decision to put up the picture of the menorah, Becky Thomas, who lives near the Schnitzers, said, "It's easy to go around saying you support some good cause, but this was different. It was putting ourselves in danger. I told my husband, 'Now *we know* how the Schnitzers *feel*'" (emphasis added) (Safran 83). Jan Stickney, a member of Torney's congregation, said, "[I went] to see if I could find a real menorah . . . [the store] had a blue plastic one, so I put that up. I did not *feel* that the menorah was a strange symbol to have in my house. I *felt* that it was part of my own life" (emphasis added) (Rosenblatt 30). All of these comments indicate the strong feeling of identification and empathy the community members shared with the victims of hate crimes. Their actions, as "fitting response," were guided, motivated, and performed on the basis of their individual and collective feeling states and shared experience, rather than by a single speech of a lone orator on a specific day.

Sarah Anthony, President of the Billings Human Rights Coalition, organized a protective vigil (in the St. Vincent Hospital parking lot across from Beth Aaron) to be held during the synagogue's Sabbath services (Rosenblatt 30). On Friday, December 10, about 150 people participated in the vigil. The Schnitzers, Rabbi Cohon, and Anthony, spoke to the crowd from the bed of a pickup truck (30). Cohon "lit a menorah and blessed it, saying that it symbolized the human spirit, and, 'You cannot stifle it.'" Before leading the congregation into the synagogue, Cohon "quoted . . . Edmund Burke's observation on apathy: 'The only thing necessary for the triumph of evil is for good men [sic] to do nothing'" (Dobb 99). When Tammie Schnitzer spoke, "a few skinheads arrived, glowering at the crowd"; when she saw them, she said, "Leave our babies alone!" (Dobb 99). Of the event, Anthony recalls, "That vigil was the most heartening moment in the last year . . . because there was such *pain around the whole event*. But standing . . . [there] on that cold night, looking at the candles, with all the people standing around us . . . it seemed that they were really with us, really there" (emphasis added) (Rosenblatt 30). Hope and altruism, or in climate measures, "warmth" and "support," was propagated by the local churches and grassroots human rights groups. This nonviolent resistance to the hatred, actively supported by the community and its leaders, furthered the change in the rhetorical climate of Billings.

Encouraged by the responses of the local churches and their congregations, the local newspaper took a bold step. On December 8, it ran an editorial that encouraged citizens to "place a menorah in your window . . . so that these haters can see that we all stand together" (*Billings Gazette* "Put a Menorah" B1). David Crisp, then assistant region editor of the *Billings Gazette*, thought of a way to extend the churches' campaign of support and solidarity for the Jewish community (*Editor & Publisher* 3). Why not print a full-page ad with a menorah on it, so that readers of the paper could cut it out and post it on their windows at home and at their places of work? On December 11, 1993, the *Billings Gazette* did just that. The full-page ad featured an enormous drawing of a menorah, candles blazing, surrounded by a rousing text of solidarity for "harmony," for "the principle of religious liberty," and against neonazi hatred.[45] It is estimated that the menorah image was posted on windows of between 4,000–10,000 homes, schools, churches, and businesses in Billings (Dobb 99; Hartsig and Wink 55; Rosenblatt 30).

Even the local "sporting goods store got involved by displaying" on their large, raised road sign a message of solidarity: "Not in our town! No Hate. No Violence. Peace on Earth" (Ehli, "Message of Support" A1; Harsig and Wink 55). The store's manager, Rick Smith, described his decision to trade "promoting . . . sales" for promoting social justice: "I read about this family, and I thought, 'What can we do, what can we say?' . . . [so] we decided we could make a statement to our community supporting this family and our police department . . . now was the time to speak out" (Ehli, "Message" A1). The feeling states of the people acting in the town influenced the media, which, in turn, influenced the people further.[46] Finally, the climate of hope overtook that of hate and fear. Literally, the community's "window" to its world was one of unity and collective support for the victims of the hate crimes.

Unfortunately, by not acknowledging the structural violence and causes of neonazi activity, there was space for setbacks. With the community's "fitting response" of solidarity, the skinheads retaliated with violent guerrilla tactics as "fitting responses" of their own. All of the altruistic action "enflamed" the "anti-Semitic vandals," who then proceeded to smash "a glass door at the Evangelical United Methodist Church and two windows displaying the paper menorahs at the First United Methodist Church," as well the windows of six homes also displaying the picture (*Editor & Publisher* 3; McCracken, "Windows with Menorahs Broken" A1). Rev. Tim Hathaway, pastor of the church, reportedly felt "vulnerable" but said, "Silence doesn't work. We need to take a stand in the midst of this, even if it's scary. What would Jesus do? I think he'd take a stand" (Olp, "Vandalized Churches" A5). Police Chief Inman, for his part, continued to stand his ground as well: "For every vandalism that is made, I hope that 10 other people put menorahs in their windows" (McCracken, "Windows with Menorahs Broken" A1). The fear tactics, then, were not working as the hate-mongers had intended. Instead, the town's climate of hope was becoming ever more recalcitrant.

Still, the neonazis continued their efforts. During the night of the vigil, "a brick and two rounds of gunfire shattered the windows at Billings Central Catholic High School . . . [where the school marquee read] 'Happy Hanukkah to our Jewish friends'" (Rosenblatt 30; Gaub, "Hands of Hate Strike" B1). More grisly still was the bow-and-arrow killing of a cat belonging to a family who had put a menorah in their window (Rosenblatt 30). The sporting goods store's billboard (featuring the nonviolent message) was shot at (*Billings Gazette*, "Violence Begets Violence" C10; Hartsig and Wink 55). Also, on December 15, six non-Jewish families had windows broken where menorahs were up (McCracken, "Windows with Menorahs" A1; Rosenblatt 30). Two windows were shot up by air rifles (Gaub, "Hands of Hate Strike" B1). Car roofs were stomped, and car windows were smashed (Gaub, "Windows Smashed" C4; Dobb 100). One car was left with the note "Jew lover" (Rosenblatt 30). After these retaliations by the hate groups, however, such incidents have abated. At least for today, a climate of hope prevails, however uneasily, over that of fear and hatred.

The Billings hate groups, for the time being, have retreated. The incidence of hate crimes have dropped in Billings "because the town had responded so well and so quickly to the hate crimes" (Rosenblatt 30). Dobbs reports that "the Schnitzers and others believe that the events of 1993 created a lasting solidarity in

Billings" (100). The churches that were targeted, and the Billings Gazette received hundreds of letters of support from across the United States (Olp, "Vandalized Churches" A5; *Billings Gazette*, "Billings' Solidarity Extolled" A4). The threatening phone calls, fliers, and property damage have been infrequent. At the same time, however, as pastor Freeman remarks, "You get the *feeling* that any time, anything could happen" (emphasis added) (*Not in Our Town*). Freeman has also said, "We're sitting on a tinderbox. What scares me the most is that the bigots are recruiting in the schools" (Rosenblatt 30). Freeman's observations, like Inman's, point to the problem of ignoring structural violence, which fosters the burgeoning of hate groups to begin with.[47] Until that issue is fully addressed, the climate of hope is all the more tenuous.

Dénouement

A portentous dénouement to these events is that Tammie Schnitzer and Sarah Anthony were each visited at their homes on separate occasions by James Pace, a leader among the skinheads (Rosenblatt 31; Safran 126). In March 1994, Pace was let into the Schnitzer's home by her young son:

> [S]uddenly Tammie found herself face to face with . . . Pace . . . "He said he wanted to see what a Jewish home looked like." *Frozen*, she watched as he strolled into her living room and seated himself. . . . "He told me *something big was going to happen* and showed me the swastikas tattooed on his chest. Then he left." (emphasis added) (Safran 126)

The "feeling" of being "frozen," and that there exists a probability for immanent change is, again, another sign of the competing rhetorical climates of fear and hope. Since then, Schnitzer has been accompanied by friends on her morning jog (Schnitzer, "Interview"; Safran 126), and the Schnitzers "keep their shades pulled down and often do not answer the phone" (Rosenblatt 44). The strain of the events caused the Schnitzers' marriage to crumble. Schnitzer herself felt compelled to have an elaborate security system installed in her home (Schnitzer, "Interview"). In addition, Chief Inman resigned under pressure from city officials, which has left a potential vacuum in Billings's nonviolent leadership (32). Also, the celebration of good triumphing over evil has been cast in doubt, with "people . . . wondering if the strong community response . . . would have been accorded . . . [an African American] or Hispanic family" (Rosenblatt 44). This highlights the fact that as long as the structural violence remains ignored, the potential for the climate of hate to return to ascendance will also persist.

The conditions for the rhetorical climate of hope and hate exist simultaneously, and as Rosenblatt observes in his report, "the atmosphere remains tense" (30). To ensure that hope prevails, it is up to local law enforcement officials and community members to continue the altruistic vigilance and solidarity against the hate groups while also examining the social, cultural, and material conditions that cause hate groups to form in the first place. As in many towns nationwide and worldwide where this kind of altruistic community support is missing, the structural violence of passive law enforcement agencies and the apathy of local citizens ensures that a climate of hate and fear endures.

DISCUSSION: UTILITY OF RHETORICAL CLIMATE CONSTRUCT

A rhetorical climate is to be distinguished from a speech text or *context*. Text, in the classical tradition, comes from the lone persuader. Likewise, context is what is most often studied as the standard, preliminary portion of any analysis of public address or other standard forms of rhetorical criticism. The preceding case demonstrates a way to handle multiple texts and a more dynamic, embodied sense of context. This case shows that the theoretical construct of a rhetorical climate can be useful and applicable to a more expansive range of persuasive communication events and texts.

This case shows that the construct of a rhetorical climate, as analytical tool, is useful. Critics can use the notion of a rhetorical climate to learn, understand, and explicate more fully the scenarios in which collectives of people, texts, and actions collide. In the case study just examined, had only *context*, or a *single text* within it been considered, the resulting study would have been very different. The successful altruistic campaign of the townspeople could have been seen as individually centered and spurred exclusively by the manly, John Wayne–style stance of the police chief. Or the comments of Tammie Schnitzer, as a targeted mother who courageously fights back, could have been examined as the primary focus of a different rhetorical study.

In other words, the traditional paradigm of rhetorical criticism usually promotes the rhetorical excellence of one single person, while other players, especially women and members of minority groups, recede into the shadows of the background. However, in light of a rhetorical climate, the rhetors, texts, and events become diffuse, collective. A rhetorical climate moves critics away from the comfortable grounding of the single text/single orator paradigm. Such diffusion opens room in rhetorical analyses for examining the chorus of meanings exposed through expressions of feelings, and how those meanings structure and motivate people to think, feel, and behave. This floating, unanchored approach also embraces the silence of the oppressed, who often must communicate in alternate ways. Silence, as alternately expressed (e.g., mood changes, weeping, or absence from work), is deemed as persuasive and as worthy of investigation as the most rousing speech.

A Leaderless, Nonviolent Theory

In traditional rhetorical criticism, it is likely that the critic would have analyzed Chief Inman's influential press statements in one study, or perhaps the *Billings Gazette*'s exposés on the hate crimes in another. Yet another study could focus exclusively on the symbol of the menorah itself, as drawn by the children or reproduced in the newspaper. These are all very individualistic orientations, in which one person (usually a white man) would get all the credit for the "success" of resolving or deescalating the conflict. Yet in the case just examined, the focus was on the descriptions of myriad factors, especially the expressions of feeling states of many women and men. These variables combined to influence the rhetorical climate and resulting actions of the inhabitants in that climate.

The combination of altruism, spread among communications networks ranging from the interpersonal to the town's journalists,[48] with the reinforcing rituals and belief systems of grassroots activists and religious organizations, all interpellated to foster a rhetorical climate of hope. This is a collectivistic, nonviolent orientation, involving the risk of sacrifice. In this case, mainly the windows of schools, churches, houses, and cars were sacrificed in order to make a neighbor feel safer, as well as to persuade the "skinheads" to stop their campaign of hatred and intimidation.

At the same time, and while there was no room in this particular study to deal with the problem, a rhetorical climate does enable us to recognize the plight of the neonazis as victims themselves. Hate group members' backgrounds often reveal they are victims of structural violence, such as poverty or child abuse; their actions can be understood in their own particular rhetorical climates (McCracken "Ex-white supremacists" A1).[49] Nonviolent theory recognizes the inherent flaws, contradictions, and conflicts that come with being human. Adversaries may be everywhere, but we can still coexist, with understanding, perseverance, and at times, sacrifice. The term "enemies" is as much a misnomer as "victims" and "victors" are misnomers, for as Gandhi wrote, "In the dictionary of . . . [nonviolent action], there is no enemy" (65).[50]

In a nonviolent view, there is less of a sense of a definitive "winner" or "success." Nonviolent struggle is not an end, but rather it is a means to handling conflict that is an inevitable part of life. Nonviolence is, as the pacifist A. J. Muste once said, not a means to an end but "a way." Much rhetorical criticism is concerned with "effective persuasion," with "success," or even with "eloquence" and textual beauty (for is not eloquence a testament to a kind of success or effectiveness?). Such criticism focuses on the individual (in Vatz's or Porrovechio's views) and the material text or context as "backdrop" (in Andrews's view). Individual-oriented criticism also makes it easy to overlook the struggles of groups or the triumphs or pitfalls of human cooperation, mutual interdependence and social influence. The waning popularity of studies on the rhetoric of social movements is a testament to the allure of individualism and materialism in much current critical orientation.

Scholars in organizational communication know well the importance of "climate" on the behaviors and actions of persons living and acting within a particular social milieu. In their study of industrial relations, Dastmalchian, Blyton, and Adamson contend that climate "has generally been viewed as a variable, or set of variables, that represents the *norms, feelings,* and *attitudes* prevailing at a workplace" (emphasis added) (31–32). They observe that such a diffuse, intangible definition has been viewed as questionable because it lacks clear "boundaries," it relies too much upon "aggregate data" which are not precisely "linked," and, overall, which are simply too "ambiguous" or "volatile" (31–32). They believe, however, that "such ambiguity is more methodological than conceptual" (31). Further, they note that individual variants among the determining "aggregate" factors do not impede a researcher from obtaining a clear picture of the climate being investigated (33). This perspective enables rhetorical critics to turn away from individual texts and orators, and toward collective texts and groups of rhetors.

Likewise, James Nave offers organizations a clear method for assessing their respective climates, and notes that the key factors in a climate are "*feelings . . . communication . . .* practices. . . . [and] *motivation* and *morale*" (emphasis added) (14–18). In addition, Berlin posits that people experience the world "interactively." As human beings, says Berlin, we "constantly attempt to make sense of and adapt to the events going on around us and within us to do whatever seems in the best interest of our goals and enhances our *feelings* of security and predictability" (emphasis added) (326). The concept of climate encompasses these interactive and motivational variables of human actions. Groundbreaking studies in cognitive theories and the social sciences, as well as in medicine, corroborate that intuitions and feelings are not only *not* irrational, but that they constitute human bases for sound reasoning, decision-making, and action. In short, new studies indicate that as human beings, our very rationality is based in feelings.

By conceptualizing rhetorical climates, critics can view various texts or acts as secondary, interrelated agents that work in concert to form a specific, if ephemeral, end result. In using rhetorical climate as an analytical tool, criticism is turned around so that we see the world through its *community*, through the feeling states of people working together to create social meanings and to make things happen.

Acknowledging the concept of a rhetorical climate enables critics to gain better insight into how structural (systemic or institutional) violence operates on its victims. Hate crimes, for instance, have been shown to *bodily* affect their victims, increasing the propensity for lethargy and inaction on the part of the victim (Lieberman 36; Nelson 50).[51] A climate imbued with structural violence, and reinforced by hate crimes, fosters social alienation. Saleebey notes that "[a]lienation rests on subjugation of the body and is often accompanied by a sense of numbness and lethargy, little access to bodily energies and resources, or peculiar bodily sensations" (115). If it can be shown that the rhetorical climate in other places and times contributed to the communities' inability to respond collectively and actively, the simplistic tendency toward creating heroes and villains becomes more complex. For instance, in the Billings case, victims of structural violence encompass both the makers and recipients of hate propaganda and terrorism (McCracken, "Ex-white Supremacists" A1).

CONCLUSION

Historian Carl Becker coined the phrase "climate of opinion" years ago and made it useful. Rhetorical critics can also learn from theorists in organizational communication who have long discussed the impact of "climate" on the day-to-day running of businesses. Scholars in organizational communication have been concerned with such intangibles as "employee morale" or developing on-the-job working "environments" that are free from sexual harassment and discrimination. Such studies constitute analysis of microclimates of rhetorical potentialities, change, and action. Sexual harassment laws, rationales for probable cause, legal statutes, and rules for understanding conduct in business and academic settings are based on the idea of assessing affective atmospheres or communication climates. If hard-nosed business managers are intrepid enough to ask for descriptions of intangibles in the corporate realm, why shouldn't rhetorical critics be able to do the same in the social realm?

Rhetorical theorists and critics have tended to rely on the more scientifically replicable notions of text or rhetor. Text is physical, material, and normally presented by the lone individual. Context has tended to be viewed as a static, structured moment in time, which tethers the range of critical vision. By focusing on single texts, critics may be more vulnerable to losing sight of the suasory force of collective actions as equally persuasive alternatives to a text produced by a single rhetor.

By expanding context and situation to include rhetorical climates, collective action may be better appreciated. "Climate is an intersubjective phenomenon that in its continuous structuring and restructuring affects individuals' actions and organizational outcomes" (Falcione, Sussman, and Herden 203). Through an appreciation of climate as a viable theoretical construct, rhetoric becomes decentralized. Accounts of events and perceptions of people existing within specific time frames can be revisited to establish rhetorical climates. If we follow organizational and other social scientific studies, we discover that attitudes, descriptions of feeling states or even body states such as the illnesses of "sick-building syndrome" or "yuppie flu" are very much intertwined. Just because something may appear to be invisible (in that it exists primarily perceptually) does not mean that it does not exist or that it does not influence the world in which we live.

Climate is interactional; it is ever moving, shifting, changing, and unpredictable. Climate is frequently "silent" or alternately voiced. Less visible than a text readily retrieved from an archive, climate relies on assessing changes in bodies, attitudes, feeling states, and environmental factors of whole communities. Climate is "a *joint* property" of people in specific locales and organizational environments (italics theirs) (Falcione, Sussman, and Herden 203). Climate depends more on descriptions than on obvious materialities. If we look beyond its apparent "ambiguity" or "fuzziness," climate can be revelatory as a theoretical construct (Dastmalchian et al. 31; Glick 606). Communication studies often incorporate fuzzy logic or knowledge maps revealing complex contributing factors in a problem situation. Therefore, purposefully *not* being precise can sometimes, perhaps paradoxically, yield the most clarity for understanding a given conflict or scenario. Above all, acknowledging the existence of rhetorical climates enables people who are politically and juridically voiceless and disenfranchised to speak as a collective, to be taken seriously, and thus to become empowered.

For the analysis of the rhetoric of social movements, collective action, organizations and corporations, or government agencies and community groups, the critical utility of the rhetorical climate construct is eminent. In particular, where there are groups of people who work in concert to achieve an end, the rhetorical climate is often more powerful, motivating, and actualizing in its suasory force than the specific speeches that occur in the climate itself. The focus shifts from "good man speaking well" to all people interacting rhetorically. In many cases, it is the climate itself that mobilizes and moves people. In addition, where people gather, the use of social norms, rituals, or even religious overtones of gatherings can, in light of the theory of conservation of previous gains, work to reinforce meanings and memories for the people involved (Donald 357).

The case in Billings, Montana, shows that the rhetoric of the human orientation toward cooperation and nonviolent action needs to be addressed, especially in view of the fact that their opposites have been researched *ad infinitum*. As Kenneth Burke has amply demonstrated, attitudes are important motivators for people existing in a particular place and time. Indeed, "[setting] a moral tone" is crucial to offsetting a sociosymbolic climate of violence (Martin 322), which myriad nonviolent activists from Rosa Parks to Martin Luther King, Jr., have proven (Galtung 27–30).[52] As the foregoing case in Billings, Montana—in "Big Sky country"—illustrates so well, key aggregates of the nonviolent social climate include civic responsibility and organized, compassionate action (Serow 107; Olson 400). The physical environment also clearly factors into the feeling states that form a rhetorical climate (Saleebey 112). A rhetorical climate as a theoretical construct may lend itself to being more forgiving and understanding, and less judgmental, of human behavior.

A rhetorical climate, like a passing storm, contains transitory and less readily visible elements, which can be daunting for the researcher to assess in order to conceive of the overall climate of a situation. Nevertheless, such obstacles are not insurmountable; they only require investigating areas normally outside the realm of conventional rhetorical criticism. Prior conceptualizations of rhetorical situations or contexts simply do not pay sufficient attention to—alas, even disavow—the play of force of the affective.[53] Until recently, traditional methodology has taught critics to seek tangible replicability. However, groundbreaking scientific studies in human cognition indicate that studies of affect are long overdue.[54] Just as an understanding of context enables critics to learn from texts, an understanding of rhetorical climates can enable critics to understand *social* and *feeling* states that propel people to act. It is now thought that "*true*" public or collective action operates more efficiently *without* persuasion coming from one person, and that the most persuasive element in a situation is each person in a group holding a "sense of responsibility and willingness to make sacrifices" (Mathews 403).[55] This view has important implications for developing rhetorical theory along collectivistic lines.

There is considerable supporting data for the view that a "climate [can be] more significant [in effecting behavior changes on the part of persons] than the type of leadership or the personal style" of a rhetor who "desires to motivate or lead people in a certain way" (Al-Shammari 32). People interacting within a given climate can experience a "shift in perspective" that is "in part . . . a function of self-discovery. When seeking to address a problem, for example, communities often will begin by looking for *the* solution. Eventually, however, they will discover that they *are* the solution" (emphasis in original) (Mathews 404). Such an orientation supports the nonviolent view that the conflicts are cyclic and inevitable, as well as that positive feelings and attitudes must be continually refreshed and renewed; there is no discrete, neat, tidy ending.

In much rhetorical criticism, the power to shift audience perspectives is still often studied via one person as the source of influential messages, while the power of the environment itself to move people to act (or not to act) has been marginalized to the status of a "backdrop." Conversely, contemporary social scientific studies provide evidence that alternative or collective voices and environmental cues are vital sources of influence.[56]

As shown in the case analyzed above, physical environment, feelings, and "moral imagination" are rhetorical. Being acted on and persuaded entails feeling states, experiences, anticipations, actions, and reactions. Rhetoric as an individualistic endeavor has focused on clear-cut equations featuring an orator, an audience, a material text, and a context or background. Bitzer's rhetorical situation, however, enables critics to blur such boundaries. To that blurring the concept of a rhetorical climate adds a collective orientation that values descriptions of personal attitudes and feelings that anticipate social actions. Fluid and quietly urgent, a rhetorical climate exists in its very contingency.

In a rhetorical climate, total *experience* supersedes oratorical texts and unique or socially privileged individuals as the foremost fonts of rhetoric. However inarticulate they may be, involuntary bodily and emotional expressions of frustration, anger, and fear or joy, hope, and kinship cannot be dismissed as outcasts of the rhetorical canon. Nor can a rhetorical climate be dismissed as "merely metaphorical." Embracing feelings and intuitions as rhetorical data enhances rhetorical criticism because it strengthens the critical capacity for revealing material and ideological injustices. The construct of a rhetorical climate helps us to expose the more easily ignored oppressions and socioculturally sanctioned silences that are suffered by children, women, and people of minority status.

CHAPTER 8

{🐍}

Conclusion:
Toward a Theory of Nonviolent Rhetoric

In a world where violence seems pervasive and all conquering, it is important to remember that it need not be that way; and, to a greater degree than most of us are led to believe, it really is not that way. Much peace exists and is believed in: the greatest world visionaries from presidents to poets do not wish to be remembered for conducting or commemorating wars, respectively, but rather, for creating and sustaining peace and justice. In order to create peace, justice must be advanced. For justice to be attained, people must persuade others that injustices exist and that they can be rectified. All of this requires a mastery of language, persuasion, verbal or visual symbols, and, increasingly, mass media: this is the stuff of rhetoric. Nonviolent rhetoric, that persuasion which is used to promote justice in order to create peace, is ubiquitous, powerful, and effective. The nonviolent collapse of British imperial rule over India; the successes of the Civil Rights movement in the United States to overcome segregation and Jim Crow laws; the largely peaceful fall of the Iron Curtain from the former Soviet Union; the end of Apartheid in South Africa; the persistent protests of meetings of the International Monetary Fund (IMF) and World Trade Organization (WTO); and protests against the war on Iraq increasingly show a global consensus that nonviolence thrives. The interrelationships among postcolonialism, the environment, developing nations' economies, and dependence on foreign oil are problems for everyone—not just the wealthy few—to solve. All of these world-changing events show that the rhetoric of nonviolence has made historic and peaceful changes, that nonviolence works, and that it is here to stay. Despite the terrible events of September 11, 2001, and the violent reactions in its aftermath, nonviolence will continue to be the most significant means of positive world change in the coming decades because, unlike large weapons and sitting-duck navies, it is accessible, at least in some degree, to every man, woman, and child on the planet.

Each of the case studies in the preceding chapters has provided insights into what nonviolent rhetoric is, how it functions, what its advantages and disadvantages are in terms of reaching various audiences in different social, political, and cultural milieus. This final chapter summarizes and examines the implications of the theoretical constructs discussed in the case studies. Ideally, these concepts will eventually lead toward the development of a theory of nonviolent rhetoric. This final chapter also suggests some reasons why it is useful for students and practitioners of rhetorical criticism to attain a working knowledge, understanding, and appreciation of nonviolent theory. At the same time, students and practitioners of nonviolence are invited to reap the benefits that a better understanding of rhetorical theory could yield.

INFORMING RHETORICAL THEORY
WITH NONVIOLENT THEORY

Nonviolent theory offers rhetorical scholars a window of opportunity for revitalizing rhetorical theory and criticism. Some rhetorical criticism has been encumbered by hidden assumptions of "human nature" that are steeped in the worldview that hierarchical power and violence are foundational and are, therefore, inevitable. Such a circumscribed perspective on human potentiality can lead to an unnecessarily cynical view of both human communicative interaction, as well as set unnecessary limits on democratic and egalitarian politics.

Theorists of rhetoric often seek to use rhetorical theory for the goal of exposing oppression and social injustice and praising rhetorical efforts at fostering justice. It can be difficult to create criticism that is supportive of justice, nonviolence, and peacemaking when worldviews used toward that end might unintentionally hamper one's efforts. Nonviolent theory can be useful to rhetorical critics in reaching the aims of promoting social justice and unveiling injustices.

Unfortunately, the study of nonviolent rhetoric has, on the whole, been left in the dust in the field of rhetorical criticism. After the 1960s and 1970s, nonviolent rhetoric all but disappeared in terms of theoretical discussion and critical attention that is informed by a solid understanding of nonviolent theory. In searches of revered anthologies of rhetorical criticism or in publications in the main speech communication journals from the 1970s onward (aside from the occasional essay on Dr. Martin Luther King, Jr., or perhaps on Gandhi), the keyword *nonviolence* yields lamentably little.

On a surface level, this attenuation of interest can be attributed to nonviolent rhetorics having been assumed to have been completely overtaken by other, more "real" or "pragmatic" rhetorics. Popular rhetorics of violence and war have held

center stage. The critical abandonment of nonviolent rhetoric, however, was facilitated by other more complex and interrelated factors, which I will recap here.

First, nonviolent rhetoric is a rhetoric that is usually convoluted and open-
ended.[1] As such, it does not fit well into, nor does it lend itself well to, the accepted and standard modes of rhetorical criticism it has been practiced since the
field of speech communication sprouted in the 1920s. This point is perhaps made
clearest by my work on the climate construct in chapter 7 of this book. The climate
construct bypasses the limits of individualistic orientation to rhetorical criticism
and enables the critic to assume a more collectivistic perspective. This collectivistic perspective can also be helpful in highlighting the political action of groups
that have been largely left out of the canon: women, people of color, people of
oppressed ethnic, religious, or political affiliations, and even children.

Indeed, shortly after the bedroom window of Tammie Schnitzer's son was
smashed, and before the town's menorah campaign had begun, Schnitzer heard
the doorbell ring. It was her neighbor and her neighbor's daughter at the front
door. The little girl, says Schnitzer, took her son, Isaac's hand, and led him to the
broken window. Speechless, Schnitzer watched as the little girl taped to the window a drawing she had made of a menorah. That little girl, Schnitzer avers,
showed everyone the right thing to do (Schnitzer "Speech"). The construct of a
rhetorical climate enables critics to be more encompassing of the rhetoric and
actions of people traditionally ignored in rhetorical criticism.

Second, nonviolent rhetoric has been misread as being "naive," "passive,"
"religious," and hopelessly utopian or utterly impractical. Nonviolent rhetoric
often has been (mis)judged by critics who espouse the prevailing view that presupposes that humans are "naturally" or "always already" predisposed to violent,
oppressive, and hierarchical modes and uses of power. Since the "truth" of this assumption is deemed incontrovertible, proponents of this view find nonviolent
rhetoric to be hopelessly lacking in *realpolitik* and, therefore, not rhetorically interesting. Both the rhetorics of Kiro Gligorov of Macedonia and Aung San Suu
Kyi of Myanmar (Burma), however, reveal the clear, calculated benefits that the
tailored usage of nonviolent rhetoric can bring.

Clearly, the lack of insightful publicity of nonviolent rhetoric does not necessarily mean that such rhetoric has no place or real effect in the actual workings
of society and the political world. It simply means that peace activists could benefit from becoming more aware of how their persuasive and symbolic attempts
will be perceived; many activists and other practitioners of nonviolence need to
develop more media savvy, and could do so through attaining at least a working
knowledge of rhetorical theory. Also, the notion that nonviolence is the fluffy,
nonsubstantive opposite of *realpolitik* should be questioned. When asked about

the practicality of the Truth and Reconciliation Commission's work in South Africa, Archbishop Desmond Tutu acknowledges openly that many people feel it is not worthwhile. Tutu argues, however, that "without forgiveness, there is no future."[2] Amnesty for unspeakable inhumanity, says Tutu, is the "price" South Africans must pay for peace. Tutu concludes that nonviolence is indeed very much oriented to *realpolitik* because it enables a more peaceful future to occur at all. Tutu has recognized that the country cannot move forward without understanding and, where humanly possible, forgiveness for the atrocities that took place during the long reign of apartheid. Tutu knows that the means to creating a peaceful new South Africa must be nonviolent. Of the work of the Commission to grant pardons to the perpetrators as a means to creating a process of healing and forgiveness, Tutu states,

> It is not enough to say let bygones be bygones. Indeed, just saying that ensures it will not be so. Reconciliation does not come easy. Believing it does will ensure that it will never be. We have to work and look the beast firmly in the eyes. Ultimately you discover that without forgiveness, there is no future. (Greer 4)

Forgiveness takes time. The Commission's work, albeit imperfect, since the fall of apartheid can be lauded for its long-term view, as well as for acknowledging the "price" of peace.

On the other hand, reconciliation has been rightly criticized by those who understand that more than interpersonal explanations are at stake. More work needs to be done to deal with the cultural and political violence that occurs through the sociopolitical structures and institutions that facilitated the interpersonal violence. Gross economic disparities need to be addressed. As one white South African puts it: "Can it be true that we got away with it?" These are the problems of transitional justice that must be grappled with in places ranging from Bosnia, Croatia, Kosovo, to Rwanda and in our own backyard here in the United States. There has been no symbolic reparation, nor even a mere apology, to Native Americans or African Americans for the well-documented historical genocides of ethnic cleansing, cultural "reeducation," and slavery.[3] And although it represents a step in the right direction, reparations of Japanese Americans who were interned in labor camps during WWII have been criticized for being too little, too late. The long-term jailings of nearly 1,000 mostly Muslim Americans, post 9/11, without trial have also been decried. Moreover, as chapter 3 indicates, the history of successes in nonviolence is absent from our educational curriculum in general, so topics such as the Japanese-American internment or the problems of the Patriot Act are seldom taught in most schools. Until the problems of the past have been addressed in a nonviolent manner, in which nonviolence and its rhetoric is clearly understood, historically based ethnic and racial injustices will continue, especially through the structurally hidden inner workings of political and economic systems.

The process of teaching and learning about nonviolence in theory and practice can be a powerful, symbolic start to a long road to recovering from centuries of race- and class-based violence. Nonviolence operates on a *kairos* of its own. Thus a long-term philosophy of healing time, combined with the nonviolent values of risk-taking, reconciliation, patience and a redefined sense of reason, can all be associated with the rhetoric of the humane arguer (Johnstone). These perspectives point the way toward a more prominent space in the canon for a specifically nonviolent rhetoric.

Tutu has been noted for saying, "Love thy enemy—it will ruin his reputation."[4] This kind of spiritual and religious form of nonviolent rhetoric, accompanied by a wry sense of humor, is the hallmark of other nonviolent practioners. Take Aung San Suu Kyi. Through a visually oriented form of nonviolent rhetoric, Suu Kyi has garnered much international attention for the plight of the people of Burma, in the totalitarian state otherwise known as Myanmar. Suu Kyi gains much-needed media attention in two key ways. One, she plays the essentialized part of Woman, in a modernized version of the "cult of true womanhood." She also enacts a subversive role as democratizer and modernizer by updating ancient, revered goddesses and packing them into her persona as a powerful, if mortal, sexy goddess of democracy.

Suu Kyi's nonviolent rhetoric relies on this visual sense. Her rhetoric depends on the mass media's endless need for themes like sex, heroism, beauty, elitism, and drama. While these themes may downplay the very real sacrifices Suu Kyi has made to promote a democratic vision for Burma's future, her nonviolent message has been flamboyant enough to gain token western sympathy, if not real economic and political support. Still, if South Africa is any indication as to how a more democratic society can take root out of a totalitarian state that is an abyss of systematic human rights abuses, gaining sympathy is an undeniably important first step in the right direction. After sympathy gains world attention, internal pressures, coupled with internationally applied economic and political sanctions, may one day topple the wealthy dictators as well as the sponsors and perpetrators of human rights abuses.

Another reason why the flourishing and prominence of nonviolent rhetoric in cultures and countries worldwide has gone largely unremarked on, unnoticed, and unanalyzed by theorists and scholars in rhetorical criticism is the predominately male, Eurocentric orientation in much of rhetorical criticism (until, say, the last 20-odd years). James Herrick notes that "the vast majority of writers acknowledged as shaping" the field of rhetorical theory "have been men" (256). Herrick adds that "excluding women from the rhetorical mainstream has resulted in the loss of women's meanings and thus . . . in the loss of women themselves as members of the social world" (257). Chapter 4 illustrates how popular culture and mainstream views of women in film contribute to both the loss of appreciating nonviolence and the loss of valuing women's voices and meanings. One of the aims in this book has been to participate, along with valuable works of rhetorical criticism such as *Women Who Speak for Peace*, in remedying this gap in scholarship.

The overarching rationale of this book is that if only rhetorical critics understood nonviolent theory better, perhaps our mission of using scholarship to subvert symbolic and linguistic oppression could be better served. Nonviolent theories offer a means to engage in a critical discourse that fights oppression. Joan Bondurant writes, "Throughout Gandhi's writings runs the quiet insistence that individual will and reason can effect social and political change" (35). Rhetoric is invoked implicitly here because discourse is a powerful means to expressing not only one person's will, but also, as we saw in chapters 6 and 7, the collective will. Willpower, risk-taking, openness to self-change, and tolerance are characteristics of nonviolent rhetoric. As chapter 6 indicates, other defining characteristics of nonviolent rhetoric include (but by no means is this list exhaustive; nor need *all* of these qualities be present at the same time) the following:

- it empathizes with, rather than demonizes, the opponent(s);
- it portrays all people as deserving of human rights, equality, and respect;
- it generally eschews metaphors that are violent (and that, therefore, confirm and condone violent behaviors);
- it relies on mutually agreed on feelings, facts and history;
- it is culturally respectful and aware;
- it relies on a sense of community and mutual responsibility;
- it evinces stubborn noncooperation with actions or systems perceived to be unjust;
- it displays an *ethos* of being an underdog; and
- it shows caring for the earth's ecosystems and creatures.

Rather than being based solely on coercion, hierarchy, and leadership, nonviolent rhetoric is informed by a more lateral and diffuse notion of power sharing. Nonviolent power comes from a kind of cooperative energy; it can be a compassionate energy that is the antidote to that institutionalized and oppressive disciplinary power that Foucault describes.

A nonviolent rhetoric seeks to channel people's energies and passions properly into constructive, practical activities that are, ideally, democratic and peace-yielding. As chapter 7 illustrates, the power of the *collective* to fight social, political, and cultural forces that constitute systematic, structural, and institutional violence needs to be taken into account. The willpower and rhetorical efforts of many peace-minded groups to nonviolently counteract oppression never really disappeared from the world in the 1960s and 1970s. Rather, it was primarily the *critical valuation and focus* on nonviolence that disappeared. There are countless individuals and many groups whose nonviolent rhetorics have flourished and continue to play a role in societies the world over. The courage of the people of East Timor in August of 1999 to risk their lives to take part in a vote for independence is yet one more example of the power of nonviolent rhetoric; it also points to the relationship of nonviolence to democracy. Considering the focus of journal articles and books in rhetorical criticism, many researchers have yet to have caught up with, much less understand, nonviolence as a continuing force for social change.[5] Of course there are exceptions, but I am concerned with the rule. To be sure, for scholars of communication theory who specialize in study areas such as interpersonal or organizational conflict, methods of nonviolent conflict resolution are more familiar. Communication theory tends to take more of an empirical form of scholarship, whereas rhetorical theory tends to be more qualitative. Moreover, each branch generally forms a distinct body of scholarship that tends to be published in its own, specialized journals. One concern in this book has been to note this distinction and to urge scholars of rhetoric and public address to more sufficiently engage with nonviolent texts and nonviolent theory because (1) such texts may be better illuminated by this theoretical grounding and (2) the field of rhetorical theory and criticism could be revitalized by this shift toward a more expansive, auspicious view of humanity's potential for achieving peace with justice.

Demystifying Nonviolence

Admittedly, there are good reasons why scholars of rhetoric and public address have seldom engaged with nonviolent theory. Nonviolent theory is not the most well articulated theory to date. Its terminology is still under development and key terms and concepts are even contested. The recalcitrant mystery surrounding nonviolence seems to render it suspect in the eyes of most people. Many people are skeptical about nonviolence and think of it as "just a philosophy for hugging trees at high tide and full moon" (McCarthy 9). However, nonviolence can be rather tough-minded and practical. Kiro Gligorov of Macedonia employed nonviolent rhetoric for the vital aim of keeping a small, weak, budding democracy from deteriorating into civil war. Macedonia has, thus far, and however tenuously, maintained a state of relative peace in the war-ridden Balkans. Macedonia's neighboring republics, in not only the utter absence of nonviolent rhetoric, but also with the media and policy-driven attention to violent rhetoric, have been unable to resist violence. One way this book is instructive to rhetorical critics is that it shows that nonviolent rhetoric is not a relic of the past, nor is it passive or impractical. This book shows how nonviolent rhetoric can be deconstructed, that it is not overly mysterious, and that it is alive and well in today's political world. Each of these case studies indicates ways that nonviolent rhetoric is both interesting and practical, and why it merits our critical attention.

In Marshall Rosenberg's popular book, *Nonviolent Communication: A Language of Compassion* (published in 1999), the relative strength of the individual is vastly overestimated while the key issue of structural violence is almost completely ignored.[6] Other books that purport to feature peace or nonviolence as communicative means fall short, too. Francis Beer's *Meanings of War and Peace*, for example, perhaps ought really to have been named *Meanings of War* because not a single definition—or even a full paragraph—of the book is devoted to any discussion of peace. In this way, scholars of rhetoric miss out on the potential insights that real analysis of meanings of peace and nonviolence might bring. The analysis of peace and nonviolent rhetoric in this book helps reveal both its strengths and limits at many levels beyond the interpersonal. These case studies also complicate and provide a more nuanced perspective on nonviolent communication and rhetoric than either Rosenberg's self-help, pop psychology genre or Beer's peace-is-war perspective can provide. In short, a crucial feature of this book is that it extends existing theories of nonviolent communication processes while questioning some of the more simplistic assumptions built into popular versions or facile interpretations of nonviolent theory.

For example, in chapter 7, the construct of a *rhetorical climate* further places into question the tendency, often evident in criticism, toward revering personal agency and having an overconfidence in the "rugged individual" to bravely handle oppression or conflict. The concept of a rhetorical climate lends itself well to studies that deal with the more subtle problems of structural and institutionalized violence. The concept of a rhetorical climate also complicates the forensic tradition of debate. The competitive, agonistic approach that is evident in much of the history and theory of rhetoric is only part of the story (Herrick 262). Instead of simplifying conflict into Us-Them dichotomies, the rhetorical climate construct encourages the critic to look into social, political, environmental, or other influences that foment conflict. Pure binaries of right and wrong, plus the need for judgmental, moral arguments, become less relevant to conducting criticism. So, too, does the rhetorical climate construct encourage a less individualistic perspective. Not unlike Kenneth Burke's comic frame, the notion of a rhetorical climate is an encompassing move that welcomes diverse people in conflict back into the human fold, rather than casting them out and dehumanizing them for their respective deviances or telltale signs of "otherness."

The implications of reexamining the role of community based agency are compelling. Examining nonviolent discourse and the ways it fosters constructive collectivistic action also challenges notions of violence as being intransigent, even in places like the Balkans or Northern Ireland. Ascertaining rhetorical climates can help highlight the existence of structural violence, such as, for instance, Orthodox ethnic Macedonian or Serbian discrimination against Muslim ethnic Albanians, or Protestant discrimination against Catholics, which results in gross economic disparities and continued conflict.

Simona Sharoni, Professor of Peace and Conflict Resolution, asserts that while society actively fosters military groups (both formal and informal, such as paramilitaries) that are crucial to both identity formation and to economic solvency of families in many societies, there are very few "alternatives [to violence] that are appealing" as well as economically helpful to people, especially "the younger generation" (qtd. in McCandless 24). Much nonviolent rhetoric precedes the necessary recognition on the part of the wider public of problems, which Patricia Hill Collins calls "intersectionality," that is, the interconnected problems of "racism, sexism, and gender discrimination" (Sharoni, as qtd. in McCandless 69; Collins "Intersections" 62). The promotion of justice that is designed to deal with problems of structural violence often begins with nonviolent rhetoric and social activism.[7]

Some aspects of rhetorical theory overlap with nonviolent theory, such as Aristotle's sense of rhetoric as "an offshoot of ethics," or Sonja Foss and Cindy Griffin's "invitational rhetoric." Through valuing different traditions of reasoning and social action, we can refresh our sense of rhetoric as a nonviolent means to creating positive social change. Nonviolent rhetoric operates by aiming to penetrate the thought and belief systems, the attitudes, the morale of oppressive or totalitarian systems and disciplinary structures. Nonviolent rhetoric helps clear the way for a renewed and honest public opinion and debate to reside within social and political systems. If language and rhetoric are understood as significant shapers of the way we perceive reality, then they can also be seen as a means to alter that reality and the social and physical entailments of it. Rhetoric is at the heart of cultural change. Cultural change can occur to foster peace just as much as it has been documented to foster war. The role of nonviolent rhetoric in fostering peace need no longer be underestimated. By demystifying nonviolent rhetoric, critics can contribute to promoting peace.

Redefining Processes and Time

Rhetoric, like nonviolence, is invested in notions of time. Classical theories of rhetoric were concerned with timing in a good speech. That particular knack of knowing the right thing to say or do in a particular moment in time was called *kairos*. Nonviolent theory has an interesting way of looking at time. Unlike much of the modern world culture's obsession with time and time-saving efficiency, the nonviolent perspective values fluidity and flexibility as well as a long-term approach to problem solving. In the 19th century, Thoreau and Tolstoy's thought gave way to Gandhi's philosophy of nonviolent direct action and rhetoric. Gandhi was *an* influence on Dr. Martin Luther King, Jr., in the early to mid-20th century, however, it is crucial to highlight the vital, deep influence that King's own father and grandfather had on his nonviolent work in civil rights. Gandhi is often erroneously credited as being the primary or sole influence on King's thought, when it was the rich tradition of the African American community and church that was steeped in nonviolent modes of civil resistance and communication.[8] This common misattribution, that is, citing King's sole source of inspiration as Gandhi while excluding his own, more influential family members, is further evidence that racism exists in culture and through curricula that exclude an accurate understanding of the history of minorities and women.

Political activists who employ nonviolent rhetoric, such as the Dalai Lama, Rigoberta Menchu, and Aung San Suu Kyi, have seen the value in taking the long view; time is not seen with the impatience that our speed-oriented culture takes. Criticism of Archbishop Tutu's work with the Truth and Reconciliation Commission in South Africa in part centered on how time-consuming the process of fact finding and reconciliation has been, and also on how many of the cases that were investigated remain open-ended and unresolved. Such criticism is typical of the modern obsession with perfect efficiency in terms of both time and results. It ignores the very real success the *process itself* has had in consciousness-raising and in moving forward constructively. As Joanna Macy, a professor and activist in human rights and preventing nuclear proliferation, states:

> I have come to suspect that our culture is in a denial of time. In addition to the problems of time speeding up—with the nanosecond measurement used in computers, and so on—there is a fear and loathing of time and, seemingly, a need to conquer it which, I suggest, comes from a patriarchal mindset that has the same view toward matter. . . . The challenge which I find myself pondering over is how to re-inhabit time. (qtd. in Ingram 147–48)

There is no reason to discredit the very real perspective in nonviolence that for a just peace to be achieved and maintained, it may take longer than just the span of one lifetime.

The process of healing is terribly slow, especially in societies in which transitional justice is at issue. This process is far slower than most modern norms for efficacy routinely allow. Nonetheless, the slow pace does not exclude the important role that nonviolent rhetoric and activism plays in creating a potential for transitional justice to be ultimately meaningful or successful. Standard measures of rhetorical success expand and become more forgiving of mistakes made along the way; forgiveness and healing entail making mistakes, trying, and sometimes failing. Gandhi himself called his life's mission his "experiments" with nonviolence; yet his sometimes imperfect work toward developing nonviolence in theory and practice continues to be refined, expanded, and improved by subsequent generations.

Through patience and a long-range perspective, the need for violence is reduced. As Johnstone has noted about our human tendency to make "excuses" so we can go to war, violence is ever the expedient in a conflict situation. The urgency of a given conflict situation can be channeled into what Gandhi called "feverish activity." This activity is positive energy; it is the humanizing willpower that challenges disciplinary power; it stems from the tolerant, humane, risk-taking arguer (Johnstone). Such motivated and other-oriented energy fosters an opting for the just way, the nonviolent way, of handling conflict situations.

Observers of nonviolent social movements may misconstrue the patient laying of the groundwork of the truth as "buying time" for the adversary. Dr. King was, and Aung San Suu Kyi of Myanmar (Burma) is, often criticized by those who misunderstood the slow pace with which nonviolent change often occurs. Nonviolent actors realize that using violence to topple systems often results in begetting anew violence. It did not go without notice, for example, the irony of President Clinton's public statement in the wake of the Columbine High School shootings in Colorado in 1999. While Clinton intoned that children needed to learn that violence was not the right way to handle conflicts, the U.S. armed forces were partaking in over 60% of the bombing raids over Kosovo and Serbia—violent raids that time and again resulted in the killing and maiming of scores of innocent civilians. Later, even the Pentagon admitted that their estimates of accurately hit targets were grossly overinflated.

As April Carter has noted, "One central tenet in the theory of nonviolence is that there must be congruence between ends and means. Means that are ignoble or destructive . . . will corrupt the ends . . . The belief that a just society could only be attained by good means was at the heart of Gandhi's philosophy and is maintained by later theorists of nonviolent struggle" (214). Nigel Young vouches for Carter's position, in stating that "the removal of an elite by coup no more guarantees real change of structure than the assassination of one member of that elite; too often the methods of the opponent are imitated—and its structures reproduced" (218).

One implication of this book is its revaluation of a form of political rhetoric that has been mostly forgotten in the field of speech communication, among other disciplines, for over two decades. For instance, had policy makers and rhetorical critics paid more attention to the nonviolent rhetoric of the likes of Ibrahim Rugova or Kiro Gligorov over 10 years ago, perhaps preventive measures might have been put into place to avoid the Kosovo conflict and war. There is a very practical rationale behind the nonviolentist's need to speak and behave non-violently: to do so, it is posited, will help ensure peace in the long run. It is worthwhile to wonder what might happen if observers paid more attention to nonviolent rhetoric in conflicts all over the world.

Instead, observers, diplomats and pundits, reporters and researchers have focused almost exclusively on violent rhetoric. It could be truly paradigm shifting were social critics and policy makers to focus at least as much (if not more) on non-violence than violence. Structurally violent institutional arrangements often follow popular violent rhetorics. Lives were needlessly destroyed by McCarthyism's red scare rhetoric; the cold war rhetoric that built great military might has also wrought massive environmental destruction; today, the continued, silent sanctioning of hate rhetoric in the U.S., passed off as "free speech," or "anti-terrorism" increasingly continues to incite gullible people to harm or even murder others on the basis of their race, gender, ethnic affiliation, or other defining characteristics.[9] Chapters 3 and 4 help illustrate how our cultural orientation and understanding of violence can often blind us to the very real possibilities of nonviolence in constructively managing conflicts.

Free speech itself, as protecting speech that fosters and incites murder, needs also to be reexamined in terms of a new world order. In the past, especially considering the United States' bellicose history, hate speech was a necessary and vital means to inciting people to sign up for the military and to fight in foreign wars. Propaganda campaigns in support of wars rely on the cultural norm of hate speech. In World Wars I and II, it has been well documented that the Japanese and Germans were particularly vilified through hate rhetoric. During the Vietnam War, historic hatred of Japanese as "representative Asian" translated fluidly into calling the Viet Cong awful, dehumanizing epithets. When the first Gulf War began, cartoonish signs appeared around my workplace at a government contractor near the Pentagon, with a parody on old Camel cigarette ads: "I'd walk a mile to smoke a Camel." Only here the picture was of a person riding a camel, in the target crosshairs of a rifle. It is not difficult to conclude that in a militaristic culture such as ours, an "extreme tolerance" for hate speech is necessary to propagate a culture of war. Post 9/11, hate speech often hides behind patriotism.

Because peace and nonviolent rhetoric calls into question the sanctity of various forms of hate speech, its very existence endangers the longevity of economies and cultures like ours that are propped up by the military. No wonder, then, in 2002, two mild-mannered peace activists found themselves inexplicably detained and unable to board their flights: they discovered that someone in the U.S. Government had put their names on the *same* "no fly" list as suspected members of the Al Quaeda terrorist network. This was later deemed a "mistake" by the government. It is a rather telling mistake, indeed, because on a literal and symbolic level, so misunderstood is peace activism, that government bureaucrats deemed *activism for peace* as dangerous as terrorist violence and activism for war. At the same time, this should also be a call for peace activists to better articulate nonviolent aims, methods, and imagery to the mainstream public so that peace activism can be understood for what it is: an integral part of the design of a healthy and working democracy.

Western society tends to focus heavily on, and sanction, violent rhetoric, while ignoring nonviolent rhetoric, aside, perhaps, from the occasional sermon. The research conducted and summarized in this book leads me to conclude that this emphasis on violence can circumscribe our inclination and ability to make peace in our own lives, as well as in our communities. This overemphasis on moralizing about violence also appears to impact international diplomacy: Some argue that President George Bush II's infamous "Axis of Evil" phrase undid years of subtle, behind-the-scenes diplomatic work—real progress toward peaceful relations—in the countries he identified as "evil," especially Iran. In contrast to such violent and forceful rhetoric, the work in chapter 7 indicates compelling ways that nonviolent rhetoric creates positive, constructive social change that can serve as a model for other communities experiencing conflicts and violence stemming from intolerance. Nonviolent rhetoric appears to operate in cross culturally universal ways so that it can be tailored to deal with conflicts in diverse places. Cross-cultural understanding is desperately needed to bridge the Christian-world/Muslim-world divide that has deepened in the post-9/11 era.

In the view of the nonviolent theorist, to use violence, contrary to the mythic paradigm of might and power under which many political analysts of many governments currently labor, mainly operates rhetorically to validate and sanction further violence. Even the government has a term for this: "blowback," of which Osama bin Laden and company are prime examples. Zealously protecting hate groups whose rhetoric promotes violence and intolerance is now being questioned due to exigencies created by Timothy McVeigh, Columbine, and 9/11. Of course, the concern now of the American Civil Liberties Union (ACLU) and others is that the pendulum is swinging too far in that direction, and that the free speech and civil rights, even of alleged terrorists, need to be protected. However, what is clear is that there is real cause for concern with regard to hate rhetorics, especially in societies where poverty and lack of education that emphasizes critical thinking can lead to public susceptibility to hate propaganda. In developed nations, industries and organizations whose products are deemed pernicious to the health of the general public or to the democratic stability of a country are often taxed and heavily regulated by legislation and litigation (i.e., cigarettes, drugs, or Nazi paraphernalia). Perhaps one day hate speech, like tobacco or pollution, will be considered a threat to the health of the general public. Maybe hate rhetorics can be seen as indicators of a conflict that needs resolution, active prevention, and intervention, rather than reactive litigation, usually after innocent people have already been killed. It is telling that to gain a government security clearance or citizenship in the United States, one needs to sign a statement affirming that one is not a member of the Communist party. This seems outdated, even silly, considering that the statistically more real threat to democracy today appears to be a belief in hatred or a membership in organizations that promote intolerance, hate, and terrorism. The United States, like other countries, has yet to have caught up with perceiving the most pressing rhetorical threats of the times.

The threats that exist in a multicultural and diversely peopled world are threats that single out specific persons for specific defining attributes. In light of the research presented in chapter 7, it seems that governments instead ought to ask whether or not applicants for citizenship or government jobs condone injuring other persons based on religious, political, economic, gender, sexual orientation, ethnic affiliation, and other defining attributes of "otherness." In the long run, preventive nonviolence appears to be more of a realistic and practical—as well as cost- and life-saving—approach to fostering both peace and democracy. One contribution this book makes is that it focuses on nonviolence as one useful means to fostering respectful cooperation as both the process and the end product of democracy.

TRANSFORMING PERCEPTIONS OF POSSIBLE PEACE THROUGH RHETORICAL MEANS

The rhetorical notion of humans as beings who are conceived through language also points the way to nonviolence. Language structures not only our interactions with others, but also our sense of self-identity. Henry Johnstone, as a rhetorical scholar, believes this occurs through the risk factor that occurs in the process of reasoned and fair argumentation (9). Johan Galtung, a peace studies scholar, emphasizes that structural violence is imbedded in our very language structures and that violence as internalized in one's self identity must therefore be exposed (10–14). Galtung explains how we usually only think of violence in terms of it being "personal" or the "subject" of some "drama." Galtung notes that simple and identifiable "subject-verb-object" relationships seen in most Indo-European languages serve to keep the focus on individual persons, when the source of even greater violence is hidden and "built into structures" (11). This hidden violence is not so easily expressed in language, and if it cannot be expressed, it is more difficult to protest about.

As Foucault finds with the rhetoric of disciplinary institutions, the rhetoric of social experience as practiced *en masse* also needs to be examined. Galtung explains that interpersonal violence (which he calls personal violence) is more easily protested, whereas institutional, disciplinary, impersonal violence (which he calls structural violence), is more difficult to pinpoint and express. The diffuseness of structural violence is a difficult property to address, but it is one that nonviolence can aid in aggregating, identifying, and decrying.

Galtung offers the example of "when one husband beats his wife there is a clear sense of personal violence, but when one million husbands keep one million wives in ignorance there is structural violence." Correspondingly, "in a society where life expectancy is twice as high in the upper as in the lower classes, violence is exercised even if there are no concrete actors one can point to as directly attacking others, as when one person kills another" (11). Galtung argues that because "personal violence shows," whereas structural violence is more difficult to observe, analyze, and articulate (12), researchers in the academy should reflect that "a research emphasis on the reduction of personal violence at the expense of a tacit or open neglect of research on structural violence leads, very easily, to acceptance of 'law and order' societies" (13). This is an important reason why rhetorical scholars' inquiry should not be limited to speeches and to rhetorical artifacts that decry only personal, observable violence. Instead, inquiry should, in Johnstone's words, "expand and consolidate" toward exposing the diffuse texts of structural violence while shifting the focus toward making a permanent "escape" into the realm of peacemaking (8–9).

The case studies in this book constitute a call to read the hidden social texts of inequalities buried in language. These case studies illustrate how rhetoric can serve to obscure violence by hiding it in silences or terminologies of hierarchy and respect. The research of nonviolent scholars paves the way for rhetorical scholars to question the institutional language of authority and discipline. By understanding the "hidden" language of structural violence, rhetoricians can use their analyses as a tool to fight such "silent" oppressions as those revealed in deadly statistics or courtroom rhetoric. The eloquence of Jonathan Harr's *A Civil Action* (1995), the haunting, nonfiction book describing the failure of the American justice system, is a testament to the fact that inquiry into structural violence can make for gripping, page-turning analysis.

Meanwhile, the rhetorical examination of the successes and failures of peace symbols that are used in nonviolent peace activism should also prove instructive to peace activists. In the current, conservative political and economic climate that is exacerbated by centralized, corporate media structures, peace activists cannot continue to operate with the same doggedly idealistic, 1960s-era beliefs that just being right means one's side of the story will be reported that way. Peace activists concerned with creating exposure for nonviolent change must become more media savvy and rhetorically aware so as to present messages that can promote and effect change under arduous circumstances. To a certain extent, the stereotype of the hippie-garbed, drum-beating, Kumbaya singing, stoned peace protester is an accurate one, at least insofar as the mainstream TV viewer or newspaper reader sees images of these kinds of persons routinely in the news. Yet all of the research and activism of peace activists and scholars summarized in this book indicates that, to the contrary, they are exceedingly smart, hard-working people. This disjuncture between perception and reality can be overcome. But peace activists will need to work extra hard in the coming years to counter the stereotypical image and replace it with a fresh, new, innovative rhetoric that can penetrate the media monoliths and mainstream public stereotypes. In short, laypersons and rhetorical critics alike can benefit from understanding nonviolent theory and perspectives as much as peace and justice activists can benefit from understanding rhetorical processes such as persuasion, audience identification, and media analysis and adaptation.

CONCLUSION

Conflict among people is as old as the beginnings of our species. Increasingly, however, we are learning that many methods of peaceful conflict resolution are just as old. The notion that violence and war is a "normal" and history-drenched phenomenon for humankind needs to be balanced with the archaeologically and historically proven fact that humans have been equally interested in creating and maintaining peace on the interpersonal, community, national, and international level. The imbalance in the reporting of this human record needs to be acknowledged. To that end, this has been an introductory exploration into the rhetoric of nonviolence. The goal of this book has been to identify specific constructs of discourse and communication practices that foster peacemaking so as to develop a foundational conception of nonviolent rhetoric. The spotlight in this book has been on the interrelationships among nonviolence, rhetoric, and promoting peace-oriented and egalitarian democracies.

Each of the case studies explored some of the distinct forms of nonviolent rhetoric. Chapters 2 and 3 provided a background and raison d'être for this study. Chapter 4 offered a popular culture perspective on nonviolence. Chapter 5 took the traditional approach of looking at a "good man speaking well," while emphasizing the advantages and disadvantages for a politician of employing a practical and pragmatic mode of nonviolent rhetoric. Chapter 6 focused on the role of essentializing in nonviolent rhetoric, as well as the importance of appetizing visual presentation in a mass-mediated, global nonterritory. Chapter 7 emphasized the spontaneous and collectivistic appeal of nonviolent rhetoric.

Each case study reveals how a better understanding of the connection between rhetorical theory and nonviolent theory can be put to practical applications. This research supports a rationale for *preventive* politics that entails a solid understanding of nonviolent rhetoric. This research focuses on the role nonviolent rhetoric plays in the complex and paradoxical business of *conjoining diversity*, which is a gargantuan peacemaking process desperately needed all over the world.

Finally, I hope these case studies spur questions and discussion about the implications that nonviolent rhetoric holds for the universal expansion of human rights in a nonterritorial sense. Nonviolent rhetorics seem to point toward a changing global political landscape in which sovereignty and inhumane versions of capitalism are increasingly being challenged. As Virginia Woolf said, "I have no country, my country is the whole world" (as qtd. in McCandless 69). The protests in numerous cities worldwide, in the early 2000s of the World Trade Organization and World Bank, and global protests of the war on Iraq in 2003, indicate that nonterritorially oriented nonviolent political action is here to stay.

Gradually, national sovereignty as an excuse for ignoring human rights abuses, including those related to capitalistic ventures, is coming under attack. So, too, does the notion of "free speech" become problematic when modern hate speech is (1) tacitly sanctioned by corporate institutions and discourses of hegemonic intersectionality; (2) so alluring to the uneducated or vulnerable audiences to whom it is most often directed; and (3) so deadly to those people against whom the diatribes are directed. At present, there are no hard-and-fast answers to the questions growing from these case studies, but this body of research shows that more attention needs to be paid to nonviolent rhetoric and perspectives.

By surveying these case studies, we see that nonviolent theory challenges, agrees with, and sometimes contradicts existing rhetorical criticism as it is commonly practiced. While we have studied the world of adversarial relationships, conflict, difference of belief, rhetorical critics have not done quite as well with understanding the practices of seeking for mutual identification, cooperation, and learning how to live more sensitively with diversity and adversity.[10] Nonviolent theory offers to the rhetorical theorist and critic added insights into the conduct of debate over public policy, political activism, and communication forms that support or decry authoritarian structures of society. Nonviolent theory espouses democratic visions for public debate in openly mediated channels. Nonviolent theory challenges the history[11] and traditional views that often characterize rhetoric as inherently "power over" people by showing that rhetoric can, and often does, mean "power with" people.

This book is an exploration of how nonviolent theory supports the notion that humans can argue fairly and arrive at mutual understanding through a risky process of tolerance and self-conversion. Nonviolent theory shows that rhetoric can fulfill the classical, Isocratean ideal of *paideia*: nonviolent rhetoric can be an educational tool to achieve Gandhian ideals of uplifting all human beings by mutually valuing and respecting one another. Nonviolent theory posits that language and culture, our ways of creating and perpetuating our reality, can be devoid of, or impose minimal, aggression. Indeed, human beings are believed to be inherently "amiable," or at least possessing far less aggression than traditionally thought. On the other hand, aggressive energies, when channeled via cultural and structural violence into hate rhetoric, can foster debilitating climates of fear that lead to violence. Conversely, altruistic energies, when channeled through nonviolent rhetoric, can create more peaceful communities. Nonviolent rhetoric supports more peace-minded means to handling, or better yet, *preventing* conflict situations.

The implications for theorizing a nonviolent rhetoric are made manifest. From the research of nonviolent theorists, it is clear that human beings are creatures often schooled in violence, and, as such, we can just as well be schooled in nonviolence. As Henry Johnstone advises, we need not take a "cynical view of human nature" (6). Nonviolent theory provides new insights not only into our uses of communication, but also into the very real human potential for peacemaking that is so desperately needed for coexistence in a world of confusing diversity. Nonviolent rhetoric, however fallible, undeniably channels peacemaking through local, regional, or international *realpolitik*.

Rhetoric and Nonviolence

This Appendix provides a brief look at how theories of nonviolence relate firmly to rhetoric. I will refer to rhetoric in two different, but interconnected senses. There is rhetoric as human communication and rhetoric as shaping our actions. Rhetoric comprises a rich tradition of study descended from such Classical thinkers as Aristotle and Plato. Still, 2,500 years later, and despite remarkable historic movements in nonviolence such as those of Mohandas K. Gandhi in India and Martin Luther King, Jr., in the United States, theories of rhetoric have largely excluded theories of nonviolence. This gap in scholarship exists to the detriment of rhetorical theory.

Kenneth Burke, the great 20th-century scholar of rhetoric, wrote that, "Even if any given terminology is a *reflection* of reality, by its very nature as a terminology it must be a *selection* of reality; and to this extent it must function as a *deflection* of reality" (45). Rhetoric, then, structures our very reality. It shapes our belief systems and our perceived potentialities. Another question revisited in various forms in each of the case studies examined here is this: What does it mean for our reality—indeed for our human potential for survival on this planet—if nonviolence and a peaceful orientation to handling conflict are better understood?

Language, persuasion, and the symbols that constitute the realm of rhetoric have long been regarded as the repository of our worldly facades. From the way we relate to people on an interpersonal basis to the way we perceive the public speeches of our politicians, we are trained to be wary, cynical disbelievers. Some scholars, such as Sally Miller Gearhart, have argued that rhetoric as we know it is inherently violent, than any attempt to persuade is an act of violence. But this is just one side of the story. There exist and have always existed resilient people like civil rights leader Medgar Evers or human rights activist Harry Wu, who have risked their lives to tell the truth, to persuade, to use language and rhetoric for the best interests of humankind. The legacies of such people are often lost amid a language and rhetoric of might, power, and a de facto reverence for war-making and violence (Tolstoy 177–95; Huxley 195–203).

In today's pop culture, rhetoric is frequently synonymous with hollow, empty discourse. Rhetoric's negative (and often, violent) connotations have been emphasized in myriad studies, including Gearhart's "The Womanization of Rhetoric." Gearhart went so far as to say that "any intent to persuade is an act of violence" (195). There is, however, another side to rhetoric that can be emphasized through an understanding of nonviolence in theory and practice (Holmes 1–6). An understanding of nonviolent theory also endows social observers and critics with a modicum of hope for humanity. An open-minded understanding of nonviolence enables us to recover a sense that communication can be used both idealistically and practically. From a nonviolent perspective, there is room for a renewed sense that rhetoric can be a force for active social change; rhetoric can be a means to managing conflict without, or at least with minimal, violence.

In his brilliant introductory essay, "Gandhi and the One-Eyed Giant," a preface to *Gandhi on Non-Violence*, Thomas Merton, the famous monk-scholar-sage, draws a clear boundary around the interrelationship between nonviolent action and persuasion. He discusses the classical notions of selfless political action, and notes the centrality of words in creating a space for social change. "It is in the public and political realm that [one] shares *words* and deeds, thus contributing [one's] share of action and thought to the fabric of human affairs," Merton writes: "Now, the public and political realm is that where issues are decided in a way worthy of free [people]: *by persuasion and words, not by violence*" (emphasis added) (7). Thus, nonviolence and rhetoric meet in the public sphere of action and speech.

Definitions of rhetoric from centuries past and present relate to Merton's definition of the ideal nonviolent political actor and action. Aristotle defined rhetoric as a "faculty of observing [or discovering] in any given case [all] the available means of persuasion" (24). In Kenneth Burke's theories of rhetoric, humans are symbol using and abusing beings—beings who are characterized by traits like cooperation, identification, and persuasion. Burke, especially in his use of the comic frame, can be said to offer us a framework for understanding nonviolent rhetoric in contemporary theory. For Merton, an agent of nonviolent change is someone who opts to use "persuasion and words" rather than "violence" to accomplish goals in society. Equipped with what Aristotle called a special "faculty," people gauge situations and stubbornly refuse to support violent regimes or politics. Using what Burke emphasized as rhetorical, that is, words, symbols, and human bodies, people cooperate to challenge and sometimes topple injustices. That is what nonviolent rhetoric is all about.

There are the likes of popular figures, such as the Dalai Lama or Thich Nhat Hanh, best selling writers, and jet-setting lecturers, whose nonviolent rhetoric advises us to incorporate nonviolent modes of behavior into our everyday lives in order to further world peace. There are scholars and activists like bell hooks or Alice Walker who encourage us to shed the shackles of structurally violent habits and to live and work to create justice, which fosters peace.

Clearly, we see there are politicians, thinkers, and doers everywhere with whom we associate a nonviolent worldview and peaceful persuasion. Aside from moral and ethical guidelines, however, we lack a set of criteria that enable us to examine and break down the fuzzy imaginary line between rhetoric that on the one hand aids violence from rhetoric on the other that aids nonviolence. It is vexing to evaluate rhetoric in terms of nonviolence and an orientation toward peacemaking when so much of the rhetorical tradition is steeped in the notion that might rules.

Much has been written in the field of rhetoric about violence, but precious little has been written about rhetoric vis-à-vis nonviolence. In addition to Gearhart, rhetorical scholars such as Stephen Browne note that rhetoric itself has long been synonymous with brute violence (55). The opposition of violence and nonviolence is clearly an unsatisfactory pairing. In theory and practice, there is really a continuum and symbiotic relationship between nonviolence and violence. We need to trouble our conventional ways of understanding rhetoric.[1] Even if we were to oppose rhetorics of violence to rhetorics of peace, the comparison remains unsatisfactory. All such comparisons are inherently lopsided because only a tiny fraction of rhetorical theory is written on peace-oriented rhetoric, whereas vast volumes of writing have been devoted to the alluring topic of war rhetoric.

An important component of nonviolent theory and activism to the *satyagraha* (roughly translated as soul-force; Truth-force; and love-force) of Gandhi's practice is persuasion. Thus the focus is on the interrelationship between nonviolence and rhetoric. In this appendix, I describe some of the main forms of nonviolent persuasion and communication. So that each of the case studies of this work as whole make more sense, I briefly summarize here literature from peace studies and nonviolent theory. I posit that persuasion and human communication—rhetoric—can be nonviolent and peace minded when it exists in the spirit and context of promoting justice and human rights. As Crosswhite has said, "The great tradition of rhetoric" is not so focused on "remedying . . . deficits" such as fixing grammar mistakes, but rather "as the realization of a certain kind of human potential" (4). The "human potential" that I believe is so powerful both rhetorically and socially is nonviolence. My assumption is that a better understanding of the connection between rhetorical theory and nonviolence theory can aid in practical applications. This practical knowledge can be used to help transform human interactions into a more peaceful ones.

FORMS OF NONVIOLENT RHETORIC

In her seminal book, *Conquest of Violence: The Gandhian Philosophy of Conflict*, Joan Bondurant cites as a fundamental rule of *satyagraha* in action the "[p]ropagation of the objectives. . . . Propaganda must be made an integral part of the movement. Education of the opponent, the public, and participants must continue apace" (38). Normally, one might take issue with the use of propaganda, since it is considered a coercive or violent form of persuasion, yet Bondurant is adamant that this form of persuasion is for the "education of the opponent, the public, and participants." The rhetorical intent of nonviolent "propaganda" is merely to promote awareness and understanding of the issues at hand, the problems that activists have with a given opponent, and the strategies that the nonviolent activists will undertake to overturn the perceived injustices. In this context, Bondurant's invoking "propaganda" can be seen as synonymous with softer terms, like public relations, or even with the classical notion of *agon* (debate in the public sphere) or critical thinking. Rex Ambler states that "the opponent has to be helped to *read* our actions by generous *explanation* and by the *general tone* of the campaign" (emphasis added) (200). Thus, the nonviolent text, as written, spoken, or enacted, is reflexive; the opponent, as audience, is also a *participant*, and must be instructed as to how to engage; the opponent must be trained, in a sense, to read the text, the discourse, or the actions as *rhetoric*.

A fine example of such a "propaganda" text that trains its audience in the principles of love, peace, and nonviolence would be Dr. Martin Luther King, Jr.'s "Letter from a Birmingham Jail." Here, King addresses the misconceptions and misgivings his adversaries hold regarding the progress of the civil rights movement, while he educates them and the public about the strategies of nonviolent action (which often seem mysterious to the uninitiated). King clearly states his objective: "I am in Birmingham because injustice is here" (68). King clears the smoke away from the nonviolent tactics, informing his detractors, who refused to remove symbols and laws perpetuating racism from the city, "We had no alternative except to prepare for direct action, whereby we would present our very bodies as a means of laying our case before the conscience of the local and the national community" (69). King draws up ethical, moral, and legal arguments firmly on his side. He invokes the democratic ideal of "human rights" while reminding his opponents that even the "Supreme Court's decision of 1954 outlawing segregation" is yet to have been fulfilled. Thus, through truth, through myriad examples of the courage of nonviolent activists in the face of intimidation and suffering, King reveals the injustices of those who oppose him, especially the members of the clergy, whom he addresses specifically. In short, King's rhetoric trains and educates his audience in how to *read* anew the events of recent history.

Rhetoricians have, thus far, focused most on King's manifest stylistic elements; critics have trailed off into side discussions of whether or not, or how much, King plagiarized some of his messages of peace and nonviolence. These sidebars miss the point of nonviolence and rhetoric together. By focusing on such peripheral issues, we have to a certain extent hindered our ability to understand both rhetoric and nonviolence as a cohesive whole. More than a masterpiece of style or superior argumentation, King's rhetoric in general, and this letter in particular, constitute the educational "propaganda" of Bondurant's nonviolent schema. King's texts remain free from any of the pejorative connotations that the word "propaganda" normally carries in the context of rhetoric as supporting the ends of war and violence. To heck with style: King's is a lesson in nonviolence and rhetorical praxis. It is "propaganda" in a campaign of nonviolence that exudes compassion—even for one's adversary—and a fervent desire for mutual understanding. Understanding rhetoric through the lens of nonviolence recovers the *content* of King's message and shifts emphasis from the message's mere trimmings to its focus on and appeals to justice and human rights.

Written texts can provide powerful nonviolent rhetoric. As part of the "agitation" step in the *satyagraha* campaign, Bondurant cites "an active propaganda campaign together with such demonstrations as mass-meetings, parades, slogan-shouting" (40). Again, we see that this rhetoric is firmly contextualized in the nonviolent escalation of the conflict through public awareness and public relations gambits, such as the New York City protest of police racism and brutality in the murder of Amadou Diallo. This extended mass protest provides a contrasting example to King's public "Letter." It is an instance when the nonviolent activists are not the sole authors of the "educational" text written for the public. The cooperation with newspapers (52) and other media figures importantly in educating the public about key issues of contention. This method of joining with members of the media to foster an environment of critical thinking and debate is crucial to the success of a nonviolent social movement. At the same time, relying on the media to announce the message also supports the notion that nonviolence requires certain preconditions for it to succeed. An open and relatively free media is one of those preconditions.

Other recent examples of such a media-oriented form of "agitation" would be the "Million Man March" and the "Million Woman March" respectively, which entailed massive preparations, "propaganda" articles in major newspapers covering and explaining (hence, educating) the public of the purposes of the marches. Beyond the texts promoting education and awareness in the general public are the texts of the speeches that conclude the marches. Another kind of dramatic "text" to read is the actual symbolic act of marching peacefully under the watchful eye of the public and the authorities. This kind of symbolic action spurs media coverage as well as public-policy debate. In the best of cases, legislation and other proactive social work are initiated to foster positive changes that redress the grievances of those who are marching or enacting the other forms of nonviolent symbolic action.

Looking closer at the various kinds of rhetoric that fall under Bondurant's general label of "propaganda," we see that nonviolent action relies heavily on *texts purveyed publicly*. Gene Sharp, one of the best known scholars of nonviolent action, lists the above-described forms of nonviolent texts among "198 Methods of Nonviolent Action" (473). He cites, for example, "formal statements," "communications with a wider audience," "group representations," "symbolic public acts," "processions," and "drama and music" (473–74). Any rhetorical theorist would have to agree that these forms of nonviolent action all fall within the range of typical research interests. Appendix Table 1 below lists examples of the types of texts that lend themselves to nonviolent interpretation and rhetorical analysis.

From this representative selection of Sharp's examples of nonviolent action as listed in Appendix Table 1, we see that nonviolent theory and action are firmly planted in the realm of rhetoric. Rhetoricians tend to focus on ways that humans use communication and persuasion as resistance to oppression, yet they routinely ignore the fact that nonviolent engagement in conflict is a *special mode of persuasion* with a distinct history of success. What I believe is happening is that sometimes critics are stuck in a rut of invoking social theories and theories of rhetoric that are heavily based in our understanding of violent or hierarchical representations of communication and human existence. Because of this orientation, when we examine rhetorical acts, such as those like King's cited above, rhetoricians may be losing insights into the nature of rhetoric itself. Simply put, nonviolent action and rhetoric stem from a universal tradition and discourse of compassion and empathy that spans the globe and encompasses all major political, religious, and philosophical traditions through time.

Much of rhetorical theory follows the "reasoning" or "logical" tradition, which tends to value the scientific or mathematic perspective. A scientific perspective might be the Darwinian one, for example, that internalizes some sort of fight for survival and naturalizes it into an accepted state of human affairs, and a way to understand conflicts in life as various kinds of violences or war. Such a perspective is not particularly hopeful for humankind. For instance, rhetorical scholar Mark Moore writes that "cynicism" is today's definitive rhetorical trope.[2] In other words, it has been my experience that rhetorical theory is often informed by essentializing human beings as aggressive or violent, à la Freud. This is not to say that rhetoric, or scholars of rhetoric, ought to become the "heavy" in this study. Quite the contrary: rhetoric is a useful foundation and the love of my scholarly life.

APPENDIX TABLE 1.
EXAMPLES OF NONVIOLENT RHETORIC

Formal Statements	Public speeches; letters of opposition or support; declarations by organizations and institutions; signed public statements; declarations of indictment and intention; group or mass petitions
Communications with a Wider Audience	Slogans, caricatures, and symbols; banners, posters, and displayed communications; leaflets, pamphlets, and books; newspapers and journals; records, radio, and television; skywriting and earthwriting
Group Representations	Mock awards, group lobbying, picketing, mock elections
Symbolic Public Acts	Displays of flags and symbolic colors; wearing of symbols; prayer and worship; delivering symbolic objects; protest disrobings; destruction of own property; symbolic lights; displays of portraits; paint as protest; new signs and names; symbolic sounds; symbolic reclamations; rude gestures
Drama and Music	Humorous skits and pranks; performances of plays and music; singing
Processions	Marches; parades; religious processions; pilgrimages; motorcades

Source: Gene Sharp, "198 Methods of Nonviolent Action" (473-74).

What I would like to merely emphasize, however, is that there is an underlying sense of "reason" or "logical reasoning" in much theory that goes something like this: since people have always been at war (actually or metaphorically), this rationale goes, we always *will* be at war. Therefore, critics may sometimes apply incommensurate or overly constricting standards to measure the "logic" or "effectiveness" of a form of discourse that may operate on different planes of socially constructed reality. Nonviolent rhetoric often operates on emotional, moral, or ethical levels of reasoning; indeed, it may, at times, exist beyond the bounds of traditional scientific conceptions of order and logic. We may dismiss nonviolence hastily because nonviolence does not always fulfill the scientific requirement for perfect replicability, cool cynicism, or the desired degree of detachment in order to prove its success.

Traditional, accepted notions of reason are points of contest. My perspectives on rhetoric complement other views that are now being played out in the context of current issues in discourse. Books such as *The Argument Culture* by Deborah Tannen or Carter's *Civility* capture such discussions that are up in the air. For instance, an important perspective in the debate over how college writing courses, including rhetoric, ought to be taught, is put forth by feminist scholars Tina LaVonne Good and Leanne Warshauer:

> As James Crosswhite writes, "The teaching of writing is nothing less than the teaching of reasoning . . . It is an attempt to develop and to strengthen the abilities of the individual people to imagine, to reason, and to judge in the medium of writing." However, in our society, reason has been gendered male, and the tenets of reasoned discourse have been strictly prescribed, relegating any other discourse that may contain elements of the personal, the narrative, or any hint of emotion to the sphere of the "non-academic," the "unacceptable" and, we would argue, the "feminine." This puts students who wish to engage in alternate modes of reasoning at a disadvantage. (Good and Warshauer)

Thus they observe how the rhetorical tradition, at least how it has played out in the writing curriculum, has been able to circumscribe definitions of what is or is not accepted as proper rhetoric. The debate over what rhetoric was, is, or ought to be makes it important to question status quo theoretical presuppositions.

As these kinds of definitions and what is accepted as rhetoric and as science change, however, so must our understanding of nonviolence. Harold Pepinsky, a professor of criminology and an advocate of nonviolent approaches to the criminal justice system, believes that a nonviolent worldview may be more closely identified with formulations of chaos theory, which allow for, indeed even call for, the "strange attractors" of unpredictable events (44–49). According to him, the chaos that nonviolent approaches often invite, stands opposed to logical or rational strictures on which our worldview—as descended from the Enlightenment—relies on to judge rhetorical texts and events. Pepinsky goes so far as to assert that "the fruit of our own peacemaking efforts lies beyond our power of empirical verification" (60). Starting from Aristotle himself, a major influence on much of the tradition of rhetorical theory, it is clear that rhetoric has traditionally been bound in tight strictures of logic and empiricism. As Pepinsky observes, we need to acknowledge new perspectives that may not always fit past methods of observing rhetorical situations.

To see where these new perspectives lead, let's return to the examples that began this book. The peace processes in Northern Ireland or between the Israelis and Palestinians resemble more closely what one would expect from chaos theory.

Two steps forward, one step back, to the side, or out altogether are moves that bet-ter characterize the bumpy ride of these negotiations for peace settlements in highly volatile and historically violent regions of the world. The operative peace and conflict theories that underpin the hard-hitting, complex negotiations have produced concrete results that leave both the peoples and their leaders at least a little optimistic. At the same time, the worldview of the glum inevitability of human violence is challenged. The nonviolent rhetoric surrounding these events confirms that human beings, against the grain of the *ce sera, sera* worldview, *need not* always be at war.

At the forefront of all such talks is a rhetoric that reflects a Bondurant-styled propaganda of peacemaking. The media receive hopeful statements and pro-nouncements from the participants of the negotiations; nonviolent rhetoric abounds. The stratified process of communication in community becomes less or-dered, and more fluid, like chaos theory (Pepinsky 4). In nonviolent theory, the rhetoric of a negotiator for peace can be seen as revealing a truth, the truth that the opponents with whom one is negotiating are just human beings like the rest of us. Rhetoric that obfuscates this fundamentally nonviolent perspective can, then, be seen to fall on the violent side of this crooked and rather arbitrary conceptual divide between violence and nonviolence.

Gandhi believed that secrets were an evil in society.[3] "Truth," he said, "never damages a cause that is just" (33). In this way, we see that negotiations that expose oppressions such as ethnocentrism, violent ultranationalism, racism, sexism, and homophobia not only confirm our "community" as human beings, but they also serve to expose the secrets of the social order and the violent structures that are perpetuated within that order. The media exposés on the murder of Matthew Shepard in Wyoming and the nationwide outpouring of support for his family and friends, for instance, expose to the squeamish the so-called ugly truth that a por-tion of the public is gay; by exposing this "secret" and celebrating it, right-wing opponents of homosexuality must face this fact and come to grips with it. The fundamental rehumanization, through nonviolent rhetoric, of a "fag" or a "bloody IRA soldier," a "murderous Israeli" or a "Palestinian terrorist" into human beings who have lives, histories, families, is part of the nonviolent process of compassion, forgiveness, and understanding. Rehumanization occurs through revealing the paucity of epithets. In Kenneth Burke's terms, it is rhetorical consubstantiation par excellence.

Moreover, the fact that negotiations for peace and concomitant long-term media coverage occur shows the patience and long view that characterizes the non-violent perspectivist's will to change the situation gradually yet steadily, as well as to reject violence, where possible, and often the expediency that comes with vio-lence. Expediency and efficiency are typical and universal modern measures of effectiveness and success. Yet the nonviolentist's perspective is more open to taking a long-range approach to problem solving and conflict resolution. As Pepinsky observes, "[p]eacemaking takes a long, long time" (59). Pepinsky aptly remarks that "those who respond to violence with compassion may . . . appear to open themselves to further victimization" (59). For the modern rhetorical theorist who applies traditional rules of style, logic, or effectiveness to speeches and symbolic action, the vulnerability and painstaking slowness of the goals expressed in nonviolent rhetoric appear to be counterproductive and, at times, illogical.

While King's rhetoric, which is often solely analyzed for *style* while the critic all but ignores the nonviolent message, it is just as common to find, as in some criticism of the Dalai Lama's rhetoric, that nonviolent rhetoric is disparaged for being unstylized and too plain. These critical problems are easily surmounted if we begin to take a different view, if we start to apply different measures of effectiveness, and if we look beyond stylistic tropes or a lack of them. By simply looking at rhetoric from a fresh perspective, nonviolent rhetoric, and perhaps rhetorical theory in part, can be expanded, better understood, and appreciated anew.

Thus far we have looked at several examples of nonviolent action and its attendant rhetoric. Differences have been highlighted between how traditional, theory-oriented rhetorical scholars have viewed human action and rhetoric, and how they might be viewed differently in light of nonviolent theory. The possibility for defining rhetoric anew as a legitimate form of nonviolent action and communication will be investigated next.

RHETORIC AS TRUE NONVIOLENT ACTION

Persuasion is not necessarily violent (or even coercive) when it is performed in the context of true nonviolent action. True nonviolent action means action that is aimed at resisting oppression, either purposefully or unwittingly. For example, terms such as *nonviolent crime* usually do not entail true nonviolence. Someone may commit a white-collar crime out of greed, such as embezzling money from a bank one works for. Because the crime is committed without physically or perhaps even financially damaging other persons, the crime is called "nonviolent." Such an action, however, is unrelated to nonviolence as I mean it in this book. Nonviolent as a description means that actions are committed to deal with issues of justice and injustice.

Here is a brief survey of nonviolent literature that includes some potential redefinitions of rhetoric that are made possible through taking a nonviolent perspective. I will first explain further this notion of true nonviolent action. There are no fast-and-simple definitions of nonviolence. There are, however, characteristics that are easily identifiable in what Lloyd Bitzer referred to as the "rhetorical situation"—a scenario of conflict in which the people involved experience an "exigency" on which they feel they need to act.

The elements of nonviolence in conflict scenarios include a desire to remediate injustice through careful planning (often aimed at creating a rhetorical situation), self-sacrifice, risk, courage, honesty, willpower or energy, and in some cases "suffering without retaliation" (*Gandhi on Non-Violence* 46). The ability to risk receiving—and sometimes to suffer—the blows of one's opponents (whether literal or figural) with no aim for revenge is what often distinguishes nonviolence in action from violence in action.[4] In his essay, "Ahimsa, or the Way of Nonviolence," Gandhi wrote:

> Suffering is the law of human beings; war is the law of the jungle. But suffering is infinitely more powerful than the law of the jungle for converting the opponent and opening his ears, which otherwise are shut, to the voice of reason. . . . if you want something really important to be done you must not merely satisfy the reason, you must move the heart also. The appeal of reason is more to the head but the penetration of the heart comes from suffering. It opens up the inner understanding in man. Suffering is the badge of the human race, not the sword. (174)

Gandhi's insight that "you must move the heart also" hearkens back to Aristotle's call to use *pathos*, or emotional appeals, to move the passions in order to effect persuasion. Nonviolent rhetoric actively seeks to draw on the chaotic, disorderly, emotional side of human beings. The nonviolent actor seeks to broach conflict, even sometimes to escalate it, but with minimal violence to people on all sides of the argument. The goal is not to hurt anyone or to use self-sacrifice with abandon, but rather to *educate* people to come to terms and to negotiate with better understanding, as well as with a renewed sense of commonality and humanity. This educated connection to one's adversary and rehumanizing propaganda is evident in the example of the rhetoric that is the essence of King's "Letter from the Birmingham Jail."

Clearly, for the rhetorical critic and student of nonviolent theory, *risk* is one of the defining criteria of rhetoric in argumentation.[5] Henry Johnstone, in his essay, "Some Reflections on Argumentation," explains how a violence of a sort occurs in dysfunctional argumentation. He makes the connection between rhetoric and humanity. In so doing, he confirms the rehumanizing effect that is a trait of nonviolent rhetoric. Johnstone writes that when two parties are arguing a point (or are negotiating as part of a peace process), "[T]he person with the totally closed mind cuts himself [sic] off from the human race" while, in contrast, "the person willing to run the risks involved in listening to the arguments of others is open-minded" and, therefore, "human" (3). Johnstone maintains that a "tension" exists in the more humane arguer (5). This tension features nonviolent and peace-minded attributes, such as "tolerance, intellectual generosity, or respect" (5). Johnstone believes that "the risk a person takes by listening to an argument is that he may have to change himself. It is the self, not any specific belief or mode of conduct, that the arguer's respondent wishes to maintain" (4). Rhetoric, then, can foster nonviolence because the change is self-initiated and self-driven, according to these standards for a fair argument. The persuasion is not coercion of another, per se, but rather a consciously self-initiated change of mind. So King's letter from jail, or the negotiations for peace, are scenarios that involve *educating* and then causing a *self-changing* in one's political opponent. Above all, from this perspective, arguing, as it exists in rhetoric, features a fundamentally nonviolent aim: "[A]rgumentation," writes Johnstone, "is a device for avoiding the need to resort to violence" (6). When the educational argument from one side fosters the ability of the arguer on the other side to initiate self-imposed, self-driven change, and to invite, through ethical means, the risks of such a change, rhetoric can be said to carry the characteristics of nonviolence.

Nonviolent rhetoric operates on an emotional level to remind the adversary of a shared, universal humanity. Evoking human emotions can be as useful in offsetting violence as it is to incurring it. Conversely, using logic and discourse devoid of emotion can entail violence since logic often involves arbitrary or superficial groupings and systematic thinking.[6] The use of a grouping or essentializing mind-set has been shown to promote "deindividuation," which can lead to aggressive behavior (Rubin, Pruitt, and Kim 88–90). In short, the logical move to grouping, categorizing, or essentializing of people often creates dehumanization. Aggressiveness occurs "because dehumanization makes the universal norm against harming other human beings seem irrelevant. If Other is less than human, the norm does not apply" (90). Thus, nonviolent rhetoric aims to reactivate norms that Pepinsky and other nonviolent theorists believe are inherent in humans. Pepinsky places such norms under the rubric of "responsiveness," meaning "compassion" and "enduring relations of mutuality and respect" (48). Nonviolent rhetoric rehumanizes by fracturing tidy categories of groups while also aggregating humans as a global whole. Paradoxically, nonviolent rhetoric focuses and thrives on visions of harmony and unity, as well as ruptures and fissures.

Gene Sharp concentrates on the human tendency toward cooperation as the font of the rhetorical power of nonviolence. In his essay, "The Techniques of Nonviolent Action," he defines the process as opposite from the "efficiency"-oriented schemas of violent engagement in conflict. Sharp states that "Nonviolent action is based on a different approach: to deny the enemy the human assistance and cooperation which are necessary if he is to exercise control over the population. It is thus based on a more fundamental and sophisticated view of political power" (224–25). A crucial means to exerting noncooperation with one's adversary is rhetoric. Noncooperation is achieved through communicative persuasion, or rhetoric, ranging from "purely verbal dissent" to carrying out "humorous pranks" (226). According to Sharp, these tactics, if conducted with a sense of understanding, can be effective because of the very chaos they invite.

Sharp's research indicates that nonviolence, often through its element of surprise, can "counter . . . violence in such as way that [opponents] are thrown politically off balance in a kind of political *jiu-jitsu*" (228). The purpose of this creative disorder "is to demonstrate that repression is incapable of cowing the populace, and to deprive the opponent of . . . support, thereby undermining his ability or will to continue with the repression" (228). For these goals to be achieved, communication must take place.

In the 1980s, South Africa, for example, was a communications crossroads for the world in the sense that American and European investors were continually reminded of its shameful apartheid system by calls for divestment from investors and other constituents. With the repressions and injustices of the apartheid regime continually splashed across news headlines around the world, the old, structurally violent system could not hold. Today, Nelson Mandela, once a "criminal" under apartheid, went on to become, through a largely nonviolent process, the new president of that nation. The eventual release of the findings of the Truth and Reconciliation Commission (TRC), led by its eloquent nonviolent leader, Archbishop Desmond Tutu, is witness to the nonviolent spirit with which the country is moving, however painfully slowly and imperfectly, out of a long period of social and structural violence. Even the TRC's last-minute concession to exclude its findings about the complicity in human rights abuses of former president F. W. DeKlerc is a nonviolent text, a speaking symbol. The censored text about DeKlerc exists in the form of a large, black square covering the text of a page in the volume. Without words, and while making a peaceful concession so as to be able to publish the historic tome at all, that censored square block is a symbol of the hatred and violence that is past; it becomes, quite literally, a page in history. Even shrouded in mystery, the reader surmises the damning spot represents DeKlerc's complicity. Without words, then, the truth is out. The reader is called on to pardon but not necessarily to forget; the reader is invited to move forward in the name of nonviolence, peace, and humanity. Truth, forgiveness, patiently forging ahead—this is the stuff of nonviolent rhetoric.

Meanwhile, the rhetoric of nonviolent movements that exist in repressive, totalitarian states is more easily suppressed. In places such as Myanmar (Burma) or China, where communications are more closely monitored and limited by the authorities, nonviolent successes remain tenuous. Nonviolent campaigns (and rhetoric), are more successful when certain supports are present, including freedom of the press and free speech, which are severely limited in countries like China. Here in the United States, too, as communication networks become increasingly centralized, freedom of information becomes curtailed.[7]

At the same time, the chaos of technological advances can help spread nonviolent rhetoric. More developing nations are moving into computer-based networks of commerce and communications. Advances in technology in developing and industrialized nations alike improve many citizens' access to information. Possibilities are appearing on the horizon for nonviolent action and rhetoric to transcend the structurally violent systems of repression that occur in places where political or economic constraints exist. Htun Aung Gyaw, for instance, runs an internet consortium called the Civil Society for Burma, which is a global resistance network (Ryan 12). Htun Aung Gyaw says, "We organize conferences over the Internet . . . [and] have a chat room where we meet to discuss strategy" (Ryan 12). New information is continually smuggled into and out of the country so that pro-democracy groups can continue to resist the military regime there.[8]

These examples show how rhetoric can be conceived of as both a part of nonviolent theory and praxis. These examples illustrate some ways that nonviolent rhetoric arises, several forms it takes, and the contextual requirements for nonviolent rhetoric to flourish. Next is a brief overview of a key obstacle that seems to prevent rhetorical theorists and other social critics from acknowledging and integrating nonviolent theory into mainstream theoretical paradigms.

PRESUMED PEACEMAKERS

At present, it would be impossible to "prove" that human nature is inherently nonviolent. Myriad books and articles have been devoted to that purpose, which I do not seek to replicate here.[9] This section merely provides a cursory overview of that literature. The purpose of this overview is simply to provide a framework for my assumption that, while human nature may or may not be necessarily nonviolent or peaceful, human beings as social and political collectives do possess great potential to manage conflicts nonviolently.

One reason why critics of nonviolence dismiss it is that they presume that human beings are basically violent animals and that we mirror a vicious, harsh natural environment. In the 19th century, Leo Tolstoy began to debunk this view by calling human violence "the product of public opinion" rather than some natural state of being (178). Tolstoy argued that our "consciousness" was responsible for "the present order of society based on violence," and as such, we could change our minds and thereby change society (178–79). Tolstoy, like Karl Marx, pointed to the structural violence of the wealthy and powerful exploiting the poor[10];

moreover, he drew attention to the rhetoric that perpetuated the violence, the "sculpture . . . poetry. . . jubilees" that glamorize the myths that humans are unequal and violent (180).

Tolstoy had reason to hope for social change because he saw that "public opinion condemns violence more and more" (185). By revealing the power structures hidden in the roles of government, the church, and the military, Tolstoy shows us that rhetoric resides in roles that people play and the discourses in which they engage. He envisioned the ultimate transcendence of the truth that violence arises from the interplay between and among people, their roles, and the unjust power structures in which they engage through their discourses. Tolstoy believed that, "A time is coming, and will inevitably come, when all institutions based on violence will disappear because it has become obvious to everyone that they are useless, stupid, and even wrong" (186). Judging from the past two decades of world history, including much nonviolent social action and progress in South Africa, the Philippines, East Timor, and Northeastern Europe, to name a few, there may be hope that Tolstoy's prophecy is gradually coming to fruition.

Often, the government, religions, the military, and other key institutions and systems thrive on a rhetoric of aggression. Michel Foucault's *Discipline and Punish* recounts the many ways oppressive power is enacted through rhetoric. Foucault traces the existence of state and social power and its juridical, economic, scientific, and political ramifications from systems of punishment and social control in the 17th, 18th, and 19th centuries up to the present time. From the 19th to the 20th centuries, in particular, power in its disciplinary form shifted from public display to private and interpersonal modes. Disciplinary power was exerted and diffused through the institutions of the factories, schools, military, sanitariums, hospitals, and prisons, all of which resemble each other both architecturally and organizationally. By the very subtle nature of the organization of each of these into tableaux mapped onto grids, with people reduced to being case studies recorded, tracked, and supervised, the options for resistance become gravely diminished. Foucault notes that this kind of organized control over "malicious minutiae" operates so as to stop any unregulated movement of people within the system (226). In a disciplinary institution or society, people, and power circulate in a more or less orderly fashion.

But cracks appear in this system of power when "compact groupings of individuals wander about the country in unpredictable ways" (219). Foucault acknowledges that "counter-power" consists in "agitations, revolts, spontaneous organizations, coalitions—anything that may establish horizontal conjunctions" (219). Thus, we see the opportunity for nonviolent action and rhetoric to manifest itself. On the whole, however, he maintains that the result of institutions and their methods is the "normalizing" of the repressive forces of power (183). The process occurs through the intense "pressure to conform to the same model" (82), through analysis, standardization (184), and objectification (187) of everything, especially human beings.[11] According to Foucault, power disciplines and punishes us through its "visible" yet "unverifiable" presence (201).

The only final option for resistance exists in Foucault's ironic and paradoxical demand that "we must hear the distant roar of battle" in the very words and "discourses that are in themselves elements" of the "strategy" of much that exemplifies scientific discipline (308). He believes that discourses "produce" oppressive power (194); therefore, perhaps, so too can some kind of alternative, anti-institutional discourses create counterpower. I join a growing number of students and scholars of peace and conflict studies in positing that nonviolent rhetoric represents precisely this sort of counterpower.

Likewise, Ashley Montagu, an anthropologist, has noted the role that rhetoric has played in promoting the worldview that human beings are naturally "aggressive" and characterized by "innate depravity" (5). Montagu states that literature like Darwin's *Origins of the Species* or William Golding's *Lord of the Flies*, or even a seemingly innocuous stage play like *West Side Story*, operate so as to "supply [people] with an easy 'explanation'" for the world's ills (9). Another way that rhetoric has been used to shape and perpetuate violent systems equally points the way for a rhetoric that can reform those same systems so as to function nonviolently. Christine Sylvester, a political scientist, observes that businesslike rules for speaking, such as *Robert's Rules of Parliamentary Procedure*, set up "intricate barriers to communication" instead of allowing for an equally possible, nonviolent, and free form mode of speech that is "usefully disorderly" (37–38). These examples further confirm Foucault's idea that systems of control, hierarchy, and violent power thrive by suppressing creative and "useful disorder."

Moving toward nonviolence that is a counter to hegemonic power, Hocker and Wilmot affirm that an important step in conflict management is sometimes to ignore rules of etiquette. "Raising one's voice," they say, "may not be as great a sin as stifling it" (64).[12] People can become nonviolent, as well as circumvent violence, through creativity, inventiveness, a sense of community, and spontaneity. Finding and expressing one's voice is an important part of fostering a community that values peacemaking and strives, however imperfectly, toward achieving a sense of harmony.

From the nonviolent theorist's perspective, achieving harmony in community is not as utopian and improbable an ideal as we have been led to believe. Montagu believes, for example, that, "Everything points to the non-violence of the greater part of early man's life, to the contribution made by the increasing development of cooperative activities" and he also notes that "the invention of speech" as a crucial factor that defines humans and their communication as fundamentally being *nonviolent* (8). In short, Montagu's research leads him to posit that much of modern society, a society of Foucault's discipline/punish paradigm, has used rhetoric to train us to feel that we should be absolved of our societal sins (such as crime or socioeconomic inequality) "by shifting the responsibility for [such problems] to our 'natural inheritance,' our 'innate aggressiveness'" (11). Montagu believes that our institutions and communication systems ought to tell the truth about the real causes of social problems and violence, "namely, the many false and contradictory values by which, in an overcrowded, highly competitive, dehumanized, threatening world, [humans] so disoperatively attempt to live" (17). Montagu's theory supports the notion that rhetoric fitting a discipline/punish schema fosters "false" violent social structures.[13] His perspective also recuperates a nonviolent sense of rhetoric because it points the way to justice, to regaining a sense of humanity at our core, which is characterized by "amiability" (14).

Prominent scientists have decried the power of language and culture to promote war. *The Seville Statement on Violence*, originally published in 1986 and reprinted in 1990, is an overlooked rhetorical document that is of note to rhetorical theorists and peace scholars alike. Written by world-renowned scientists, it affirms that "warfare is a peculiarly human phenomenon and does not occur in other animals" (221). The scientists maintain that language and culture are the reasons for war, not "natural" biological makeup. "Warfare," they write, "is a product of culture. Its biological connection is primarily through language" (221). Consequently, they believe that culture can be ameliorated to a nonviolent equilibrium, as evidenced by the "cultures which have not engaged in war for centuries" or only in certain epochs (222). Theorists of peace and conflict studies and of rhetoric are examining further how this role of language in culture—how rhetoric—figures importantly in our perceptions of reality and the viability of nonviolence in conflict management.

On a more middle theoretical ground than the authors just mentioned, William James allows that humans do have aggressive tendencies, but he believes these tendencies can simply be channeled to constructive pursuits rather than to violence and war (213). Pepinsky supports this view in noting our human "drive [is] to be responsive" and "compassionate" rather than aggressive (48). James maintains that the rhetoric of history and literature like the *Iliad* perpetuate the prevalence of violence in society by rationalizing its very "irrationality" and rendering it "fascinating" (215). James argues that notions of "peace" have been subverted to mean "competitive preparation for war" (217). As Patricia Hill Collins states, "peace without justice constitutes an illusion" (8). Likewise, Jacques Ellul's *Propaganda: The Formation of Men's Minds* (1965) and Michael Sherry's *In the Shadow of War: The United States Since the 1930s* are books that recount in great detail how the meaning of peace, through the manifest institutions of contemporary society, becomes subverted actually to mean war.[14] Here again, scholars both in rhetoric and peace studies are benefiting from a better understanding the sociolinguistic processes by and through which true peace is stunted and thwarted.

James demonstrates the difficult, and seemingly inferior, rhetorical position that the pacifist or nonviolentist is placed into because we must argue for a "negative," an absence of war. This pacifistic lack, this void of imagery, as a negative, pales in its allure compared to the thrilling "positive," the visible, tangible "horror" of war that many cultures amplify and condone (220). The rhetorical stance that James recommends to counter this problem is for pacifists "to enter more deeply into the aesthetical and ethical point of view of their opponents," in other words, create a positive and known quantity, "a moral equivalent of war" that will replace the perceived void (220). James believes that military values like "intrepidity, contempt of softness, surrender of private interest, obedience to command" can all be accommodated through nonviolent programs of public works (222). Konrad Lorenz, by the same token, believed that human overflows of energy (in the form of aggression or otherwise) could be channeled into the positive realms of art, science, and medicine (236). Today, from rhetorical legacies of figures like John F. Kennedy ("Ask not what your country can do for you—ask what you can do for your country"), ostensibly nonviolent programs like the Peace Corps or Habitat for Humanity show the plausibility of James's and Lorenz's arguments. It is possible to find positive, tangible, and rewarding substitutes for war-making and violence.

Finally, it is helpful here to return to Johnstone's point about the relationship between rhetoric, risk taking, argumentation, and humanity. The rhetorician's perspective tends to confirm that humans are not fundamentally violent, but rather that we are fundamentally nonviolent and desire to be peaceful. In response to the claim that argumentation is merely "a device for avoiding the need to resort to violence," Johnstone maintains that

> This is a cynical view of human nature, since it regards [our human] capacity for argument as no more than the product of a transient enlightenment—an unstable victory over the irrational forces that define [us]—and it regards argument itself as no more than an expedient. If argument is in fact a mere expedient to avoid violence, then we ought to consider as most successful that argument which has the greatest soporific effect. More fundamentally, the standard view is in direct contradiction to the history of human hostility. Throughout recorded time, [people] have always based their conflicts upon arguments. Every war has been preceded by the search for an excuse for fighting. To find examples of violence not based upon argument, we must look to the annals of psychopathology. This fact shows that normal human violence already presupposes argument. (7)

Thus, Johnstone's perspective as a rhetorical scholar supports the positions of other social theorists who question the durability of the position that humans are fundamentally depraved, violent, and warlike.

Johnstone goes on to say that "argument is a defining feature of the human situation. . . . It is . . . to introduce the arguer into a situation of risk in which open-mindedness and tolerance are possible" (7). Johnstone calls for students of rhetoric to engage in philosophical inquiry that invites counterarguments and looks beyond the mere "facts" at hand (8). To exist in our "human milieu," says Johnstone, we must engage first and foremost "values" (8). Questioning the veracity of some sort of human of innate depravity, through the mere engagement of one's interlocutor, begins a process that, in the words of Johnstone, is "an attempt to expand and consolidate the [peace-minded and just] world into which the escape has been made" (8). I reiterate, then, that my purpose here is to "expand and consolidate" both the project of nonviolent theory and the vital relationship that rhetorical theory has in the practice of nonviolence. This is our "escape," in the nonviolent mode, into a discursive world where peacemaking is possible. Through the expansion of the discursive realm, of the word, of all things rhetorical, expansion of culture becomes possible. If we can nurture a cultural orientation toward peacemaking and nonviolence, according to the theories of the scientists in the *Seville Statement*, the reality of achieving more peace in the world is inevitable.

We have just looked at ways that rhetoric can be seen as a form of nonviolent action and how nonviolent action is rhetorical. Nonviolence is a form of persuasion and communication that aims to minimize the violence found in conflict situations. Nonviolentists strive stubbornly to attain social justice through revealing social and political injustices and through subverting disciplinary, oppressive, and institutional forms of power. As this glance at the literature shows, culture, history, and rhetoric serve to perpetuate the myth that humans are naturally "aggressive" beings, rather than beings who are just as much, if not more, cooperative and "amiable."

APPENDIX 2

Address of Kiro Gligorov to the
UN General Assembly, September 30, 1993
(Official UN Translation)

At the outset, it is my pleasure to extend to you, Sir, my sincere felicitations on your election to the presidency of the General Assembly at its forty-eighth session. In discharging your important duties, you can count on the support and cooperation of my delegation. Your wide experience and diplomatic skills are a valuable asset for the success of this important session of the General Assembly.

This is the first time that my country, the Republic of Macedonia, is attending a session of the General Assembly as an independent State committed to making its full contribution to the enhancement of world peace and the promotion of international cooperation.

The Republic of Macedonia is a country with foreign policies based on the principles of peace, friendship and cooperation. We see the interdependence of interests and mutual respect as the future of successful international cooperation. An important element of our foreign policy is to promote good-neighbourly relations and to incorporate the principles of the new European architecture in the crisis-ridden region of the Balkans. Such a foreign policy is consistent with the internal development of the Republic of Macedonia, which is oriented towards a market economy, a State of law, human rights and harmony in inter-ethnic relations.

By attaining its independence in a peaceful and legitimate manner, the Republic of Macedonia has kept the peace and forestalled a spill-over of the war into the southern Balkans. The comprehensive efforts of the past two years have changed our historic position from a bone of contention to a factor for peace and stability in the Balkans. Pursuant to this, the endeavours of the delegation of the Republic of Macedonia in the course of this session will be aimed at strict compliance with the United Nations Charter; support for all measures that enhance international peace and security; the democratization of international relations in all spheres; the advancement of human rights and freedoms to the utmost degree; the promotion and development of a policy of good-neighbourly relations; forestalling the proliferation and use of weapons of mass destruction; and the enhancement of preventive diplomacy in settling disputes.

The adverse situation of the world today is a source of concern to all of us. We are not fully satisfied with the efforts of our Organization nor especially with the results it has achieved in resolving current sources of tension. We accept the assertion that the world today is not threatened by a new world war and that the use of nuclear arms is not very likely. But the fact remains that the number of serious and potential military conflicts is increasing. The efforts of our Organization to find peaceful solutions have been enormous. Regrettably, the results have not always been productive, owing to a certain extent to the absence of a wider implementation of preventive diplomatic measures and activities.

I take this opportunity to emphasize the extraordinary significance of the historical accord between Israel and the Palestine Liberation Organization for peace in the Middle East and the development of world relations. All those who have contributed to its signing deserve our special recognition.

In this context, I am deeply convinced that, despite all difficulties, we will soon be speaking of South Africa as a region of successful development and human dignity. Let us hope that the forces of peace in that region will ultimately prevail over the forces of regression and apartheid.

I must reiterate our deep concern over the perpetuation of the war in Bosnia and Herzegovina, the threat of a spill-over and a wider destabilization of our region. In dead earnest we, a country situation in the immediate vicinity, see this as the threat of an all-out Balkan war. The situation in Bosnia and Herzegovina is extremely grave, tragic and incomprehensible. The most terrible post-cold-war drama is unfolding in the heart of Europe: massive killings, massive destruction, over 2 million refugees, insane acts of ethnic cleansing and genocide. Numerous international conferences and activities have been undertaken in order to bring an end to this war. The Security Council has adopted numerous resolutions. Let us all hope that peace in Bosnia will finally become a reality.

An end to the war in Bosnia and Herzegovina is a first and essential step. However, permanent peace in Bosnia and Herzegovina will not be possible without compliance with, and upholding of, the fundamental principles of international law, the United Nations Charter and the principles of the Conference on Security and Cooperation in Europe (CSCE), namely that borders cannot be changed by force; that the international community does not recognize or accept "ethnic cleansing"; and that the rights of minorities must be respected.

Without these preconditions, not only will permanent peace in Bosnia and Herzegovina be impossible, but a precedent will be set which will incite new conflicts. To condone the use of force and military superiority for territorial expansion and redrawn borders would exacerbate other, less heated tensions, especially in the ethnically mixed Balkans and the countries of Eastern Europe. It would in fact mean condoning the potential for permanent inter-ethnic wars.

The Republic of Macedonia is vitally interested in seeing an end to the war in Bosnia and Herzegovina, forestalling a spill-over and attaining peace on lasting foundations. For these reasons, and out of concern for our own security and for peace and stability in the region, we have undertaken a number of timely preventive measures in cooperation with the United Nations. In this context, I would like to stress the key role played by Security Council resolution 795 (1992) of December 1992 for the deployment of a contingent from the United Nations Protection Force (UNPROFOR) in the Republic of Macedonia.

The decision of the Security Council, to which the Secretary-General made a great contribution, has proved to be justified, timely and efficient. It has demonstrated the enormous advantages of preventive diplomacy. The peace-keeping forces of the United Nations, strengthened by the United States contingent, are of great importance for our security and for sustaining peace and stability in the region. Our cooperation with these forces is exemplary, and it will remain so in the future. This step has greatly increased the feelings of security and trust in the peace-keeping activities of the United Nations on the part of the citizens of the Republic of Macedonia.

As a country and as a people, our permanent interest lies in peace and cooperation in the Balkans. In the same spirit, our efforts are aimed at establishing good-neighbourly relations with all our neighbours and at resolving all existing problems with our southern neighbour. The war in Bosnia and Herzegovina, the implementation of United Nations sanctions against Serbia and Montenegro, and the remains of bloc divisions prevalent until recently prevent the Balkans from functioning on natural regional principles. Economic and cultural ties, communications, the free flow of people, goods and ideas have practically been severed. This is indeed a depressing situation. In order to prepare for the twenty-first century and a Europe of open borders and cooperation, it is essential that the Balkans undergo major changes. This is in the interest of all the peoples and all the countries in this region. Those are the reasons why Macedonia has adopted policies of good-neighbourly relations, peaceful settlement of problems and development of overall economic, political and cultural cooperation among the countries of the Balkans. We are truly convinced that, in the interest of peace and stability, the international community will ardently support these process in the Balkans. The principles of the Conference on Security and Cooperation in Europe and the processes within the European Community are the only options for peace, stability and economic revival in the Balkans. However, this also implies that all the Balkan States, which have chosen the European option, must be enabled to achieve gradual integration into the European Community.

We are all dissatisfied with the stagnation of the world economy in the past year, the deterioration of the economic situation in the world, and the economic situation in certain countries and regions. The number of people affected by unemployment, poverty and hunger is on the rise. For developed countries, recovery from the recession has been slower than expected, hindering their increased participation in the development of the developing countries and countries in transition.

Because of this situation, and because of our firm conviction that the period after the cold war must not grow into a period of economic conflicts, we believe that much more can be done to seek a way out of the world's current economic and social difficulties. In this context, I am convinced that the forty-eighth session of the General Assembly will serve as firm encouragement for an increase in world demand and for liberalization of world trade. A very important prerequisite for the realization of this goal is the successful outcome of the Uruguay Round of the General Agreement on Tariffs and Trade (GATT) negotiations, encouraged by the Tokyo summit. It is also essential to resolve the issue of arrears and that of access by developing countries and countries in transition to international financial markets. All of these activities support the view that only development generates new development, while stagnation brings only regression and poverty.

Enhanced protection of human rights is justifiably receiving greater priority in the work of our Organization. We are concerned by the fact that in the past year, violations of human rights have reached epidemic proportions. We feel that the Vienna Conference on Human Rights is a very positive step in the right direction, and we hope that the Declaration and Action Programme adopted at that Conference will contribute greatly to ending the unfavourable [sic] developments in this area today.

The negotiations in Vienna have clearly shown that current mechanisms for implementing existing human rights instruments are not efficient, and that much improvement is needed, particularly in the rights of ethnic, religious and linguistic minorities. A significant step in this direction has been taken by the adoption last year of the Declaration on minorities. The next steps which our delegation will support are the commencement of operations of the Commission on Human Rights according to the Declaration on the Rights of Persons Belonging to National or Ethnic, Religious and Linguistic Minorities, and an examination of the need for setting up a United Nations high commission for minorities, with headquarters in Geneva.

I would like to point out that all unresolved issues involving ethnic minorities can well lead to future military conflicts, particularly in certain regions of the world, thus endangering international peace. Hence it is essential to take immediate preventive measures in this area as well.

The Republic of Macedonia is a European country in transition, a landlocked country, a country of transit and a developing country. These factors contribute to the economic difficulties of my country. The situation is further complicated by the consequences of the United Nations sanctions imposed on Serbia and Montenegro. I would immediately like to emphasize that we have strictly complied with the implementation of the sanctions. As a result, this year alone, our gross national product has been cut in half. External trade has been reduced considerably, transport costs have increased immensely, and other indirect damage has occurred as well.

Today, the survival, democracy and economic development of the Republic of Macedonia are fundamentally dependent on assistance from the international community. Otherwise, it is very possible that social tensions, and the probable collapse of the economy, will bring about a new crisis spot. I am deeply convinced that, in accordance with Article 50 of the Charter and Security Council resolution 820 (1993), the United Nations and the Security Council will be in a position to provide us with concrete forms of assistance.

It is inconceivable to expect a small country to bear the damage of an international action of this type on its own, without solidarity and timely assistance. Aid should be provided now as a preventive measure, instead of after the outbreak of those likely social clashes which may grow into new conflicts.

In this spirit, the delegation of the Republic of Macedonia at this session will lay out our direct proposals regarding the problem of compensation for damage incurred as a result of implementing the sanctions, the problems deriving from the position of landlocked countries, and other issues related to peace and cooperation.

The strengthening of the United Nations in all aspects, in the post-cold-war period, is of vital importance to the Republic of Macedonia. My country belongs to a group of countries that can survive and develop only in conditions without war, in a world where peace and stability are not threatened, where international cooperation will be conducted without obstacles and discrimination, and a world where everyone will have respect for human dignity.

In this context, the delegation of the Republic of Macedonia will make its full contribution to the successful work of the forty-eighth session of the General Assembly and to strengthening the Organization.

Early History of Macedonia

Philip of Macedon "absorbed the tribes of 'inland Macedonia' into his kingdom from 358 BCE onwards" (Hammond 122).[1] This was to include "the territory between Lake Lychnidus (today [it is called] Lake Ohrid) and the river Nestos into Macedonia" (Poulton, *Macedonians* 14). Thus Philip "extended the kingdom of Macedon to its 'natural' geographic area" (Poulton, *Macedonians* 14). Philip "admired Greek thought and . . . employed Aristotle to teach [his son] Alexander" (Poulton, *Macedonians* 15). When Alexander the Great reigned, Macedonia's territory extended all the way into Asia (Hammond 125). Alexander "turned a chaotic region, backward by the standards of the day and on the periphery of the Hellenic world, into a world power" (Perry, *Miracle* 113). Alexander's untimely death in 323 BCE resulted in dividing "his huge empire . . . into three parts—Macedon (including Greece), Syria, and Egypt" (Poulton, *Macedonians* 15). By 167 BCE the "expansion and consolidation of Roman power saw the Balkans and Macedonia once more revert to their old role as a border region, this time marking the zone between Latin- and Greek-speaking cultures, and between western and eastern halves of the empire" (16). During the fourth century CE, the Roman "empire was divided . . . north along the river Drina—which was the border in the twentieth century between Serbia and Bosnia" (16-17).

Later, by the sixth century CE, the Slavs, "an Indo-European people originating in east-central Europe" had settled in the area (4). In 681 CE, the first Bulgarian state was founded, and would later expand to include Macedonia by the ninth century (19). The once matriarchal and later, pagan, tribes in the region were converted to Christianity by St. Cyril and St. Methodius (11; 19). By 886 CE, their disciples, St. Kliment and St. Naum, had created the Slavic-language alphabet, Cyrillic, and "established the first seat of Slavic higher learning in Ohrid" (Vesilind 127). The religion, combined with the unique language (now totally distinct from the Greek), served to create the roots of a strong Slavic culture and what would later evolve into regional nationalism (Poulton, *Macedonians* 19-20).

In the 10th century, the ruler Samuil of the Bulgarian empire was uprooted from his seat of power in Macedonia by the Byzantine emperor Basil II, "and Macedonia once again fell firmly under Byzantine control till 1230" (20). By "1282, Milutin, the Serbian king, took Skopje from Byzantium and by the end of the century had established hegemony over much of the Balkans and penetrated deeply into Macedonia" (21). Milutin was succeeded by Stefan Dušan, whose "empire stretched from the Danube to central Greece and from the Drina to western Thrace" (21). During the Serbian and Byzantine era Jews and Roma (Gypsies) settled in Macedonia. But Serbian control of Macedonia ended in 1355 after Dušan's death, and the "chronic disunity in the Balkans allowed the Ottoman Turks, an Asiatic people who had gradually eroded away the ailing Byzantine empire, to invade the peninsula through Macedonia" (21). The last of the Serbs were defeated at Kosovo Polje in 1389,[2] and by 1453, the Ottoman Turks had taken over Constantinople, which marked the ending of the Byzantine empire (21).

The Ottoman empire would endure the longest of any of the preceding dominions over Macedonia, in carrying over until the early 20th century. In 1903, modern Macedonian nationalism briefly flickered in the form of "an abortive uprising . . . launched by the Internal [*Vnatrešno*] Macedonian Revolutionary Organization (VMRO)," one that "failed to create an autonomous Macedonia within the Ottoman Empire" (Perry, *Miracle* 114).[3] The VMRO revolt did, however, achieve a symbolic gain, called the "Ilinden uprising," by "taking over Kruševo for [an entire] week. . . . There was even an attempt to form a kind of revolutionary government" (Poulton, *Macedonians* 57).

N o t e s

CHAPTER 1

1. "Police Brutality." Narr. interview. Diane Sawyer and Forrest Sawyer. *Good Morning America*. ABC. March 26, 1999.

2. There are two general camps of theory in the contemporary field of rhetoric and rhetorical criticism. First, there is what Michael Leff refers to as the "theory of the text," in which a given speech, letter, or other rhetorical artifact is seen as containing its own, unique eloquence and logic. Leff believes that through a "close reading and rereading of the text" one can ascertain a rhetorical theory that may only be applicable to that particular piece and none other. In the other camp of theory, there is the more traditional sense of theory as a unified set of criteria (methods, hypotheses, assumptions, *topoi*, genres, etc.) that ought to be applicable to *all* rhetorical artifacts.

For discussions of the "theory of the text," see: Leff, Michael C. "Interpretation and the Art of the Rhetorical Critic." *Western Journal of Speech Communication* 44 (1980): 345; Leff, Michael C. "Textual Criticism: The Legacy of G. P. Mohrmann," *The Quarterly Journal of Speech* 72 (1986): 380.

For general overviews of what theory making is all about in rhetoric and criticism of rhetoric, see: Medhurst, Martin J. "Introduction: The Academic Study of Public Address: A tradition in Transition." In *Landmark Essays on American Public Address*, ed. Martin J. Medhurst. Davis, CA: Hermagoras Press, 1993: xi–xliii; Benson, Thomas. "Introduction: Beacons and Boundary-Markers: Landmarks in Rhetorical Criticism." In *Landmark Essays on Rhetorical Criticism*. Davis, CA: Hermagoras Press, 1993: xi–xxii; Nothstine, William L., Blair, Carole, and Copeland, Gary A. "Invention in Media and Rhetorical Criticism: A General Orientation." In *Critical Questions: Invention, Creativity, and the Criticism of Discourse and Media*, eds. William Nothstine, Carole Blair, and Gary Copeland. New York: St. Martin's Press, 1994: 3–12.

3. Journals that tend to publish empirical studies in communication theory include (but are not limited to), for example: *Communication Monographs; Communication Quarterly; Communication Reports; Communication Research; Communication Review; Communication Studies; Communication Theory*.

4. Journals that tend to publish qualitative studies in rhetorical theory or cultural studies include (but are not limited to), for example: *Quarterly Journal of Speech; Rhetoric and Public Affairs; Southern Communication Journal; Text and Performance Quarterly; Western Journal of Communication*.

5. He goes on to say that students learn of

> Thoreau as an eccentric, antisocial crank rather than as someone intimately involved in the political issues of his day . . . Jane Addams as a founder of modern social work, but never as one who risked her career and reputation with her opposition to World War I. And . . . [Martin Luther] King as a "dreamer" rather than as a savvy politician with a radical economic critique of American capitalism.

These are all ways that history serves to undermine nonviolence as a valid theory and concept. David Cochran, "An Underground Tradition," *The Progressive* 59 (1995): 37.

6. Theodore Herman, "A Conceptual Framework of Nonviolence for Peace Research," *International Journal of Group Tensions* 21 (1991): 6.

7. Gene Sharp, "Beyond Just War and Pacifism: Nonviolent Struggle Towards Justice, Freedom, and Peace," *Ecumenical Review* 48 (1996): 240.

8. Harry W. Bowen, "Does Non-Violence Persuade?" *Communication Monographs* [*Today's Speech*] 11 (1963): 11.

9. Bowen lists some of the preconditions under which "non-violent action change[s] the course of events in favor of its users" (31). This does indicate an acknowledgment that nonviolence can work, that it can persuade, yet it is still equivocal because Bowen notes among such preconditions that "non-violent resisters realistically admit that many enemies will not be converted either in thought or in deed to the civil rights cause by non-violent techniques" (31). Bowen's statements distort the effectiveness of nonviolence by downplaying its ultimate successes. This is so because if "events have been changed in favor" of the nonviolent activists, then "many enemies"—or at least those deemed crucial and powerful enough to make social change—already been "converted . . . to the cause" (Bowen 11, 31).

10. Richard Fulkerson, "The Public Letter as a Rhetorical Form: Structure, Logic, and Style in King's 'Letter from Birmingham Jail,'" *Quarterly Journal of Speech* 65 (1979): 121.

11. Fulkerson, 122, 136.

12. Cochran, "An Underground Tradition" 37.

13. Donald Smith, "Martin Luther King, Jr.: In the Beginning at Montgomery," *Southern Speech Journal* 34 (1968): 15–16.

14. Malinda Snow, "Martin Luther King's 'Letter From Birmingham Jail' as Pauline Epistle," *Quarterly Journal of Speech* 71 (1985): 332.

15. "Peace-oriented" should be distinguished from "peaceful" since the engagement of conflict in order to attain justice may necessarily involve discomfort on the part of some or all of the parties involved in the conflict. The goal is to achieve social and political justice with the minimum amount of violence, that is, with peace as a way, method, and rationale for doing things, not just a lofty end-goal. But if discomfort and anger occurs, for example, from the nonviolent taking over of the space of an adversary, such as sitting at lunch counters to oppose segregation, the action can still be deemed "peace-oriented" even if it is not situationally "peaceful."

CHAPTER 4

1. In this essay, all quotes from Gandhi that appear under headings are from the book *Gandhi on Non-Violence*.

2. That these films may not have reached as "mass" an audience as others is a red herring; Ono and Sloop have reminded critics of the value of not focusing exclusively on mass media or rhetoric that is intended for the largest audience (39).

3. I would qualify my point on conservative perspectives by noting that such critical perspectives as those provided by postmodern or poststructural film criticism, or critical explorations of race, class, or gender issues are heuristic, but the fact remains that they all issue from what to me is a clearly nonviolent goal: to use scholarship to reveal social inequalities and how persuasive structures in film and/or society perpetuates such structures.

4. Norman Clark believes the Isocratean tradition is a way to share power with the audience; it is a "service"-oriented rhetoric (112–13). Clark has called to critics to fulfill their "duty . . . for the public good and train their own minds so as to help their fellow [people]" (113). This means, at least in part, critics must look for ways to overcome stultifying critical and theoretical perspectives that have placed unnecessary constraints on our abilities "to help" people.

5. Holmes further identifies nonviolence as being qualified or unqualified, indicating the shades of commitment that one has in dealing with violence in every day life:

> What is nonviolence? To answer this requires looking beyond a few specific acts on specific occasions; it requires considering how people would act under various kinds of circumstances, and why. Particularly relevant here are circumstances in which most people are confronted with violence. Most of us are nonviolent most of the time; this is as true of those who approve of the use of violence in some circumstances as of those who do not. . . . to understand nonviolence requires understanding something of the nature of violence. For a commitment to nonviolence . . . involves the renunciation of violence . . . [and] may assume the form of nonresistance, passive resistance, or nonviolent direct action . . . Rosa Parks' act [of refusing to give up her bus seat to a white person] was an act of passive resistance. It was a refusal to comply with a directive, hence a refusal to acquiesce in the requirements of an unjust system.

So in addition to renouncing violence of either a physical or a psychological sort (or both), the nonviolentist must be prepared to offer some account of how one responds to the violence or wrongdoing of others (1–2). Thus Holmes reveals the range of options and views that exist in various nonviolent philosophies from Buddhism, to Christianity, to Jainism, and so on.

6. It is especially of note that many wealthy United Nations member countries, which profited from, in some cases, *centuries* of plundering of nations that are now developing countries, now refuse to forgive debts to the same countries that made the rich nations rich.

7. Gandhi worked throughout his career to discredit the cultural obsession, in India in particular, but worldwide in general, with the class system. Gandhi felt that artificial social hierarchies constituted a vile form of violence. Today nonviolent theorists such as Johan Galtung recognize such violence under the rubric of structural violence.

8. I myself would rate *The Spitfire Grill* as a "B+" movie. Nor is the rhetoric in the film entirely unproblematic. As it operates on some levels as a rhetorical appeal for mercy and nonviolence, it is by no means flawless.

9. Kohn reiterates the fact that "communication is improved through cooperation," which depends on the key nonviolent aggregates of sensitivity, other-orientation, and trust (150). Kohn, A. *No contest: The case against competition* (Boston: Houghton Mifflin Company, 1986).

10. Montagu states that

What, in fact, such writers do, in addition to perpetrating their wholly erroneous interpretation of human nature, is to divert attention from the real sources of [hu]man's aggression and destructiveness, namely, the many false and contradictory values by which, in an overcrowded, highly competitive, dehumanized, threatening world, he so disoperatively attempts to live. It is not [hu]man's nature, but his nurture, in such a world, that requires our attention. (17)

Thus we see that the canonical Western texts have deep influences on our cultural outlook toward life and violence. Only by questioning the validity of the rhetoric in these texts can we begin to uncover a socially empowering, nonviolent perspective.

11. "The greatest criminality is found in positions of wealth and power" concludes Pepinsky (9). Enron is a prime example.

12. The latter, as the ultimate, last resort of nonviolence in action is conducted in the name of "liberty and democracy," for in this context self-sacrifice is deemed "no less brave . . . than violent resistance . . . because it will give life" to the many through the taking of the life of only the few (Gandhi, 47).

13. See, for example: A. Ruth Fry, ed., *Victories without Violence: True Stories of Ordinary People Coming through Dangerous Situations without Using Physical Force* (Santa Fe: Ocean Tree Books, 1986); and Louise Hawkley and James C. Juhnke, eds., *Nonviolent America: History through the Eyes of Peace* (Newton, KS: Mennonite Press, 1993).

CHAPTER 5

1. In *Balkan Babel*, Sabrina Ramet notes that in "contrast with the United States, where historical memory is quite short, peoples in the Balkans talk about events in 1389, 1459, 1921, 1948, 1970-1971, as if they were fresh" (40).

2. As one elder Macedonian patriot, Tome Bonevski, puts it:

Macedonians have always been the victims in war . . . My grandfather died fighting the Turks, and my father was left an orphan when he was only three. I joined the Partisans during World War II and got our nation back . . . We fought for Macedonia for 500 years . . . and it should be known: This piece of land is Macedonia and will always be Macedonia! (Vesilind 125)

3. See, for example: Garret, Mary and Xiao, Xiaosui, "The rhetorical situation revisited," *Rhetoric Society Quarterly* 23, 1993: 30-40; Xiao, Xiaosui. "From the Hierarchical Ren to Egalitarianism: A Case of Cross-Cultural Rhetorical Mediation." *Quarterly Journal of Speech* 82 (1996): 38-54; Xiao, Xiaosui. "China Encounters Darwinism: A Case of Intercultural Rhetoric." *Quarterly Journal of Speech* 81 (1995): 83-99.

4. In terms of "technique," Sharp offers three correlative "methods" for conducting this pragmatic form of nonviolence:

1) . . . symbolic actions . . . called *nonviolent protest and persuasion* . . . such [as] demonstrations . . . marches, parades and vigils . . . 2) withdrawal or the withholding of social, economic, or political cooperation . . . described as *noncooperation* . . . 3) nonviolent intervention . . . [which] means sit ins, nonviolent obstruction . . . invasion and parallel government." (*Technique* 149-50)

5. At the same time, however, Bowen qualifies the potential rhetorical impact of nonviolent rhetoric, saying that "non-violent appeals to public sympathy are futile unless they attract political support and threaten dire economic consequences to opponents" (*Realistic* 10). In view of the Tiananmen Square debacle, Bowen's qualifier rings true, for, as another nonviolent scholar has noted, the students had neither the political backing of the masses of Chinese people, nor the political support to gain the rights they sought (*Mean* 9).

6. Ralph Summy writes that for every violent metaphor we have, there is a nonviolent alternative. Summy states that "with awareness of the problem, plus a modicum of imagination, everyone can contribute to the nonviolent transformation of language" (577). Summy gives such examples as changing "dressed to kill" into "dressed to thrill" or taking the biblical expression of "kill the fatted calf" and transforming it to "reaping the ripened grain" (573; 577). See; Summy, Ralph, "Nonviolent Speech." *Peace Review* 10 (1998): 573-78.

7. In terms of cross-cultural exchange in this milieu, Prosser has

> hypothesized . . . that the more abstract the crisis, the more symbolic the language and the more specific the tension of an actual war threat, the more direct the language [used will be] . . .
>
> The rhetorical use of basic elements of nature—wind, fire, water, the life cycle of [hu]man[s], and seasonal analogies to sowing, planting, and harvesting—cut across cultural boundaries as analogous themes to allow leaders of radically different backgrounds to transcend . . . divisive frames of reference with meaningful and timely messages for their fellow leaders. (273)

8. As Richard Spence, a historian of the Balkans puts it, each Balkan nation has its own myth of a greater land mass that does have some grain of truth to it in history. Borders in the Balkans have ebbed and flowed like tides over the centuries, which complicates border disputes and leaves room for nationalist extremists to claim more territory for their respective countries.

9. Hammond states that Herodotus further

> distinguished that pre-Temenid kingdom, which he evidently located within 'the territory Macedonis' . . . from the land beyond the river which was 'another land of Macedonia' and from 'the rest of Macedonia,' the latter including the region near 'the Gardens of Midas' below Mt. Bermium . . . In the phrases 'another land of Macedonia' and 'the rest of Macedonia' Herodotus had in mind not the pre-Temenid kingdom but the Macedonia of his own day." (121)

Thus, over time, the geographical Macedonia, as well as the varying peoples within that region, remained relatively constant in terms of name recognition and regional affiliation.

10. Even Romania, "while not contiguous with Macedonia . . . did make claims regarding the Vlach" ethnic people living in Macedonia; such claims were made with a view toward gaining territory from Bulgaria (Poulton, Macedonians 61). Romanian "propaganda" attempts were largely unsuccessful, however, since the Vlachs had been, for the most part, "hellenized" (Poulton 61-62).

11. Zimmerman also notes that the United States erroneously ignored the tortuous Balkan past and thus

> underestimated the potential for conflict in the region. Apparently the U.S. Congress, in particular, treated [Yugoslavia] as if it were Poland, Czechoslovakia, or Hungary: it would merit

their support only if communism were swept away, democracy installed, and the brutal dictatorship from the center eliminated.

But the Congress didn't see that Yugoslavia fit none of the stereotypes; that nationalism,
not communism, was the problem; and that the first democratic elections, by sweeping nationalists to power, had made the problem worse. (130)

As the fumbling attempts at negotiations on the unfolding crisis in Yugoslavia progressed
among member nations of the European Union, it is clear that they suffered from similar
shortsightedness as the Americans.

12. The Hungarian intellectual, George Konrad, writes:

The West considered the former Yugoslavia an artificial creation, despite 21 nationalities having lived there together over many years without ethnic civil war and despite Yugoslavia having been able to protect its sovereignty against the Soviet Union without outside help, as it had
resisted Hitler's Germany. The West forgot about the 1 million war dead, the executions on
both sides and the memories of that as a cultural legacy. It forgot that the collapse of a federal
state with its restraining framework would make ethnicity the chief principle of orientation for
individuals. On land where the population is mixed, however, the principle turns neighbors
who have lived together in peace into enemies. ("Nationalism Unleashed")

13. Serbia was also backed by powerful allies including Russia and France.

14. The troops were placed in the singularly "unique" position since "it wasn't accurate to talk about a JNA 'invasion,' since the JNA was in its own [if *de facto*] country" (Zimmerman 143).

15. The 1990s witnessed many foreboding ethnic struggles inside Macedonia. In
1992, rumors that "an arrested Albanian youth had been killed by Macedonian police,"
spread through Skopje and caused riots to ensue (Kaufman 234). In 1993, "a series of
shootings at the Albanian-Macedonian border . . . contributed to further [ethnic] tensions"
(237). In the summer of 1997, "ethnic Macedonian police officers pulled down an Albanian flag from the city hall in Gostivar, a mostly [ethnic] Albanian town [in Macedonia],
and crushed a local demonstration, killing three [ethnic] Albanians and injuring 186"
(Boudreaux). Although a Macedonian parliamentary panel later found the officers guilty of
using excessive force, the failure to prosecute the officers angered ethnic Albanians
(Boudreaux). Misha Glenny, among other Balkan scholars, maintains, "[a] breakdown in
relations between Macedonia's Slav majority and Albanian minority would provoke an internal collapse" of Macedonia proper (102) and would very likely lead to an all-out Balkan
war (Kaufman 238).

16. In a gesture of conciliation toward the Greeks, Gligorov negotiated to modify the
flag so that the current Macedonian flag now only features eight rays, instead of the original sixteen rays. Unofficially, however, Macedonians, especially in the diaspora throughout
the industrial centers of Europe, the United States, and Australia, display the sixteen-ray
flag as a gesture of approval (or nostalgia) of an old, idealized, perhaps mythic version of
greater Macedonia.

17. It is true that extreme nationalists in Macedonia vaunt such aspirations, but on
a practical level, realizing such ideas would be far from likely. With the withdrawal of the
JNA from Macedonia in 1991, nearly all of Macedonia's weapons were removed from the
country. At present, the Macedonian army is too small and ineffective to serve as more
than an augmentation of the civil police force.

18. President Gligorov was the butt of a glaring gaff in diplomacy when, on meeting with the Bulgarian president, it was declared that no interpreter was needed. Macedonians were outraged at the implication that the Macedonian language, and by correlation, the nation, were simply a part of Bulgaria (Kaufman 237).

19. Perry also comments that

President Gligorov, a former communist functionary in the Yugoslav bureaucracy, managed to weld . . . [Macedonia] together at the start of the 1990s. Although he spent his professional life in Belgrade and was not a well-known figure in Macedonia, he rose to the occasion. Gligorov has been the personification of the Macedonian state. He has been able to mediate problems and insure interethnic peace. He is respected, if not liked, by all sides. (117)

20. Gligorov's positions include serving as

secretary general of the government of the Federal People's Republic of Yugoslavia from 1945 to 1947; assistant to the minister of finance from 1947 to 1952; deputy director of the Federal Administration for Economic Planning and Development from 1952 to 1955; secretary of economic affairs of the Federal Executive Council from 1955 to 1962; member of the Federal Executive Council from 1962 to 1967; and vice president of the Federal Executive Council from 1967 to 1969. From 1974 to 1978 he was the president of the National Assembly . . . of the Socialist Federal Republic of Yugoslavia and a professor at Belgrade University. He also served as a member of the Central Committee of the League of Communists of Yugoslavia. (Perry, *Politics* 32)

21. Gligorov, Kiro, "Address to the United Nations General Assembly, forty-eighth Session, 30 September 1993." *United Nations Publication* A/48/PV.10, October 14, 1993: 1–4.

22. Tragically, not all negotiators and UN members hold such a staunch nonviolent perspective. The Dayton Accords resulted in handing over much of the disputed land to Serbia (or Croatia)—land that was obtained through the violent and systematic process of "ethnic cleansing" involving mass exoduses and genocide during the civil war.

23. Misha Glenny maintains that while NATO may not have caused the "exodus of Albanians from Kosovo . . . its actions have worsened the problem" (Glenny "Victims"). The flood of refugees into Macedonia, at its peak, increased Macedonia's entire population by a whopping 12%, which former Prime Minister Georgievski says "would be like having 20 million Mexicans coming in to the United States in one day" (Gall).

24. Unfortunately for the public relations of Macedonia in 1999, the pragmatic nonviolent reactions and rhetoric of Gligorov and other Macedonian heads of state have worked to their disadvantage, arousing suspicion and moral outrage among many Western audiences. However, as events unfolded, in the wake of the bombing of the Chinese embassy and increasing occurrences of civilian casualties from NATO bombs gone awry, Macedonia eventually garnered a modicum more understanding and sympathy (Hopper 10A; Gall).

25. In a recent interview, Gligorov summarized Macedonia's predicament: "[O]ur capacities allow us to absorb only about 20,000 refugees. But what is also true is that we have to abide by international conventions and that we have to take in all individuals who seek to save their lives and the lives of their children and families" (King).

CHAPTER 6

1. Craig R. Whitney, "Burmese Opposition Leader Wins the Nobel Peace Prize," *New York Times* (15 October 1991), A10.

2. See: Twine, Richard, "Essentialism." Online. Internet. August 20, 1999. Available: http://www.cc.emory.edu/ENGLISH/Postcolonial/Essentialism.html.

3. For instance, Adler and Ling read too literally Gandhi's "love thy enemy" dictate and they attempt to personalize it to situations of domestic violence, their implication being that nonviolence wrongly forces women to submit to oppression and violence against them. A more expansive and apt reading of Gandhi's works as a whole reveals that he disapproved of a great deal of cultural violence against women. Clearly, he was famously personally shortsighted and contextually situated in some practices today deemed "sexist," such as his having a "traditional" marriage in which his wife's wishes were often subordinated to his own, or viewing women primarily as mothers. However, Gandhi's biographer, Sudhir Kakar, writes that Gandhi "adamantly opposed" the practice of "the marriage of old men with young girls" (as qtd. in Clement, 162). Kakar goes so far as to say that "Gandhi was an enthusiastic champion of women's rights" (163). Gandhi asserted that women ought to express their rights: "I want women to learn the primary right of resistance," he said (164). See: Clement, Catherine, *Gandhi: The Power of Pacifism*. Trans. from the French, Ruth Sharman (New York: Harry Abrams, 1996).

4. Minnich was a student of Hannah Arendt.

5. Minnich does not use the concept of "natality" literally. I interpret her use of natality as a nonviolent sense of the fullness and rich potential of all humans as creative beings. Thus natality as a term and concept escapes what might be seen as a heterosexist bias toward male/female reproduction. Natality, above all, represents the nonviolent fulfillment and actualization of the self and Other in family, society, work, and other life-sustaining relationships or activities.

6. Oddly enough, as the media take on this highly visible role, the media in some ways become less noticeable; the media are to some extent taken for granted in free democracies as being "truly objective," when in reality they are ruled by governmental policies and large, multinational corporations with highly circumscribed editorial policies. Such policies, in their totality, often plug a socially conservative and structurally violent worldview. Major media outlets such as CNN or ABC news may be considered socially conservative as compared to more independent media entities such as Pacifica Radio or FAIR (Fairness and Accuracy in Reporting), which rely more on independent reporting that is designed to present facts than on corporate, profit driven news agendas that are established to increase ratings and gain viewers or readers by offering titilating, but often factually or rhetorically skewed, stories. The social conservatism of ABC news, for instance, is evident in the recent story about the numerous women who were sexually assaulted in the summer of 2000 in New York City's Central Park, while police failed to intervene. In one ABC news program, a reporter wondered whether the victims, some of whom were clad only in shorts and swimsuit tops, were somehow asking for it. Such commentary is socially conservative in that it harkens to the old excuse that was often a way for rapists to escape being charged: "She asked for it" because of what she was wearing. Such commentary is socially conservative, for instance, because it not so subtly reveals the conservative worldview that women ought to totally cover up, be proper, not go out unescorted, and so on. See: "Central Park Sexual Attacks" Democracy Now!, Pacifica Radio News, June 20, 2000; "Rape:

The Victim as Suspect," Prod. Susan Scheftel and Gail Boehm, Pacifica Radio, Pacifica Radio Archive, Archive no. E2BC1526.01. Los Angeles, 1973; "Unreliable Sources" by Norman Solomon; interviewed by Pamela Burton, Pacifica Radio Archive, Archive no. E2KZ1880. Los Angeles, Dec. 1990. For the problems of inaccuracy in the media generally, see: Herman, Edward S., "The Media's Role in U.S. Foreign Policy," *Journal of International Affairs*, Summer 1993, vol. 47, no. 1, pp. 23-45. Other helpful resources include: Michael Parenti's *Inventing Reality*; Noam Chomsky's recent books; anything by Neil Postman, especially the book, *Amusing Ourselves to Death*. Also, see the essay collection, *The Public Voice in a Democracy at Risk*; *Propaganda: The Formation of Men's Attitudes*, by Jacques Ellul. Also useful are recent works by Herbert Schiller, Bagdikian, Amand Mattelart, or Ron Bettis.

7. Kenneth Woodward notes, for example, that "His encompassing smile, his devouring laugh, his engaging humility and nonjudgemental manner have made the Dalai Lama the most benign and welcome figure on the stage of world religion" (32). See: Woodward, Kenneth, "A Lama to the Globe." *Newsweek* 16 Aug. 1999: 32-35.

8. David Wallechinsky, "How One Woman Became the Voice of Her People," *Parade Magazine* (19 January 1997), 1; 4-5.

9. Craig Whitney, p. A10.

10. Norwegian Nobel Committee, "The 1991 Nobel Peace Prize," in *Freedom from Fear and Other Writings*, ed. by Michael Aris (London: Viking, 1991), 236-37.

11. International awards, honors and appointments to Daw Aung San Suu Kyi include the following: 1990 Honorary Fellow. St Hugh's College (Oxford, UK); 1990 Thorolf Rafto Award for Human Rights (Norway); 1991 Sakharov Prize for Freedom of Thought (European Parliament); 1991 Nobel Peace Prize (Oslo, Norway); 1991 Honorary Member, International PEN (Norwegian Center); 1991 Humanities Human Rights Award (USA); 1991 Honorary Member, International PEN (Candian Center); 1992 Marisa Bellisario Prize (Italy); 1992 Annual Award of the International Human Rights Law Group (USA); 1992 Honorary President, Students' Union London School of Economics and Political Science; 1992 Honorary Member, International PEN (English Centre); 1992 Honrary Life Member, University of London Union (UK); 1992 Honorary Professional Fellowship, Law and Society Trust (Sri Lanka); 1992 Honorary Doctorate in Political Science, Thammasat University (Thailand); 1992 International Simon Bolivar Prize (UNESCO); 1992 Prix Litteraire des Droits de l'Homme (Nouveaux Droits de l'Homme, France); 1992 Honorary Member, World Commission on Culture and Development (UNESCO); 1993 Member, Academie Universelle des Cultures (Paris); 1993 Rose Prize (arbejderbevaegelsens Internationale Forum/International Forum of the Danish Labour Movement, Copenhagen); 1993 Victor Jara International Human Rights Award (Center for Human Rights and Constitutional Law, Los Angeles, USA); 1993 Member of the Advisory Board, Francois-Xavier Bagnoud Center for Health and Human Rights, Harvard University; 1993 Honorary Doctorate of Law, University of Toronto (Canada); 1993 The Freedom of the City, Commune of Giugliano, Italy; 1993 Bremen Solidarity Prize (City of Bremen, Germany); 1994 Honorary Doctorate, Philosophy and Letters, Free University of Brussels; 1994 Honorary Adviser, Forum of Democratic Leaders in the Asia-Pacific; 1995 The Freedom of the City, Aversa, Italy; 1995 Liberal International Prize for Freedom (UK); Honorary Doctorate of Laws, Queen's University, Canada; 1995 Jawaharlal Nehru Award for International Understanding (for 1993), India;1995 Gandhi Award, Simon Fraser University, Canada (to be awarded in October); 1995 Honorary Doctorate of Civil Law, University of Oxford

(awaiting collection in person). See: Ko Soe Pyne, *Free Burma*. Online. Accessed August 18, 1999. http://metalab.unc.edu/freeburma/assk/assk.html.

12. Gayle Kirshenbaum, "Aung San Suu Kyi," *Ms.* 6 (1996), 56–57.

13. David Wallechinsky, p. 5.

14. Josef Silverstein, "The Idea of Freedom in Burma and the Political Thought of Daw Aung San Suu Kyi," *Pacific Affairs*, 69 (1996), 211–28.

15. Karan Thapar, "Burmese Days of Reckoning," *The Spectator* 263 (August 12, 1989), 13.

16. Thapar 13.

17. Thapar 13.

18. At the time of the award announcement, her family did not even know if Suu Kyi had been apprised of her award. Consequently, the speech that was delivered by her son, Alexander Aris, contains only one paragraph—an excerpt from her previous writings—that was actually written by Suu Kyi herself. It is likely that the rest of the speech, entitled "The Revolution of Spirit," was written by Michael Aris, Suu Kyi's husband and editor of her book, *Freedom from Fear*. Aung San Suu Kyi, "The Revolution of Spirit," in *Peace! By the Nobel Peace Prize Laureates: An Anthology*, ed. by Marek Thee (Mayenne, France: Unesco, 1995), 433–35. Preceding the text of the speech is the following descriptive commentary: "Aung San Suu Kyi. Nobel Peace Prize Laureate 1991. Leader of the democratic movement in Burma; Advocate of human rights and reconciliation. Acceptance speech read by her son, Alexander Aris."

19. In Burma, crowds of more than four persons constitute "illegal gatherings" and are immediately subject to arrest and/or martial orders.

20. Marina Budhos, "Update on Aung San Suu Kyi," *Ms.* 7 (March/April 1997), 25.

21. See: "Aung San Suu Kyi." Online. Internet. August 18, 1999. Available: http://www.dfn.org/Voices/Asia/burma/assk.html.

22. John Pilger, "Slave Nation" p. 70.

23. Archbishop Desmond Tutu, who is also a Nobel peace laureate for his nonviolent work first opposing, then dealing with the aftermath of apartheid South Africa, avers, "International pressure can change the situation in Burma. Tough sanctions, not 'constructive engagement,' finally brought about a new South Africa. This is the language that must be spoken with tyrants, for it is the only language they understand." John Pilger, p. 70.

24. Caroline Nath, "Burma: War of Nerves," *World Press Review* 13 (February 1996), 31. Of course, precise definitions of "imprisoned" and "harmed" as well as "large-scale" remain to be defined by the U.S. State Department and Congress. Both of these political bodies are ever under pressure from oil lobbying interests who contend, correctly, that if U.S. companies do not have access to the rich oil reserves in Burma, then European countries will simply take them.

25. Suu Kyi released the statement: "I have been so fortunate to have such a wonderful husband, who had always given me the understanding I needed. Nothing can take that from me." See: "In Remembrance: Michael Aris." *Tricycle: The Buddhist Review* (Summer 1999) 8.

26. "Inside Burma: Land of Fear: A Special Report by John Pilger." Documentary film. Oley, PA: Bullfrog Films. Produced by Carlton, UK. 1997.

27. Aung San Suu Kyi, *Freedom from Fear*.

28. Anonymous, "Burma: Phooey to 80%," *Economist* 316 (1990): 29–30.

29. Karan Thapar, 13.

30. Anonymous, "A Woman of Subtlety," *Economist* 322 (1992): 90.

31. David Wallechinsky, 1.

32. Steven Erlanger, "Burmese Whose Silenced Voice Echoes," *New York Times* (October 15, 1991), A11.

33. Michael Aris, "Introduction," in *Freedom from Fear*, xvi–xvii.

34. See: Free Burma Coalition. Online. Accessed 19 August 1999. http://www.free burmacoalition.org.

35. The sarong takes on political significance, as it is worn by the various ethnic groups in Burma. It symbolizes the solidarity that she encourages among the often factious ethnic groups. The brightly colored patterns of the sarong's fabric starkly contrasts the drab military uniforms worn by her political adversaries in SLORC/SPDC.

36. David Wallechinsky, 4.

37. See, for example: Xiaosui Xiao, "From the Hierarchical Ren to Egalitariansim: A Case of Cross-Cultural Rhetorical Mediation," *The Quarterly Journal of Speech* 82 (1996), 38–54. Xiao shows how Eastern rhetoric emphasizes the "humanistic" (38) and the "interdependent and collectivistic aspects of human life" (52).

38. The association of elitism, class snobbery (and its economic entailments in colonialism or postcolonialism) with nonviolent theory and practice remains problematic. This problem is large enough to merit a study in and of itself, which is far beyond the focus and scope of this particular study.

39. Ms. Spencer took the initiative to use her high-profile personage and lavish lifestyle to attract major media attention to issues such as promoting the international ban on landmines. As a "smiling professional," Spencer actively sought out photo opportunities evoking intense pathos. Shortly before her death, with cameras rolling, she sat chatting with a child on her lap and was surrounded by children whose limbs were mere nubs as the result of landmine explosion "accidents."

40. Hartley notes that the excluded "they" includes "criminals, political extremists, drug traffickers, paedophiles, juvenile offenders and . . . immigrants (207). Also, Asian countries consist of "Theydom." Suu Kyi, in subject position of both Asianness and "political extremist" tainted by the strangeness of nonviolence to conservatives, appears to need elitist symbols in order to cross over into the realm of "Wedom" and inclusion in the media.

41. Mary Ann Rentz, "The Cabinet Member as a Representative of the President: The Case of James Watt," *Communication Studies*, 38 (1987): 94–110.

42. Rentz, p. 98.

43. Rentz, 101; 106. Rentz observes that in the case of President Reagan, Secretary of the Interior James Watt served as his "mouthpiece" so that "Reagan was able to distance himself from the controversial policy" of his administration—thus Reagan achieved optimal rhetorical distance. As a result, Rentz concludes that a rhetor can "continue an unpopular position" by using "its active advocate," that is, a representative speaker—a medium/mediator—to "remain relatively free of contamination."

44. Clearly, as the daughter of a Burman national hero, Aung San Suu Kyi is special and unique. But both her rise to leadership of the democratic movement, and her persisting influence, could not have been sustained by her beautiful body alone: a strong leader is required for any social movement to thrive and endure. It has been remarked that the labeling of intelligent, successful women as *special* is a routine, hegemonic discursive practice. In addition to the word *special* having the ring of being a euphemism for "slow" or "retarded," feminist rhetorical scholars have noted the word's other associations. Such women

are perceived as being unique, unusual—like freaks of nature. They are the chosen few who have unusual access to patriarchal privilege and power. Their success is seen as the result of a combination of luck and the right connections, and only occasionally due to intellectual abilities (and even then, their freakishness is emphasized). See, for example: Adrienne Rich, *Ms.* 8 (1979): 43; Carole Spitzack and Kathryn Carter, "Women in Communication Studies: A Typology for Revision," *The Quarterly Journal of Speech,* 73 (1987), 401–23; Barbara Beisecker, "Coming to Terms with Recent Attempts to Write Women into the History of Rhetoric," 141–47.

While the charge that greatness in women only occurs due to unusual circumstances is more problematic for women in overcoming stereotypes and prejudices, the same charge has been levied against great men, according to historian Arnold Toynbee. Toynbee maintains that several preconditions must exist for a truly "great" leader to emerge in history. These preconditions are: (1) a "reciprocity between the leader and [her/] his followers; (2) opportunity or the right timing; (3) faith of the people; (4) "instances of simultaneity . . . that counts for most"; and (5) "psychological insight and sympathy" for others. Arnold Toynbee, "The Leader," in *Time and the Philosophies.* (London: Unesco, 1977): 231–42.

45. Josef Silverstein, 211–28.

46. She has a proven ability to think both "in theory and the abstract": Suu Kyi holds an undergraduate degree from Delhi University and a postgraduate degree from the Oxford University, England.

47. Were she to leave Burma, SPDC is prepared to forbid her reentry into Burma. Her sons and (now deceased) spouse, also, have only been able to visit her on rare occasions, due to SLORC interventions and restrictions on their travel into and out of Burma. During the early years of her house arrest, she was prevented from seeing her family, apparently SLORC leaders believed this separation would serve as sufficient incentive for her to leave Burma. To date, she has remained in Burma.

48. Anonymous editorial commentary. See: Aung San Suu Kyi, "Letter from Burma: A Fishy Episode," *Utne Reader* 78 (1996): 70.

49. Mark Johnson's research focuses on the complex processes of meaning making. Specifically, he explores the dynamic relationship of the body and cognition in human reasoning processes. Johnson contends that "physical appearance is a physical force" (7). See: Johnson, Mark, *The Body in the Mind: The Bodily Basis of Meaning, Imagination, and Reason* (Chicago: University of Chicago Press, 1987).

50. Gayle Kirshenbaum, 57.

51. Karan Thapar, 13.

52. See, for example: Riane Eisler's work "describes a way of life based on equality, nonviolence, and harmony with nature 'a partnership way' that was the basis of prehistoric Goddess-worshiping societies and offers a model for developing a sustainable and equitable future." Eisler, Riane, *The Chalice and the Blade* (New York: Harper Collins Publishers, 1988). Also, author Leonard Shlain maintains that due to the left brain cognitive emphasis in literate societies, logical, "masculine" gendered traits, including aggression and violence, have been overemphasized. Shlain contends that right brain, intuitive, and inner-awareness tendencies have been quashed by literate societies. Shlain argues, however, that with the rise of increasing pictorialization of current societies all over the world, "feminine" gendered tendencies such as equality and nonviolence are once again ascending to a status of strong social force today. Shlain, Leonard. *The Alphabet Versus the Goddess: The Conflict between Word and Image* (New York: Viking, 1998).

53. See, for instance: Smith, Huston, *The World's Religions* (San Francisco: Harper, 1991); Stone, Merlin, *When God Was a Woman* (Boston: Beacon Press, 1976); Pollack, Rachel, *The Body of the Goddess. Sacred Wisdom in Myth, Landscape, and Culture* (Great Britain: Element Books Limited, 1997); Monahan, Patricia, *The Book of Goddesses and Heroines* (New York: Dutton, 1981).

54. Ian Harris, 192.

55. In fact, "south Asia" is a locale Sardar concedes is possibly one of "the most misogynist, patriarchal and male chauvinist regions on earth" (24). It is critically vital to note, however, that the abstract region of "Asia" or the descriptor of "Asian" must not be seen as too generic, even if there are certain commonly shared attributes across cultures and countries deemed Asian. For example, Chinese rhetoric is quite different from Indian rhetoric.

56. The SPDC's surveillance tactics include "housechecks," that is, the mandatory registrations of all households and members and vistitors to them; "random checks" by special police in the "middle of the night"; "intelligence units"; and strictly monitored travel through "Myanmar's fourteen states and divisions" (Matthews 10).

57. Aung San Suu Kyi, as quoted on p. 52, in Alan Clements and Leslie Kean, *Burma's Revolution of the Spirit: The Struggle for Democratic Freedom and Dignity* (New York: Aperture Foundation, 1994).

58. Gayle Kirshenbaum, 57.

59. Josef Silverstein, 212.

60. Sardar puts "Burma" in quotations because he feels the name Myanmar (which SLORC renamed the country by decree and without civilian input) should be used in the media. The name Burma, for Sardar, reveals "unconscious nostalgia for the [British] Empire" (24). Sardar is suspicious of what he calls "the colonial project of making the world more like the west" (24).

61. Madeleine Albright writes, for instance, of her visit to Burma in 1995 when she spoke with a SLORC representative and expressed the U.S. government's support for Suu Kyi's position:

> The general insisted that the SLORC's approach is the best way to guarantee stability and that the Burmese people support its efforts to rebuild the economy and ensure law and order. "Even at midnight," he said, "you can walk around town without danger; that is why the Burmese people have such happy faces." I replied that during a lifetime of studying repressive regimes I had found the smiling quotient in many of them to have been quite high. Authoritarian leaders often delude themselves that they are loved, but the smiles they see are usually prompted not by affection, but fear.

Thus the smiles are an illusion manufactured by the military's hard handed rule.

63. G. P. Mohrmann confirms that

> there is a linguistic tendency to make the abstract concrete and that this strain toward palpability and movement becomes . . . [key to] the metaphorical texture of . . . discourse. . . . it seems equally clear that these same forces are integral to our understanding of the power exerted by spatial metaphors. Certainly, both the strain toward palpability and the subtle indications of local motion are fundamental to . . . [certain] spatial images. (148)

63. Lawrence W. Rosenfield, "Central Park and Civic Virtue," 224.

64. John Pilger, "Slave Nation," *Utne Reader* 78 (November 1996), 66–71.

65. Xiaosui Xiao, "From the Hierarchical Ren to Egalitariansim: A Case of Cross-Cultural Rhetorical Mediation," 52.

66. Gail Presbey, 248.

67. Lauren, Paul G., "Moral Choice and Human Rights." Lecture. The V. N. Bhatia Lecture on Excellence in Education. Washington State University, Pullman, April 29, 1999.

CHAPTER 7

1. There is a nexus between rhetoric and democracy that is covered in this case:

> Iris Young's concept of communicative democracy, particularly the relationship between argu-
> ment and rhetoric, provides additional support for [this chapter's] argument about the impor-
> tance of feelings and emotions. The Billings response to hate crimes might qualify as an
> example of what Young calls "greeting." The argument about climate [in this chapter] is also an
> argument about the communicative preconditions for an inclusive democracy.

I thank Dr. Nancy Love, Penn State University, for making this insightful connection. Love, Nancy, Letter to author. September 9, 1999. For the discussion of communicative democracy, see: Young, Iris, Justice and the Politics of Difference (Princeton: Princeton University Presss, 1990): 92–94.

2. But in discussing symbols, Burke cites the example of the poet, whose symbols are actually "symbolistics" that are replete with feeling, with attitudes. It is such attitudes which render the poetry so powerful, rather than the mere symbols that the poet invokes. He writes that the poetic, symbolistic word "signalized an *attitude*," and that the poet chose a particular word "not because it names an *image* but because it names an attitude" that goes far beyond a mere "descriptive . . . function" normally associated with images or symbols (emphasis in original) (242–43).

All the "poetic categories," moreover, proffer equally powerful claims to their respective attitudes. Frames for viewing poetic renditions of reality, such as comedy, tragedy, satire, burlesque, or grotesque, all draw on unique, respective "attitudinizings of the frame" (40). Wrapped inside each rhetorical situation are Kenneth Burke's notions of "perspec-tive" and "attitudes." In *Attitudes toward History*, Burke notes the socially "bridging" func-tion of the effect that "attitudes" have on how history plays out, describing this effect as "the organizing of a unifying *attitude*" (emphasis in original) (92). Burke distinguishes be-tween symbols and attitudes, but consistently shows how each interrelates to the other.

Of symbols, Burke emphasizes the attitudinal: "A symbol is a vessel of much more content than is disclosed by its 'face value' as a label. Words may contain *attitudes* much more complex and subtle than could possibly be indicated in the efficient simplifications of a 'practical' dictionary" (emphasis added) (329).

Attitudes which are contained in each frame (comic, tragic), or window to the world, are crucial to this discussion because they reveal how situations flow through people's minds (individually, collectively), and call on a *special feeling* to color the way the drama un-folds or the crisis is to be resolved or at least *experienced*. Cultural or social outsiders in a historical setting are seen by the insiders as being "culturally dispossessed" because their new ideas, according to the insiders, "are felt as [mere] attitudes, rather than as 'truth'" (40–41). In this way Burke shows how history plays itself out among the backdrop of the feeling states—attitudes—of the players through time, whether in real life (Hitler, Stalin) or on the stage (*MacBeth*, *Othello*). Beyond attitudes, what is known more simply as "context" has equally figured into how rhetorical critics have broached the metaphorical notion of "climate," yet not gone quite far enough.

3. Andrews proposes that the critic's perspective on context should be viewed in this way:

> In a speaking situation . . . there is always a speaker, a message produced by that speaker, an audience responding to that message, and a complex context made up of a multiplicity of factors ranging from prevailing ethical standards and the importance of the issues involved to the size and temperature of the room and the speaker's energy level. The critic has to deal in some way with all these constituents one by one. (16)

4. Depending on the state and jurisdiction, hate crimes in the United States are also called "bias crimes" or crimes of "malicious harrassment."

5. This phrase is from Ed Lamoureux, Editor, *Journal of Communication and Religion*.

6. Thich Nhat Hanh, the Buddhist monk (whom Dr. Martin Luther King, Jr., called "a scholar of immense intellectual capacity"), notes that, clearly, understanding context is just as important as understanding a text:

> Everything Jesus and the Buddha taught was to a particular person or group on a particular occasion. We must try to understand the context in which they spoke in order to understand their meaning. If we just analyze their words, we may miss the point. (76)

7. Moreover, speaking events often exclude the politically underprivileged, silencing their voices, and hence perpetuating structural violence; whereas acting events such as peaceful gatherings, riots, or other emotional manifestations of social conflict might be viewed in a new light, giving voice to those normally silenced by status quo social structures.

8. Interpellation, from the French, *interpellé*, connotes a "hailing," a "Hey, you there!"—thus an ideological "subject" is being continuously called out to respond in and through language. Maurice Charland describes interpellation in this way:

> Interpellation occurs at the very moment one enters into a rhetorical situation, that is, as soon as an individual recognizes and acknowledges being addressed. An interpellated subject participates in the discourse that addesses [her/] him. Thus, to be interpellated is to become one of Black's personae and be a position in the discourse . . . [So] interpellation has a significance to rhetoric, for the acknowledgement of an address entails an acceptance of an imputed self-understanding which can form the basis for an appeal . . . [Also] interpellation occurs rhetorically, through the effect of the addressed discourse. [But] interpellation does not occur through persuasion in the usual sense, for the very act of *addressing* is rhetorical. It is logically prior to the rhetorical *narratio*. In addition, this rhetoric of identification is ongoing, not restricted to one hailing, but usually part of a rhetoric of socialization. Thus, one must already be an interpellated subject and exist as a discursive position in order to be a part of the audience of a rhetorical situation in which persuasion could occur. (217)

For Charland's disscussion, see: Charland, Maurice, "Constitutive Rhetoric: The Case of the *Peuple Québéqois*," in *Critical Questions: Invention, Creativity, and the Criticism of Discourse and Media*. eds. William Nothstine, Carole Blair, and Gary Copeland (New York: St. Martin's Press, 1994): 211–32. See also: Dickinson, Greg, "Memories for Sale: Nostalgia and the Construction of Identity in Old Pasadena," *Quarterly Journal of Speech* 83 (1997): 1–27.

9. Even the question mark in the pamphlet's title seems to reflect the symbolic uncertainty the writers had with the concept of climate.

10. I found the pamphlet in 1996 prominently displayed in racks with other brochures and pamphlets, both at Penn State's Women's Studies Department and at the Women's Center on campus. Perhaps the target audience for the pamphlet was assumed to understand, through a sense of shared persecution, what a climate is, chilly or otherwise.

11. There is also a need to distinguish the word *climate* from the word *culture*. Unlike climate, as part of a critic's perspective, "culture" has been defined clearly by many theorists, from anthropology to communication. "Culture" generally comprises historically transmitted beliefs, ideals, rituals and customs of human groups. So, whereas "climate has been viewed as a shared perception, culture has been characterized more as a shared belief or assumption . . . [C]limate has tended to be employed as a descriptive concept, while much of the discussion on culture has been imbued with a prescriptive or normative slant" (Dastmalchian, Blyton, and Adamson 33). Therefore, the concept of a *human social climate* provides a more descriptive way of looking at things; certainly culture can be part of a description of a perceived reality, but climate and culture are not synonymous.

12. "Women are 9 times more likely than men to quit jobs because of sexual harrassment [perpetrated against them and/or other female coworkers], 5 times more likely to transfer, and 3 times more likely to lose jobs." "Sexual Harrassment: Facts and Figures." Handout. Center for Human Rights. Pullman: Washington State University. 1998.

13. In addition, it should be noted that over "3 million [MBTIs] are administered annually in the U.S." while the test is "also used internationally and has been translated into many languages, including Japanese, French, Spanish, Korean, German, Danish, Swedish, and Chinese" (Briggs Myers 1).

14. Ironically, Porrovecchio himself states that "[a] graduate student is treated to a theoretical field as vast as the status quo allows. But that expansive terrain of possibilities is likely to be constrained by the manner in which critics use and promote the theories that are available" (56). I am positing that the status quo has tended to "constrain" the theoretical shift I make here. This shift is away from the individualism of the rhetor and toward an expansive view of rhetoric that is collectivistic and audience based.

15. For further reading on climate, see: Falcione, Raymond L., Sussman, Lyle and Herden, Richard P, "Communication Climate in Organizations." *Handbook of Organizational Communication: an Interdisciplinary Perspective.* Ed. Fredric M. Jablin (Newbury Park: Sage, 1987), 195–225; Falcione, Raymond L. and Kaplan, Elyse A., "Organizational Climate, Communication, and Culture." *Communication Yearbook* 8. Ed. R. N. Bostrom (Beverly Hills: Sage, 1984), 285–309; Denison, Daniel R., "What Is the Difference Between Organizational Culture and Organizational Climate? A Native's Point of View on a Decade of Paradigm Wars." *Academy of Management Review* 21 (1996): 619–54; M. Patterson, M. West, and R. Payne, "Collective Climates: A Test of Their Socio-Psychological Significance." Discussion Paper No. 94. Sept. 1992. Online, Corporate Performance and Work Organization. Internet. January 29, 1999. Available http://cep.lse.ac.uk/papers/discussion/dp0094.html.; Benjamin Schneider et al., "A Passion for Service: Using Content Analysis to Explicate Service Climate Themes." *Journal of Applied Psychology* 77 (1992): 705–16; Drory, Amos, "Perceived Political Climate and Job Attitudes." *Organization Studies* 14 (1993): 59–71.

16. Meanwhile, the suasory influence of the singular unit of "good man speaking well" grows moot; it becomes diluted and absorbed into the collective.

17. Earlier, Carl L. Becker highlights the value of Whitehead's terms, "climate of opinion." Becker writes that "Whether arguments command assent or not depends less on the logic that conveys them than on the climate of opinion in which they are sustained" (5). This climate is comprised of "instinctively held preconceptions in the broad sense, that *Weltanschauung* or world pattern—which . . . [imposes upon certain persons in an historical setting] a peculiar use of the intelligence and a special type of logic" (5). Becker's position supports the notion that this type of climate can silence some and empower others socially, for he observes that

> If we would discover the little backstairs door that for any age serves as the secret entranceway to knowledge, we will do well to look for certain unobtrusive words with uncertain meanings that are permitted to slip off the tongue or the pen without fear and without research; words which, having from constant repetition lost their metaphorical significance, are unconsciously mistaken for objective realities. (47)

This shows how social meaning and perceptions play a role in our processes of reality construction. Carl L. Becker, *The Heavenly City of the Eighteenth-Century Philosophers* (New Haven, CT: Yale University Press, 1960).

18. Falcione and Kaplan state that the "International Communication Association (ICA) has made a commendable effort to clarify . . . climate research" (299). The ICA created a "Communication Audit" is comprised of five "instruments . . . (1) questionnaire survey, (2) interviews, (3) network analysis, (4) communication experiences instrument, and (5) communication diary" (299). Falcione and Kaplan believe that "the ICA Communication Audit is one of the more sophisticated and carefully designed efforts to measure the communication systems of organizations" and it is therefore reliable (299).

19. I also pay homage to the notion of a "climate of opinion" or one that is perceived by certain demographic groups, such as that of a "chilly climate."

20. Becker highlights the factor of beings moving through time and simultaneously feeling emotion as an important consideration in a given climate. He writes: "memory of past and anticipation of future events work together . . . so that in a real sense the specious present as held in consciousness at any time is a *pattern of thought* woven instantaneously from the threads of memories, perceptions, and anticipations" (emphasis added) (121). It is this "pattern of thought" that is like an attitude, it frames the action(s) that will unfold.

21. Berlin states that people, as social beings

> live . . . within a system of socially constructed institutions, rules, and relationships that in some sense provide [them] with a set of prestructured meanings—a social reality that [they] can conform to, rebel against, or understand in . . . idiosyncratic ways but that [they] cannot completely escape or ignore. (331)

22. If one asks, "Alternately to what?" the answer is "alternately to the dominant or norm." There is a variation or divergence from the hegemonic norm or the expected and understood reality. An alternate reality is a reality that is just as real, though is often less visible, than the climate of normalcy that people who participate in hegemony experience. In the wake of the April 20, 1999 shootings at Columbine High School in Littleton, Colorado, reports arose that the two student gunmen surfed violent web sites, subscribed to

neonazi ideology, listened to violent music lyrics, played ultraviolent video games, and so on. It was a cold, callous, and violent emotional climate in which these two students, and their alleged peers in their clique, "The Trenchcoat Mafia," existed. These students' rhetorical climate can be said to have existed *alternately*, apart from a hegemony of "normal" understanding, and therefore less perceptibly, to the students and faculty at the school as well as to the boys' parents and families.

23. See, for example, Branham and Pearce's "models of . . . text-context relations" (23-27).

24. Robert Kully's essay, "Rabbi Isaac Mayer Wise: His Language of Anti Anti-Semitism" provides ample evidence of the strong anti-Semitic sentiment in America in the 1800s. Kully remarks that "as the Jewish population in America multiplied, so did the prejudice against the Jews . . . between 1850 and 1900 . . . Hatred of Jews became fashionable" (166).

25. Johan Galtung defines violence as "the cause of the difference between the potential and the actual, between what could have been and what is . . . [it] is that which increases the distance between the potential and the actual, and that which impedes the decrease of this distance" (9-10). Galtung lists many types of violence, ranging from the physical and psychological; negative and positive approaches to influence; and material (object) and personal (subject) violence (10-11). He clarifies that much violence "is structural," that is, it is "built into structures" and thus seems invisible (11). The danger of this invisibility, according to Galtung, is that it then appears the so-called natural state of affairs, and even worse, that our "ethical systems . . . will easily fail to capture structural violence in . . . [our] nets" so that we focus on overt or personal violence, such as "murder," while "ignorance" may be more socially detrimental (11). Structural violence operates, exists, and is perpetuated in a rhetorical manner:

> It is not strange that attention has been focused more on personal than structural violence. Personal violence shows. The object of personal violence perceives the violence, usually, and may complain—the *object of structural violence may be persuaded not to perceive this at all*. . . . Structural violence is *silent*, it does not show—it is essentially static. . . . Thus a research emphasis on the reduction of personal violence at the expense of a tacit or open neglect of research on structural violence leads . . . to acceptance of "law and order" societies [emphasis added]. (12-13)

Thus Galtung explains how structural violence is made to seem a normal part of social order, when in reality it functions to warp that order and prevent human beings from reaching their highest level of self-actualization. See: Johan Galtung, "Violence and Peace," *A Reader in Peace Studies*, eds. Paul Smoker, Ruth Davies, and Barbara Munske (New York: Pergamon Press, 1990): 9-14.

26. Structural violence occurs where systems, such as police departments, large corporations, and other social bureaucracies serve to perpetuate wrongdoing by ignoring—either passively or actively—problems such as hate crimes, which feature interpersonal violence. Through socially organized acceptance, the perpetuation of both structured and interpersonal violence becomes an entrenched societal norm.

27. This case has been the real-life basis for a children's book, a made-for-television movie, a PBS documentary, and a social movement with an organizing web site, respectively. See: Cohn, Janice, *The Christmas Menorahs: How a Town Fought Hate* (Morton Grove, IL: Whitman, 1995); "Not in This Town." Perf. Kathy Baker and Adam Arkin. USA Network. April 19, 1997; *Not in Our Town*. Video Documentary. Series: We Do the Work. Dir. and

Prod. The Working Group. California, PBS, 1994; "Not in Our Town." Online. Not In Our Town Campaign. Internet. April 26, 1999. Available: http://www.igc.org/an/niot/.

28. Antonio Damasio, who is head of the Department of Neurology at the University of Iowa College of Medicine, remarks that even phrasing the prognosis of a patient's potential for recovery can impact that individual's recovery itself. With regard to the individual, Damasio states that a single prognosis, phrased as a "ninety-five percent success rate," will be far more well received by a sick patient than to say that there is a "five percent failure rate."

29. The Polish anthropologist Jan Kubik has shown that the visit of the Pope to Poland in 1979 was instrumental in turning the tide against the communist regime (129-52). The Pope's visit created and reinvigorated in the Polish people the hope that was a crucial prerequisite to starting a patriotic catharsis (148-49). Without the Pope's visit and the reflowering of spiritual faith, the organizing and rhetoric of the Solidarity movement would simply not have taken hold as it did.

30. In *Origins of the Modern Mind*, Merlin Donald discusses the cognitive phases of human evolution, starting with the simplest episodic culture, to which, in successive evolutionary advances, mimetic, mythic, and theoretic cultures appeared. Through the conservation of previous gains, human beings today operate in cognitive states that maintain each of these mental mapping systems (1991). What organized religion does is foster this fourfold state to reinforce beliefs, motivations, and activity patterns among the faithful.

31. Weaver observes that

> The discourse of the noble rhetorician . . . will be about real potentiality or possible actuality, whereas that of the mere exaggerator is about unreal potentiality. Naturally this distinction rests upon a supposal that the rhetorician has insight . . . given insight, he has the duty to represent to us the as yet unactualized future . . . During the Second World War, at the depth of Britain's political and military disaster, Winston Churchill likened the future of Europe to "broad sunlit uplands." . . . the hope which transfigured this [situation] . . . was not irresponsible . . . [because] the rhetorician talks about both what exists simply and what exists by favor of human imagination and effort. (20)

32. David Mathews remarks that one "aspect of banding together is that it requires an affirmative *will* to act—not a momentary enthusiasm inspired by some charismatic figure, but a sustained commitment of many people over a long period of time, even if it means making sacrifices" (emphasis in original) (400).

33. Or conversely, Damasio's research indicates that "bereavement . . . leads to a depression of the immune system . . . One *can* die of a broken heart" (emphasis in original) (120).

34. Jan Kubik's analysis of the fall of Communism in Poland echoes Weaver's point that hope can change a situation. Kubik shows that it is the Pope's visit to Poland which serves as a catalyst for activating the Polish people to rise up in Solidarity and reject the Communist leadership. In Kubik's words, "For most Poles the pope's visit was an unusually *cathartic* experience" (emphasis in original) (148).

35. See, for example: Moore, Mark P, "From a Government of the People, to a People of the Government: Irony as Rhetorical Strategy in Presidential Campaigns." *Quarterly Journal of Speech* 82 (1996): 22-37. Moore maintains that widely held cynical attitudes of voters are tapped into by candidates as a rhetorical strategy to win at the polls.

36. Damasio believes that "most ethical rules and social conventions" actually are derived from "simpler . . . drives and instincts" (125). He affirms that these drives "contribute . . . albeit indirectly, to survival and to the quality of survival" (125).

37. This stands refreshingly in opposition to Freud's clichéd views on a "naturalized" human aggression or Burke's similar views on people being "goaded by hierarchy."

38. Damasio describes case after case in which patients, because they have experienced damage to the areas of the brain that support feelings and sensory perception, are to a great degree incapacitated and unable to reason logically. Further, he cites sociopaths who are able to commit and usually repeat crimes "in cold blood" because their "decline in rationality is accompanied by diminution or absence of feeling" (178).

39. In Fall of 2000, a civil case brought suit against Butler and his organization. Butler lost, and the compound was closed down. However, Butler maintains his organization now from a new suburban home nearby, and the Aryan Nations members marched in their annual parade. Their presence is still keenly felt in Northern Idaho and Washington state.

40. Philip Wander notes, however, that in the particular instance referred to here, Heidegger's speech was not at all related to anti-Semitism, but rather to "an audience's general, collective, and personal concrete knowledge and experience." Wander, Phillip C., Letter to the author. May 18, 1999.

41. For an excellent analysis that deconstructs Nazi rhetoric, see: Scanlan, Ross, "The Nazi Rhetorician," *Quarterly Journal of Speech* 37 (1951) 430-40. For discussions that cover Nazi attempts at specifically creating climates of feeling, experience, and action, see also: Bosmajian, Haig A., "The Sources and Nature of Adolf Hitler's Techniques of Persuasion," *Communication Studies* 25 (1974): 240-48; Bosmajian, Haig A., "Nazi Persuasion and the Crowd Mentality," *Western Journal of Speech Communication* 29 (1965): 68-78; Bosmajian, Haig A., "The Persuasiveness of Nazi Marching and Der Kampf um Die Strasse," *Communication Quarterly* 16 (1974): 240-48; Delia, Jessee G., "Rhetoric in the Nazi Mind: Hitler's Theory of Persuasion," *Southern Communication Journal* 37 (1971): 136-49.

42. Current research on this conception of proponents and adherents of neonaziism is, however, changing. As middle-class children are increasingly recruited into hate groups or ideologies during the junior high school and high school years, as well as through the Internet, stereotypes of neonazis as being poor or uneducated are being broken. Also, in the Pacific Northwest, affluent businessmen have underwritten hate groups with enormous financial support. Such support has enabled vast, and, unfortunately, influential, direct mail propaganda campaigns to occur.

On a different level, as Myrlie Evers Williams states, intolerance has changed so that today, one needs perhaps to be more wary of the person in the "Brooks Brothers' suit" than the skinhead on the street. See: Williams, Myrlie Evers. Speech. Washington State University. February 17, 1999.

43. Of the murder, Inman said, years later,

> I have no doubt that had Portland risen up against the hate-mongers when they first got going, the impact of the skinheads would have been substantially reduced. We could not get community support to say, "not in our town." (as qtd. in Rosenblatt 26)

44. There are many such examples of spontaneous and creative solidarity. Telushkin gives the following example:

> Consider the case of Ian O'Gorman, a ten-year-old boy in Oceanside, California, who was diagnosed with cancer. The doctors prescribed ten weeks of chemotherapy, during which, they warned him, all his hair would fall out. To avoid the anxiety and pain of watching his hair gradually disappear, the youngster had his entire head shaved.

One can only imagine Ian's *feelings* a few days later when he returned to school, prematurely bald, and found that the thirteen other boys in his fifth grade class, and their teacher as well, greeted him with their heads completely shaved. (emphasis added) (155)

This same kind of support has been repeated nationwide by other children as well as by spouses supporting their partners undergoing chemotherapy.

45. Above the picture of the menorah, the text of the ad read:

On December 2, 1993, someone twisted by hate threw a brick through the window of the home of one of our neighbors: a Jewish family who chose to celebrate the holiday season by displaying a symbol of faith—a menorah—for all to see. Today, members of religious faiths throughout Billings are joining together to ask residents to display the menorah as a symbol of something else: our determination to live together in harmony, and our dedication to the principle of religious liberty embodied in the First Amendment to the Constitution of the United States of America.

Below the picture of the menorah, the text continued:

We urge all citizens to share in this message by displaying this menorah on a door or a window from now until Christmas. Let all the world know that the irrational hatred of a few cannot destroy what all of us in Billings, and in America, have worked together so long to build. (*Billings Gazette*, "Solidarity Symbol" A12)

46. Such rhetoric protesting the hate crimes fulfills a dual function. On one level, it is selfless. On the other level, part of the power of creating a subordinate text, such as is seen in protest rhetoric, is that it is self-actuating. "The rhetoric is basically self-directed, not other-directed in the usual sense of that term, and thus it can be said to be fulfilling an ego-function" (Gregg 74). The "self-hood" of a subordinate group is constituted "through expression" (74). Gregg, Richard B, "The Ego-Function of the Rhetoric of Protest" *Philosophy and Rhetoric* 4 (1971): 71–91.

47. According to Jim Cleaver, a supervisor at the FBI in Montana, "Domestic hate groups are something that we don't take lightly." Hate crimes, when purveyed by phone or U.S. mail, constitute violations of "several federal laws, including civil rights laws and communications laws" (McCracken "Symbol of Unity" A9). However, the FBI and state or local law enforcement agencies tend to use a reactive, rather than a proactive stance toward these groups (*Billings Gazette*, "Hate Groups Get Aggressive" A7; "Reward Fund" A9).

48. Cooke states that the media can serve as a positive counter-influence to a climate in which hate crimes have taken place: "Discretion . . . and the sensitization of the local news media has improved the climate for victims" (49).

49. In this light, we may be tempted to compare a rhetorical climate to Antonio Gramsci's notion of the "hegemonic bloc." Gramsci wrote:

Previously germinated ideologies become "party," come into conflict and confrontation, until only one of them, or at least a single combination, tends to prevail, gaining the upper hand and propagating itself throughout society. It thereby achieves not only a unison of economic and political aims, but also intellectual and moral unity, posing all questions over which the struggle rages not on a corporate but on a universal plane. It thus creates the hegemony of a fundamental social group over a series of subordinate groups. (as qtd. in Anderson 19)

But from the nonviolent perspective, there can be no "upper hand"; there is only understanding. Gramsci's desire to articulate the possibility for "a new, homogeneous, politico-economic historic bloc, without internal enemies" appears to exclude the possibility for a nonviolent perspective.

50. Gramsci's notion of a "hegemonic bloc" seems to perpetuate the utopian wish for a world without conflict, "without compromise" (19). A nonviolent worldview esteems conflict as healthy, provided it is handled in creative ways that minimize physical or mental hurt to all parties involved in the long run.

51. A rhetorical climate of violence and hate might better account for the inaction of many Jews (which has been decried by Elie Weisel, Hannah Arendt, and others) during the rise of Nazism in pre–World War II Germany. Likewise, the seeming inability of minority groups in the inner cities to overcome gangs, drugs, and welfare-dependency, might also become more understandable to those who have not been subjected to a lifelong rhetorical climate of violence that both causes and perpetuates inaction and despair.

52. In addition, Galtung notes that as subjects of history, both nonviolence and women are often overlooked in favor of men and violence. On violence in history, Galtung states, "stories of violent resistance, ending with a decisive battle and the hero emerging as the national leader (or as the martyr, having been defeated), follow [a] linear, male meta-narrative faithfully" and are therefore more easy and popular to report and consume (29). With regard to women and their relative invisibility in history, Galtung believes that

> events will register more easily, the more they are identified with male and non-lower class leaders like M. K. Gandhi or M. L. King, Jr. A major event emanating from black, lower class women . . . would not easily register with person with the opposite rank configuration. As women are prominent in nonviolence, this factor alone accounts for some of the invisibility. (26–27)

Since the nonviolent case that I analyze in this discussion features both nonviolence and women leaders, it is surprising that it was reported as extensively as it was in the media. Galtung further comments that nonviolence and the media do not mix well: "nonviolence [is] almost hopelessly unsuited for reporting. Not only is there not necessarily any leader . . . there is no [specific] beginning and . . . no end. Reports will focus on the drama in the middle" (30). Admittedly, this would be true, too, with my reporting of the events in this discussion, since Billings (among other cities) continues to grapple with hate crimes to this day, and also had problems for years prior to the drama I retell.

53. As stated by an anonymous reviewer.

54. Berlin asserts

> that at least on some level the environment matters . . . [it is] worth our while to explore the ways in which constructive approaches to individual change might enlarge our understanding of [social] dilemmas . . . [and] affirm a relationship between the person and his or her social and physical environments. (332)

55. Mathews believes that persuasion from one source makes the persuasion seem "illegitimate" in the eyes and ears of the audience: "Legitimate public opinion results from the interactions that citizens have with one another. Working to shape opinions collectively renders them legitimate, genuine, and authentic" (403). He also concludes that this interaction and

the blending of different perspectives, eventually causes us to see things differently. And it is those different perspectives that allow us to be creative and discover ways to do things that we did not know before . . . Citizens in communities that are accustomed to interactive public talk will not tolerate panel discussions and *speeches*. They insist on engaging one another (emphasis added). (404)

56. Saleebey echoes Foucault's views (in *Discipline and Punish*). Saleebey states that

[t]he hegemony of science and the "technical/rationalist" . . . professions over ordinary culture has been accomplished largely by disembodying individuals and groups of individuals, by separating the world of cognition from the corporeal world, and by identifying the body and its parts as targets of technical curiosity . . . the world of bureaucracy, science, and the professions . . . [seems] oddly blasé about the sensuous, visceral side of life, although they may see the body as a disease or as a social problem . . . [as] in the case of violence and aggression, for example. Yet the body's urges, promptings, and energies; its frailties and calamities; and the environment's support or subversion of the body are more than a small part of self-identity and moral imagination. (112)

CHAPTER 8

1. Johan Galtung, "Nonviolence and Deep Culture: Some Hidden Obstacles." *Peace Research* 27 (1995): 21–37.

2. A major U.S. study on forgiveness was released in August 1999 that lends support to Tutu's assumptions. The study revealed that people who are able to forgive past transgressions of others are generally healthier, live longer, and tend to be happier than their grudge-holding counterparts.

3. See, for instance: Takaki, Ronald. *A Different Mirror: A History of Multicultural America* (Boston: Little, Brown, 1993).

4. See: *On the Trail of Mark Twain with Peter Ustinov*, Part Two: "A Riddle at Every Turn/Such a Wonderful Thing." PBS. KUID, Moscow. September 1, 1999. Peter Ustinov interviews Archbishop Desmond Tutu and asks, in the context of South Africa's horrific Aparteid past, "How can one forgive the unforgivable?" Tutu argues that a nonviolent program of forgiveness is the only way that the nation can move forward, and that nonviolence constitutes the most pragmatic, *realpolitik* there is.

5. Give or take a few articles, essays in rhetorical criticism that specifically feature nonviolence are limited to the following: Bowen, Harry W., "Does Non-Violence Persuade?" *Communication Monographs [Today's Speech]* 11 (1963): 11; Allen H. Merriam, "Symbolic Action in India: Gandhi's Nonverbal Persuasion," *Quarterly Journal of Speech* 61 (1975): 190–306; Christopher L. Johnstone, "Thoreau and Civil Disobedience: A Rhetorical Paradox," *Quarterly Journal of Speech* 11 (1974) 313–22; Elizabeth Walker Mechling and Jay Mechling, "Hot Pacifism and Cold War: The American Friends Service Committee's Witness for Peace in 1950s America," *Quarterly Journal of Speech* 78 (1992): 173–96.

For literary criticism, see: Sterling Fishman, "Ernst Toller and the Drama of Nonviolence," *Midwest Quarterly: A Journal of Contemporary Thought* 7 (1965): 29–41; Daniel Born, "Nonviolence and Nationalism in Leigh Hunt's Early Liberal Rhetoric," *Nineteenth Century Prose* 23 (Spring 1996): 25–39.

6. Rosenberg asserts, for instance, that "denial of responsibility" constitutes a "kind of life alienating communication" that can be avoided by individuals owning up to their

"thoughts, feelings, and actions" (16). Of the examples he offers of this sort of "denial," he includes a teacher's remarks that she didn't like to give out grades because she felt that grades were not "helpful and they create a lot of anxiety on the part of students," yet that this teacher said she had "to give grades: it's the district policy" (18). To this observation, Rosenberg recommended the teacher "correct" her thinking to say, instead, "I choose to give grades because I want to keep my job" (18). This reversal of the situation in which a hierarchical and cultural construct that values power and distribution of favors in the form of grades, in short, a form of structural violence, is transformed unfairly and in an oversimplified manner into one individual's problem or false dilemma of trying to stay employed (as if myriad other job opportunities might be available to a woman who spent a career as a teacher). Rosenberg on the one hand complains that the world is made dangerous by the large "number of obedient, docile men," yet his theory tends to accommodate such docility by taking a social, political, or other cultural problem and pinning it onto a single person to deal with or just "accept" it. Moreover, Rosenberg contradicts himself by listing "blame" or being judgmental as one type of "punitive force" that ought to be avoided, while he himself blames others for being too "obedient" and "docile" to fight oppression such as the Holocaust.

Elsewhere, Rosenberg advocates "paraphrasing" what others might be "observing, feeling, or requesting" by asking questions that aim to guess what the other person is thinking. This interpersonal process, which is only anecdotally verified by Rosenberg as successful, flies in the face of the documented, statistically verified data and research of John Gottman. Gottman specifically targets "negative mind reading" as one communicative tactic that leads marriages to fail! See: Rosenberg, Marshall. *Nonviolent Communication: A Language of Compassion* (Del Mar, CA: Puddle Dancer Press, 1999); Gottman, John M., *What Predicts Divorce? The Relationship between Marital Processes and Marital Outcomes* (Hillsdale: Lawrence Erlbaum Associates, Publishers, 1994).

7. For instance, in *The Cigarette Papers*, Stanton Glantz, among others, recounts the collective risks involved in taking on the cigarette industry by exposing decades old memos and documentation proving that the major cigarette manufacturers and advertisers were actively deceiving the public regarding the risks of cigarette smoking. Today, cigarette manufacturers owe the U.S. government millions of dollars, and state as well as civil suits continue to plague cigarette makers. See: *The Cigarette Papers*, ed. Stanton A. Glantz (Los Angeles: University of California Press, 1996); Glantz, Stanton. *Tobacco Biology and Politics* (Waco: WRS Publishers, 1992).

8. I would like to thank Dr. Deborah Atwater, Penn State University, for suggesting that I highlight this important fact.

9. Carole Carrington is the mother of two of the four murdered women, Carole and Julie Sund, who were killed by a serial killer in Yosemite National Park in California in 1999. Carrington testified before the U.S. Congress that the category of gender needs to be added to current hate crimes statutes. Carrington believes that the serial murders of these women, like those of most serial murderers, were primarily gender based, with women as targets. See: "Interview with Carole Carrington." *Good Morning America*. ABC, August 4, 1999.

10. I would like to thank Dr. Richard B. Gregg, Department of Speech Communication, Pennsylvania State University, for helping me to articulate the problem clearly.

11. Versus what feminist scholars refer to as "herstory."

APPENDIX 1

1. See, for example, Sheila Murphy, *The Rhetoric of Nonviolent Conflict Resolution: Toward a Philosophy of Peace as a Social Construct*, Unpublished Dissertation, Department of English, University of South Carolina, 1996; Robert Allen Bode, *Mohandas K. Gandhi's Rhetorical Theory: Implications for Communication Ethics*, Unpublished Dissertation, Department of Speech, University of Oregon, 1987.

2. Moore, Mark P., "From a Government of the People, to a People of the Government: Irony as Rhetorical Strategy in Presidential Campaigns," *Quarterly Journal of Speech* 82 (1996): 22-37.

3. Of secrets, Gandhi wrote:

> No secret organization, however big, could do any good. Secrecy aims at building a wall of protection around you. *Ahimsa* disdains all such protection. It functions in the open in the face of odds, the heaviest conceivable. We have to organize for action a vast people that have been crushed under the heel of unspeakable tyranny for centuries. They cannot be organized by other than open, truthful means. I have grown up from youth to seventy-six years in abhorrence of secrecy. There must be no watering down of the ideal. (40)

With this perspective the rationalization and raison d'être of organizations, such as the CIA or the FBI, come under doubt. While a Burkean perspective views such groups as inevitable in the social hierarchy, a nonviolent perspective like Gandhi's views them as an abomination to the spirit of humanity and its growth toward fullness and equality (*swaraj*).

4. The Buddha, for example, is characterized by being "tolerant with the intolerant, mild with the violent," and by being one "who utters true speech" (in *Dhammapada* 461).

5. I would like to thank Dr. Stephen Browne, of Pennsylvania State University, for pointing this out to me and for recommending the Johnstone article. I would also like to thank James E. Burnside for the reminder that courage and the willingness to undergo suffering is one key risk of nonviolence.

6. The classic syllogism is an example of this; for example:

> Major premise: All men are mortal.
> Minor premise: Socrates is a man.
> Conclusion: Socrates is mortal.

This kind of reasoning abounds in theories of rhetoric. What this kind of reasoning ignores is the connotative baggage that terms often carry, which skews our perceptions and hence our conclusions. Look, for instance, at the "logic" of the following syllogism:

> Major premise: All women are biologically equipped to nurture.
> Minor premise: Sarah is a woman.
> Conclusion: Sarah will/must . . . (fill in the blank: get married, have children, etc.).

In this situation, we are using logic that impugns a woman's motives for her life, and which affects her career, as well as her economic status, among other things. By modern logic, the syllogism makes sense. But from a nonviolent perspective, the rhetoric of this kind of "logic" itself is damaging; it is violent because it attributes, through essentializing, categorization and systematic grouping, the life's course of a person. The predetermination of a life's course, irrespective of that life's human potentiality is what Johan Galtung could call an instance of structural violence.

7. For example, the megacorporation Disney now owns what was once a stand-alone entity, the American Broadcasting Corporation (ABC); since that take-over, there has been a marked increase in advertising plugs for Disney movies and products, especially on ABC's popular morning and evening programs, such as *Good Morning America* or *Live with Regis and Kathy Lee* and the evening show, *ABC World News with Peter Jennings*.

8. Resistance web sites include www.csburma.org and www.freeburma.org.

9. See, for instance: Lopez-Reyes, Ramon, "Fight/Flight Response and Nonvio-lence," in Chaiwat Satha-Anand and Michael Ture (eds.), *The Frontiers of Nonviolence* (Bangkok: International Peace Research Association, 1998); MacLean, Paul, "On the Evo-lution of Three Mentalities of the Brain," in Gerard Neuman (ed.), *Origins of Human Ag-gression* (New York: Human Sciences Press, 1987); Lorenz, Konrad, *On Aggression* (New York: Harcourt, Brace & World, 1966); Morris, Desmond, *The Naked Ape* (New York: Mc-Graw-Hill, 1967); Eisler, Riane, *The Chalice and the Blade: Our History, Our Future* (New York: Harper & Row, 1987); Hollins, H., Powers, A. and Sommer, M., *The Conquest of War: Alternative Strategies for Global Security* (Boulder: Westview Press, 1989); Arendt, Han-nah, *On Violence* (New York: Harvest Books, 1970); Summy, Ralph, "Nonviolent Speech," *Peace Review* 10 (1998): 573–91.

10. The theft occurs because wealthy business magnates "fleece the laborers" through low wages and deceit (194). The current trend of moving American factories over-seas is an example. Americans lose their jobs here and products such as Nike athletic shoes are made in Asia for a fraction of the cost; myriad reports show that Asian workers in such factories only earn a tiny fraction of what American factory workers earn. We, as con-sumers and wearers of Nike shoes, participate in the violent process because we are buying the product at the expense of a politically and economically disenfranchised person in both Asia and America.

11. The rhetoric of Dr. Christiane Northrop is an example of a nonviolent rhetoric of medicine that goes against the corporatized and patterned, one-size-fits-all, traditions of stan-dard medical practices. Thus, it is not science or institutions per se that are problematic, but rather the frequently inhumane way in which the science is activated or the institutions are operated that constitute the fundamental problem of science.

12. Hocker and Wilmot note that etiquette can constrain creative conflict interaction. They maintain that while it

> may be appropriate to "respect your elders" when you are eight years old, overgeneralizing that rule to include not bringing up situations that might cause conflict with respected elders when you are an adult can be much less appropriate. Learning to seek permission to speak might be fine for behavior in the third grade, but waiting for permission to speak in a bargaining ses-sion, whether formal or informal, may well assure that you will never be heard. Using polite forms may foster accommodation; overusing parliamentary procedure sometimes stifles debate. Rules of etiquette must be tempered with the exigencies of conflict behavior. (64)

This perspective is in direct opposition to Mark Kingwell's argument in *A Civil Tongue* (1995) that politeness and civility need to be emphasized in today's political environment. Kingwell's view reduces the chance for nonviolence to prevail. Politeness and etiquette can serve to mask and perpetuate oppression, which is precisely what nonviolent rhetoric seeks to unmask and subvert.

13. Montagu goes on to cite many examples of this peculiar rhetoric of "innate depravity," which he maintains perpetuates social conflict by making it an easy excuse for doing nothing to correct the problem:

> The myth of early man's aggressiveness belongs in the same class as the myth of "the beast," that is, the belief that most if not all "wild" animals are ferocious killers. In the same class belongs the myth of "the jungle," "the wild," "the warfare of Nature," and, of course, the myth of "innate depravity" or "original sin." These myths represent the projection of our acquired deplorabilities upon the screen of "Nature." What we are unwilling to acknowledge as essentially of our own making, the consequences of our own disordering in the [hu]man-made environment, we saddle upon "Nature," upon "phylogenetically programmed" or "innate" factors. (17)

Thus, Montagu shows the power that myth, and our special terminologies, or rhetorics, of that myth, continue to enable us to rationalize violence as a means to dealing with conflict.

14. See also: Chernus, Ira, "The Word 'Peace' as a Weapon of (Cold) War," *Peace Review* 10 (1998): 605–11.

APPENDIX 3

1. "Inner Macedonia" is also referred to as Upper Macedonia; Lower Macedonia includes coastal areas of Halkidiki and west across what is now northern Greece to the Pindus mountains (Hammond, 1995: 126; Poulton, Macedonians xvii).

2. This event is a major source of Serbian collective memory and nationalism. In 1989 Slobodan Milosovic returned to the "field of the blackbirds" in Kosovo where this defeat occurred, and gave the speech that would launch his political rise to power in Serbia and the "rump" Yugoslavia that remained after the country's breakup in 1991.

3. Poulton's research reveals that Macedonia's revolutionary organization

> repeatedly and confusingly changed its name, often as a reflection of the balance between pro-Bulgarian and pro-Macedonian autonomists. . . . It appears to have originally been called the Bulgarian Macedonian-Adrianopolitian Committee (BMORK—the 'O' standing for Odrin or Adrianopole). In 1902 it changed its name to the Secret Macedonian Adrianopolitan Revolutionary Organization (TMORO) while from 1905 it was first known as VMORO and then simply VMRO, where the 'V' stands for 'inner' in Bulgarian [and Macedonian]. (53)

It should also be noted here that in the 20th-century, Bulgaria has supported Macedonia's revolutionary attempts all along, while simultaneously claiming Macedonia as a republic or state belonging to Bulgaria. Bulgaria was the first nation in 1993 officially to recognize Macedonia as a republic, long before the United States and the United Nations as a whole did so.

Works Cited

CHAPTER 1

Adams, David et al. "The Seville Statement on Violence." *A Reader in Peace Studies.* Ed. Paul Smoker et al. Oxford: Pergamon, 1990. 221-23.

Ambler, Rex. "Ghandian Peacemaking." *A Reader in Peace Studies.* Ed. Paul Smoker et al. Oxford: Pergamon, 1990. 199-205.

Aristotle. *Rhetoric,* trans., W. Rhys Roberts. New York: The Modern Library, 1954.

Beer, Francis A. *Meanings of War and Peace.* College Station: Texas A&M UP, 2001.

Bitzer, Lloyd F. "The Rhetorical Situation." *Philosophy and Rhetoric* 1, 1968. 1-14.

Bode, Robert A. "Mohandas Karamchand Gandhi's Rhetorical Theory: Implications for Communication Ethics (Nonviolence)." Diss., U of Oregon, 1987.

Bondurant, Joan V. *Conquest of Violence: The Gandhian Philosophy of Conflict.* Princeton, NJ: Princeton UP, 1988.

Boulding, Kenneth E. "The Role of Organized Nonviolence in Achieving Stable Peace." *Perspectives on Nonviolence.* Ed. V. K. Kool. New York: Springer-Verlag, 1990. 3-13.

Browne, Stephen. "Encountering Angelina Grimke: Violence, identity, and the creation of radical community." *Quarterly Journal of Speech* 82 (1996): 55-73.

Buddha, "From The Dhammapada: Chapter XXVI. The Brahmin Buddha." *A Peace Reader: Essential Readings on War, Justice, Non-Violence and World Order.* Ed. Joseph J. Fahey and Richard Armstrong. Mahwah, NJ: Paulist Press, 1992. 461.

Burgess, Guy, and Heidi Burgess. "Justice without Violence: Theoretical Foundations." *Justice without Violence.* Eds. Paul Wehr, Heidi Burgess, and Guy Burgess. Boulder: Lynne Rienner Publishers, 1994. 7-35.

Burke, Kenneth. *Language as Symbolic Action: Essays on Life, Literature, and Method.* Berkeley: U of California P, 1966.

Carroll, Susan J., and Linda M. Zerilli. "Feminist Challenges to Political Science." *Political Science: The State of the Discipline II.* Ed. Ada W. Finifter. Washington, DC: American Political Science Association, 1993. 55-76.

Carter, April. "Non-Violence as a Strategy for Change." *A Reader in Peace Studies.* Ed. Paul Smoker et al. Oxford: Pergamon, 1990. 210-16.

Charland, Maurice. "Constitutive Rhetoric: The Case of the *Peuple Québéqois.*" *Critical Questions: Invention, Creativity, and the Criticism of Discourse and Media.* Eds. William Nothstine, Carole Blair, and Gary Copeland. New York: St. Martin's Press, 1994. 211-32

Clark, Norman. "The Critical Servant: An Isocratean Contribution to Critical Rhetoric." *Quarterly Journal of Speech* 82 (1996): 111-124.

Connolly, William. *Identity\Difference: Democratic Negotiations of Political Paradox*. Ithaca, NY: Cornell UP, 1991.

Crosswhite, James. *The Rhetoric of Reason: Writing and the Attractions of Argument*. Madison: U of W P, 1996.

Damasio, Antonio. *Descartes' Error: Emotion, Reason, and the Human Brain*. New York: Avon Books, 1994.

DeLuca, Kevin. *Image Politics*. New York: The Guilford Press, 1999.

Deats, Richard L. "The Global Development of Movements of Active Nonviolence." *Nonviolent Social Movements: A Geographical Perspective*. Oxford, Blackwell, 1999.

Donald, Merlin. *Origins of the Modern Mind: Three Stages in the Evolution of Culture and Cognition*. Cambridge, MA: Harvard UP, 1991.

Foucault, Michel. "About the Beginning of the Hermeneutics of the Self, Two Lectures at Dartmouth." *Political Theory* 21 (1993): 198.

——. *Discipline and Punish: The Birth of the Prison*. New York: Vintage Books, 1977.

Foss, Sonja, and Griffin, Cindy. "Beyond Persuasion: A Proposal for an Invitational Rhetoric." *Communication Monographs* 62 (1995): 2-17.

Galtung, Johan. "Peace Studies: A Curriculum Proposal." *Transnational Associations* 6, 1987: 327-330.

——. "Violence and Peace." *A Reader in Peace Studies*. Eds. Paul Smoker, Ruth Davies, and Barbara Munske. New York: Pergamon Press, 1990. 9-14.

——. "Nonviolence and Deep Culture: Some Hidden Obstacles." *Peace Research* 27 (1995): 21-37.

Gandhi, Mohandas K. "Ahimsa, or the Way of Nonviolence." *A Peace Reader: Essential Readings on War, Justice, Non-Violence, and World Order*. Eds. Fahey and Armstrong. Paulist Press, 1994. 209-13.

Gandhi, Mohandas. All Men are Brothers. UNESCO: World without War Publications, New York: 1958.

Gearhart, Sally Miller. "The Womanization of Rhetoric." *Women's Studies International Quarterly* 2 (1979): 195-201.

Good, Tina L., and Warshauer, Leanne. "Academic Discourse Meets Feminine Reasoning: What Will Happen to Their Offspring?" The Second Biennial Feminism(s) and Rhetoric(s) Conference "Challenging Rhetorics: Cross-Disciplinary Sites of Feminist Discourse." Online. Internet. 17 June 2000. Available: http://femrhet.cla.umn.edu/proposals/good_tina.htm.

Gorsevski, Ellen. Rev. of *Meanings of War and Peace*, by Francis A. Beer. *International Journal on World Peace* June 2002: 83-85.

Greer, Colin. "The World Is Hungry for Goodness: Without Memory, There Is No Healing. Without Forgiveness, There Is No Future." *Parade Magazine*, 11 January 1998, 4-6.

Herman, Theodore. "Seven Forms of Nonviolence for Peace Research: A Conceptual Framework." *Perspectives on Nonviolence*. Ed. V. K. Kool. New York: Springer-Verlag, 1990. 140-49.

Herrick, James A. *The History and Theory of Rhetoric*. Scottsdale, AZ: Gorsuch Scarisbrick, Publishers, 1997.

Hocker, Joyce L., and William W. Wilmot. *Interpersonal Conflict.* 2nd ed. Dubuque, IA: Wm. C. Brown Publishers, 1985.

Holmes, Robert L. *Nonviolence in Theory and Practice.* Belmont, CA: Wadsworth, 1990.

Huxley, Aldous. "Time and Eternity." *Philosophical Perspectives on Peace: An Anthology of Classical and Modern Sources.* Ed. Howard P. Kainz. Athens: Ohio UP, 1987. 195–203.

James, William. "The Moral Equivalent of War." *Philosophical Perspectives on Peace: An Anthology of Classical and Modern Sources.* Ed. Howard P. Kainz. Athens, Ohio: Ohio UP, 1987. 213–25.

Johnstone, Henry. "Some Reflections on Argumentation." *Philosophy Rhetoric and Argumentation.* Eds. Maurice Natanson and Henry Johnstone. University Park, PA: Pennsylvania State UP, 1965. 1–9.

Katz, Neil H. "Conflict Resolution and Peace Studies." *Annals of the American Academy of Political and Social Science* 504, July, 1989: 14–21.

Lorenz, Konrad. "On Aggression." *Philosophical Perspectives on Peace: An Anthology of Classical and Modern Sources.* Ed. Howard P. Kainz. Athens, Ohio: Ohio UP, 1987. 230–46.

McCarthy, Colman. "Why We Must Teach Peace." *Educational Leadership* 50 1992: 6–9.

McPhail, Mark. *Zen in the Art of Rhetoric: An Inquiry into Coherence.* Albany: State U of New York P, 1996.

Merton, Thomas. *Gandhi on Nonviolence.* New York: New Directions, 1965.

Montagu, Ashley. "The New Litany of "Innate Depravity," or Original Sin Revisited." *A Peace Reader: Essential Readings on War, Justice, Non-Violence, and World Order.* Eds. Joseph Fahey and Richard Armstrong. Mahwah, NJ: Paulist Press, 1994. 5–18.

Murphy, Sheila M. "The Rhetoric of Nonviolent Conflict Resolution: Toward a Philosophy of Peace as A Social Construct." Diss., U of South Carolina, 1996.

Nieve, Evelyn. "Antiwar Effort Gains Momentum: Growing Peace Movement's Ranks Include Some Unlikely Allies." *Washington Post.* December 2, 2002. A01. http://washingtonpost.com. Accessed December 4, 2002.

Pepinsky, Harold. *The Geometry of Violence and Democracy.* Bloomington: Indiana UP, 1991.

Rubin, Jeffrey Z., Pruittt, Dean, and Kim, Sung. *Social Conflict: Escalation, Stalemate, and Settlement.* New York: McGraw-Hill, 1994.

Ryan, Michael. "He Fights Dictators with the Internet." *Parade Magazine,* August 23, 1998: 12.

Shabecoff, Philip. *A New Name for Peace: International Environmentalism, Sustainable Development, and Democracy.* London: UP of New England, 1996.

Sharp, Gene. "198 Methods of Nonviolent Action." *A Peace Reader: Essential Readings on War. Justice, Non-Violence, and World Order.* Eds., Joseph Fahey and Richard Armstrong. Mahwah, NJ: Paulist Press, 1992. 473–79.

——. "The Techniques of Nonviolent Action." *A Peace Reader: Essential Readings on War, Justice, Non-Violence, and World Order.* Eds., Joseph Fahey and Richard Armstrong. Mahwah, NJ: Paulist Press, 1992. 223–29.

Sylvester, Christine. "Patriarchy, Peace and Women Warriors." *A Peace Reader: Essential Readings on War, Justice, Non-Violence, and World Order.* Eds. Joseph Fahey and Richard Armstrong. Mahwah, NJ: Paulist Press, 1994. 33–47.

Taylor, Orlando. "My Choices for the 'Top 10 Communication Events [of the 20th Century].'" *Spectra* July 1999: 2, 7.

Tolstoy, Leo, "The Kingdom of God Is Within You." *Philosophical Perspectives on Peace: An Anthology of Classical and Modern Sources.* Ed. Howard Kainz. Athens, OH: Ohio UP, 1987. 177-95.

Washington, James M., ed. *A Testament of Hope: The Essential Writings of Martin Luther King, Jr.* New York: Harper & Row, 1986.

Whitmer, Barbara. *The Violence Mythos.* New York: State U of New York P, 1997.

Young, Iris M. *Justice and the Politics of Difference.* Princeton: Princeton UP, 1990.

——. "Asymmetrical Reciprocity: On Moral Respect, Wonder, and Enlarged Thought." *Intersecting Voices: Dilemmas of Gender, Political Philosophy, and Policy.* Princeton: Princeton UP, 1997. 38-59.

——. "Communication and the Other: Beyond Deliberative Democracy." *Intersecting Voices: Dilemmas of Gender, Political Philosophy, and Policy.* Princeton: Princeton UP, 1997. 60-74.

CHAPTER 2

Andrews, Kenneth. "Creating Social Change: Lessons from the Civil Rights Movement." *Social Movements: Identity, Culture, and the State.* Eds. David Meyer, Nancy Whittier, and Belinda Robnett. New York: Oxford University Press, 2002. 105-17.

Bond, Julian. "The Media and the Movement: Looking Back from the Southern Front." *Media, Culture, and the Modern African American Freedom Struggle.* Ed. Brian Ward. Gainesville: The University Press of Florida, 2001. 16-40.

Brand-Jacobsen, Kai F., and Carl Jacobsen. "Beyond Mediation: Towards More Holistic Approaches to Peacebuilding and Peace Actor Empowerment." *Searching for Peace: The Road to Transcend.* Eds. Johan Galtung and Carl G. Jacobsen. London: Pluto Press, 2000. 231-67.

DeLuca, Kevin. *Image Politics.* New York: The Guilford Press, 1999.

Brummet, Barry. *Rhetoric in Popular Culture.* New York: St. Martin's Press, 1994.

"Fall, 1996 Patagonia Product Directory." Reno: Patagonia, Inc., 1996. 62-63.

Fisk, Larry. "Shaping Visionaries: Nurturing Peace Through Education." *Patterns of Conflict, Paths to Peace.* Eds. Larry Fisk and John Schellenberg. Ontario, Canada: Broadview Press, 2000. 170-71.

——. "Epilogue: Last Thoughts and First Principles." *Patterns of Conflict, Paths to Peace.* Eds. Larry Fisk and John Schellenberg. Ontario, Canada: Broadview Press, 2000. 206-08.

Foss, Sonja, Karen Foss, and Robert Trapp. *Contemporary Perspectives on Rhetoric.* Prospect Heights, IL: Waveland Press, 1985.

Gale, Ivan. "West Marin Women Strip for Peace." Point Reyes Light. 14 Nov. 2002. Accessed 19 Nov. 2002. http://www.ptreyeslight.com/stories/nov14_02/peace_rally.html.

Galtung, Johan. "TRANSCEND: 40 Years, 40 Conflicts." *Searching for Peace: The Road to Transcend.* Eds. Johan Galtung and Carl G. Jacobsen. London: Pluto Press, 2000. 101-90.

——, and Tschudi, Finn. "Crafting Peace: On the Psychology of the TRANSCEND Approach." *Searching for Peace: The Road to Transcend.* Eds. Johan Galtung and Carl G. Jacobsen. London: Pluto Press, 2000. 206-27.

Hastings, Tom. "Sit-ins, Protests and Strikes." E-mail to Peace and Justice Studies Association Listserv. September 23, 2002.

Hauser, Gerard. *Introduction to Rhetorical Theory*. Prospect Heights, IL: Waveland Press, 2002.

Herrick, James. *The History and Theory of Rhetoric: An Introduction*. Scottsdale, AZ: Gorsuch Scarisbrick, Publishers. 1997.

Jacobsen, Carl. "Peacemaking as Realpolitik, Conflict Resolution and Oxymoron: The Record; the Challenge." *Searching for Peace: The Road to Transcend*. Eds. Johan Galtung and Carl G. Jacobsen. London: Pluto Press, 2000. 3-25.

Klatch, Rebecca. "The Development of Individual Identity and Consciousness among Movements of the Left and Right." *Social Movements: Identity, Culture, and the State*. Ed. David Meyer, Nancy Whittier, and Belinda Robnett. New York: Oxford UP, 2002. 185-201.

Nagler, Michael. "Sit-ins, Protests and Strikes." E-mail to Peace and Justice Studies Association Listserv. September 23, 2002.

"Seattle Couple Makes Popular Anti-War Flag." *NPR Morning Edition*. By Kathy DuChamp. KUOW Seattle affiliate. November 26, 2002.

Smithey, Lee, and Lester Kurtz. "'We Have Bare Hands': Nonviolent Social Movements in the Soviet Bloc." *Nonviolent Social Movements: A Geographical Perspective*. Eds. Stephen Zunes, Lester R. Kurtz, and Sarah B. Asher. Malden, MA: Blackwell Publishers, 1999. 106-08.

True, Michael. *An Energy Field More Intense Than War: The Nonviolent Tradition and American Literature*. New York: Syracuse UP, 1995.

Walker, Jenny. "A Media-Made Movement? Black Violence and Nonviolence in the Historiography of the Civil Rights Movement." *Media, Culture, and the Modern African American Freedom Struggle*. Ed. Brian Ward. Gainesville: UP of Florida, 2001. 41-66.

Ward, Brian. "Introduction. Forgotten Wails and Master Narratives: Media, Culture, and Memories of the Modern African American Freedom Struggle." *Media, Culture, and the Modern African American Freedom Struggle*. Ed. Brian Ward. Gainesville: UP of Florida, 2001. 1-15.

Zunes, Stephen. "The Origins of People Power in the Philippines." *Nonviolent Social Movements: A Geographical Perspective*. Eds. Stephen Zunes, Lester R. Kurtz, and Sarah B. Asher. Malden, MA: Blackwell Publishers, 1999. 129-57.

Zunes, Stephen, and Lester Kurtz. "Conclusion." *Nonviolent Social Movements: A Geographical Perspective*. Eds. Stephen Zunes, Lester R. Kurtz, and Sarah B. Asher. Malden, MA: Blackwell Publishers, 1999. 302-22.

CHAPTER 3

Bowen, M. E. (1996). "The Power of Nonviolence." *Journal of Intergroup Relations* 23 (1996): 47-54.

Campbell, K. K. "The Communication Classroom: A Chilly Climate for Women? *Journal of the Association for Communication Administration* 51 (1985): 68-72.

Chetkow-Yanoov, B. "Preparing for Survival in the 21st Century, Some Approaches to Teaching Conflict Resolution in Our Schools and Universities." *International Journal of Group Tensions*, 22 (1992): 277-90.

Cochran, D. "An Underground Tradition." *Progressive* 59 (1995): 37.

Early, F. H. "New Historical Perspectives on Gendered Peace Studies." *Women's Studies Quarterly* 23 (1995): 22-31.

Eisler, R. *The Chalice and the Blade.* San Francisco, CA: Harper & Row, 1987.

Forcey, L. R. "Women's Studies, Peace Studies, and the Difference Debate." *Women's Studies Quarterly* 23 (1995): 9-13.

Gage, R. L., ed. (1995). *Choose Peace: A dialogue between Johan Galtung and Daisaku Ikeda.* East Haven, CT: Pluto Press.

Galtung, J. "Nonviolence and Deep Culture: Some Hidden Obstacles." *Peace Research* 27 (1995): 21-37.

Genser, L. M. "Peace Education—A Response to Violence in Detroit." *Perspectives on nonviolence.* Ed. V. K. Kool. New York: Springer-Verlag, 1990. 238-46.

Hall, R. M. "The Classroom Climate for Women." *Journal of the Association for Communication Administration* 51 (1985): 64-67.

Hart, R. P. "Teaching Persuasion." Eds. J. A. Daly, G. W. Friedrich, and A. L. Vangelisti. *Teaching Communication: Theory, Research, and Methods.* Hillsdale, NJ: Lawrence Erlbaum, 1990. 105-14.

Herman, T. "A Conceptual Framework of Nonviolence for Peace Research." *International Journal of Group Tensions* 21 (1991): 3-15.

Hubbard, A. S. "Killing the Messenger": Public perceptions of nonviolent protest. *Perspectives on Nonviolence.* Ed. V. K. Kool. New York, NY: Springer-Verlag, 1990. 118-27.

Hunt, M. M. "Teaching Peace—A Conscious Decision." *Adult Learning* 3 (1991): 29.

Katz, N. H., and J. R. Kendrick, Jr. "Lessons from Action Research on Nonviolence. *International Journal of Group Tensions* 20 (1990): 335-50.

Kohn, A. *No Contest: The Case against Competition.* Boston: Houghton Mifflin Company, 1986.

Kool, V. K. Preface. *Perspectives on Nonviolence.* Ed. V. K. Kool. New York: Springer-Verlag, 1990. v.

Leyden, M. "Alternatives to Violence: An Educational Approach. *Perspectives on nonviolence.* Ed. V. K. Kool. New York: Springer-Verlag, 1990. 231-37.

McCarthy, C. Speech to the Peace and Justice Studies Association. Washington, DC., 2001.

——. "Why We Must Teach Peace." *Educational Leadership* 50 (1992): 6-9.

Parry, A. "Choosing Nonviolence in a Violent World. *Education Digest* 59 (1994): 42-45.

Peterson, E. E. "Moving toward a Gender Balanced Curriculum in Basic Speech Communication Courses." *Communication Education* 40 (1991): 60-72.

Sharp, G. "Beyond Just War and Pacifism: Nonviolent Struggle towards Justice, Freedom, and Peace." *Ecumenical Review* 48 (1996): 233-50.

Troester, R., and C. S. Mester. "Peace Communication: A Survey of Current Attitudes, Curricular Practice and Research Priorities." *Western Journal of Speech Communication* 54 (1990): 420-28.

Porter, K. "Teaching Peace." *Humanist* 52 (1992): 32.

Will, D. S. "Teaching Peace through Debunking Race." *Peace and Change; A Journal of Peace Research* 18 (1993): 182-203.

Wright, J. "Getting to Peace—By Teaching Peace?" *Adult Learning* 3 (1991): 17.

Zunes, S., L. Kurtz, and S. Asher, eds. (1999). *Nonviolent Social Movements: A Geographical Perspective.* Oxford: Blackwell Publishers.

CHAPTER 4

Affron, Charles. *Cinema and Sentiment.* Chicago: University of Chicago Press, 1982.

Arnett, Robert. "Gandhi: A Screenplay Review." *Creative Screenwriting* 3 (1996): 13-15.

Bauer, Erik. "On 'The Spitfire Grill': Interview with Lee David Zlotoff." *Creative Screenwriting* 3 (1996): 55-60.

Briley, John. "On 'Gandhi' and 'Cry Freedom': Two Pivotal Scripts in My Life." *Creative Screenwriting* 3 (1996): 3-12.

Browne, Stephen. "Encountering Angelina Grimké: Violence, Identity, and the Creation of Radical Community." *Quarterly Journal of Speech* 82 (1996): 55-73.

Clark, Norman. "The Critical Servant: An Isocratean Contribution to Critical Rhetoric." *Quarterly Journal of Speech* 82 (1996): 111-24.

Courts, Roger. Letter to Author. 16 June 2000.

Dauphin, Gary. "The Spitfire Grill." *Village Voice* 27 August 1996: 45-50.

Foss, Sonja, and Cindy Griffin. "Beyond Persuasion: A Proposal for an Invitational Rhetoric." *Communication Monographs* 62 (1995): 2-17.

Galtung, Johan. "Violence and Peace." *A Reader in Peace Studies.* Eds. Paul Smoker, Ruth Davies, and Barbara Munske. New York: Pergamon Press, 1990. 9-14.

Guthmann, Edward. "Sweetness Is Artificial in 'The Spitfire Grill.'" *San Francisco Chronicle,* 23 August 1996: D3.

Hanh, Thich N. "Feelings and Perceptions." *Nonviolence in Theory and Practice.* Ed. Robert L. Holmes. Belmont: Wadsworth Publishing Company, 1990. 144-46.

Holmes, Robert L. "General Introduction." *Nonviolence in Theory and Practice.* Ed. Robert L. Holmes. Belmont: Wadsworth Publishing Company, 1990. 1-9.

How, Deson. "'The Spitfire Grill's' Pleasant Service." *Washington Post* 6 September 1996: F1.

Klady, Leonard. "Film Reviews: 'Care of the Spitfire Grill' Directed by Lee David Zlotoff." *Variety* January (1996): 65.

Lawson, Terry. "'Spitfire Grill' Serves Up More Female Bonding." *Detroit News & Free Press,* 25 August 1996: G9.

Mawson, C. O. Sylvester, ed. *Roget's Thesaurus of the English Language in Dictionary Form.* New York: The New Home Library, 1942.

Montagu, Ashley. "The New Litany of "Innate Depravity,' or Original Sin Revisited." *A Peace Reader: Essential Readings on War, Justice, Non-Violence, and World Order.* Eds. Joseph Fahey and Richard Armstrong. Mahwah, NJ: Paulist Press, 1994. 5-18.

Nakayama, Thomas, and Robert Krizek. "Whiteness: A Strategic Rhetoric." *Quarterly Journal of Speech* 81 (1995): 291-309.

Ono, Kent, and John Sloop. "The Critique of Vernacular Discourse." *Communication Monographs* 62 (1995): 19-46.

Pepinsky, Harold. *The Geometry of Violence and Democracy.* Bloomington: Indiana UP, 1991.

Petrakis, John. "'Spitfire Grill' Serves Up Solid Writing, Superior Acting." *Chicago Tribune,* 23 (August 1996): D4.

Powell, Beth. "One Out of Three Homeless Is a Vet." *Centre Daily Times* 9 November 1997, 6A.

Rafferty, Terrence. "The Spitfire Grill." *New Yorker* (September 1996): 93.

Rottenberg, Josh. "The Spitfire Grill." *Premiere* 10 (1997): 126.

Salmi, Jamil. *Violence and Democratic Society: Approaches to Human Rights.* London: Zed Books, 1993.

Simon, John. "New Directors." *National Review* 48 (1996): 94-95.

"The Spitfire Grill." *Sight and Sound* 7 (1997): 63.

Travers, Peter. "Girls Town: The Spitfire Grill." *Rolling Stone* (September 1996): 69.

Williamson, Bruce. "Movies: The Spitfire Grill Directed by Lee David Zlotoff." *Playboy* (October 1996): 28.

CHAPTER 5

"A Balkan Beacon." *Economist* 339 (1996): 56.

Ackerman, Peter, and Christopher Kruegler. *Strategic Nonviolent Conflict: The Dynamics of People Power in the Twentieth Century.* Westport, CN Praeger, 1994.

Andrews, James R. "The Ethos of Pacifism: The Problem of Image in the Early British Peace Movement." *The Quarterly Journal of Speech* 53 (1967): 28-33.

Aristotle. *Rhetoric and Poetics.* New York: The Modern Library, 1954.

Arnold, Thomas F., and Heather R. Ruland. "The 'Prehistory' of Peacekeeping." *Soldiers for Peace.* Ed. Barbara Benton. New York: Facts on File, Inc., 1996. 11-23.

Balgooyen, Theodore J. "Unusual Procedures for Extending Debate in the United Nations General Assembly." *The Southern Communication Journal* 32 (1967): 296-303.

Balkan Region (Former Yugoslavia). Map. *The Washington Post.* Online. Internet. May 18, 1999. http://www.cgi.washingtonpost.com.

Behl, William A. "The United Nations Security Council." *The Quarterly Journal of Speech* 34 (1948): 40-45.

Bennet, William. "Conflict Rhetoric and Game Theory: An Extrapolation and Example." *The Southern Communication Journal* 37 (1971): 34-46.

Benson, Thomas W. "Violence: Communication Breakdown? Focus on Recent Publications." *Intercommunication Among Nations and Peoples* 326-36. Ed. Michael H. Prosser. New York: Harper & Row, 1973.

Blinn, Sharon Bracci, and Mary Garrett. "Aristotelian Topoi as a Cross-Cultural Analytical Tool." *Philosophy and Rhetoric* 26 (1993): 93-112.

Boudreaux, Richard. "Kosovo Warfare Imperils Macedonia's Fragile Peace; Balkans: Regional Instability Only Fuels Internal Friction between the Country's Ethnic Slavs, Albanians." *The Los Angeles Times.* Online. Proquest. 20 August 1998.

Bowen, Harry W. "Does Non-Violence Persuade?" *Communication Quarterly* 11 (1963): 9-10.

——. "The Future of Non-Violence." *Communication Quarterly* 11 (1963): 3-4.

——. "A Realistic View of Non-Violent Assumptions." *Communication Quarterly* 15 (1967): 9-10.

Cohen, Raymond. *Negotiating Across Cultures: Communication Obstacles in International Diplomacy.* Washington, DC: United States Institute of Peace Press, 1991.

Dorsey, Gray L. *Beyond the United Nations: Changing Discourse in International Politics and Law, Vol. 5, Rhetoric and Political Discourse Series.* New York: UP of America, 1986.

Fromkin, David. "Dimitrios Returns: Macedonia and the Balkan Question in the Shadow of History." *World Policy Journal* 10 (1993): 67-71.

Gall, Carlotta. "Election Takes Macedonia Another Step toward Democracy." *New York Times.* Online. Proquest. Internet. November 15, 1999.

———. "Yugoslavia Neighbor Fears an Effort to 'Destabilize' It." *New York Times*. Online. Proquest. Internet. April 15, 1999.

Galtung, Johan. "Nonviolence and Deep Culture: Some Hidden Obstacles." *Peace Research* 27 (1995): 21–37.

Gligorov, Kiro. "Address to the United Nations General Assembly, Forty-eighth Session, 30 September 1993." *United Nations Publication* A/48/PV.10, October 14, 1993: 1–4.

Gandhi, Arun. "What Did Gandhi Mean by Nonviolence?" *Journal of Intergroup Relations* 20 (1993): 9–15.

Gandhi, Mohandas K. "On Satyagraha." *Nonviolence in Theory and Practice*. Ed. Robert Holmes. Belmont, CA: Wadsworth Publishing Company, 1990. 51–56.

———. *Non-Violent Resistance (Satyagraha)*. New York: Schocken Books, 1951: 3.

Ghebali, Victor-Yves. "UNPROFOR in the Former Yugoslavia: The Misuse of Peacekeeping and Associated Conflict Management Techniques." *New Dimensions of Peacekeeping*. Ed. Daniel Warner. Boston: Martinus Nijhoff Publishers, 1995. 13–40.

Glenny, Misha. "When Victims Become a Threat." *New York Times*. Online. ProQuest. Internet. April 6, 1999.

———. "Heading Off War in the Southern Balkans." *Foreign Affairs* 74 (1995): 98–108.

Gourevitch, Philip. "Comment: A War Up in the Air." *The New Yorker* (April 12, 1999): 21–22.

Hammond, N. G. L. "Connotations of 'Macedonia' and of 'Macedones' Until 323 B.C." *Classical Quarterly* 45 (1995): 120–28.

Herman, Theodore. "A Conceptual Framework of Nonviolence for Peace Research." *International Journal of Group Tensions* 21 (1991): 6.

Holmes, Robert L., ed. *Nonviolence in Theory and Practice*. Belmont, CA: Wadsworth Publishing Company, 1990.

Hooper, John. "Large Numbers of Refugees Upset Macedonia." *Moscow-Pullman Daily News*. Weekend ed. (April 10 & 11, 1999): 10A.

Kaufman, Stuart J. "Preventive Peacekeeping, Ethnic Violence, and Macedonia." *Studies in Conflict and Terrorism* 19 (1996): 229–46.

"Are NATO Airstrikes Against Yugoslavia Helping Kosovar Albanians or Worsening Their Plight?" Narr. Larry King. *Larry King Live*. CNN. New York. March 30, 1999.

Kaufer, David S., and Kathleen M. Carley. "Condensation Symbols: Their Variety and Rhetorical Function in Political Discourse." *Philosophy and Rhetoric* 26 (1993): 201–26.

Keeve, Steven. "CEELI Bestows First Award." *ABA Journal* 80 (1994): 106–07.

Konrad, George. "Nationalism Unleashed." *The Nation*. Online. Proquest. May 3, 1999.

"Kosovo Terror: Calendar Marks the Most Recent Battles in an Ancient Conflict." *USA Today*. April 5, 1999: 4A.

Lewis, Paul. "A Short History of United Nations Peacekeeping." *Soldiers for Peace*, 25–41. Ed. Barbara Benton. New York: Facts on File, Inc., 1996.

Logue, Cal, and Eugene Miller. "Rhetorical Status: A Study of Its Origins, Functions, and Consequences." *Quarterly Journal of Speech*, 81 (1995), 20–47.

Geographic Macedonia. Map. National Geographic Society. Online. Internet. May 18, 1999. http://www.nationalgeographic.com.

Marquand, Robert. "War Hits Macedonia's Fragile Peace: Refugee Crisis Threatens to Undo Recent Progress between Macedonians." *Christian Science Monitor*. April 12, 1999. ProQuest. Internet. 9+.

Mohrmann, Gerald P. "Blinking on the Brink: The Rhetoric of Summitry." *Western Journal of Communication* 31 (1967): 172–79.

Norton, Augustus R., and Thomas G. Weiss. *U.N. Peacekeepers: Soldiers with a Difference.* New York: Foreign Policy Association, Inc., 1990.

Oliver, Robert T. "The Rhetoric of Power in Diplomatic Conferences." *The Quarterly Journal of Speech* 40 (1954): 288–92.

Padilla, Leslie M. Letter. *Washington Post.* April 20, 1999, sec. A: 22.

Perry, Duncan M. "Macedonia: Balkan Miracle or Balkan Disaster?" *Current History* 95 (1996): 113–17.

——. "Politics in the Republic of Macedonia: Issues and Parties." *RFE/RL Research Report* 2 (1993): 31–37.

Poulton, Hugh. "The Republic of Macedonia After U.N. Recognition." *RFE/RL Research Report* 2 (1993): 22–30.

——. *Who Are the Macedonians?* Bloomington, IN: Indiana University Press, 1995.

Prosser, Michael. "The Role of Summitry in Conflict Resolution at the United Nations." *Intercommunication among Nations and Peoples* 257–85. Ed. Michael H. Prosser. New York: Harper & Row, 1973.

——. "Adlai Stephenson's United Nations Audience." *Communication Studies* 16 (1965): 262–71.

——. "Communication Problems in the United Nations." *The Southern Communication Journal* 29 (1963): 125–32.

Ramet, Sabrina P. *Balkan Babel: The Disintegration of Yugoslavia from the Death of Tito to Ethnic War.* Boulder, CO: Westview Press, 1996.

Rentz, Mary Ann. "Argumentative Form and Negotiating Strategy in Three United Nations Security Council Debates." *Communication Studies* 38 (1987): 166–80.

Sharp, Gene, "Beyond Just War and Pacifism: Nonviolent Struggle Towards Justice, Freedom, and Peace." *Ecumenical Review* 48 (1996): 233–50.

——. "Nonviolent Action: An Active Technique of Struggle." *Nonviolence in Theory and Practice.* Ed. Robert L. Holmes. Belmont, CA: Wadsworth Publishing Company, 1990.

——. *The Politics of Nonviolent Action.* Boston: Porter Sargent Publisher, 1973.

Spence, Richard, Lisa Carlson, and Rand Lewis. "The Balkan Conflict in Perspective." Lecture. The Martin Institute for Peace Studies and Conflict Resolution. University of Idaho College of Law Courtroom. April 6, 1999.

Starosta, William J. "The United Nations: Agency for Semantic Consubstantiality." *The Southern Communication Journal* 36 (1971): 243–54.

Vesilind, Priit J. "Macedonia: Caught in the Middle." *National Geographic* 189 (1996): 118–39.

"Yugoslav Crisis: Situation Worsens as Peace Process Continues." *UN Chronicle* 30 (1993): 4–12.

Zimmermann, Warren. *Origins of a Catastrophe: Yugoslavia and Its Destroyers—America's Last Ambassador Tells What Happened and Why.* New York: Times Books, 1996.

CHAPTER 6

"A Woman of Subtlety." *Economist* 322 (1992): 90.

Adler, Lisa and Ling, Lily. "From Practice to Theory: Toward a Feminist Reconstruction of Nonviolence." Working Paper No. 30. Program on the Analysis and Resolution of Conflicts (PARC). Syracuse University, Maxwell School of Citizenship and Public Affairs. September 1993.

"Asia's Mandela?" *Economist* 336 (1995): 12.

Benhabib, Seyla. "Feminism and Postmodernism: An Uneasy Alliance." *Feminist Contestations: A Philosophical Exchange.* New York: Routledge, 1995. 22-30.

——. "Subjectivity, Historiography, and Politics: Reflections on the 'Feminism/Postmodernism Exchange.'" *Feminist Contestations: A Philosophical Exchange.* Ed. Linda Nicholson. New York: Routledge, 1995. 113-18.

Brummett, Barry. *Rhetoric in Popular Culture.* New York: St. Martin's Press, 1994.

Budhos, Marina. "Update on Aung San Suu Kyi." *Ms.* 7 (March/April 1997): 25.

"Burma: Phooey to 80%." *Economist* 316 (1990): 29-30.

Butler, Judith. "Contingent Foundations: Feminism and the Question of Postmodernism." *Feminist Contestations: A Philosophical Exchange.* Ed. Linda Nicholson. New York: Routledge, 1995. 42-52.

——. "For a Careful Reading." *Feminist Contestations: A Philosophical Exchange.* New York: Routledge, 1995. 134-38.

Clement, Catherine. *Gandhi: The Power of Pacifism.* Trans. Ruth Sharman. New York: Harry N. Abrams, 1996.

Clements, Alan. *The Voice of Hope: Aung San Suu Kyi; Conversations with Alan Clements.* New York: Seven Stories Press, 1997.

Cochran, David. "An Underground Tradition." *Progressive* 59 (1995): 37.

Collins, Patricia Hill. "Women in Hawaii: Sites, Identities, and Voices." Book Review. *Contemporary Sociology* 27 (1998): 581-82.

——. "It's All in the Family: Intersections of Gender, Race, and Nation." *Hypatia* 13 (1998): 62-82.

——. "Intersections of Race, Class, Gender and Nation: Some Implications for Black Family Studies." *Journal of Comparative Family Studies* 29 (1998): 27-36.

——. "On Book Exhibits and New Complexities: Reflections on Sociology as Science." *Contemporary Sociology* 27 (1998): 7-11.

Connolly, William. *Identity\Difference: Democratic Negotiations of Political Paradox.* Ithaca: Cornell University Press, 1991.

Dean, Jodi. *Solidarity of Strangers: Feminism After Identity Politics.* Berkeley: U of California P, 1996.

Erlanger, Steven. "Burmese Whose Silenced Voice Echoes." *New York Times*, October 15, 1991, sec A: 11.

Fraser, Nancy. "False Antithesis: A Response to Seyla Benhabib and Judith Butler." *Feminist Contestations: A Philosophical Exchange.* New York: Routledge, 1995. 68-72.

——. "Pragmatism, Feminism, and the Linguistic Turn." *Feminist Contestations: A Philosophical Exchange.* Ed. Linda Nicholson. New York: Routledge, 1995. 157-63.

Fuss, Diana. *Essentially Speaking: Feminism, Nature & Difference.* New York: Routledge Kegan & Paul, 1989. xi-xii.

Gordon, Linda. "The Trouble with Difference." *Dissent* 46 (1999): 41+.

Harris, Ian. "Gandhi's Concept of Love." *Nonviolence: Social and Psychological Issues.* Ed. V. K. Kool. New York: University Press of America, 1993. 183-97.

Hartley, John. *The Politics of Pictures: The Creation of the Public in the Age of Popular Media.* New York: Routledge, 1992.

"In Remembrance: Michael Aris." *Tricycle: The Buddhist Review.* (Summer 1999): 8.

Ingram, Catherine. *In the Footsteps of Gandhi: Conversations with Spiritual Social Activists.* Berkeley: Parallax Press, 1990.

Jones, Kathleen. *Compassionate Authority: Democracy and the Representation of Women.* New York: Routledge, 1993.

Kirshenbaum, Gayle. "Aung San Suu Kyi." *Ms.*, 6 (1996): 56–57.

Lauren, Paul G. "Moral Choice and Human Rights." Lecture. The V. N. Bhatia Lecture on Excellence in Education. Washington State University, Pullman, April 29, 1999.

Leff, Michael. "Dimensions of Temporality in Lincoln's Second Inaugural." *The Practice of Rhetorical Criticism, 2nd Ed.* James R. Andrews. New York: Longman, 1990. 80–85.

"Letter from Burma: A Fishy Episode." Editorial. *Utne Reader*, 78 (1996):, 70.

Matthews, Bruce. "The Present Fortune of Tradition-bound Authoritarianism in Myanmar." *Pacific Affairs* 71 (1998): 7–23.

McAllister, Pam, ed. *Reweaving the Web of Life: Feminism and Nonviolence.* Pennsylvania: New Society Publishers, 1982.

Minnich, Elizabeth. *Transforming Knowledge.* Philadelphia: Temple UP, 1990.

Mitchell, W. J. T. *Picture Theory: Essays on Verbal and Visual Representation.* Chicago: U of Chicago P, 1994.

Mohrmann, G. P. "Place and Space: Calhoun's Fatal Security." *Western Journal of Communication* 51 (1987): 143–58.

Nath, Caroline. "Burma: War of Nerves." *World Press Review* 13 (February 1996): 31.

Nicholson, Linda. "Introduction." *Feminist Contestations: A Philosophical Exchange.* New York: Routledge, 1995. 3–6.

Pilger, John. "Slave Nation." *Utne Reader* 78 (November 1996): 66–71.

——. *Inside Burma: Land of Fear.* Documentary Video. Prod. and Dir. David Munro. A Carlton UK Production, 1997.

Reilly, Susan. "Picture/Theory." *Other Voices* 1 (1998): Online Journal. Accessed August 4, 1999. Available: http://www.english.upenn.edu/~ov/1.2/sreilly/mitchell.html.

Rentz, Mary Ann. "The Cabinet Member as a Representative of the President: The Case of James Watt." *Communication Studies* 38 (1987): 94–110.

Roberts, Monty. *The Man Who Listens to Horses.* New York: Random House, 1997.

Sardar, Ziauddin. "Kept in Power by Male Fantasy." *New Statesman.* August 7, 1998: 24–25.

Shlain, Leonard. The Alphabet Versus the Goddess: The Conflict Between Word and Image. New York: Viking, 1998.

Silverstein, Josef. "The Idea of Freedom in Burma and the Political Thought of Daw Aung San Suu Kyi." *Pacific Affairs*, 69 (1996): 211–28.

Suu Kyi, Aung San. *Freedom From Fear and Other Writings.* Ed. Michael Aris. London: Viking, 1991.

——. *Letters from Burma.* London: Penguin Books Ltd., 1997.

——. "The Revolution of Spirit." Speech. *Peace! By the Nobel Peace Prize Laureates: An Anthology.* Ed. Marek Thee. Mayenne, France: Unesco, 1995: 433–35.

——. "Opening Keynote Address." Speech. NGO Forum on Women, Beijing. August 31, 1995.

Thapar, Karan. "Burmese Days of Reckoning." *The Spectator* 263 August 12, 1989: 13.

Toynbee, Arnold. "The Leader." *Time and the Philosophies.* London: Unesco, 1977. 231–42.

Trachtenberg, Peter. "Dharma in the Republic of Desire." *Tricycle: The Buddhist Review* 9 (Fall 1999): 50–53; 114–17.

Wallechinsky, David. "How One Woman Became the Voice of Her People." *Parade Magazine*, (January 19, 1997): 1; 4–5.

Whitney, Craig R. "Burmese Opposition Leader Wins the Nobel Peace Prize." *New York Times*, (October 15, 1991): A10.

Young, Iris. *Justice and the Politics of Difference*. Princeton: Princeton UP, 1990.

CHAPTER 7

Al-Shammari, Minwir M. "Organizational Climate." *Leadership and Organization Development Journal* 13 (1992): 30–32.

Anderson, Paul. "The Antinomies of Antonio Gramsci." *New Left Review* 100 (1976): 5–78.

Andrews, James R. *The Practice of Rhetorical Criticism*. 2nd ed. White Plains: Longman. 1990.

Bates, Gail, and Dennis Bates. Letter. *Billings Gazette*. (January 9, 1994): sec. C: 9.

Ben-Or, Gabriel. Letter. *Billings Gazette*. (January 9, 1994): sec. C: 9.

Benoit, William L. "The Genesis of Rhetorical Action." *The Southern Communication Journal* 59 (1994): 342+.

Benson, Thomas. "Rhetoric as a Way of Being." *American Rhetoric: Context and Criticism*. Ed. Thomas Benson. Carbondale: Southern Illinois University Press, 1989. 293–22.

Berlin, Sharon B. "Constructivism and the Environment: A Cognitive-Integrative Perspective for Social Work Practice." *Families in Society* 77 (1996): 326–35.

Biesecker, B. "Rethinking the Rhetorical Situation from within the Thematic of Différance." *Philosophy and Rhetoric* 22 (1989): 110–30.

"Billings' Solidarity Extolled." Editorial. *Billings Gazette*. (January 4, 1994): sec. A: 4.

Bitzer, Lloyd F. "The Rhetorical Situation." *Philosophy and Rhetoric* 1 (1968): 1–14.

——. "The Forum: Bitzer on Tompkins (And Patton)." *Quarterly Journal of Speech* 66 (1980): 90–93.

——. "Functional Communication: A Situational Perspective." *Rhetoric in Transition: Studies in the Nature and Uses of Rhetoric*. Ed. E. E. White. University Park: Pennsylvania State UP, 1980. 21–38.

——. "The Forum: Bitzer on Vatz." *Quarterly Journal of Speech* 67 (1981): 99–101.

——. "The Forum: Bitzer on Tompkins." *Quarterly Journal of Speech* 67 (1981): 101.

Braden, Waldo W. "Myths in a Rhetorical Context." *Southern Speech Communication Journal* 40 (1975): 113–26.

Branham, Robert J., and W. Barnett Pearce. "Between Text and Context: Toward a Rhetoric of Contextual Reconstruction." *Quarterly Journal of Speech* 71 (1985): 19–36.

Briggs Myers, Isabel. *Introduction to Type: A Guide to Understanding Your Results on the Myers-Briggs Type Indicator*. 5th ed. Palo Alto: Consulting Psychologists Press, 1993.

Burke, Kenneth. *Attitudes Toward History*. Berkeley: University of California Press, 1987.

Campbell, Karlyn Kohrs. "The Communication Classroom: A Chilly Climate for Women?" *Journal of the Association for Communication Administration* 51 (1985): 68–72.

"Classroom Climate . . . A Chilly One for Women?" Pamphlet. University Park: Pennsylvania State U. 1993.

Cooke, Leonard. "Fighting Hate Crimes: The Eugene Model." *Police Chief* 61 (1994): 44, 46, 49.

"Crime Stories Come in on Top of Reader Poll." *Billings Gazette*. (December 26, 1993): sec. A: 1.

Damasio, Antonio. *Descartes' Error: Emotion, Reason, and the Human Brain.* New York: Avon Books. 1994.

Dastmalchian, Ali, Paul Blyton, and Raymond Adamson, *The Climate of Workplace Relations.* New York: Routledge. 1991.

Denison, Daniel R. "What Is the Difference Between Organizational Culture and Organizational Climate? A Native's Point of View on a Decade of Paradigm Wars." *Academy of Management Review* 21 (1996): 619–54.

Dobb, Edwin. "Not in Our Town." *Reader's Digest* (November 1994): 96–100.

Donald, Merlin. *Origins of the Modern Mind: Three Stages in the Evolution of Culture and Cognition.* Cambridge: Harvard University Press. 1991.

Ehli, Nick. "Mother Denounces Hate Crime." *Billings Gazette.* (December 4, 1993): sec. A: 1.

———. "Message of Support Replaces Sales Pitch." *Billings Gazette.* (December 7, 1993): sec. A: 1.

Falcione, Raymond L., Lyle Sussman, and Richard P. Herden. "Communication Climate in Organizations." *Handbook of Organizational Communication: An Interdisciplinary Perspective.* Ed. Fredric M. Jablin. Newbury Park: Sage, 1987. 195–225.

———, and Elyse A. Kaplan. "Organizational Climate, Communication, and Culture." *Communication Yearbook* 8. Ed. R. N. Bostrom Beverly Hills: Sage, 1984. 285–309.

Forster, Julie. "Churchgoers Asked to Unite Against Hate Crimes." *Billings Gazette.* (December 5, 1993): sec. C: 1.

Gallagher, Winnefred. *The Power of Place: How Our Surroundings Shape Our Thoughts, Emotions, and Actions.* New York: Poseidon Press, 1993.

Galtung, Johann. "Nonviolence and Deep Culture: Some Hidden Obstacles." *Peace Research* 27 (1995): 21–37.

Gantz, Walter S., Sarah Trenholm, and Mark Pittman. "The Impact of Salience and Altruism on Diffusion of News." *Journalism Quarterly* 54 (1976): 727–32.

Garret, Mary, and Xiao, Xiaosui. "The Rhetorical Situation Revisited." *Rhetoric Society Quarterly* 23 (1993): 30–40.

Gaub, Dennis. "Hands of Hate Strike at School." *Billings Gazette.* (December 11, 1993): sec. B: 1.

Gaub, Dennis. "Windows Smashed on Vehicles Across City." *Billings Gazette.* (December 31, 1993): sec. C: 4.

Glick, William H. "Conceptualizing and Measuring Organizational and Psychological Climate Pitfalls in Multilevel Research." *Academy of Management Review* 10 (1985): 601–16.

Greer, Colin. "'We Won't Tolerate Hate': How Communities and Schools Around the Country Continue to Take Action against Bigotry and Intimidation." *Parade Magazine.* (February 25, 1997): 4.

Gregg, Richard B. "'The Mind's I,' 'The Mind's We,' 'The Mind's They': A Cognitive Approach to the Rhetorical Analysis of Public Discourse." *Commmunication: Views from the Helm for the 21st Century.* Ed. Judth S. Trent. Boston: Allyn and Bacon, 1998.

Haley, Usha C. "The MBTI and Decision-Making Styles: Identifying and Managing Cognitive Trails in Strategic Decision Making." *Developing Leaders: Research and Applications in Psychological Type and Leadership Development.* Eds. Catherine Fitzgerald and Linda K. Kirby. Palo Alto: Davies-Black Publishing, 1997. 187–223.

Hall, Roberta M. "The Classroom Climate for Women." *Journal of the Association for Communication Administration* 51 (1985): 64–67.

Hall, Robert M., and Bernice R. Sandler. *Out of the Classroom: A Chilly Campus Climate for Women?* Washington, DC: Project on the Status and Education of Women, Association of American Colleges, 1984.

Hample, Dale. "The Cognitive Context of Argument." *Western Journal of Speech Communication* 45 (1981): 148–58.

Hanh, Thich Nhat. *Be Still and Know: Reflections from Living Buddha, Living Christ.* New York: Riverhead Books. 1996.

Hartsig, Jo Clare, and Walter Wink. "Light In Montana: How One Town Said No to Hate." *Utne Reader* (July 1995): 54–55.

"Hate Groups On the Rise." *World News with Peter Jennings.* ABC News. New York. February 23, 1999.

"Hate Groups." Editorial. *Billings Gazette.* (December 10, 1993): sec. A: 4.

"Hate Groups Denounced." *Billings Gazette.* (December 14, 1993): sec. C: 8.

"Hate Groups Get Aggressive." *Billings Gazette.* (January 11, 1994): sec. A: 7.

"Hate Is Not Speech: A Constitutional Defense of Penalty Enhancement for Hate Crimes." *Harvard Law Review,* 106 (1993): 1314–31.

"Hate Crimes Symptoms of Infection: Prescription: Light Shrivels Creatures of the Night." Editorial. *Billings Gazette.* (December 19, 1993): sec. C: 12.

Johnstone, Christopher L. "Electing Ourselves in 1976: Jimmy Carter and the American Faith." *Western Journal of Speech Communication* 42 (1978): 241–49.

Kohn, Alfie. *No Contest: The Case Against Competition.* Boston: Houghton Mifflin, 1986.

Kubik, Jan. *The Power of Symbols against the Symbols of Power: The Rise of Solidarity and the Fall of State Socialism in Poland.* University Park: Pennsylvania State UP, 1994.

Kully, Robert. "Rabbi Isaac Mayer Wise: His language of anti Anti-Semitism." *Quarterly Journal of Speech* 50 (1964): 166–78.

Lemert, James B. "News Context and the Elimination of Mobilizing Information: An Experiment." *Journalism Quarterly* 61 (1984): 243–249; 259.

Lieberman, Michael. "Enforcing Hate Crime Laws: Defusing Intergroup Tensions." *Police Chief* 61 (1994): 36–38, 40, 42.

Long, Connie, and Bob Long. Letter. *Billings Gazette.* (December 21, 1993): sec. A: 4.

Martin, Susan E. "A Cross-burning Is Not Just an Arson": Police Social Construction of Hate Crimes in Baltimore County." *Criminology* 33 (1995): 303–25.

Mathews, Dave. "Community Change Through *True* Public Action." *National Civic Review* 83 (1994): 400–04.

McCracken, Greg. "Windows with Menorahs Broken by Rock Throwers." *Billings Gazette.* (December 16, 1993): sec. A: 1.

——. "Menorah Remains Symbol of Unity." *Billings Gazette.* (December 17, 1993): sec. A: 1.

——. "Turning Against Hate: Ex-white Supremacists Come Out Against Crimes." *Billings Gazette.* (January 6, 1994): sec. A: 1.

McCafferty, Art. Letter. *Billings Gazette.* (December 15, 1993): sec. B: 1.

"Memories of 1993." *Billings Gazette.* (December 26, 1993): sec. F: 2.

"Menorah." Solidarity Symbol. *Billings Gazette.* (December 12, 1993): sec. A: 12.

Merton, Thomas. *Gandhi on Non-Violence: A Selection from the Writings of Mahatma Gandhi.* Ed. Thomas Merton. New York: New Directions, 1965.

"Montana Daily Reproduces Menorah to Urge Solidarity." *Editor and Publisher* (January 15, 1994): 3.

National Association of Colleges and Employers (NACE). *Planning Job Choices: 1999.* Ed. Mimi Collins. Bethlehem: NACE, 1998.

Nave, James L. "Gauging the Organizational Climate." *Management Solutions* 31 (1986): 14-18.

Nelson, Marshall W. "A Multifaceted Approach." *Police Chief* 61 (1994): 49-50.

Nevins, Norma. Letter. *Billings Gazette.* (December 28, 1993): sec. A: 4.

Not in Our Town. Video Documentary. Series: We Do the Work. Dir. and Prod. The Working Group. California. PBS. 1994.

Olp, Susan. "Vandalized Churches Get National Support." *Billings Gazette.* (January 8, 1994): sec. A: 5.

Olson, John K. "Crime and Religion: A Denominational and Community Analysis." *Journal for the Scientific Study of Religion* 29 (1990): 395-403.

Ostoj, Ruby. Letter. *Billings Gazette.* (December 22, 1993): sec. A: 4.

Patterson, M., M. West, and R. Payne. "Collective Climates: A Test of Their Socio-Psychological Significance." Discussion Paper No. 94. September 1992. Online, Corporate Performance and Work Organization. Internet. 29 Jan. 1999. Available http://cep.lse.ac.uk/papers/discussion/dp0094.html.

Poole, Marshall S. "Communication and Organizational Climates: Review, Critique, and a New Perspective." *Organizational Communication: Traditional Themes and New Directions.* Eds. Robert D. McPhee and Phillip K. Tompkins. Beverly Hills: Sage, 1986. 79-107.

Porrovecchio, Mark J. "Rethinking the Constraints: Examination, Application and Revision of 'The Rhetorical Situation.'" *The Speech Communication Annual* 12 (1998): 43-65.

"Put a Menorah in Your Window." Editorial. *Billings Gazette.* (December 8, 1993): sec. B: 1.

Quilico, Jack. Letter. *Billings Gazette.* (December 15, 1993): sec. B: 1.

"Racicot Decries Local Hate Crimes." *Billings Gazette.* (December 18, 1993): sec. B: 1.

"Reward Fund Set Up." *Billings Gazette.* (December 17, 1993): sec. A: 9.

Rosenblatt, Roger. "Their Finest Minute." *New York Times Magazine* (July 3, 1994): 23-32, 44-45.

Ryan, Michael. "How One Town Said 'No.'" *Parade Magazine.* (February 23, 1997): 5-6.

Safran, Claire. "Not in Our Town." *Redbook* (November 1994): 81-83, 126.

Sandler, Bernice R., and Roberta Hall. *The Campus Climate Revisited: Chilly for Women Faculty, Administrators, and Graduate Students.* Washington, DC: Project on the Status and Education of Women, Association of American Colleges, 1986.

Saleebey, Dennis. "Biology's Challenge to Social Work: Embodying the Person-in-Environment Perspective." *Social Work* 37 (1992): 112-18.

Schnitzer, Tammie. "Not in Our Town Movement." Speech Delivered at the Martin Luther King Human Rights Awards Breakfast of the Latah County Human Rights Task Force. Moscow, Idaho. January 16, 1999.

——. Personal interview. January 15, 1999.

Serow, Robert. "Community Service, Religious Commitment, and Campus Climate." *Youth and Society* 21 (1989): 105-19.

Sochocky, Anna, and Catherine Seigner. "Citizens Organize Against Neo-nazis." *Progressive* 53 (1989): 15.

Stewart, Bob. "Hate Crimes: Understanding and Addressing the Problem." *Police Chief* 61 (1994): 14-50.

Telushkin, Joseph. *Words that Hurt, Words that Heal: How to Choose Words Wisely and Well.* New York: Quill William Morrow, 1996.

Urman, Ernest, and Judy Urman. Letter. *Billings Gazette.*(January 9, 1994): sec. C: 9.

Vatz, Richard E. "The Myth of the Rhetorical Situation." *Philosophy and Rhetoric* 6 (1973): 154-61.

"Violence Begets Violence." Editorial. *Billings Gazette.* (December 12, 1993): sec. C: 10.

Walters, Joe. Letter. *Billings Gazette.* (December 16, 1993): sec. C: 13.

——. Letter. *Billings Gazette.* (January 14, 1994): sec. A: 4.

Wander, Phillip C. "The Third Persona: An Ideological Turn in Rhetorical Theory." *Central States Speech Journal* 35 (1984): 197-216.

——. Letter to the author. May 18, 1999.

Weaver, Richard. *The Ethics of Rhetoric.* Davis: Hermagoras Press, 1985.

White, James Boyd. *When Words Lose Their Meaning: Constitutions and Reconstitutions of Language, Character, and Community.* Chicago: University of Chicago Press, 1984.

Wilcox, Dennis L., and Lawrence W. Nolte. *Public Relations: Writing and Media Techniques.* 3rd ed. New York: Longman, 1997.

Wing, Delores M. Letter. *Billings Gazette.* (December 22, 1993): sec. A: 4.

Woodall, W. Gill, and Joseph P. Folger. "Nonverbal Cue Context and Episodic Memory: On the Availability and Endurance of Nonverbal Behaviors as Retrieval Cues." *Communication Monographs* 52 (1985): 319-33.

CHAPTER 8

Bondurant, Joan V. *Conquest of Violence: The Gandhian Philosophy of Conflict.* Princeton, NJ: Princeton UP, 1988.

Carter, April. "Non-Violence as a Strategy for Change." *A Reader in Peace Studies.* Ed. Paul Smoker et al. Oxford: Pergamon, 1990. 210-16.

Collins, Patricia Hill. "It's All in the Family: Intersections of Gender, Race, and Nation." *Hypatia* 13 (1998): 62-82.

Foss, Sonja, and Cindy Griffin. "Beyond Persuasion: A Proposal for an Invitational Rhetoric." *Communication Monographs* 62 (1995): 2-17.

Gall, Carlotta. "Election Takes Macedonia Another Step Toward Democracy." *The New York Times.* Online. Proquest. Internet. November 15, 1999.

Galtung, Johan. "Violence and Peace." *A Reader in Peace Studies.* Eds. Paul Smoker, Ruth Davies, and Barbara Munske. New York: Pergamon Press, 1990. 9-14.

Greer, Colin. "The World Is Hungry for Goodness: Without Memory, There Is No Healing. Without Forgiveness, There Is No Future." *Parade Magazine* (January 11, 1998): 4-6.

Herrick, James. *The History and Theory of Rhetoric.* Scottsdale, AZ: Gorsuch Scarisbrick, Publishers. 1997.

Ingram, Catherine. *In the Footsteps of Gandhi: Conversations with Spiritual Social Activists.* Berkeley: Parallax Press, 1990.

Johnstone, Henry. "Some Reflections on Argumentation." *Philosophy Rhetoric and Argumentation.* Eds. Maurice Natanson and Henry Johnstone. University Park, PA: Pennsylvania State UP, 1965. 1-9.

McCarthy, Colman. "Why We Must Teach Peace." *Educational Leadership* 50 (1992): 6–9.

McCandless, Erin. "Gender Analysis: A Peace Building Tool; An Interview With Simona Sharoni." *Cantilevers* 6 (Spring 1999): 23, 69.

Reardon, Patrick T., Gary Washburn, Jim Kirk, and William Gaines. "Billboard Foes Beat the System." *Chicago Tribune*. Chicago, IL; (September 11, 1997): 1.

Trachtenberg, Peter. "Dharma in the Republic of Desire." *Tricycle: The Buddhist Review* 9 (Fall 1999): 50–53; 114–17.

Young, Nigel. "Nonviolence and Social Change." *A Reader in Peace Studies*. Eds. Paul Smoker, Ruth Davies, and Barbara Munske. New York: Pergamon Press, 1990. 217–20.

APPENDIX 1

See chapter 1 list of works cited.

Index